The Political Relevance of Food Media and Journalism

Interrogating the intersections of food, journalism, and politics, this book offers a critical examination of food media and journalism, and its political potential against the backdrop of contemporary social challenges.

Contributors analyze current and historic examples such as #BlackLivesMatter, COVID-19, climate change, Brexit, food sovereignty, and identity politics, highlighting how food media and journalism reach beyond the commercial imperatives of lifestyle journalism to negotiate nationalism, globalization, and social inequalities. The volume challenges the idea that food media/journalism are trivial and apolitical by drawing attention to the complex ways that storytelling about food has engaged political discourses in the past, and the innovative ways it is doing so today.

Bringing together international scholars from a variety of disciplines, the book will be of great interest to scholars and students of journalism, communication, media studies, food studies, sociology, and anthropology.

Elizabeth Fakazis is Professor of Media Studies in the School of Design & Communication at the University of Wisconsin Stevens Point, USA.

Elfriede Fürsich is Visiting Associate Professor in the Department of Communication at the University of Pittsburgh, USA.

Routledge Research in Journalism

Global Media Ethics and the Digital Revolution
Edited by Noureddine Miladi

The Future of the Presidency, Journalism, and Democracy
After Trump
Edited by Robert E. Gutsche, Jr.

Journalistic Practices in Restrictive Contexts
A Sociological Approach to the Case of Iran
Banafsheh Ranji

The Media and Inequality
Edited by Steve Schifferes and Sophie Knowles

Newspaper Building Design and Journalism Cultures in Australia and the UK: 1855–2010
Carole O'Reilly and Josie Vine

Emerging Practices in the Age of Automated Digital Journalism
Models, Languages, and Storytelling
Edited by Berta García-Orosa, Sara Pérez-SeijoPérez-Seijo, and Ángel Vizoso

Global Pandemics and Media Ethics
Issues and Perspectives
Edited by Tendai Chari and Martin N. Ndlela

Investigative Journalism in Changing Times
Australian and Anglo-American Reporting
Edited by Caryn Coatney

The Political Relevance of Food Media and Journalism
Beyond Reviews and Recipes
Edited by Elizabeth Fakazis and Elfriede Fürsich

For more information about this series, please visit: https://www.routledge.com/Routledge-Research-in-Journalism/book-series/RRJ

The Political Relevance of Food Media and Journalism
Beyond Reviews and Recipes

Edited by Elizabeth Fakazis and
Elfriede Fürsich

LONDON AND NEW YORK

Designed cover image: © Getty Images

First published 2023
by Routledge
4 Park Square, Milton Park, Abingdon, Oxon OX14 4RN

and by Routledge
605 Third Avenue, New York, NY 10158

Routledge is an imprint of the Taylor & Francis Group, an informa business

© 2023 selection and editorial matter, Elizabeth Fakazis and Elfriede Fürsich; individual chapters, the contributors

The right of Elizabeth Fakazis and Elfriede Fürsich to be identified as the authors of the editorial material, and of the authors for their individual chapters, has been asserted in accordance with sections 77 and 78 of the Copyright, Designs and Patents Act 1988.

All rights reserved. No part of this book may be reprinted or reproduced or utilised in any form or by any electronic, mechanical, or other means, now known or hereafter invented, including photocopying and recording, or in any information storage or retrieval system, without permission in writing from the publishers.

Trademark notice: Product or corporate names may be trademarks or registered trademarks, and are used only for identification and explanation without intent to infringe.

British Library Cataloguing-in-Publication Data
A catalogue record for this book is available from the British Library

ISBN: 978-1-032-25050-2 (hbk)
ISBN: 978-1-032-25560-6 (pbk)
ISBN: 978-1-003-28394-2 (ebk)

DOI: 10.4324/9781003283942

Typeset in Sabon
by MPS Limited, Dehradun

Contents

Acknowledgements   viii
List of Contributors   x

Introduction: From the Racist Sandwich to Civil Eats: How Food Journalism and Media Are Engaging with Politics   1
ELIZABETH FAKAZIS AND ELFRIEDE FÜRSICH

PART I
Engaging with Systems of Injustice and Disparity   17

1 Influencer Activism: Visibility, Strategy, and #BlackLivesMatter Discourse on Food Instagram   19
 TISHA DEJMANEE

2 Super Bowl Food Politics: On the Menu, on the Screen, and on the Field   34
 EMILY J.H. CONTOIS

3 Agribusiness, Environmental Conflict, and Food in Travel Journalism: Image Work for the Bay of Fundy in New Brunswick   48
 LYN MCGAURR

4 Who Speaks and Are We Listening? Food Sovereign Voices in a Changing Climate   66
 ALANA MANN

PART II
Raising Questions of Legitimacy, Power, and Good Citizenship 83

5 From Bad Boys to Heroes: Culinary Philanthropy and Good Citizenship in the Age of COVID-19 85
KATHLEEN LEBESCO AND PETER NACCARATO

6 Cooking in the Time of Corona: The Politicized Domesticity of Food Journalism in *The New York Times* 100
ELFRIEDE FÜRSICH

7 Paleo and Pain Free: Reporting on Scandals of Food Celebrities 115
KATHERINE KIRKWOOD

PART III
Negotiating Regional, National, and Global Identities 133

8 Of Clay Stoves and Cooking Pots: "Village Food" Videos and Gastro-Politics in Contemporary India 135
SUMANA KASTURI

9 How the Bendy Banana Became a Symbol of Anti-EU Sentiment: British Media, Political Mythology, and Populism 153
MARY IRWIN AND ANA TOMINC

10 Heritage, Belonging, and Promotion: Food Journalism Reconsidered 167
UNNI FROM ANDREASEN AND ALBERTE BORNE ASMUSSE

PART IV
Recovering History and (Re)producing Memory 181

11 Patriotic Hens, Tomato Turbans, and Mock Fish: The *Daily Mail* Food Bureau and National Identity during the First World War 183
SARAH LONSDALE

12 Influencer before the Internet: The Extraordinary Career of Chef, Editor, and Food Entrepreneur Alma Lach 199
KIMBERLY VOSS

13 *Chef's Table* and a Collective Past: Netflix, Food Media, and Cultural Memories 210
DIANA WILLIS

Index 224

Acknowledgements

The idea that food is more than just sustenance has been a guiding motive in both our lives. Elizabeth Fakazis grew up in what she experienced as a gritty city just across the Hudson River from Manhattan, that island's glittering skyline and all it promised seemingly a world away. Her resilient divorced mother worked nights as a private duty nurse to keep the family housed and fed, which wasn't always easy. Summertime, her father would put her and her sister on a plane to Athens, Greece to spend three sunny and delicious months with their grandparents, who had left their home of generations in Sinope on the Black Sea coast of Turkey during the forced population exchanges of the early 1920s. They couldn't bring much with them, but somehow a cookbook that her great-grandmother had used in culinary school in Istanbul (Constantinople to them) survived the journey to Athens. The book, with her scribbled annotations, represents an amalgam of French sauces and techniques (the fashion of the time), and cinnamon and cumin-spiced recipes of the Greeks from Asia Minor. These experiences shaped Fakazis's deep-down, unarticulated understanding that food, culture, politics, and media impact everyday life in important ways, a feeling that she now explores in her professional life.

Elfriede Fürsich lives in a Bavarian-Bengali family, where *Schnitzel* (breaded slice of meat) and *Maacher Jhol* (fish curry) have equal standing on the daily menu. It's a family of foodies where the conversation over one meal not infrequently veers off into discussions of what to eat for the next meal. Eating in Germany, India, and the United States, she has experienced directly how cooking can heal homesickness, uphold family bonds and create new friendships. Her transnational exposure has also given her the freedom to appropriate recipes and techniques across cultures without hesitancy as she sees authenticity as an overrated concept.

These experiences have led both of us to an enduring interest in food – in the systemic conditions that result in its abundance and scarcity; in the ways it sustains families, communities, and social identities across generations, bringing people together as well as fortifying boundaries of difference and exclusion; and in the ways food is represented in media and the ripple effects such representations can have on culture, society, and politics.

We are fortunate to be asking our questions at a time when food journalism and interdisciplinary research on food are bourgeoning. They have led us to colleagues from around the world who share similar interests and concerns about how intersections of food, media, and politics influence our personal and civic lives. Indeed, one of the most significant and enduring pleasures of this project has been getting to know and collaborate with them. We are deeply grateful to all the contributors to this volume who were willing to share their knowledge, experience, and research, and who dedicated scarce resources of time, energy, and patience during a global pandemic to work with us toward the final version you are reading today.

We are also grateful to the Association for Education in Journalism and Mass Communication, especially the Magazine Media Division, and the Association for the Study of Food and Society for the opportunity to publicly present early work that eventually led to this project. Thanks, too, to all who attended our panels and offered feedback that both challenged and inspired us, to Suzanne Richardson and Tanushree Baijal at Routledge for their guidance and support, and to the peer reviewers for raising questions and offering suggestions that strengthened our work.

Finally, we are grateful to our families for stepping in to help manage daily life as we regularly stepped out to sit at our computers to make this book happen, and for offering enthusiastic encouragement, calm reassurance – and good meals!

Contributors

Alberte Borne Asmussen holds a Master of Arts in Media Studies from the School of Communication and Culture, Aarhus University, Denmark. In her thesis, *A Budding Media Coverage of Veganism and Plant-Based Food (2021)*, she critically examined the coverage of veganism and plant-based food in Danish national newspapers in 2015 and 2020. Employing quantitative and qualitative methods, the thesis drew on a framework combining research on food journalism, lifestyle journalism, and consumer journalism.

Emily J.H. Contois is Assistant Professor of Media Studies at The University of Tulsa, USA. Her research explores the intersection of food, bodies, health, and identities in US media and popular culture. She is the author of *Diners, Dudes, and Diets: How Gender and Power Collide in Food Media and Culture* (University of North Carolina Press, 2020) and co-editor of *Food Instagram: Identity, Influence, and Negotiation* (University of Illinois Press, 2022).

Tisha Dejmanee is Lecturer of Digital and Social Media at the University of Technology Sydney, Australia. Her research explores the intersection of feminist theory, media studies, critical food studies, and Asian American studies. Her forthcoming book is titled *Postfeminism, Postrace and Digital Politics in Asian American Food Blogs* (Routledge, 2021). She edited a special section on feminism and food media in *Feminist Media Studies* and has published articles on "food porn" and neoconservative ideologies on the Food Network.

Elizabeth Fakazis is Professor in Media Studies at the University of Wisconsin-Stevens Point, USA, where she teaches journalism and media studies. Her early research explored food, journalism, and gender in men's magazines and children's media, which led her to an interest in the various ways that food media intersect with the politics of everyday life. Her research interests have become an integral part of her teaching and she leads an annual study abroad program on food, media, tourism and sustainability in the Mediterranean Basin.

List of Contributors   xi

Unni From Andreasen is Associate Professor of Media and Journalism at the School of Communication and Culture, Aarhus University, Denmark, where she serves as Head of the School. She specializes in research about cultural and lifestyle journalism, especially cultural criticism across media, along with constructive journalism. Her work applies both quantitative and qualitative methods. She is co-editor of *Rethinking Cultural Criticism: New Voices in the Digital Age* (Palgrave Macmillan, 2021) and *Cultural Journalism and Cultural Critique in the Media* (Routledge, 2017).

Elfriede Fürsich is a Visiting Associate Professor at the Department of Communication, University of Pittsburgh, USA. Her research explores issues relating to media representations and criticism with a special focus on niche and lifestyle journalism in a global media system. She has investigated the impact of globalization on media ranging from travel shows and music reviews to business journalism and African Internet sites. With Folker Hanusch, she is the co-editor of *Travel Journalism: Exploring Production, Impact and Culture* (Palgrave MacMillan, 2014).

Mary Irwin is a cultural historian and TV studies specialist, and honorary research fellow in the Media, Communications and Performing Arts Division at Queen Margaret University, Edinburgh, UK. She has published extensively on contemporary and historical television. Her books include a collection on national and regional television comedy, *UK and Irish Television Comedy: Nation, Region and Identity* (Palgrave, 2022) and a monograph on historical television romantic comedy, *Love Wars: Television Romantic Comedy* (Bloomsbury, 2023).

Sumana Kasturi is an Independent Scholar living and working in Mumbai, India. Her research interests include digital media, children's communication, and feminist media studies. Her early work explored pedagogies of consumption on the Disney interactive website, and that has extended into a continued interest in young people's use of media and digital culture. Her current work has focused on Indian women bloggers and transnational cultures. She is the author of *Gender, Citizenship and Identity: Writing the Everyday* (Routledge, 2019) and is co-editor of the forthcoming *Children and Media in India* (Orient Blackswan).

Katherine Kirkwood is a content writer at Liquid Interactive. She completed her PhD at the Digital Media Research Centre at the Queensland University of Technology, Australia, where she is now a Visiting Fellow. Her dissertation entitled: *Superfood Me: Negotiating Australia's Post-Gourmet Food Culture* examined popular culture's relationship with everyday Australian food culture. Her research articulates how media and cultural texts inform and shape Australians' approach to food, their culinary interests and concerns. She is co-editor with Michelle Phillipov of *Alternative Food Politics: From the Margins to the Mainstream* (Routledge, 2019).

Kathleen LeBesco is Professor of Communication and Media Arts and Associate Vice President for Strategic Initiatives at Marymount Manhattan College in New York City. She is author of *Revolting Bodies: The Struggle to Redefine Fat Identity*, co-author of *Culinary Capital*, and co-editor of *The Bloomsbury Handbook of Food and Popular Culture*, *Bodies Out of Bounds: Fatness and Transgression*, *Edible Ideologies: Representing Food and Meaning*, and *The Drag King Anthology*, as well as dozens of book chapters and journal articles. LeBesco is also a former snack bar technician, line cook, and restaurant reviewer for *Time Out New York's Eating and Drinking Guide*.

Sarah Lonsdale is a Senior Lecturer in the Department of Journalism at City, University of London, UK. Her research explores journalism history in both newspapers and periodicals, particularly in the interwar years and with respect to gender. She has investigated the role of women foreign correspondents in challenging the agenda of diplomatic news during the 1920s and 1930s. Her latest book, *Rebel Women between the Wars: Fearless Writers and Adventurers* (Manchester University Press, 2020) explores how women journalists of the interwar years overcame obstacles to their participating in public life.

Alana Mann is Professor and Head of Discipline, Media, at the University of Tasmania, Australia. Her research focuses on the dynamics of citizen engagement, participation, and collective action in food systems planning and governance. She is a director of the food business incubator FoodLab Sydney which began as an Australian Research Council (ARC) funded project supported by the City of Sydney, TAFE NSW, and FoodLab Detroit. Her books include *Global Activism in Food Politics: Power Shift* (Palgrave Macmillan, 2014), *Voice and Participation in Global Food Politics* (Routledge, 2019), and *Food in a Changing Climate* (Emerald Publishing, 2021).

Lyn McGaurr is a University Associate at the School of Creative Arts and Media, University of Tasmania, Australia. Her research interests span environmental conflict and the media, environmental communication, environmental movements, climate change and the media, travel journalism, place-branding, tourism public relations, and social license. She is the author of *Environmental Communication and Travel Journalism: Consumerism, Conflict and Concern* (Routledge, 2015) and co-author with Bruce Tranter and Libby Lester of *Leadership and the Construction of Environmental Concern* (Palgrave Macmillan, 2017). Outside academia, Lyn has worked for NGOs and as a journalist, book editor and communications consultant.

List of Contributors xiii

Peter Naccarato is Vice President for Academic Affairs/Dean of the Faculty and Professor of English and World Literatures at Marymount Manhattan College. With Kathleen LeBesco, he is co-author of *Culinary Capital* (Berg, 2012) and co-editor of *The Bloomsbury Handbook of Food and Popular Culture* (Bloomsbury, 2018) and *Edible Ideologies: Representing Food and Meaning* (SUNY Press, 2008). With Zach Nowak and Elgin Eckert, he is co-editor of *Representing Italy Through Food* (Bloomsbury Press, 2017). He has developed and taught interdisciplinary courses in food studies at Marymount and at the Umbra Institute, an American study abroad school in Perugia, Italy. He also serves on the advisory board of the Institute's Center for Food, Sustainability, and Environment.

Ana Tominc is Reader in Food, Communication, and Media Studies at Queen Margaret University Edinburgh, United Kingdom. She has published on contemporary food discourses related to lifestyle and class, veganism and far-right cooking shows on social media, construction of culinary national identity, cookbooks, and food television in socialist Yugoslavia. She is the author of *The Discursive Construction of Class and Lifestyle: Celebrity Chef Cookbooks in Post-Socialist Slovenia* (John Benjamins, 2017), editor of *Food and Cooking on Early Television* (Routledge, 2022), and the founder of the Biennial Conference on Food and Communication.

Kimberly Voss is Professor of Journalism at the University of Central Florida, USA. Her research focuses on the historical analysis of women journalists' careers and the definition of women's news, including food. She has published five books, including *The Food Section* (Rowman & Littlefield, 2014) andmore than 30 journal articles, including a 2020 *Journalism History* article about Jane Nickerson, the first *New York Times* food editor. She is currently conducting oral histories with former food editors.

Diana Willis is a PhD student at the State University of New York at Albany. Her research focuses on the intersections of new media, food studies, and collective memory. She is interested in how new media curate traditions, represent the past, and reinforce personal, social, political, and cultural identities.

Introduction

From the Racist Sandwich to Civil Eats: How Food Journalism and Media Are Engaging with Politics

Elizabeth Fakazis and Elfriede Fürsich

The beginning decades of the 21st century have been an exciting time for those of us who love food journalism. A volatile and competitive media environment during a period of intense technological transformations has jolted the field, spurring profound anxiety followed by an infusion of creative energy birthing new publications and platforms, story structures, production practices, and framing strategies. These changes opened up space for engagement with political and social issues within its narratives and institutions in ways so unexpected that they continue to draw widespread audience interest and debate.

One of the most prominent examples of this came in the final years of the late Anthony Bourdain (1956–2018). When Bourdain, long matured out of his early bad-boy exploits, began talking about the suffering and dignity of Palestinians living through perpetual war, exploitation of immigrant labor, and persistent sexual harassment and violence in the restaurant and media industries in his social media posts, interviews, and episodes of his food and travel programs, reactions to his "auxiliary role as a political journalist" ("Anthony Bourdain" 9 June 2018) were mixed. In an interview for *Food & Wine* (Kanani 24 May 2017), Bourdain said that he was often told to stick to food and stop talking about politics, but that was an impossible task. "There's nothing more political than food," he said. "Who eats? Who doesn't? Why do people cook what they cook? It's always the end or part of a long story, often a painful one." Yet not everyone was dismayed. As David Klion of *The Nation* wrote, "Bourdain understood that the point of journalism is to tell the truth, to challenge the powerful, to expose wrongdoing ... [he] made it possible to believe that social justice and earthly delights weren't mutually exclusive, and he pursued both with the same earnest reverence" (Klion 8 June 2018).

Bourdain's willingness to "go there" – to people, places, and issues at the margins or even outside the expected boundaries of food journalism and entertainment food media's "beat" – earned him not only several Emmy nominations and awards but also recognition from the American Constitution Society and the Muslim Public Affairs Council. It was also one of the most remarked upon aspects of his work, as articles proliferated

DOI: 10.4324/9781003283942-1

before and after his death drawing attention to this turn: "Anthony Bourdain Knew There Was Nothing More Political Than Food" (*The Nation* 8 June 2018); "Anthony Bourdain Claps Back at Critics Who Say Chefs Should Stay Out of Politics" (*Delish* 8 Oct. 2018), "Anthony Bourdain's Moveable Feast: Guided by a lusty appetite for indigenous culture and cuisine, the swaggering chef has become a traveling statesman" (*New Yorker* 5 Feb. 2017), among many others. Bourdain's prestige, power, and influence as a successful celebrity chef, author, and television/documentary host allowed him to engage hot-button socio-political issues in his entertainment/food journalism and to pave the way for others with less influence who were prevented from addressing these issues or had done so but without the associated media fanfare.

Opportunities to activate the potential for stories about food to engage with important social, political, and cultural issues, long recognized by anthropology and food studies, have proliferated. In October 2021, the Food Sustainability Index (developed by *Economist* Impact and the Barilla Center for Food and Nutrition) predicted that food journalism would continue to grow, increasingly tying the food on our plates – and conventional food journalism of recipes, lifestyle, and celebratory culture – to both local and global contexts, examining supply chains and sustainability, and increasingly framing stories of food as systemic and collective, rather than individual, concerns (Food Sustainability Index 2021). Their prediction continues to be borne out in the recent work of outlets such as *Civil Eats, Serious Eats, Food52, Gravy*, and the *Food and Environment Reporting Network*; writers and editors such as Jessica Harris (*High on the Hog*), Michael Twitty (*The Cooking Gene*), Mayukh Sen (*Taste Makers: Seven Immigrant Women Who Revolutionized Food in America*), Zahir Janmohamed *(The Racist Sandwich Podcast),* Soleil Ho (*The Racist Sandwich Podcast,* food editor of the *San Francisco Chronicle*), Stephen Satterfield (*Whetstone* magazine), and Tom Philpott (food and agriculture correspondent for *Mother Jones*); and programs such as *What's Eating America* hosted by Andrew Zimmern and produced by MSNBC – among many, many others. As Mayukh Sen argued in a critical reflection of both the progress and the still stultifying limitations of food journalism for the *Columbia Journalism Review*, "in its finest form, food writing [can] function as both vivid storytelling and bracing cultural critique" (2018).

We agree with Sen that food media can function in these dual roles, and we are encouraged by the willingness of media outlets to support more complex and sometimes risky storytelling surrounding food and the efforts to diversify their ranks. Appraising the state of food journalism today, we take this book as an opportunity to interrogate its political significance: What opportunities does food offer for journalism to engage audiences with local, national, regional, and even global politics in order to provide "bracing cultural critiques," and to mobilize its legitimacy and civic and public relevance? What conditions are required to sustain and broaden the innovations and inroads of the past ten years? How are scholars around the world addressing these and related questions? What would meaningful future directions in research and in practice look like?

Our project began with a research panel on food journalism and politics (organized for the annual conference of the Association for Education in Journalism and Mass Communication in August 2020) that raised additional questions, introduced us to new colleagues exploring similar concerns, and inspired us to collaborate with others. We sent out an invitation for chapters to an interdisciplinary and international group of researchers who examine the intersections of food, media, and politics using a variety of theoretical frameworks and methods. The response was enthusiastic – and varied even beyond our expectations. The resulting collection of contemporary and historical case studies, we hope, will help us better understand the whys and hows of this provocative and increasing articulation of food, journalism, and politics by grounding it in research. It brings together disparate approaches and makes visible future directions for aligning food journalism research and practice in ways that can support journalism's economic viability, legitimacy, and relevance. Our findings can amplify the roles that food journalism and media can play in fostering equitability in social institutions and in building engaged and inclusive communities.

Food, Journalism, and Lifestyle Media

For decades, Western journalism scholars and educators have placed news at the center of their work (Zelizer 2013), and its production has afforded professional journalists legitimacy and authority as they act in "guarding the public interest, holding powers to account, turning public attention to matters of common interest, and incorporating a plurality of viewpoints" (Hanitzsch and Vos 2018, 150) with the ultimate goal of providing citizens with the information they need to participate in political life and self-government (see Norris and Odugbemi 2010).

Especially in the United States and Western democracies, serious journalism had come to be defined by its "watchdog" role of documenting abuses of power in government and business; by the concept and methods of objectivity, which included fortifying boundaries between the news or editorial functions of the press and its advertising and commercial functions; and by the imperative to address readers primarily as citizens with public responsibilities and concerns rather than as consumers with private everyday concerns. Journalism that addressed the latter (and could be found historically in newspaper women's pages and magazines), while always much appreciated by readers, was discursively devalued as frivolous, domestic, feminine, and soft in opposition to the serious, public, masculine, and hard news journalism of politics and business.

Yet increasingly, scholars have acknowledged the diversity and complexity – and argued for the political, social, and cultural significance – of journalism as it is practiced in its varied forms and functions around the world – including forms that relate to the management of lifestyle, identity, and everyday life (Hanusch 2012, 2020). As Hanitzsch and Vos explain, now "audiences are addressed less in their role as public citizens concerned with the social and political issues of the day, but rather in their role as clients and consumers whose personal concerns, aspirations, attitudes, and emotional experience become the center of attention" (Hanitzsch and Vos 2018, 156).

This growing relevance of lifestyle journalism has been linked to increasingly widespread disposable income in Western post-war societies and to a "shift from survival values to self-expression values" that this has enabled (Bauman 2000, 31). Such an increase in "wealth and prosperity leads to more options and flexibility in shaping one's identity and lifestyle, especially when lifestyle is articulated through visible attributes such as purchasable products and patterns of leisure-time activities" (Hanitzsch and Vos 2018, 157; see also Chaney 2001; Taylor 2002). In addition, institutions (such as religion, work, education, and family) that have long served as sites for identity construction have lost their authority in providing normative and powerful discourses of how identity should be thought of and performed. As a result, identity in modern societies is "more than ever an individual exercise … . Individuals are no more 'born into' their identities; identity is transformed from a 'given' into a 'task,' charging the actors with the responsibility for performing the task and for the consequences" (Bauman 2000, 31). As individuals engage in this identity work, they are presented with an often overwhelming array of options for who they can be and how they can enact their sense of self and values, especially through their consumption choices and practices. Journalism has stepped in to aid in this project through "news you can use" (Eide and Knight 1999; Underwood 2001), providing models for possible lifestyles performed through consumption as well as discursive and practical resources for managing everyday life, developing a sense of belonging in their communities, and fostering meaning and social connectedness (Bartsch and Schneider 2014). In performing these roles, journalism addresses audiences as consumers and contributes to the construction of consumer societies. Consumption becomes a performance of lifestyle, which is linked to a sense of self, but also to relationships with others, ethics, civic engagement, political participation, and ideological orientation. Thus, "journalism of everyday life" has profound political implications (Hanitzsch and Vos 2018).

To capitalize on the increasing relevance and demand for this type of journalism, traditional boundaries between hard and soft news, and between information and advertising, advocacy, and entertainment, are becoming more fluid. The category "lifestyle journalism" is extensive: it addresses "audiences as consumers, providing them with factual information and advice, often in entertaining ways, about goods and services they can use in their everyday lives" (Hanusch 2012, 5) and includes travel, entertainment, leisure, fashion, home and garden, and food. While lifestyle journalism is engaging with issues associated with news (such as Bourdain's reflections on war in Lebanon), formats associated with news have been adopting strategies of storytelling and audience engagement long associated with softer content (From 2018; Hanusch 2019). These hybrid forms also combine reporting of facts with the proffering of advice, seeking to "empower audiences by providing solutions and guidance in a highly complex modern world" (From 2018). In the process, this type of coverage usurps traditional hard news as the primary provider of information and re-engages disaffected audiences. In this way, lifestyle journalism has enormous potential to extend the reach of news by popularizing and democratizing knowledge (Hartley 2000) and "to contribute to the public sphere, albeit in perhaps different ways than traditional mainstream journalism" (Hanusch 2012, 5; see also Bird 1992; Dahlgren and Sparks 1992; Fiske 1989, 1992; Fürsich 2012; Hartley 1999; Meijer 2001).

Changing Concepts of Citizenship

Along with blurring boundaries between news and lifestyle journalism, there has been a re-evaluation of what it means to be a citizen and an effective participant in democratic societies. Scholars acknowledged that the idea of citizenship, which traditionally has often excluded people based on gender, class, race, or national origin, would benefit from moving beyond regulatory, legal, and state-connected aspects of nationality. Instead, the concept of cultural citizenship emphasizes the social, symbolic, and negotiated aspects of citizenship. Klaus and Lünenborg (2004), for example, argued that the media don't just create a rational, informed citizen, they play a significant role in the interactive and individual process of accessing symbolic resources of national identity and citizenship. This transformed notion of citizenship allows media scholars to examine the democratic affordances of various types of media and "to investigate traditional as much as popular journalism concerning its public or civic role" (Fürsich 2012, 17).

With this book, we take up this call and interrogate food journalism and media for their potential to support a democratic public sphere. John Fiske's (1989) concepts of "relevance" and "productivity" are helpful in clarifying if media content is truly "popular journalism," i.e., able to successfully engage its audiences (or users) in open interrogatory texts. Beyond formal criteria, our project also entails asking what concepts of public life and subjects of civic concern are negotiated in food media and what aspects are left behind. We are guided by more "holistic investigations of the power of media to define issues that are deemed worthy of public and popular discussion and whose voices and viewpoints are publicized and silenced" (Fürsich 2012, 19). Adapting Irene Costera Meijer's concept of "public quality," we investigate if food media as much as other types of journalism can instill "a sense of common experience and a basis for social cohesion by not excluding systematically the experiences of particular social groups, [by] the use of ordinary people's experience along with experts," and by exhibiting a capacity "for turning complex social discussions and issues into issues with clear options" (2001, 201). While food media as lifestyle journalism mostly offers advice that addresses and can be solved by individuals rather than collective problems and solutions, even private problems can have wider ramifications. Scholars should evaluate how this type of journalism negotiates social change: "The question is how the discourses and practices of lifestyle journalism narrate and relate to changing sociopolitical situations; and which social, cultural and even psychological scripts are offered to audiences to cope with these concerns" (Fürsich 2012, 16). As Mark Deuze suggested, "consumer culture and civic engagement seem to be interconnected and co-creative rather than opposing value systems, and as such function to make the daily remix of work, life and play just a little bit easier" (Deuze 2009, 21).

Questioning Lifestyle Empowerment and Reclaiming the Political

Even as we embrace the importance of lifestyle media in contemporary public life, we reject naively celebrating its democratic or civic potential. Tania Lewis, for example, warns that lifestyle is grounded in an "individualistic, consumption-oriented conception of the relation between selfhood and the social, where rather than being constrained by traditional forms of identity such as class, race, or gender, the individual is seen as a site of endless choice and potential transformation" (Lewis 2008, 5). She argues that performing lifestyle increasingly means recognizing oneself as belonging to broader affective communities, or communities of shared tastes, as well as being part of a body politic "with domestic space and everyday life increasingly colonized by discourses that assume a merger between consumer choice and behaviour and the duties and responsibilities of citizenship" (Lewis 2008, 5). Her question remains valid: "Does the displacement of public/national concerns onto the space of private, domestic consumption represent the death of a 'common public culture' ... or rather are we seeing a more complex redefinition of the boundaries and sites of citizenship and politics?" (Lewis 2008, 58).

Laurie Ouellette, amongst others, has explained that along with intensified commodification the success of lifestyle media has been tied to a problematic neoliberal ideology that weakened the state, public institutions, and the common good, while helping "create a model of citizenship that puts more emphasis on private institutions, individual choice and self-empowerment than before" (Ouellette 2016, 75). In her work on governmentality, lifestyle, and reality media, Ouellette shows how this ideological positioning has forged lifestyle entertainment into technologies that recreate citizens "as entrepreneurs of the self who must take responsibility for their own welfare" in an era when collective systems and public goods are systemically underfunded, privatized, or abandoned (Ouellette 2016, 80). Food media may popularize discourses of food ethics and politics, but structural solutions are often limited or absent, as, for example, Bell, Hollows, and Jones (2017) criticized. Instead, activist discourses are coopted in lifestyle media in the service of building commercial brands, thereby diluting their messages and disempowering their democratic potential (Phillipov 2016).

Digital media provide an intensified platform for lifestyle management. The wellbeing of the citizen is no longer understood "as a responsibility of the state but of the 'good' self-governing citizen who uses media as a tool to access the lifestyle expertise of a range of new cultural intermediaries, from celebrity chefs to 'ordinary' people" (Phillipov 2016, 93) as influencers (see Lewis 2008, 2020; Ouellette and Hay 2008; Rousseau 2012). This extreme focus on the individual does not preclude food media from presenting personal lifestyle choices as means of "investing in – and articulating – ethical, social and civic concerns, particularly those tied to notions of responsible and sustainable consumption" (Phillipov 2016, 93; see also Bell and Hollows 2011; Lewis 2020). But for food media and journalism to escape the neoliberal, and ultimately anti-democratic trappings of hypercommodified lifestyle media and to actually mobilize sustainable transformation, a special effort will be necessary. We purposively ask in this book for the "political" relevance of food media. It seemed to us that terms such as "civic importance," "public significance," or "popular potential" could not capture what is at stake. Expecting a *political* capacity reconnects food journalism and lifestyle media more directly to the original task of journalism to produce a democratic public sphere. Adapting Michael Goodhart's concepts (Goodhart 2018) for our project, being "political" means for the media to remain actively engaged in the project of change towards a more equitable world for all and to stay committed to the neverfinished project of democracy.

Food Journalism/Media

In this book, we use both food "journalism" and "media," often in the same phrase or sentence, as a way of acknowledging the conceptual and practical difficulties of maintaining clear boundaries between journalism and other forms of non-fiction media. Our less categorical approach is based on several considerations: the limitations of the traditional approach of defining journalism as news in spite of the variety of narratives, practices, audiences, and outlets that exist on the ground; the challenge in maintaining clear boundaries between journalistic forms produced for distribution on platforms that operate very differently (i.e., newspapers, consumer magazines, documentaries, blogs, Instagram, and other social media) and between producers that include those who have been professionally trained as journalists either through specialized education or professional experience, and those who haven't; and the problem of establishing clear boundaries between journalism and other nonfiction media when we take into account how audiences use, experience and learn from media in integrated ways.

And yet, the need and desire to distinguish journalism as a separate category of cultural production with important and still relevant unique standards and practices persist among researchers, practitioners, and audiences. We, too, feel this need, believing that journalism must continue to be defined by its accuracy, information, and watchdog functions, in addition to its many other possible roles such as entertainment, advocacy, literary, or community building. Maintaining the balance between the former and the latter influences our use of "journalism" in this volume, and allows us to include researchers examining everything from tabloid and broadsheet news, regional public television, culinary blogs, YouTube videos, travel magazines, advertising, recipes and menus, Netflix documentaries, and social media accounts , among others. Nevertheless, we also feel the pull to follow other researchers in not imposing an artificial isolating bubble around "journalism," but treating it as a form of cultural production that contributes to and is shaped by the broader media environment. So we use both concepts in tandem – journalism and media – to draw attention to the position of food as a journalistic genre and topic and its long history of straddling news, entertainment, and lifestyle on a wide variety of platforms. We embrace the way it is brought into being and maintained by the contextual tensions that animate it, that give it its purpose and protocols, its legitimacy, its failings, and its potential.

Food Media as a Site of Negotiation

Along with producing routine news related to the production, consumption, and regulation of food, media are increasingly covering in a more focused way food and its connections to broader social, political, and economic concerns, including climate change, environmental health, labor practices, immigration policy, racism, sexual harassment and violence in the food and culinary industries, food deserts, animal welfare, and international conflicts, among others. In addition to lifestyle and entertainment media addressing social problems and political solutions within the limits permitted by the logic and economics of their formats and production models, established and innovative news organizations also are reporting on food issues using a variety of narrative forms and business models. For example, FERN (Food and Environment Reporting Network), was founded in New York City in 2010 as a non-profit news organization producing investigative and explanatory reporting on food, agriculture, and environmental health by partnering with journalists working in various national media, such as *The Washington Post, Aljazeera America, National Public Radio, Mother Jones, The New Republic, Cooking Light, Eating Well*, as well as numerous local and regional outlets. The founders, all veteran reporters, wanted to support both the increased production of high-quality food news in particular and investigative reporting in general, which they understand to be an expensive yet critical function of journalism and one that has been severely curtailed as newsrooms cut their budgets and reduce their staff. On the US West Coast, another non-profit food news organization, *Civil Eats*, was founded in 2009 in California with similar intent to support the work of journalists and consistent critical coverage of food policy, farming, health, and the environment in order to "build economically and socially just communities" (civileats.com). These and other media outlets are finding ways to produce food news that confront the ongoing critical challenges of the media industry by building audience interest and loyalty with a sustainable financial grounding that flexibly adapts to technological change.

At the same time, food media have become sites for engaging identity politics and social justice in the media industries themselves. Critical questions of how media select, frame, and tell stories about food, which journalists get assignments, whose perspectives are routinely privileged, and which audience's interests and needs are taken into account in editorial decision-making are commanding critical attention from scholars and journalists alike. Motivated by the election of Donald Trump to the U.S. presidency in 2016 on a populist, anti-immigration platform and the growth of social movements such as Black Lives Matter, #MeToo, and others, many food media responded by turning inward and reflecting on their own power structures, policies, and production practices – and by seeking to diversify their full-time staff and contributors and the types of stories they supported to the extent that food writers of color "were startled by the degree to which editors asked them to write about their identities" (Sen 2018). But as Sen notes, this diversification was not without its problems, introducing a complex tokenism as journalists of color were pigeonholed into writing about food associated with "their" racial and ethnic identities, and focusing on their struggles with racism, sexism, and other systemic discrimination and violence – while at the same time being asked to modify their perspective to meet their editors' expectations and demands. As Korsha Wilson, who writes about food media, race, and class, observed, editors wanted stories told from their perspective: "They want me to be the face of it, but when it comes time for me to tell it from my point of view, they're like, no, no, we wanted you to tell it how we would tell it, but black" (quoted in Sen 2018). The question remains whether this engagement will lead to the infrastructure and commitment needed to support diverse storytelling in a consistent way, or if what food writer and publisher Stephen Satterfield described as "this responsive, reactionary moment" will remain just that – a fleeting response to broader national politics.

This combination of factors provides us with opportunities to further interrogate food journalism, its still largely unexcavated history, and its distinctive contributions to public culture and discourse. Beyond our focus on food media, this research provides broader insights into how journalism in general responds to moments of crisis that require change: the redefinition of its roles, audiences, and boundaries; a reassessment of its policies and practices; and a renewed endorsement of its relevance, authority, and legitimacy. With this book, we have seized these opportunities by bringing together scholars who are addressing these issues to help us understand food journalism and media's ability to generate forms that may be better able to represent the diversity of lived experience and to integrate a politics of consumption and lifestyle with a politics of collective action aimed at systemic change.

Outline of the Book

The contributors to this volume bring an international and interdisciplinary perspective to our understanding of food journalism and media. Their research in Australia, Canada, Denmark, India, the United Kingdom, and the United States highlights similarities and differences in journalism philosophies, practices, and scholarship in a globalized media landscape. Their projects tap into the continued expansion of food journalism and media in recent years with a special eye on understanding the economic, technological, political, and cultural forces behind them. Even though these chapters vary in terms of subject, theoretical frameworks, and methodology, we have organized them into four sections that correspond to the main concerns of this book. Read in dialogue with each other, they offer insights into the problems and promises of food journalism/media as practiced today. Moreover, they review achievements and gaps in current research and find overlooked historical connections; and they present suggestions for future directions in both research and practice.

Part One introduces the broad questions at the heart of this volume, centering on how food journalism and media engage in political issues beyond the production, distribution, marketing, and consumption of food. Specifically, this section addresses the varied ways food journalism and media engage with systems of injustice and disparity while obfuscating or illuminating systemic social problems. In Chapter 1, Tisha Dejmanee takes an intersectional feminist and media studies approach to analyzing food bloggers' engagement with #BlackOutTuesday, a digital action that was part of the wave of international Black Lives Matter protests. She explains the tensions inherent in how this community orchestrated influencer activism and discussions of race within their branded food platforms. While she notes several limitations to these posts – including adherence to neoliberal ideals of individualism and personal responsibility as well as consumer activism – Dejmanee argues that they generally demonstrated a high degree of self-reflexivity that challenged the norm that food bloggers should refrain from using their platforms to voice "controversial" or "political" opinions. In Chapter 2, Emily Contois explores the politics of Super Bowl food, analyzing how food sections and commercials framed the inclusion or exclusion of vegetables in Super Bowl menus while endorsing particular notions of gender that collide with evolving cultural concerns over health, wellness, and performance optimization. These collisions grow all the more apparent when comparing Super Bowl food culture before and during the COVID-19 pandemic. Her analysis reveals the roles food media play, and could play, within consumer spectacles like the Super Bowl. This chapter complements the author's previous work on "dude food," the recent marketing of food traditionally coded as feminine to men, and the ways that gendered identities are performed through food (Contois 2020). Chapter 3 examines how and under what conditions travel/food journalism engages with environmental conflict by analyzing the intersection of seafood, the impact of fish farming, and tourism in the Bay of Fundy, New Brunswick, Canada, a destination that relies partly on its seafood culture and "pristine" waterways to attract tourists. Drawing on her previous work on travel and environmental journalism, Lyn McGaurr uses interviews with local environmental activists and tourism professionals, along with analyses of articles, websites, and news reports to explicate the conditions that enable corporations and government agencies to maintain a discursive advantage in media representations of environmental conflict. Her case study supports the argument (e.g., Phillipov 2016) that when lifestyle media invest in particular foods that have local significance but fail to critique their chains of production, they increase the space for dominant players to deploy diluted discourses of sustainability and authenticity in their public relations and marketing campaigns. Finally, in Chapter 4, Alana Mann examines how journalists and other media producers can contest classism and racism embedded in food systems by going beyond superficial inclusion of "other" voices in the stories they tell about food-related problems and solutions. The author argues that while food media that incorporate the voices of frontline workers in fields, kitchens, food service, and processing lines can reveal unequal power relations in food systems, they also run the risk of reducing the autonomy of those voices in media discourse by reproducing paternalistic framings of the "powerless" in stories about food insecurity and related climate changes. Drawing on Sabiha Ahmad Kahn's (2020) notion of "food sovereign voices," the chapter instead suggests concrete strategies that can help produce more equitable, contextualized, and powerful food media narratives.

Part Two examines changing concepts of "good citizenship" – on the part of food journalism/media producers, their sources, and their audiences – with a special focus on questions of legitimacy and power. In Chapter 5, Kathleen LeBesco and Peter Naccarato document the changing representations of celebrity chefs from the "bad boy" persona of Anthony Bourdain's early work to the chef-heroes of the popular Netflix series *Chef's Table*, changes that began before but accelerated during the first two years of the COVID-19 pandemic. Using their concept of "culinary philanthropy," the authors illustrate how chefs and consumers affirm their identities as good citizens through their food practices, and in and through their engagement with food journalism/media. However, they criticize such framing to the extent that such philanthropic posturing serves to protect rather than challenge existing power dynamics and to reinforce capitalist values and traditional gender ideologies. In Chapter 6, Elfriede Fürsich explores how food journalism changed in response to the COVID-19 pandemic. Her analysis of the *New York Times* Food section finds that its journalism expressed a new type of domesticity that straddled neoliberal and holistic positions. Many articles exemplified an increasingly inward perspective that linked the food coverage to a neoliberal domesticity connected to individualism, self-optimization, and commodified approaches to personal happiness. However, the liminoid aspects of the pandemic as a global media event also generated openings for a "politicized domesticity," marked by an outward perspective related to the sustainability of food production, service, and consumption that emphasized systemic problems, collective solutions, and the hope for a better future for all. Chapter 7 examines the responsibility journalists have to rigorously interrogate claims by high-profile social media influencers. Katherine Kirkwood investigates two cases, that of Australian influencers Belle Gibson and Pete Evans, both of whom were implicated in misleading their followers by recommending diets to prevent or cure serious illnesses like COVID-19 and cancer. The author argues that even though journalists eventually exposed Gibson and Evans' deceptions, their initial uncritical coverage afforded these influencers an unwarranted legitimacy that was potentially harmful to the health and well-being of their vast audience. She connects these scandals to concurrent transformations in food media and journalism such as tabloidization and digitalization that enabled the problematic rise of these personalities to lifestyle celebrities.

Part Three turns our attention to the ways that food journalism and media construct, perform, or contest regional, national and global identities. In Chapter 8, Sumana Kasturi interrogates the "village food" YouTube videos that have emerged as a popular category in Indian food media, depicting great-grandmothers and village elders in rural settings cooking traditional recipes on clay stoves and over wood fires while attracting millions of viewers. The author situates these videos in the context of traditional and contemporary Indian gastro-politics, such as political battles over vegetarianism, "taboo foods," and indigenous foodways. Kasturi explains how social media platforms allow ordinary people to participate in online food cultures by creating culinary counterpublics that challenge the dominance of elite, urban food discourses in legacy and international media. Chapter 9 explores the relationship between national identity, international politics, and food by analyzing how the "bendy banana" became a powerful symbol in Euromyths – exaggerated or invented stories about activities and regulations of the European Union written for tabloids but often echoed in broadsheet newspapers published in the United Kingdom. Mary Irwin and Ana Tominc trace the multivarious historic and metaphorical representations of bananas that could be activated to galvanize anti-EU sentiment and help shore up support for Brexit. Chapter 10 investigates how innovative food journalism can strengthen sub-national identity, foster audience loyalty, and promote economic development. Unni From Andreasen and Alberte Borne Asmusse detail how the Danish regional television station TV2/FYN organized a "live journalism" Smoked Cheese Day event on the island of Funen to increase engagement with its coverage of the economic and cultural impact that the declining popularity of the traditional cheese is having on the region. Extending scholarly debate on constructive journalism, live journalism, and food journalism, From and Borne clarify how food as a specific beat can facilitate engagement and community building and become "valuable news" in a local context.

Finally, Part Four connects food journalism and media to dimensions of history and memory as public or political action. Sarah Lonsdale takes us back to World War I in Chapter 11. She documents how food journalism published in a variety of sections in the *Daily Mail* during the war employed service journalism to help citizens, especially women, navigate the crisis, and participate in the war effort through gardening and careful management of rationed food resources. This coverage not only boosted national identity and fortified reader loyalty but also framed women's participation in civic life as worthy of full citizenship rights, including the still elusive right to vote. In Chapter 12, Kimberly Voss draws attention to the gender politics of (food) media history and archives by documenting the achievements of Alma Lach (1914–2013), in her time well-known in Chicago for her food writing, television appearances, cooking school, consultancy, and entrepreneurship. The chapter is based on Lach's personal archive that includes more than 3000 cookbooks, personal notebooks, cooking ephemera, and promotional materials. Voss explains how Lach played a significant role in her community and in the development of food journalism in newspapers, magazines, television, and branded content. She was also a forerunner of today's complex integration of food journalism with other genres of food media and even the entrepreneurial femininity of online influencers. Chapter 13 rounds out this section by examining "history-in-the-making." Diana Willis scrutinizes the use of autobiographical, historical, and collective cultural memories in representations of chefs' lives in the Netflix series *Chef's Table* as a locus of contemporary negotiations of identity and elite authenticity. Willis explains how the series' individual profiles and its overall aesthetic approach rest on the premise that food practices serve as important markers of social status. The episodes are wrapped in an "authentic" elite discourse high on culinary capital, while cultural memories of family history, rootedness, and locality distance the audience from current systemic problems in and beyond the food industry.

The Political Relevance of Food Media and Journalism

Overall, this book brings a wide variety of assumptions, topics, and methods to the nexus of food, journalism, media, and politics. By allowing for a flexible definition of "journalism" and "politics," we tried to generate an inclusive, complex, and diversified platform for research and knowledge production. We see the main contribution of this volume as stimulating a lively debate on the political relevance of food media. Journalism and media have always been produced under specific but constantly evolving regulatory, economic, and technological circumstances; food journalism/media are no exception. Global challenges related to the climate crisis, the ongoing pandemic, and the persistent social and economic inequities across and within borders provide the current context of concern. The advantage of narrating and elucidating intricate issues through mediated stories of the production, distribution, consumption, and waste of food is its immediate and direct relevance for everyone: "We are what we eat!" But we hope this book provides new incentives to demand from food and lifestyle media even more: Food journalism/media remain relevant if they actively accept their public role and recognize that critical awareness of the circumstances of our everyday lives are a pre-condition and catalyst of political action and change.

References

"Anthony Bourdain's Colleagues Pay Tributes." 2018. *The Quint*. June 9, 2018. https://www.thequint.com/hotwire-text/anthony-bourdain-s-colleagues-pay-tributes#read-more.

Bartsch, Anne and Frank M. Schneider. 2014. "Entertainment and Politics Revisited: How Non-escapist Forms of Entertainment Can Stimulate Political Interest and Information Seeking." *Journal of Communication* 64:369–396.

Bauman, Zygmunt. 2000. *Liquid Modernity*. Cambridge: Polity.

Bell, David, and Joanne Hollows. 2011. "From *River Cottage* to *Chicken Run*: Hugh Fearnley-Whittingstall and the Class Politics of Ethical Consumption." *Celebrity Studies* 2:178–191.

Bell, David, Joanne Hollows, and Steven Jones. 2017. "Campaigning Culinary Documentaries and the Responsibilization of Food Crises." *Geoforum* 84: 179–187.

Bird, Elizabeth. 1992. *For Enquiring Minds: A Cultural Study of Supermarket Tabloids*. Knoxville: University of Tennessee Press.

Chaney, David. 2001. "From Ways of Life to Lifestyle: Rethinking Culture as Ideology and Sensibility." In *Culture in the Communication Age*, edited by James Lull, 75–88. London: Routledge.

Contois, Emily J. H. 2020. *Diners, Dudes, and Diets: How Gender and Power Collide in Food Media and Culture*. Studies in United States Culture. Chapel Hill: The University of North Carolina Press.

Dahlgren, Peter and Colin Sparks (eds.) 1992. *Journalism and Popular Culture*. London: Sage Publications.

Deuze, Mark. 2009. "Journalism, Citizenship and Digital Culture." In *Journalism and Citizenship: New Agendas in Communication*, edited by Zizi Papacharissi, 18–28. New York: Routledge.

Eide, Martin and Graham Knight. 1999. "Public/Private Service: Service Journalism and the Problems of Everyday Life." *European Journal of Communication* 14(4):525–547.

Fiske, John. 1989. *Reading the Popular*. Boston: Unwin Hyman.

Fiske, John. 1992. "Popularity and the Politics of Information." In *Journalism and Popular Culture*, edited by Peter Dahlgreen and Colin Sparks, 45–63. London: Sage.

Flagler, Madison. 2017. "Anthony Bourdain Claps Back at Critics Who Say Chefs Should Stay Out of Politics." *Delish*. Oct. 8, 2018.

Food Sustainability Index 2021. https://impact.economist.com/projects/food-sustainability/

From, Unni. 2018. "Lifestyle Journalism." *Oxford Research Encyclopedias*. 10.1093/acrefore/9780190228013.013.835.

Fürsich, Elfriede. 2012. "Lifestyle Journalism as Popular Journalism: Strategies for Evaluating its Public Role." *Journalism Practice* 6(1): 12–25. 10.1080/17512786.2011.622894.

Goodhart, Michael E. 2018. *Injustice: Political Theory for the Real World*. New York, NY: Oxford University Press.

Hanitzsch, Thomas, and Tim P. Vos. 2018. "Journalism beyond Democracy: A New Look into Journalistic Roles in Political and Everyday Life." *Journalism* 19(2):146–164.

Hanusch, Folker. 2012. "Broadening the Focus: The Case for Lifestyle Journalism as Scholarly Inquiry." *Journalism Practice* 6(1): 2–11.

Hanusch, Folker. 2019. "Journalistic Roles and Everyday Life: An Empirical Account of Lifestyle Journalists' Professional Views." *Journalism Studies* 20 (2): 193–211. 10.1080/1461670X.2017.1370977.

Hartley, John. 1999. "What is Journalism? The View From Under a Stubbie Cap." *Media International Australia* 90: 15–33.

Hartley, John. 2000. "Communicative Democracy in a Redactional Society: The Future of Journalism Studies." *Journalism Studies* 1(1): 39–48.

Kanani, Rahim. 2017. "The World According to Anthony Bourdain." *Food & Wine*. May 24, 2017.

Keefe, Patrick Radden. 2017. "Anthony Bourdain's Moveable Feast: Guided by a Lusty Appetite for Indigenous Culture and Cuisine, the Swaggering Chef has Become a Traveling Statesman." *New Yorker*. Feb. 5, 2017.

Klaus, Elisabeth and Lünenborg, Margreth. 2004. "Cultural Citizenship. Ein Kommunikationswissenschaftliches Konzept zur Bestimmung kultureller Teilhabe in der Mediengesellschaft." *M&K - Medien und Kommunikationswissenschaft* 52 (2): 193–213.

Klion, David. 2018. "What Anthony Bourdain Gave Us." *The Nation*. June 8, 2018.

Lewis, Tania. 2008. *Smart Living: Lifestyle Media and Popular Expertise.* New York: Peter Lang.

Lewis, Tania. 2020. *Digital Food: From Paddock to Platform.* Oxford: Bloomsbury Academic.

Meijer, Irene Costera. 2001. "The Public Quality of Popular Journalism: Developing a Normative Framework." *Journalism Studies* 2(2): 189–205. 10.1080/14616700120042079.

Nichols, John. 2018. "Anthony Bourdain Knew There Was Nothing More Political Than Food." *The Nation.* June 8:218.

Norris, Pippa, and Sina Odugbemi. 2010. "Evaluating Media Performance." In *Public Sentinel: News Media and Governance Reform,* edited by Pippa Norris, 3–29. Washington, DC: World Bank Publications.

Ouellette, Laurie. 2016. *Lifestyle TV.* Routledge Television Guidebooks. New York, NY: Routledge.

Ouellette, Laurie, and James Hay 2008. "Makeover Television, Governmentality and the Good Citizen." *Continuum* 24:471–484.

Phillipov, Michelle. 2016. "The New Politics of Food: Television and the Media/Food Industries." *Media International Australia* 158(1): 90–98. 10.1177/1329878X15627339.

Rousseau, Signe. 2012. *Food Media: Celebrity Chefs and the Politics of Everyday Interference.* Oxford: Berg Publishers.

Sen, Mayukh. 2018. "Where Food Writing Leads." *Columbia Journalism Review.* Fall 2018. https://www.cjr.org/special_report/food-writing-race-identity.php

Taylor, Lisa. 2002. "From Ways of Life to Lifestyle: The 'Ordinari-ization' of British Gardening Lifestyle Television." *European Journal of Communication* 17:49–493.

Underwood, Doug. 2001. "Reporting And the Push for Market-Oriented Journalism: Media Organizations As Businesses." In *Mediated Politics: Communication in the Future of Democracy,* edited by W. Lance Bennett and Robert M. Entman, 99–116. New York: Cambridge University Press.

Zelizer, Barbie. 2013. "On the Shelf Life of Democracy in Journalism Scholarship." *Journalism* 14 (4):459–473. 10.1177/1464884912464179.

Part I
Engaging with Systems of Injustice and Disparity

1 Influencer Activism: Visibility, Strategy, and #BlackLivesMatter Discourse on Food Instagram

Tisha Dejmanee

In June 2020, mainstream attention to the Black Lives Matter movement in the wake of George Floyd's murder led to #BlackOutTuesday, a digital action that attracted widespread engagement from celebrities and digital influencers on Instagram. Devised by Brianna Agyemang and Jamila Thomas, two Black women music executives, #BlackOutTuesday was a call for the music industry to pause and reflect on their participation in structural racism (an affiliate hashtag #TheShowMustBePaused was also circulated) (Donoughue 2020). This action was widely represented on Instagram by a black square and was incredibly popular, with estimates that 14.6 million #BlackOutTuesday posts were published on June 2, 2020, the designated day of action (Bursztynsky and Whitten 2020).

Black Lives Matter, as a social movement and political ideology, was formed in 2013 by Alicia Garza, Patrisse Cullors, and Opal Tometi as "an ideological and political intervention in a world where Black lives are systematically and intentionally targeted for demise" (Garza 2016, 23). While built on a history of using audiovisual evidence to rally against State-sanctioned violence toward Black people, the unprecedented capacity for recording and circulating such evidence in the digital age has supported the sustained growth of the movement (Jackson, Bailey, and Foucault Welles 2020; Lebron 2017). #BlackLivesMatter, as a widely circulated hashtag on social media, has also facilitated the spread of information required to sustain the movement. It has been used in recruitment for the movement by offering opportunities for sustained reflection and engagement around racial issues and movement ideologies (De Choudhury et al. 2016), providing a sense of collective identity for disparately-located activists across a sustained time period (Mundt et al. 2018), and creating a digital counterpublic to mobilize identity-based political action (Jackson, Bailey, and Foucault Welles 2020). While #BlackOutTuesday was related to the use of #BlackLivesMatter on Twitter, the way it was made hypervisible through the accounts of celebrities and influencers on Instagram led to widespread criticism of "performative activism" and "optical allyship," where non-minority influencers participate in trending digital actions primarily to boost their own social and financial capital (Ashe 2020; Mercado 2020).

DOI: 10.4324/9781003283942-3

I explore this perception of influencer activism as optical allyship through an analysis of the food blogging community's engagement with #BlackOutTuesday on Instagram. Food bloggers are digital influencers who build online brands through the performance of stylized, hegemonic femininity and high-quality food content. As influencers whose brands and livelihoods are often predicated upon the production of aspirational, commercially-aligned lifestyle content, the food blogging community has historically adopted a strictly apolitical and artificially cheerful tone that has been described as "no serious conflict, no controversy, no cynicism, no snark" (Fortini 2011). However, #BlackOutTuesday offers a moment to explore how the conventions of this digital food culture are negotiated to allow for social activism, and the tensions inherent to such challenges. Drawing on a sample of Instagram accounts by prominent food bloggers, I perform a qualitative discourse analysis of the caption text produced in posts affiliated with #BlackOutTuesday and Black Lives Matter to explain the characteristics of influencer activism. In my analysis, I explore the efficacy of this action by asking: What actions were recommended by the community? What language around race and racism was used? How did food influencers portray themselves and their roles within this movement? How did they negotiate the language of activism within the cultivated performances of their brands and digital identities?

In my findings, I note a conflation of protest with the brand strategies of the attention economy, as well as a tendency to rely on neoliberal individualism and consumer politics as activist strategies. Additionally, I point out the ways that the visibility of this action was determined by the pre-established hierarchies and algorithms of Instagram and the food blogosphere, which worked to reproduce situational, rather than structural, understandings of racism. At the same time, I reject accusations of optical allyship within this influencer community, drawing on evidence of a high degree of self-reflexivity among the bloggers in this sample and the use of this action to challenge the expectations of apoliticism within the food blogosphere. In turn, this response demonstrates the malleability of the food blogosphere, which has the capacity to both reproduce and rupture hegemonic norms as an expression of user-generated digital food politics.

Food Bloggers, Instagram, and Self-Branding Strategies

Food blogs are digital food media that feature the narratives, photographs, and recipes of food that is produced in the home of an individual, typically female, blogger. As food blogs have become established as a digital genre, they have built a reputation for high production values as well as for publishing intimate and stylized performances of feminine domesticity (Dejmanee 2015; Matchar 2015; Presswood 2019), and these qualities have developed hand-in-hand with the food blogosphere's rise as a particularly lucrative site for marketers. As such, while food blogs mimic performances of casual and effortless domestic labor, content is strategic and carefully calculated within self-branding logics that require food bloggers to consciously construct their digital identities, content, and overarching narratives as commodities that cohere with commercial logics (Hearn 2008).

This allegiance to commercial logics leads to the celebration and reproduction of hegemonic identity discourses, notably postfeminism as food bloggers "exacerbate distinctions between men and women and provoke middle-class anxieties about having children, finding a husband, and securing the comforts of home" (Salvio 2012, 35). Moreover, the sites are embedded in a postrace discourse, as the dominant whiteness of the food blogosphere is unremarked upon and race is often articulated only through practices of commoditization, appropriation, and colonization. The resulting ambivalence, which is characteristic of "post-" ideologies, is further amplified through the digital affordances which shape and constrain meaning on food blogs. For instance, as food influencers become microcelebrities who "accumulate a following on blogs and social media through textual and visual narrations of their personal, everyday lives" (Abidin 2016a, 86) and perform "relational labor" through "regular, ongoing communication with audiences over time to build social relationships that foster paid work" (Baym 2015, 16), digital intimacies become inseparable from profit-accumulation strategies. It is such ambivalence that has undoubtedly produced polarized responses to the food blogosphere, with many trivializing the genre and its emphasis on personal narratives or disparaging the content produced as self-promotional and inauthentic. Echoes of this denigration of food bloggers and their work became prominent in the wake of the community's response to #BlackOutTuesday on Instagram.

While my focus is on food influencers who have attained digital visibility through the production of food blogs, Instagram accounts are an increasingly important cross-promotional platform for food bloggers, and Instagram is used strategically and deliberately by influencers as an extension of their brand management practices (Cotter 2019). Due to the labor-intensive process of food blogging, many bloggers use Instagram not only to cross-publicize new posts and recipes that are published to their blogs, but also during moments when they are unable to regularly update their blogs. Moreover, Instagram is increasingly attracting US users, with Pew Research hailing it as the country's third most popular social media platform after YouTube and Facebook, and it is particularly popular amongst young people, with 71 percent of 18-to-29-year-olds claiming to use the platform (Auxier and Anderson 2021).

A growing body of research has explored Instagram as a platform for activism, particularly in regard to issues of gender, representation, and embodiment (e.g., Butkowski et al. 2020; Baker and Walsh 2018; Caldeira and De Ridder 2017; Ging and Garvey 2018; Mahoney 2020), which are well suited to the platform's demographics and visual emphasis. A further strand of work has explored how influencers utilize Instagram to disseminate activist and social justice messaging, such as "realfooders" who post content on nutrition and dietary patterns on Instagram (Gil-Quintana, Santovena-Casal, and Riaño 2021), and female environmental influencers who post about veganism and the zero-waste movement (Quintana Ramos and Cownie 2020). However, the current study builds on this discussion by focusing on food bloggers who are participating in Black Lives Matter discourse, which typically falls outside the purview of their brand's content focus. It is this emergence of race-based activism and protests from a community which is predominantly non-Black and has historically been understood as apolitical that attracted criticisms of optical allyship. In this study, I seek to complicate this claim, while simultaneously acknowledging some of the limitations of the #BlackOutTuesday action and influencer activism.

The *Saveur* Food Blog Awards

The sample for this study was derived from the Instagram accounts associated with food blogs that were finalists for the *Saveur* Blog Awards between 2009 and 2019. The *Saveur* Blog Awards, organized annually by *Saveur* magazine, are one of the highest forms of recognition for food bloggers with tens of thousands of nominations received for these awards each year (Saveur 2019). From the complete list of award finalists over the past decade, I compiled a sample of food blogs that were active, published in English, and adhered to the definition of food blogs set out above. While the resulting sample is not necessarily representative of the food blogosphere as a whole, it is relevant to understand the blogosphere not as an index of blogs, but as a site structured by flows of power that are governed by the rules of visibility and profits in a digital attention economy. In this hierarchy, the more visible blogs attract an exponential amount of influence, and thus, due to the publicity generated from being *Saveur* award finalists, I would regard this as a highly influential sample of food bloggers. From this sample of food blogs, I viewed the corresponding Instagram accounts and collected 167 posts on #BlackOutTuesday and Black Lives Matter published from 96 unique Instagram accounts in June 2020. It is relevant to note that this sample reflected the dominant whiteness of the wider food blogging community as Black food bloggers authored only 7 of the 96 Instagram accounts and 20 of the 167 posts.

I performed a qualitative thematic analysis of the 167 #BlackOutTuesday and Black Lives Matter posts, drawing on a grounded theory approach (Corbin and Strauss 1990). Employing open coding of Instagram caption text, I identified the recurrent, salient themes that emerged across all posts and then used a process of clustering to determine the dominant thematic categories, with a focus on discourses around activism and race. This process resulted in the identification of six themes: (1) education,

(2) personal experience, (3) amplifying and muting content, (4) self-reflexivity, (5) empty statements, and (6) anger, self-promotion, and self-care for Black food bloggers.

Themes of #BlackOutTuesday on Food Instagram

Education: Learning, Listening, and "Doing the Work"

References to learning and education appeared extensively across this sample, supporting the idea that a key contributor to racism is ignorance and that this could or should be combatted by taking personal responsibility for learning about racism, its history, and the perspectives of Black Americans. For instance, Joy of *Joy the Baker* writes, "Looking at my privilege and the things I can take for granted is uncomfortable. But I do it often because it is part of the work … If you're uncomfortable right now - yes, good, use it. Use it to stay aware and self-examine and donate and sign petitions and educate yourself." This framing – where overcoming racism is expressed as a personal journey for self-betterment – aligns with the ethos of neoliberal individual responsibility, also demonstrated through the widespread circulation of the phrase "doing the work," which suggests the difficult and arduous process of anti-racism as a moral imperative, as well as analogizing activism with entrepreneurialism, where the agency, creativity, and gumption of the individual is critical to producing a successful outcome.

This focus on education was supported by sharing links to books, resources, and accounts of anti-racism educators: Michelle of *Nom Nom Paleo* posts an image of @jane_mount's book suggestions, while Sara of *Sprouted Kitchen* writes that she is "listening to and amplifying the voices of: @rachel.cargle @austinchanning @theconsciouskid @ohhappydani @blackcoffeewithwhitefriends." It is likely that this emphasis on information-seeking as action may have been particularly resonant within the food blogging community as it maps onto dominant food and health discourses that compel personal investment in food research, particularly for women and mothers, as compulsory for the correct performance of contemporary food work (Cairns, Johnston, and MacKendrick 2013). As food blogs are key sites for disseminating food knowledge and pedagogies, the same infrastructures for knowledge exchange are readily used to accommodate a shift in focus from food to racism.

Personal Experience

It is unsurprising, given the intimate tone cultivated by food blogs and the personal storytelling promoted by the Instagram platform, that #BlackOutTuesday posts were often articulated through very personal language and experiences. This was evident in the use of the highly emotive language that is prevalent across the food blogosphere – many bloggers confessed that they felt heartbroken, disgusted, sad, horrified, and overwhelmed while also suggesting that love, joy, and hope were routes to overcoming racism. As Beth of *Budget Bytes* writes, "Taking a pause. I can't think about food right now and pretend everything is okay. I'm pressing pause on food to take a moment to grieve ... My heart is breaking for all the lives lost ... But I'm hopeful. I believe we can be better." The personal experiences shared by this group also included confessions of their privilege and ignorance, as well as their personal pledges to take specific actions to overcome racism. For instance, Kate of *Cookie and Kate* writes, "I was born into privilege, and my heart is heavy with injustice ... Considering myself a non-racist is not enough. I have work to do and I will do it ... I'm contemplating how to become a more active part of the solution, both in my personal life and through this platform." A small number of posts also documented attendance at or observation of protests as part of their personal experiences. The fact that the majority of influencers in this sample were non-Black highlighted the clear disjunct between sharing personal experiences and the issue of racism, which many bloggers had not personally experienced.

The influence of postrace discourse – in which the myth of a colorblind and meritocratic society leads to the taboo of acknowledging or discussing race (Bonilla-Silva 2003; Joseph 2018) – was evident as many bloggers expressed feelings of uncertainty, discomfort, and hesitation when talking about racism. Michelle of *Hummingbird High* confesses, "I hesitated posting something for too long because, truthfully, I was struggling"; while Sara of *Sprouted Kitchen* acknowledges, "I don't know how to speak on racism correctly." However, some bloggers also drew on these feelings to note the necessity in this moment of overcoming their discomfort to speak up and use their platforms to take a public stand against racism.

Amplifying and Muting Content

The language of muting or pausing content, and inversely, amplifying the content and voices of Black and minority influencers, was widely used across this sample. For example, Sarah of *Broma Bakery* explains, "in support of the current happenings in the world, I am joining the #amplifymelanatedvoices movement ... this means I won't be posting anything on my feed this week, June 1st–7th, to give more visibility to black and POC voices." Such language was central to the articulation of #BlackOutTuesday, and was practiced by pausing content but also tagging and publicizing Black content creators and their accounts.

While amplifying the accounts and content of Black food bloggers was a practice that was enthusiastically taken up by non-Black bloggers, some of the Black bloggers whose accounts were suddenly made hypervisible often alluded to being overwhelmed by new followers, and some expressed uncertainty about the lasting impacts of this fleeting surge in visibility as a result of the movement. As Black blogger Benjamina of *Carrot and Crumb* writes, "There are plenty of new faces here so hello ... What a week. So much to process, so many more conversations to have but hopeful that people's words will be followed up by actually putting in the work."

There was also a tendency for this action to perpetuate a myopic understanding of racism, for instance suggesting that the lack of representation within the food blogging community was the problem rather than a symptom of larger structural problems, including the bias encoded into algorithms, Silicon Valley, Instagram, and the commercial sponsorship model through which success and visibility is granted. That is, when the problem was framed simply as the "lack of visibility" of Black content creators, it became easy to address this problem by taking action – by tagging, following, and amplifying Black creatives – without further interrogation into the structure of racism itself. Moreover, the form of this digital action also meant that when non-Black account holders participated in this action by amplifying or muting content, they also potentially generated greater visibility and value for their own brands, making it difficult to distinguish philanthropy from self-promotional strategy. This can be seen in the post by Alexandra of *Alexandra's Kitchen*, "I'll be holding virtual cooking classes through Zoom via @airsubs. Classes will be $25 each and capped at 50 attendees per class. All of my proceeds will go to a charity that supports the BIPOC community," in which the personal brand and business are purposefully merged with the Black Lives Matter movement.

Self-Reflexivity: "Instagram Is Not Real Life"

Discourse in this sample demonstrated a high degree of self-reflexivity about the action. This included explaining the purpose and intent of the movement, circulating information about protests and practices for participating, and noting that actions, phrasing, or comments had been influenced by dialog with Black individuals and activists.

Bloggers also referenced the criticism and loss of followers that resulted from their participation in #BlackOutTuesday. This made clear the considered calculation of participation as part of a broader brand strategy, which sometimes resulted in defiance – for instance, Michelle of *Nom Nom Paleo's* exclamation, "no, I'm not going to stick to food," in response to attempts to denigrate or silence political discussion by lifestyle bloggers – and other times resulted in meeker reassurances that bloggers would 'get back to cooking soon,' for instance by Deb Perelman of *Smitten Kitchen* and Marisa of *Food in Jars*. In a similar fashion, bloggers demonstrated self-reflexivity about perceived criticisms of their participation as optical allyship, or as superficial and fleeting. This was sometimes evidenced in the language used – for instance, Marie of *Food Nouveau* writes, "Do the work. Instagram is not real life" – while other bloggers (such as Kate of

Cookie and Kate and Linsdey of *Dolly and Oatmeal*) acknowledged their own complicity with structural racism, and documented plans for structural change within their own brands and work. However, self-reflexivity was signaled most pertinently through the length of captions – which averaged 137 words per post, an unusually long average for the Instagram platform – and the number of bloggers who posted more than once on the topic of racism or Black Lives Matter. These patterns of posting suggest that bloggers were eager to demonstrate their participation was part of an ongoing commitment to racial justice, and was genuine and thoughtful rather than simply motivated by the desire to join a trend.

Empty Statements

A small number of posts in the sample engaged in empty statements, which were short posts either just employing the hashtag #BlackLivesMatter, or phrases that were commonly circulated on social media during this time, notably "I understand that I can never understand" (e.g., Astrid, *The Sweet Rebellion*). While such phrases reflected notions of solidarity, support, and a stance against racism, they lacked substance and their primary goal was to signal support for and participation in the movement.

Anger, Self-Promotion, and Self-Care for Black Food Bloggers

The data produced by Black-identified food bloggers within this sample was comparatively small, featuring only 20 posts, and further skewed by the fact that two bloggers were responsible for publishing 65 percent of these 20 posts. However, while this sample was small, their response to the #BlackOutTuesday action was significant as Black-identified bloggers were spotlighted, having their accounts tagged and amplified by others within the community. This meant they were often compelled to use this moment to publicize their brands, cookbooks, and blog labor. For instance, Kimberly of *The Little Plantation* intertwines her experiences of identity with her professional brand as she writes,

> Being a POC means I have always had to work harder to achieve the same things my white colleagues get. I've never been bitter about it, instead it has simply resulted in an INSANE work ethic … It also means I can proudly say that my #eatcaptureshare photography challenge is one of the BEST ones on this platform and my ecourse one of the best you'll ever sign up to because I usually out work everyone in this space.

Additional themes present within this sample included attention to grief, mental health, and self-care of Black activists and the Black community. As Lazarus Lynch of *Son of a Southern Chef* writes, "Our pain is far too deep for one tweet or one protest or one anything … Our grief is multifaceted and multilayered. We must empower each other while we do the work." Finally, Black bloggers used this action to call out racism within the food blogging community. As Angela of *Kitchenista* writes, "I see those of you who have blacked out and muted but those comments are turned off ... The very least you can do is directly deal with the racist comments your own audiences spew. Deal with that before you tag me as your black blogger of the week for performative activism."

Protest Language as Brand Strategy

The dominant discursive themes and practices from this sample of food bloggers reflect the tensions inherent to influencer activism, as social movement messages take place within an influencer culture that is popularly understood to be driven by self-promotional interests and commercialized communication practices. It is clear that Instagram's platform vernacular had a distinct influence on #BlackOutTuesday. This was most salient in the use of language in this sample, with the words "amplify" and "mute" prominently circulated and emphasizing the spreadability of digital content as, in and of itself, central to the success of protest actions. The reliance on such language and actions reflects the conflation of online activism with digital brand strategy within an attention economy in which likes, shares, and retweets typically serve as measures of success (van Dijck 2013) and in which cross-promotional activity that highlights other creatives' work and profiles is commonly used to engender goodwill within a digital community (Ryan 2018). However, when this same logic is applied to social movement action frames, such language fails to offer a barometer for distinguishing between more or less valuable or accurate content and tends to portray civil rights as an individual project of self-education and/or communication, both of which elide an understanding of the necessity for structural reforms and collective action in the fight for racial equality. Moreover, this discourse demonstrates a continuing reliance on neoliberal logics whereby individuals and their choices – including where to allocate their money or which accounts are worthy of amplification – are viewed as the key drivers of social change.

Moreover, while action to tag and spotlight Black Instagram content is intended to highlight the lack of diversity within digital influencer spaces, it also tends to mistake the symptoms of structural racism with structural racism itself. To this end, while temporarily and artificially boosting the circulation of creative content and the accounts of some Black individuals may serve a purpose within the influencer community, it does not encourage reflection on the deeper flaws of the attention economy which systematically benefits white content creators who perform aspirational hegemonic lifestyles and identities. As noted in the examples above, many Black food bloggers appeared to be overwhelmed by the instant surge in the attention their accounts and brands received, and some expressed discomfort and skepticism at the value of such action even where it brought much attention to their work. It is possible to see from these reactions that Black food bloggers who are the supposed beneficiaries of this action had very little control over or buy-in to such amplification strategies.

Finally, the language of amplifying and muting had the effect of highlighting the trend-based nature of information spread on social media. Many of the same phrases, resources, and words were highly circulated and repeated as part of the action, notably the statement "I understand that I will never understand, but still I stand," quotes by antiracism activist Rachel Cargle and links to her account, and the digital infographic produced by @ohhappydani. This structuring of #BlackOutTuesday as a trend guaranteed a rapid surge in visibility and attention to an issue across a wide range of media, which was reflected in the broad coverage and participation in this action. However, trends are also transient and fleeting, embedding an inevitable obsolescence into this action that is antithetical to the long-term commitment to structural change that the Black Lives Matter movement is advocating.

These criticisms of #BlackOutTuesday certainly give context to the claims of optical allyship as it is clear that influencer activism tends to fall within hegemonic discourses around neoliberal individualism and consumer politics. Nevertheless, it is also somewhat unreasonable to expect the food blogosphere to be a site of radical challenge to hegemonic ideologies around race. It is important to attend to the realities of ambivalence that structure the possibilities for food bloggers' visibility and identity performance and, on this note, I would generally reject the accusations of optical allyship for this particular influencer community. Instead, food bloggers overwhelmingly demonstrated an awareness of their role within the limits of their platforms and the genre of food blogging and sought to challenge these limits and expectations in the course of their participation in #BlackOutTuesday.

Many bloggers used #BlackOutTuesday to vocalize and denounce the expected apoliticism of the food blogosphere. In particular, the expectation that food bloggers' visibility and influence was predicated on their tacit agreement to refrain from voicing political opinions and that they should "just stick to food" echoed the argument that the visibility of the postfeminist subject is predicated upon her silence on feminism (McRobbie 2008) and that discussion about race is stifled through postrace discourse (Bonilla-Silva 2003). Food bloggers pointed out the privilege inherent to designating racism as a "political" topic rather than a lived reality and challenged the expectation that bloggers refrain from using their vast platforms to discuss social issues. Several bloggers also used this discussion to relate these conventions directly back to the commercialization of the blogosphere, evidencing a self-reflexivity of the ways that branding strategies are often at odds with social justice imperatives. While such criticisms did not necessarily facilitate a better response to Black Lives Matter, they demonstrated a critical awareness of the commercial logics and algorithms that reproduce political silencing and the invisibilization of Black digital content, and self-reflexivity about the limits food influencers inherently faced when trying to participate in this movement. #BlackOutTuesday thus served as a collective awakening of and challenge to the ways the genre of food blogging has worked to dampen political discussion.

Admittedly, at times the incorporation of Black Lives Matter content within the pre-existing commercial tenor of digital food content revealed an awkward fit. Discussion of the serious and fatal topic of structural racism within the determinedly cheerful and capricious tone of digital food blogs involved an abrupt and sometimes awkward shift in tone. In a few instances, this was navigated through flippant or fleeting references to Black Lives Matter that was offensive to the topic matter at hand, for example, Ashlae of *Oh Lady Cakes* writes, "Here's a photo of a really delicious thing with a reminder that BREONNA TAYLOR'S KILLERS STILL HAVEN'T BEEN ARRESTED." However, the vast majority of Black Lives Matter posts were thoughtful and action-oriented, and either demonstrated or incited multiple forms of action, including learning and seeking further educational resources; muting one's social media feed or listening to others and reflecting on events; amplifying the work and platforms of Black content creators; as well as financially supporting the cause through donations to social organizations or Black businesses. Additionally, food bloggers often drew on the established brand strategies of professional blogging to demonstrate their commitment to social justice with tactics such as donation matching, fundraising, and giveaways of food, cookbooks, and cooking classes used to raise money for various social justice organizations. This discussion reveals that while food bloggers are not activists and predominantly not Black, their potential contributions to the Black Lives Matter movement are material. Additionally, they work to challenge some of the structural flaws which contribute to apoliticism within the food blogosphere and draw attention to the disjunct that arises from their engagement with activism within this commercialized environment.

Food bloggers have built their digital presence upon personalized lifestyle media, not activism centered around race and social justice. Yet, it is too easy to dismiss their contributions, and I am wary of specific critiques of this participation in activism for several reasons. First, while it is always going to be a struggle to meaningfully incorporate allies into racial justice movements, particularly given the emphasis on sharing personal experiences on social media that has drawn such powerful responses to sustain hashtag activism over the past few years, it seems that accusations of optical allyship are often intertwined with criticisms of influencers and their content as being frivolous, narcissistic and superficial (Abidin 2016b). Food bloggers in particular are routinely denounced and subjected to constant criticism from strangers while their content is exploited and appropriated for profit by mainstream media companies and platforms. My analysis suggests that on the whole, participation in #BlackOutTuesday was thoughtful and sustained, even though it necessarily took place within the parameters of the commercialization and self-branding strategies that make the blogosphere legible. Second, I would argue that it is more productive to acknowledge the role that allies and information dissemination have in the growth of digital activist movements and to cultivate this relationship by guiding specific and thoughtful ways to develop meaningful responses. This inevitably leads to a dilution of the message, as the spreadability of social content is traded off against central control over message and collective action frames. Yet this process, described as "connective action" by Bennett and Segerberg (2013, 2012), also demonstrates the rapid scaling up and widespread mobilization of social movements through affinity coalitions that becomes possible through the communicative capacities of social media.

I suggest that as niche digital communities of influencers work together to challenge racism within the fields in which they have the expertise, such networks of digital allies can generate impactful contributions to the Black Lives Matter movement by addressing structural racism as it is encountered in multiple spaces. For food influencers, this might involve a focus on the many ways in which race and food activism go hand-in-hand, for instance through a focus on the environmental impacts and working conditions around food production chains, the social structures that lead to food deserts, and the moralization of discourses around health and food work. Such work would build on one of the most enduring legacies of the food blogosphere, which is the vast gift economy that is generated by the community, performing everyday knowledge exchange of food cultures, food work, and food pedagogies that have clearly provided tangible benefits for a very broad audience. This gift economy and its networks have been used in #BlackOutTuesday to circulate information about intersectionality, structural racism, white privilege, and allyship – cultural knowledges that, like much food knowledge, are not readily available through traditional social institutions and their communication mechanisms. I regard these as powerful and important forms of allyship that hold the potential for further benefits to digital social movements and demonstrate the political potential of the everyday, user-generated content of the food blogosphere.

Conclusions

As influencer activism, like influencer marketing, undoubtedly begins to play an increasingly prominent role in social movement strategy, the relevant questions to ask are not whether influencers should be taken seriously and whether or not their contribution is legitimate, but how to meaningfully incorporate and harness the visibility of this influence within growing digital activist movements. This involves accounting for the limitations of the platform, but also performing the kinds of self-reflexivity that are evidenced in this community – how to participate thoughtfully, meaningfully, and in dialogue with activists and social movements.

This study presents the findings on just one digital influencer community but provides strong evidence that food influencers who participated in #BlackOutTuesday, on the whole, did so in ways that were thoughtful and self-reflexive. The willingness of a core group of food influencers to actively participate in the movement challenged norms within the food blogosphere for bloggers to refrain from using their digital influence to voice "controversial" or "political" opinions, as well as the expectation that idealized postfeminist subjects accept political silencing in exchange for cultural visibility and influence. Bloggers engaged in multiple calls for action and demonstrated a willingness to embark on consciousness-raising around race and structural racism. While there were moments where the departure from the norms and logics of the food blogosphere resulted in awkward and limiting responses to and perspectives on racism, on the whole, there was not a lot of evidence that bloggers were engaging in this action solely for personal gain or individual acclaim.

While optical allyship and performative activism are undoubtedly real phenomena, it is important to resist jumping onto the bandwagon of the criticism of female social media influencers as generally frivolous and narcissistic. Influencer activism operates by the same mechanisms that have given rise to large and profound hashtag movements, and this inevitable expansion of activist messaging into mainstream and high visibility sectors should be encouraged.

References

Abidin, Crystal. 2016a. "Visibility Labour: Engaging with Influencers Fashion Brands and #OOTD Advertorial Campaigns on Instagram." *Media International Australia* 161(1): 86–100. 10.1177/1329878X16665177.

Abidin, Crystal. 2016b. "'Aren't These Just Young, Rich Women Doing Vain Things Online?': Influencer Selfies as Subversive Frivolity." *Social Media & Society* 2(2). 10.1177/2056305116641342.

Ashe, Lauren. 2020. "The Dangers of Performative Activism." *VoxAtl*, June 23, 2020. https://voxatl.org/the-dangers-of-performative-activism/.

Auxier, Brooke, and Monica Anderson. 2021. "Social Media Use in 2021." *Pew Research Center*, April 7, 2021. https://www.pewresearch.org/internet/2021/04/07/social-media-use-in-2021/.

Baker, Stephanie A., and Michael J. Walsh. 2018. "'Good Morning Fitfam': Top Posts, Hashtags and Gender Display on Instagram." *New Media and Society* 20(12): 4553–4570. 10.1177/1461444818777514.

Baym, Nancy K. 2015. "Connect with Your Audience! The Relational Labor of Connection." *The Communication Review* 18(1): 14–22.

Bennett, Lance W., and Alexandra Segerberg. 2013. *The Logic of Connective Action*. Cambridgeshire: Cambridge University Press.

Bennett, Lance W., and Alexandra Segerberg. 2012. "The Logic of Connective Action." *Information, Communication & Society* 15(5):739–768.

Bonilla-Silva, Eduardo. 2003. *Racism Without Racists: Color Blind Racism and the Persistence of Racial Inequality in America.* New York: Rowman & Littlefield.

Bursztynsky, Jessica, and Sarah Whitten. 2020. "Instagram Users Dlood the App with Millions of Blackout Tuesday Posts." *CNBC*, June 2, 2020. https://www.cnbc.com/2020/06/02/instagram-users-flood-the-app-with-millions-of-blackout-tuesday-posts.html.

Butkowski, Chelsea P., Travis L. Dixon, Kristopher R. Weeks, and Marisa A. Smith. 2020. "Quantifying the Feminine Self(ie): Gender Display and Social Media Feedback in Young Women's Instagram Selfies." *New Media & Society* 22(5):817–837.

Cairns, Kate, Josee Johnston, and Norah MacKendrick. 2013. "Feeding the 'Organic Child': Mothering Through Ethical Consumption." *Journal of Consumer Culture* 13(2): 97–118.

Caldeira, Ana Sofia P., and Sander De Ridder. 2017. "Representing Diverse Femininities on Instagram: A Case Study of the Body-Positive @effyourbeautystandards Instagram Account." *Catalan Journal of Communication & Cultural Studies* 9(2):321–337.

Corbin, Juliet M., and Anselm Strauss. 1990. "Grounded Theory Research: Procedures, Canons, and Evaluative Criteria." *Qualitative Sociology* 13(1):3–21.

Cotter, Karen. 2019. "Playing the Visibility Game: How Digital Influencers and Algorithms Negotiate Influence on Instagram." *New Media & Society* 21(4):895–913.

De Choudhury, Munmun, Shagun Jhaver, Benjamin Sugar, and Ingmar Weber. 2016. "Social Media Participation in an Activist Movement for Racial Equality." *Proc Int AAAI Conf Weblogs Soc Media* 2016:92–101.

Dejmanee, Tisha. 2015. "'Food Porn' as Postfeminist Play: Digital Femininity and the Female Body on Food Blogs." *Television and New Media* 17(5):429–448.

Donoughue, Paul. 2020. "What the #BlackoutTuesday Movement Means and Why It Turned Your Instagram Dark." *ABC News*, June 3, 2020. https://www.abc.net.au/news/2020-06-03/instagram-went-dark-for-black-out-tuesday-heres-why/12315146.

Fortini, Amanda. 2011. "O Pioneer Woman!" *The New Yorker*, May 9, 2011. https://www.newyorker.com/magazine/2011/05/09/o-pioneer-woman.

Garza, Alicia. 2016. "A Herstory of the #BlackLivesMatter Movement." In *Are All the Women Still White?: Rethinking Race, Expanding Feminisms*, edited by Janell Hobson, 23–28. Albany: SUNY Press.

Gil-Quintana, Javier, Sonia Santoveña-Casal, and Efren Romero Riaño. 2021. "Realfooders Influencers on Instagram: From Followers to Consumers." *International Journal of Environmental Research and Public Health* 18(4):1624.

Ging, Debbie, and Sarah Garvey. 2018. "'Written in These Scars Are the Stories I Can't Explain': A Content Analysis of Pro-Ana and Thinspiration Image Sharing on Instagram." *New Media & Society* 20(3):1181–1200.

Hearn, Alison. 2008. "'Meat, Mask, Burden': Probing the Contours of the Branded 'Self'". *Journal of Consumer Culture* 8(2):197–217.

Jackson, Sarah J., Moya Bailey, and Brooke Foucault Welles. 2020. *#HashtagActivism: Networks of Race and Gender Justice.* Boston: MIT Press.

Joseph, Ralina. 2018. *Postracial Resistance: Black Women, Media, and the Uses of Strategic Ambiguity*. New York: NYU Press.

Lebron, Christopher J. 2017. *The Making of Black Lives Matter: A Brief History of An Idea*. Oxford: Oxford University Press.

Mahoney, Cat. 2020. "Is This What a Feminist Looks Like? Curating the Feminist Self in the Neoliberal Visual Economy of Instagram." *Feminist Media Studies*. Epub ahead of print 20 August 2020. 10.1080/14680777.2020.1810732.

Matchar, Emily. 2015. *Homeward Bound: Why Women Are Embracing the New Domesticity*. New York: Simon & Schuster.

McRobbie, Angela. 2008. *The Aftermath of Feminism: Gender, Culture and Social Change*. London: SAGE.

Mercado, Mia. 2020. "3 Ways to Practice Non-Optical Allyship & Actually Be Useful." *Bustle*, June 5, 2020. https://www.bustle.com/p/what-is-optical-allyship-3-ways-to-be-actively-anti-racist-22956518.

Mundt, Marcia, Karen Ross, and Charla M. Burnett. 2018. "Scaling Social Movements Through Social Media: The Case of Black Lives Matter." *Social Media & Society* 4(4):1–14.

Presswood, Alane L. 2019. *Food Blogs, Postfeminism, and the Communication of Expertise Digital Domestics*. Lanham and London: Lexington.

Ramos, Irene, and Fiona Cownie. 2020. "Female Environmental Influencers on Instagram." In *Influencer Marketing: Building Brand Communities and Engagement*, edited by Sevil Yesiloglu and Joyce Costello. Routledge.

Ryan, Maureen E. 2018. *Lifestyle Media in American Culture: Gender, Class, and the Politics of Ordinariness*. London: Routledge.

Salvio, Paula M. 2012. "Dishing It Out: Food Blogs and Post-Feminist Domesticity." *Gastronomica: The Journal of Food and Culture* 12(3):31–39.

Saveur. 2019. "Meet the Winners of the 2019 SAVEUR Blog Awards." *Saveur*, August 29, 2019. https://www.saveur.com/winners-2019-saveur-blog-awards/.

van Dijck, Jose. 2013. *The Culture of Connectivity. A Critical History of Social Media*. New York: Oxford University Press.

Yang, Guobin. 2016. "Narrative Agency in Hashtag Activism: The Case of #Blacklivesmatter." *Media and Communication* 4(4):13–17.

2 Super Bowl Food Politics: On the Menu, on the Screen, and on the Field

Emily J.H. Contois

Every year on a Sunday in early February, millions of Americans eat from an indulgent spread, as they watch on television a highly anticipated football game interspersed with cinematic commercials and a stunning halftime musical performance. As one of the nation's last remaining mass media spectacles, the Super Bowl is an American ritualistic holiday that celebrates commercialism and overconsumption in culturally meaningful but also contradictory ways. Although food, football, commercials, and musical entertainment comprise the event, a story in the *New York Times* muses humorously and existentially, "If a football game is watched without beer and wings, was it ever really watched at all?" (Laskey 2021). Along with the action on the field, football food matters and has stories to tell.

In this chapter, I analyze a specific genre of food media—the content produced annually to promote the Super Bowl—to evaluate its political and transformative content and potential. I draw from food media covering Super Bowl party food, placing it within the sports media context of multi-million-dollar TV commercials and the game of football, as played and promoted by the National Football League (NFL). Fans and scholars can see a more complete picture of the Super Bowl by analyzing these elements in concert with one another and through the circuits between them, especially when food lies at the center. As I will show, the diets of individual athletes influence Super Bowl food culture, at the same time that the snacks featured in Super Bowl ads shape the menus published by food writers. While not a straightforward story of cause and effect, I consider these dynamics within the food politics of Super Bowl party menus, drawing insights from media studies, food studies, sports studies, and gender studies. I focus specifically on the exclusion or inclusion of vegetable dishes to demonstrate how these menus endorse particular notions of gender, which collide with evolving cultural concerns for health, wellness, and performance optimization.

These collisions grow all the more apparent when comparing Super Bowl food culture before and during the COVID-19 pandemic. For this chapter, I researched Super Bowl menus, recipes, food rankings, advertisements, and player diets across various media. Overall, I examined a rich corpus of texts

DOI: 10.4324/9781003283942-4

to draw generative comparisons between typical Super Bowl food rules and the menus offered by major food media outlets for the 2021 Super Bowl, which took place during the COVID-19 pandemic and before vaccines were widely available to the public. I explored food section coverage of the Super Bowl from three national newspapers from geographically disparate locations (*New York Times, Los Angeles Times,* and *Washington Post*), nationally recognized food media websites (such as *Bon Appétit, Food & Wine,* and *Food Network*), and other websites publishing such content, ranging from *CNN* and *USA Today* to *E! Online* and *Sports Illustrated*. I tracked and analyzed Super Bowl ads featuring food and beverage brands through the Ad Age Super Bowl Ad Archive. Analyzing the football food politics of these various texts reveals what role food media play, and could play, within consumer spectacles like the Super Bowl.

Not a Day for Salads: Typical Super Bowl Food Rules

Like the American Thanksgiving meal, there are ingredients, dishes, flavors, and cooking techniques considered traditional and even culturally required at a Super Bowl party. Bearing such cultural weight, Super Bowl menus most often include foods like potato skins, chips dunked in numerous dips, and beer, as well as meaty foods like chicken wings, pizza, chili, and just about anything involving bacon. Many restaurants and bars offer such items during the Super Bowl, while at-home parties serve up these various foods buffet style with myriad dishes crowding tables or countertops. Super Bowl foods also boast a specific flavor profile, which Chef Andrew Rea summarizes for *CNN*, "Think cheesy, crunchy, saucy, spicy, bacony … preferably all at the same time" (Thompson 2021). Even for non-football fans, as Alex Beggs writes for *Bon Appétit* with intended snark and humor, "We get a random winter day to gorge on cheesy, saucy, meaty snacks because we have something, at least ONE THING, to cheer for" (Beggs 2021). Acknowledging the typical codification of Super Bowl food, *New York Times* food writer Sam Sifton declares in one of his weekend newsletters, "I'll make chicken wings, because I'm an American. Also, pizza. And nachos, of course. Sometimes it's good just to steer into the clichés, celebrate them, make them your own" (Sifton 2018).

Sifton characterizes many of these recipes as "dude food" (Sifton 2020). I define this food genre as "comfort food but with an edge of competitive destruction" (Contois 2020, 21). This destruction can arise from exaggerated flavors (extra spicy!) or ingredients (more bacon!), massive portion size, or disregard for moderation and nutritional balance. As Beggs wrote, Super Bowl Sunday is like Thanksgiving, a day widely embraced to "gorge," a holiday that is *about and for* not just eating but eating a lot. One Super Bowl fan told the *New York Times* he planned to eat "some sort of Velveeta cheese dip thing—a splurge food I don't normally have—and then I'll balance it out with some celery sticks" (Creswell 2021). Given this central tension between excess and moderation, the makers of Super Bowl menus typically defend a commercialized feast day of celebratory overeating.

Menus that shift Super Bowl food norms document more than changing tastes. They capture American identity on the move, especially evolving notions of health and social inclusion that are personal and political, communal, and capitalistic. These negotiations are made most apparent not by tracking typical Super Bowl menus, but by their culinary outcasts. The primary gastronomic reject at Super Bowl parties has been vegetables. A 2014 ranking of the best and worst Super Bowl party foods from *E! News* dismissed salads, veggie trays, and fruit platters as too healthy to accompany the big game (Mullins 2015). The same year, a *Huffington Post* list included kale chips among "11 Foods that Don't Belong Anywhere Near a Super Bowl Party" (Orchant 2014). The author scoffed, "Chips are a requirement. Kale is exactly the opposite," a snarky sentiment reinforced by her claim, "This day is not a day for salads." Notably, these food rules diverge from reality, as market research data indicates that vegetables, like finger-food-friendly baby carrots, are actually the top food eaten at Super Bowl parties (Hellmich 2014). Nevertheless, ostracizing feminized and "healthy" vegetables is so typical on Super Bowl menus that it's conventional, revealing how gender shapes football party food.

Cultures the world over code meat as masculine food. Meat eating constructs manhood itself, on Super Bowl Sunday and every other day, too. In her foundational work, *The Sexual Politics of Meat: A Feminist-Vegetarian Critical Theory*, Carol J. Adams argues that Western cultures link the welfare of women, animals, and the environment, as they connect meat with men, virility, power, and appetite, but fuse vegetables to women, characterizing both as placid and passive (Adams 1990). Adams proposes veganism as an engaged feminist politics capable of righting such power imbalances. It's no wonder then that Super Bowl party menus typically resist vegetables, both literally and symbolically.

These notions of meat-fueled masculinity, virility, and power also shape football. As a sport routinely described as ferocious, intense, and tough, football endorses and enacts conventional masculinity, which has health implications beyond the dietary. Masculine conventions require a man to "face danger fearlessly, disregard his risks, and have little concern for his own safety," as Will Courtenay has documented (2000, 10). Football requires such masculine performances on the field. As a result, critics, commentators, viewers, and even some players have protested NFL rules that sought to make the game safer to play, penalizing hits and maneuvers that can cause concussions and other injuries like chronic traumatic encephalopathy (CTE), a degenerative disease believed to be caused by blows to the head (Bachynski 2019; Bell, Applequist, and Dotson-Pierson 2019). Cultural norms of masculinity, NFL rules and injuries, and the food served on Super Bowl Sunday are each implicated in football culture. Football masculinity requires balancing the strident acceptance of risk, danger, violence, and aggression with the subtle pursuit of safety, care, calmness, and gentleness. These stereotypically gendered dynamics also inform Super Bowl food media.

The Super Bowl's inherently gendered anti-vegetable norms have remained prominent, even in recent years. In January 2018, *Food & Wine's* "Super Bowl Food" webpage highlighted a party tip from celebrity chef Michael Symon, who sneered, "Who eats vegetables at a Super Bowl party? You eat fried food!" (Symon 2018). In 2019, *Men's Health* published a list of 20 healthy Super Bowl snacks for men following stricter training diets, but recommended nary a produce item except for guacamole (Schubak 2019). In 2019, *CBS Sports* published a ranking of Super Bowl foods, including quiche as the worst (an item the list's author conceded, "I only included this so that I can ridicule it,") and veggies on a tray, writing that "veggies are underappreciated," but also that "Super Bowl Sunday just doesn't always seem like the best place and time for our garden friends" (Benjamin 2019; Contois 2021). That year, *Sports Illustrated* also included a veggie platter on their Super Bowl Party foods ranking, but described it as "a good option for your vegan, vegetarian or rabbit friends," offering up a ham-fisted approach to dietary inclusivity (Staff 2019). Such belittling of meat-free eaters as small, furry creatures again demonstrates how patriarchal culture oppresses women and animals, as meat-eating constructs gendered power, marginalizing and denigrating veganism and vegetarianism.

Super Bowl commercials also write the culinary grammar of the Super Bowl party menu, including its anti-vegetable sentiments. Unlike typical television commercials, which viewers skip or view inattentively, Super Bowl ads, at least since Apple's famed "1984" commercial, comprise what Matthew McAllister calls spectacular consumption and commercial celebration (McAllister and Galindo-Ramirez 2017; McAllister 1999). He argues that viewers do not even consider these commercials as ads, "but as celebrated forms of culture in-and-of-themselves" (McAllister and Galindo-Ramirez 2017, 55). By my own count from the Ad Age Super Bowl Ad Archive, the number of food and beverage commercials held steady from 2016 to 2021, representing approximately one-third of the brands that purchase multi-million-dollar Super Bowl ad time. With the vegetable-adjacent exception of Avocados from Mexico (Greenaway 2013), various brands of beer, soda, candy, chips, and fast food make up the bulk of the food and beverage ads each year—foods and drinks often included in Super Bowl spreads, revealing the flow between the ads on the screen and Super Bowl celebration rituals in homes and bars.

Specific Super Bowl commercials have also made the case for meat and against vegetables. Chevrolet Silverado's 2014 Super Bowl commercial "Wheatgrass" cut to the heart of the football food imaginary, as the brand spent $4.25 million for a 30-second ad. As a gleaming white truck with a behemoth barbecue grill in tow pulled up to a tailgate party, John Cusack's voiceover recited a poem-like ode:

> A man.
> A man and his truck.
> And tofu, and veggie burgers, and raw kale salads
> Be … damned.

In so many words, the commercial sentenced these vegetable-based options to eternal football damnation. At the tailgate, men and women in the ad chow down on meats of every size, shape, and sauce, each expertly prepared by the truck-driving grill master, who proudly displayed numerous masculine conventions: a full beard, plaid shirt, and carnivorous appetite. The commercial incited such ire from vegetarians, vegans, and profanity watch groups alike that later airings modified the final line of the commercial to "all fine, just not today." While this revision softens the degree of denigration, the updated commercial nevertheless excludes vegetables from Super Bowl spreads, embracing meat instead.

Beyond gender conventions surrounding meat and vegetables, Super Bowl culinary rules also express a degree of class-based resistance against foods considered too posh, and by extension too inauthentic, to grace the football table. Just as it banished kale chips (perhaps also viewed as an elitist, Millennial, and liberal food), a *Huffington Post* list proclaimed that "fancy cheese" did not belong, universalized with the claim, "Tiny, fancy foods are for other parties. This party is for big, messy, overblown foods" (Orchant 2014). Similarly, a 2012 DIRECTV commercial for NFL Sunday Ticket landed its joke by framing tapenade as too highbrow, as antithetical to the unpretentious simplicity that governs football and its food (*NFL Sunday Ticket: Fridge* 2012). Overall, Super Bowl food communicates the enduring (albeit debatable) notion that football, every NFL team, and the cities in which they reside represent blue-collar, working-class, "American" values (McQuade 2015; Newman 2011). Furthermore, sports studies scholars Maria J. Veri and Rita Liberti assert that despite the diversity of tailgaters across the country, tailgating as a cultural ritual remains encoded as white, a racial logic that also influences tailgate food and cooking, and Super Bowl parties (Veri and Liberti 2019; 2013). Typical Super Bowl menus and parties, then, reinforce dynamics of power along lines of gender, race, and class, exclusions that vegetables make particularly visible.

Super Bowl LV: Small, Cozy, Safe—and Vegetable-Friendly

Compared to previous years' festivities, Super Bowl LV in 2021 was in a word, different. Given the COVID-19 pandemic, concerns usually sidelined by football's masculine norms took the center field: safety, moderation, comfort, and health. In-person attendance at the game was limited to 25,000 people, bars in some states were closed, and news sources reported public health fears that Super Bowl Sunday would become "Superspreader Sunday" (Caron 2021). Numerous news articles encouraged fans to adopt safety measures, such as celebrating only with the family with whom they lived (Kirsch 2021). The pandemic shaped the game's advertising as well (Hsu 2021). Rather than seeking to entertain or shock, brands aimed to "comfort and connect" (Anderson 2021).

Related to food, the online delivery services DoorDash and Uber Eats both ran Super Bowl ads for the first time, in part due to the profits generated by limits on in-door dining and other stay-at-home orders. Likely to combat the public perception of their business models as much as promoting community connection, DoorDash's commercial emphasized neighborhood shopping, while Uber Eats endorsed eating local. Chipotle also ran an ad for the first time, which pondered how a burrito "could change the world" by reshaping the food system. In the commercial, an altruistic young boy excitedly tells his (quite disinterested) sister that the burrito in his hand "could change how we plant things, water things, grow things, pick things, move things, and transport things" with positive results for farmers and the climate. Compared to the typical, funny Super Bowl ads for Snickers, Doritos, or Mountain Dew, these brands' focus on food system issues was unique.

The pandemic also shaped Super Bowl food media coverage, ushering in a new set of food rules. Many writers focused on safety, recommending that fans watch the game and eat outdoors, forego communal dishes and buffet-style options, and stay six feet apart while eating. *CNN Underscored* offered recipes for "the coziest game day ever," an adjective antithetical to typical Super Bowl celebrations (Thompson 2021). Similarly, the *New York Times* offered recipes for an alliterative "tiniest tailgate," encouraging fans to alter their Super Bowl traditions like eating in "a crowded bar" and instead "delight … from the comfort (and safety!) of your home" (Sichynsky 2021). The *Times* and the *Washington Post* offered advice on how to host "a smaller, safer gathering" with recipes easy to "scale down" for intimate gatherings or even for just oneself (Sonde 2021). In these ways, the pandemic necessitated curtailing some of the Super Bowl's traditional excess.

Given these safety concerns and restrictions, the established items on Super Bowl menus may have played an even larger ritualistic role. Their presence marked a normalcy that the times themselves could not manifest. As such, chicken wings—a food that American culture typically views as masculine and uniquely fused to sports entertainment—still topped most Super Bowl menus in 2021 (Contois 2018). But, as Jacob Bogage warned in the *Washington Post*, "America, we have another crisis. We're running out of chicken wings" (Bogage 2021). During the pandemic, demand for chicken wings was seven percent higher than usual, perhaps as eaters stuck at home sought to find bar food, the community, and fun of going out delivered to their door (Bogage 2021).

Despite the ongoing Super Bowl status of chicken wings, the pandemic cracked the door open for vegetables, long precluded, to take a more equitable seat at the big game's table. Food writers took a number of approaches to add or highlight vegetables within their proposed Super Bowl menus. Some food columnists still emphasized the celebratory indulgence of the holiday, while creating a small space for vegetables, too. Ben Mims of the *Los Angeles Times* embraced the Super Bowl as "always a great excuse to toss the green juice and cauliflower rice for the day and indulge in some fun food … that we all probably haven't had for the past year, since we can't go to the bars and restaurants that serve them" (Mims 2021). Alongside wings, nachos, and chips, Mims offered a "vegan spinach artichoke number that frees the veggies from all that heavy dairy and instead adds creaminess with blended Marcona almonds" (Mims 2021). Mims' vegan option framed dairy as something to be escaped from, repeating ongoing diet culture and wellness discourses that demonize certain foods (Contois 2015). It is unclear whether this was meant to appeal to vegans or to entice non-vegans to try the recipe too, but it nevertheless promoted an explicitly vegan Super Bowl recipe.

The *New York Times* also expanded classic Super Bowl food with five food categories: wings, all things buffalo-style flavor, dips, vegetarian, and chili. The author conceded, "Maybe [vegetarian is] not a traditional football food category," but framed these recipes as necessary for vegan and vegetarian fans, as well as "satisfying" choices, "so you can just say 'no' to the meat sweats" (Laskey 2021). These veggie options accommodate vegan and vegetarian eaters, but still somewhat marginalize them within Super Bowl food. The author specifically describes these snacks as "satisfying," seeking to combat stereotypes that masculine appetites demand satisfaction, which vegetables supposedly cannot deliver (Kiefer, Rathmanner, and Kunze 2005; Wardle et al. 2004). While pro-vegetable, the language of "just say no to the meat sweats" posits a critique of eating too much meat, even on Super Bowl Sunday. But the choice of phrase worrisomely likens excessive meat consumption to drugs, evoking Nancy Reagan's Just Say No campaign, at the same time that it endorses meat-eating as an issue primarily of personal choice, downplaying the influence of the broader food system and marketing. Food writers are still negotiating if and how to include vegetable-forward dishes within Super Bowl menus and how to frame such inclusion, given the history of these menus and some readers' potential resistance to them.

Some food sections included a number of vegetarian or vegan dishes but called attention to them in varyingly subtle ways. Another *New York Times* piece featured 17 recipes. Two clearly drew attention with their recipe titles: Bean-Rich *Vegetarian* Skillet Chili and *Vegan* "Queso" made with cashews rather than cheese (italics added). While a recipe for vegan queso may seem unusual to some Super Bowl eaters, even *Food Network* included a recipe for it among their selection of eight "game-day greats" in 2021. Other recipes in the *Times* round-up offered potential vegetarian substitutions, such as Bricklayer-style Nachos with tofu rather than beef, and Buffalo Cauliflower rather than chicken wings, while other recipes were quietly vegetarian-friendly for all: Air-Fryer French Fries, Chile Verde Guacamole, Spinach Artichoke Dip, Mozzarella in Carrozza, Cheesy Pan Pizza, and Olive Oil Brownies with Sea Salt (Sichynsky 2021). The *Washington Post* similarly included Vegan Artichoke Tofu Ricotta, marked as vegan, and Hot Buffalo Chicken Dip with instructions for how to make it without chicken, along with a number of dishes universally vegetarian and with multicultural flare: Greek-ish Potato Nachos, Bean and Barley Chili, Baked Black Bean and Corn Taquitos with Mango Salsa, Curried Pumpkin Seeds, Harissa-Roasted Carrot and Bean Dip, Savory Cereal Snack Mix, Patti LaBelle's Macaroni and Cheese, and a snacking cake (Sonde 2021).

What do these vegetables mean within the 2021 Super Bowl menus? If typical dude food nutritionally communicates the potential violence of football and normative masculinity, as well as the Super Bowl's ritualized excess, what cultural and political work do these vegetables perform? There was a time when I predicted that including more vegetables on Super Bowl menus might mark steps toward inclusion, diversity, and equity that would traverse the menu, screen, and field (Contois 2018). In some ways, vegan and vegetarian dishes do transgress the masculine norms of the Super Bowl, but these pandemic vegetables are far more ambivalent, in at least two ways.

First, instead of sincere inclusion or a notable shift in American diets, these vegan and vegetarian Super Bowl dishes represent voraciously expanding market logics for plant-based consumption. A 2018 Gallup poll estimated that 5 percent of Americans consider themselves vegetarian, the same as 20 years prior, though that number doubles among respondents who identify politically as liberal; even fewer are vegan (Gallup Inc. 2019; Judkis 2018). As a *Washington Post* headline put it, "You might think there are more vegetarians than ever. You'd be wrong" (Judkis 2018). What *has* changed in more recent years is increasing consumer openness to eating some or more vegetarian or vegan foods. Gallup polls released in January 2020 found that 41 percent of Americans had tried a plant-based meat product with very similar rates by gender and race (Piper 2020). Plant-based product options are expanding, as is consumer interest and spending. But consumers do not appear to be adopting exclusively vegan or vegetarian diets in any greater numbers. Furthermore, meat consumption in the US and globally is actually increasing (Blaustein-Rejto and Smith 2021; Bentley 2019). As Derek Thompson convincingly wrote in *The Atlantic*, "Plants are becoming the fourth meat" (Thompson 2020).

These Super Bowl menus follow a similar pattern. Overtly vegetarian and vegan recipes are a small inclusive gesture, but they also represent an expansion of Super Bowl food to include more options, to meet the growing market availability of such products. Considering the interplay between Super Bowl commercials and party menus, the 2021 ad lineup included an ad for Oatly, a plant-based milk product. While the inclusion of more plant-based fare appears on the surface to be a Super Bowl menu change, it is a transition in keeping with the Super Bowl's established culture of celebratory indulgence and rampant consumption.

Second, vegetables played a larger role both on Super Bowl LV menus and on the field in player diets, though media conversations on the topic reinforced individualized notions of performance optimization rather than discussing health, risk, and masculinity in more socially progressive ways. While food writers and fans may have historically eschewed vegetables on Super Bowl Sunday, they make up 80 percent of what Buccaneers quarterback Tom Brady eats (Sargent 2016). Tom Brady's eating has shaped his brand in recent years, especially his "TB12 Diet," which he published as a book in 2017, along with snacks, supplements, and basic exercise equipment. Coupled with his career success on the field, Brady's diet has become a media fascination. Brady's mostly vegan diet is not primarily about wellbeing, animal welfare, or climate crisis, though. Brady's personal chef, Allen Campbell, shares that he became interested in "plant-based diets because that's where all the nutrition is" (Sargent 2016). Scholar Gyorgy Scrinis categorizes such an approach as "functional nutritionism," that is, eating according to nutritional edicts that emphasize food components rather than whole foods or food culture, and not to just fulfill nutritional needs but to achieve optimization (Scrinis 2015). Such an approach bears a heavier mantle given the financial stakes of professional football and its annual championship at the Super Bowl.

At times, journalists cover Brady's diet as far more than one player's strict and effective training regime (Henson 2019). A *Boston Globe* article, titled, "Around the NFL, QBs Are Training and Eating the Tom Brady Way," asserted that vegan or nearly vegan eating, playing at a lower weight, and training for flexibility and function rather than power and strength alone "is a movement being led by Tom Brady" (Volin 2017). In interesting ways, "the Tom Brady way" pushes back against masculine norms that privilege power and strength over flexibility and longevity. The sports dietitian for the Kansas City Chiefs (who played the Buccaneers in Super Bowl LV) said, "We've got a lot more players these days who want to be plant-based, and we do have vegan players on the roster" (Rosenbloom 2021). Players increasingly view veganism as a "performance hack," which again situates it not within individual, animal, or planetary wellbeing, but rather the techno-fetishistic frame of life hacking (Berger 2018; Thomas 2014).

Whether concerned with peak performance, winning seasons, or a new football training philosophy, the story of Brady's vegan-adjacent eating is also about aging and career longevity. Most articles on Brady's diet open with his age (Kita and Adebowale 2021; St Clair 2019). He is credited with winning the most Super Bowl rings *and* being the oldest signed player in the league at 43 years old, referred to as "the ageless wonder" (Heck 2020). Tom Brady's diet and advanced age have made him a sports media fascination, in part, because masculinity norms often link manhood to a youthful, strong, and vigorous body, constructing the aging male body as one that is vulnerable, at risk, and less masculine. Elderly people are commonly portrayed as ungendered, which for older men represents lacking or losing masculinity (Spector-Mersel 2006). While men can, and do, negotiate new understandings of masculinity as they age, media often provide contradictory exemplars. Tom Brady shines as a sports media beacon of age-defying optimization, an achievement due, at least in part, to vegetables. Within this context, vegetables are re-signified from earthly, feminine, and weak into a proto-scientific source of masculine strength. Brady's diet and its considerable media coverage reveal another circuit linking Super Bowl food themes from the field to the screen and to everyday eaters.

Conclusions

At the epicenter of food media, sports media, and the COVID-19 pandemic, Super Bowl LV animated shifting discourses about food, identity, and wellbeing. They collided on the menus offered by food writers, on the screen in Super Bowl commercials created to comfort as much as entertain, and on the field, where the oldest player in the NFL led his team to victory, fueled, at least in part, by vegetables. Indeed, vegetables, plant-based meats, vegetarianism, and veganism played an evolving but ambivalent role in this Super Bowl story and within American life more broadly. This shifting meaning of vegetables and meat-free eating reveals the ongoing tensions within American identity that the Super Bowl animates each year: pressure to consume and restrain, to win and demonstrate good sportsmanship, to go hard but also be safe, to be a man but of the right sort. With regard to gender specifically, Tom Brady's verdant diet demonstrates how vegetables can be culturally rewritten as "appropriately" masculine and Super Bowl savvy. Nevertheless, he, and other athletes, seem to endorse vegan eating primarily to cut a competitive edge on the field rather than to negotiate newly inclusive gender norms throughout society or to address the pressures of climate change.

The Super Bowl's food politics also reveal how food media remain embedded within the power structures of consumer spectacle. Although food writers expanded and diversified their menus in new ways for Super Bowl LV, these vegetable dishes are still tied to established norms that promote celebratory excess more so than mindful moderation, tradition instead of transformative change, and individual optimization rather than collective access. For example, given the primarily entertainment context of Super Bowl commercials, hardly any writers (food or otherwise) covered the Chipotle commercial that sought to spotlight food system issues on a national stage, even if to simply sell more burritos. Or in the case of the chicken wing shortage, food writers covered the supply chain hiccup more so as a gastronomic oddity of concern for Super Bowl celebrations than as an imperative food production critique. This missed opportunity grew all the more glaring as global supply chain issues further multiplied and became front-page news in subsequent months, as the pandemic's effects lingered. Although food media possess real potential to rewrite cultural norms and inform political processes, Super Bowl food media ultimately remain constrained by the capitalist logics operating on the menu, on the screen, and on the field.

Acknowledgments

This chapter began as an essay in *Nursing Clio*, "Not a Day for Salads: The Football Food Rules of the Super Bowl," February 1, 2018, https://nursingclio.org/2018/02/01/not-a-day-for-salads-the-football-food-rules-of-the-super-bowl/, which I am thankful to expand upon here. I am grateful to Mark Brewin, Conor Heffernan, the members of the University of Chicago US History and Culture Workshop, and this volume's editors for their very helpful feedback on previous drafts of this chapter.

References

Adams, Carol J. 1990. *The Sexual Politics of Meat: A Feminist-Vegetarian Critical Theory*. New York: Continuum.

Anderson, Mae. 2021. "Super Bowl Ads Aim to Comfort and Connect." *ABC News*, February 5. https://abcnews.go.com/Politics/wireStory/super-bowl-ads-aim-comfort-connect-75703555.

Bachynski, Kathleen. 2019. *No Game for Boys to Play: The History of Youth Football and the Origins of a Public Health Crisis*. Chapel Hill: University of North Carolina Press.

Beggs, Alex. 2021. "Is It Ever Okay … to Skip the Super Bowl but Keep the Super Bowl Snacks?" *Bon Appetit*. February 1. https://www.bonappetit.com/story/super-bowl-etiquette-2021.

Bell, Travis R., Janelle Applequist, and Christian Dotson-Pierson. 2019. *CTE, Media, and the NFL: Framing a Public Health Crisis as a Football Epidemic*. Lanham: Lexington Books.

Benjamin, Cody. 2019. "2019 Super Bowl Food: 15 Popular Super Bowl Party Snacks, Ranked from Worst to First." *CBS Sports*. February 3. https://www.cbssports.com/nfl/news/2019-super-bowl-food-15-popular-super-bowl-party-snacks-ranked-from-worst-to-first/.

Bentley, Jeanine. 2019. "U.S. Per Capita Availability of Red Meat, Poultry, and Seafood on the Rise." USDA Economic Research Service, December 2. https://www.ers.usda.gov/amber-waves/2019/december/us-per-capita-availability-of-red-meat-poultry-and-seafood-on-the-rise/.

Berger, Sarah. 2018. "NFL Players' Surprising Performance Hack: Going Vegan." *CNBC*, September 9. https://www.cnbc.com/2018/09/07/nfl-players-are-going-vegan.html.

Blaustein-Rejto, Dan, and Alex Smith. 2021. "We're on Track to Set a New Record for Global Meat Consumption." *MIT Technology Review*, April 26. https://www.technologyreview.com/2021/04/26/1023636/sustainable-meat-livestock-production-climate-change/.

Bogage, Jacob. 2021. "The Super Bowl Is Coming. And We're Running out of Chicken Wings." *Washington Post*. February 2. https://www.washingtonpost.com/business/2021/02/02/chicken-wing-shortage-super-bowl/.

Caron, Christina. 2021. "Is Your Super Bowl Party a Superspreader Event?" *New York Times*, February 4. https://www.nytimes.com/2021/02/04/well/live/super-bowl-parties-covid.html?action=click&module=RelatedLinks&pgtype=Article.

Contois, Emily J.H. 2020. *Diners, Dudes, and Diets: How Gender and Power Collide in Food Media and Culture*. Chapel Hill: University of North Carolina Press.

Contois, Emily J.H. 2015. "Guilt-Free and Sinfully Delicious: A Contemporary Theology of Weight Loss Dieting." *Fat Studies* 4(2):112–126.

Contois, Emily J.H. 2018. "The Spicy Spectacular: Food, Gender, and Celebrity on Hot Ones." *Feminist Media Studies* 18(4):769–773.

Contois, Emily J.H. 2018. "Not a Day for Salads: The Football Food Rules of the Super Bowl." *Nursing Clio*, February 1. https://nursingclio.org/2018/02/01/not-a-day-for-salads-the-football-food-rules-of-the-super-bowl/.

Contois, Emily J.H. 2021. "Real Men Don't Eat Quiche, Do They? Food, Fitness, and Masculinity Crisis in 1980s America." *European Journal of American Culture* 40(3):183–199.

Courtenay, Will H. 2000. "Engendering Health: A Social Constructionist Examination of Men's Health Beliefs and Behaviors." *Psychology of Men & Masculinity* 1(1):4–15.

Creswell, Julie. 2021. "Super Bowl Means Snacking, Even Without Parties." *The New York Times*, February 5. https://www.nytimes.com/2021/02/05/business/super-bowl-snacks-food-delivery.html.

Gallup Inc. 2019. "What Percentage of Americans Are Vegetarian?" Gallup.com, September 27. https://news.gallup.com/poll/267074/percentage-americans-vegetarian.aspx.

Greenaway, Twilight. 2013. "How Did Avocados Become the Official Super Bowl Food?" *Smithsonian Magazine*. January 30. https://www.smithsonianmag.com/arts-culture/how-did-avocados-become-the-official-super-bowl-food-8332793/.

Heck, Jordan. 2020. "The Oldest NFL Players in the 2020 Season." *Sporting News*, September 5. https://www.sportingnews.com/us/nfl/list/oldest-players-nfl-2020/1sipv6l05rqd019gmauw5ermxd.

Hellmich, Nanci. 2014. "Pass the Super Bowl Sunday Plate: Chips, Pizza, Veggies." *USA Today*, January 22. https://www.usatoday.com/story/news/nation/2014/01/22/super-bowl-foods-eating/4671109/.

Henson, Milla. 2019. "What Tom Brady Eats in a Day Is Nearly Impossible for 'Regular People.'" *Sportscasting* (blog), December 15. https://www.sportscasting.com/what-tom-brady-eats-in-a-day-is-nearly-impossible-for-regular-people/.

Hsu, Tiffany. 2021. "Super Bowl Commercials: To Address or Avoid the Pandemic?" *The New York Times*, February 3. https://www.nytimes.com/2021/02/03/business/media/super-bowl-commercials.html.

Judkis, Maura. 2018. "You Might Think There Are More Vegetarians than Ever. You'd Be Wrong." *Washington Post*, August 3. https://www.washingtonpost.com/news/food/wp/2018/08/03/you-might-think-there-are-more-vegetarians-than-ever-youd-be-wrong/.

Kiefer, Ingrid, Theres Rathmanner, and Michael Kunze. 2005. "Eating and Dieting Differences in Men and Women." *Journal of Men's Health and Gender* 2(2):194–201.

Kirsch, Melissa. 2021. "Super Bowl in Quarantine." *The New York Times*, February 5. https://www.nytimes.com/2021/02/05/at-home/newsletter.html.

Kita, Paul, and Temi Adebowale. 2021. "Here's What Tom Brady Eats Every Day, and on Game Day." *Men's Health*, January 22. https://www.menshealth.com/nutrition/a19535249/tom-brady-reveals-insane-diet-in-new-book/.

Laskey, Margaux. 2021. "Best Super Bowl Recipes: Wings, Chili and More." *The New York Times*, February 5. https://www.nytimes.com/article/super-bowl-recipes.html.

McAllister, Matthew P. 1999. "Super Bowl Advertising as Commercial Celebration." *The Communication Review* 3, (4):403–428.

McAllister, Matthew P., and Elysia Galindo-Ramirez. 2017. "Fifty Years of Super Bowl Commercials, Thirty-Two Years of Spectacular Consumption." *The International Journal of the History of Sport* 34(1–2):46–64.

McQuade, Dan. 2015 "The Results Are in: Every Single US Sports Team Is Blue-Collar." *The Guardian*, March 31. http://www.theguardian.com/sport/blog/2015/mar/31/the-results-are-in-every-single-us-sports-team-is-blue-collar.

Mims, Ben. 2021. "The Best Game-Day Foods, Whether You're Watching One or Not." *Los Angeles Times*. January 31. https://www.latimes.com/the-best-game-day-foods-whether-youre-watching.

Mullins, Jenna. 2015. "The Best and Worst Super Bowl Party Food, Ranked." *E! Online*. January 30. https://www.eonline.com/news/619899/the-best-and-worst-super-bowl-party-food-ranked.

Newman, Kathy. 2011. "Hard Day's Work: The Super Bowl and the Working Class." *Working-Class Perspectives* (blog), February 4. https://workingclassstudies.wordpress.com/2011/02/04/hard-days-work-the-super-bowl-and-the-working-class/.

"NFL Sunday Ticket: Fridge." 2012. *Vimeo*. Accessed April 5, 2021. https://vimeo.com/48325772.

Orchant, Rebecca. 2014. "11 Foods That Don't Belong Anywhere Near A Super Bowl Party." *Huffington Post*, January 17. https://www.huffingtonpost.com/2014/01/17/worst-super-bowl-food_n_4610497.html.

Piper, Kelsey. 2020. "Can You Guess Which Americans Are Most into Plant-Based Meat?" *Vox*, January 29. https://www.vox.com/future-perfect/2020/1/29/21110967/gallup-poll-plant-based-meat-vegan-climate-animals.

Rosenbloom, Cara. 2021. "Perspective | Here's What Players Eat before, during and after the Super Bowl." *Washington Post*, February 2. https://www.washingtonpost.com/lifestyle/wellness/super-bowl-diet-brady-mahomes/2021/02/02/14bf4592-657f-11eb-886d-5264d4ceb46d_story.html.

Sargent, Hilary. 2016. "Meet the Chef Who Decides What Tom Brady Eats—and What He Definitely Doesn't." *Boston.com*, January 4. https://www.boston.com/sports/new-england-patriots/2016/01/04/meet-the-chef-who-decides-what-tom-brady-eatsand-what-he-definitely-doesnt.

Schubak, Adam. 2019. "These Tasty Super Bowl Snacks Won't Pack on the Pounds." *Men's Health*, December 4. https://www.menshealth.com/nutrition/g25960202/healthy-super-bowl-snacks/.

Scrinis, Gyorgy. 2015. *Nutritionism: The Science and Politics of Dietary Advice*. New York: Columbia University Press.

Sichynsky, Tanya. 2021. "17 Super Bowl Recipes for the Tiniest Tailgate." *New York Times*, February 4. https://www.nytimes.com/2021/02/04/dining/super-bowl-recipes-tailgate.html.

Sifton, Sam. 2018. "What to Cook This Weekend." *The New York Times*, February 2. https://www.nytimes.com/2018/02/02/dining/what-to-cook-this-weekend-newsletter.html.

Sifton, Sam. 2020. "What to Cook This Weekend." *The New York Times*, January 31. https://www.nytimes.com/2020/01/31/dining/what-to-cook-this-weekend.html.

Sonde, Kari. 2021. "Our Best Super Bowl Recipes Deliver Big Flavor for a Smaller Watch Party." *Washington Post*, February 1. https://www.washingtonpost.com/food/2021/02/01/game-day-super-bowl-recipes/.

Spector-Mersel, Gabriela. 2006. "Never-Aging Stories: Western Hegemonic Masculinity Scripts." *Journal of Gender Studies* 15(1):67–82.

St Clair, Josh. 2019. "Inside Tom Brady's Offseason Diet and Fitness Routine." *Men's Health*, August 6. https://www.menshealth.com/fitness/a28578925/tom-brady-gym-and-fridge-tour/.

Staff, S. I. 2019. "SI's Ultimate Ranking of Super Bowl Party Foods." *Sports Illustrated*, January 31. https://www.si.com/eats/2019/01/31/best-super-bowl-party-foods-snacks-appetizers-ranking-most-popular.

Symon, Michael. 2018. "Super Bowl Food." *Food & Wine*, February. https://www.foodandwine.com/holidays-events/super-bowl.

Thomas, Matthew. 2014. "Life Hacking: A Critical History, 2004–2014." Dissertation, University of Iowa. https://ir.uiowa.edu/cgi/viewcontent.cgi?article=7138&context=etd.

Thompson, Courtney. 2021. "Have the Coziest Game Day Ever with These Delicious Snack Recipes." *CNN Underscored*, February 5. https://www.cnn.com/2021/02/04/cnn-underscored/super-bowl-food-ideas/index.html.

Thompson, Derek. 2020. "The Capitalist Way to Make Americans Stop Eating Meat." *The Atlantic*, January 10. https://www.theatlantic.com/ideas/archive/2020/01/why-2020s-will-be-peak-meat-america/604711/.

Veri, Maria J., and Rita Liberti. 2019. *Gridiron Gourmet: Gender and Food at the Football Tailgate*. Fayetteville: University of Arkansas Press.

Veri, Maria J., and Rita Liberti. 2013. "Tailgate Warriors Exploring Constructions of Masculinity, Food, and Football." *Journal of Sport & Social Issues* 37(3):227–244.

Volin, Ben. 2017. "Around the NFL, QBs Are Training and Eating the Tom Brady Way." *The Boston Globe*, August 17. https://www.bostonglobe.com/sports/patriots/2017/08/17/around-nfl-qbs-are-training-and-eating-tom-brady-way/2hpOwhcZZmIBPYLXtArfkN/story.html.

Wardle, Jane, Anne M. Haase, Andrew Steptoe, Mareem Nillapun, Kiriboon Jonwutiwes, and France Bellisie. 2004. "Gender Differences in Food Choice: The Contribution of Health Beliefs and Dieting." *Annals of Behavioral Medicine* 27(2):107–116.

3 Agribusiness, Environmental Conflict, and Food in Travel Journalism: Image Work for the Bay of Fundy in New Brunswick

Lyn McGaurr

Food consumption and production are popular topics in travel journalism. Experiencing fresh ingredients close to their source is often used to signify an authentic engagement with locals and their culture. Given the increasing critical coverage in food media of sustainable foodways, the question is in what ways do travel media take on problematic issues such as environmental impact? In particular, this chapter seeks to better understand the relationship between lifestyle media, agribusiness, and tourism through a case study of travel journalism about a region in Atlantic Canada promoted to holidaymakers through its local seafood tastes and traditions, but to its trading partners through its industrial-scale aquaculture.

By examining this tourism destination as a primary site of travel/food journalism production, my analysis finds that local loyalties can contribute to the invisibility of contested foodways in the genre even when environmentalists are media-savvy and networked into resident communities and economies. This finding can help explain conditions that enable corporations and governments to maintain a discursive advantage in environmental conflict. The case study supports Michelle Phillipov's (2016) argument that when lifestyle media invest particular foods with significance but fail to critique their chains of production, they increase the space for dominant players to deploy diluted discourses of sustainability and food movements in their public relations and marketing campaigns.

Travel Journalism, Food, and the Environment

The journalistic domains of political life and everyday life are increasingly inter-related (Hanitzsch and Vos 2018, 160), and there are, inevitably, political dimensions to lifestyle journalism's production, representations, and strategic significance (Banjac and Hanusch 2020; Duffy and Ashley 2012; Fürsich 2002, 2012; Hanusch 2019). Those dimensions are enacted in editorial decisions to include, or pressure to ignore, political conflicts in travel content.

Within the broad scope of lifestyle journalism, my own work (McGaurr 2016, 2015, 2010; McGaurr, Tranter, and Lester 2015) and that of Ben

DOI: 10.4324/9781003283942-5

Cocking (2020) have attended to the intersection of environmental conflict and travel journalism. One of the examples I foregrounded in my previous work concerned international travel journalists' investigations and re-presentations of the potential impact of a proposed pulp mill on the reputation of Tasmanian food and wine (McGaurr 2015). In that instance, the restaurateur interviewed by travel journalists did more than simply invest the food he served close to its source with significance as an alternative to less artisanal, less sustainable production practices; he explicitly entered the political fray via travel journalism to express his concern about the mill. That case study was valuable because it demonstrated how a close examination of discourses, networks, and strategies in the local food and wine sector could help explain the rare presence in travel features of campaigning food politics arising from environmental conflict (McGaurr 2015). Nevertheless, the case had limitations for food media studies because although the company responsible for the proposed pulp mill had recently bought a major vineyard, the development at issue was to service the forestry industry rather than the food sector. This made me curious about what I might find by examining a case in which food production itself was central to an environmental conflict in a tourism destination promoted for its culinary experiences.

Cuisine can be a primary motivation for a holiday (Becker 2008), making portrayals of food cultures, restaurants, and locally sourced ingredients mainstays of travel journalism (Brett and Pinna 2015; Pan and Ryan 2008). As evidenced by my Tasmanian case study, the very essence of the genre – research about place, conducted *in* place – can afford access to local knowledge by which travel journalists can test tourism claims about place-branded food (McGaurr 2015). Moreover, the provocative culinary travel series of Anthony Bourdain demonstrates that the genre is also capable of using food as "a conceit ... to have a conversation about the culture, politics, struggles and triumphs of people around the world" (Henry 2018). Yet travel journalism is regularly assumed to be less rigorous than other categories of lifestyle and news media for its reluctance to take a critical stance (Becker 2008), and research largely bears this out. Despite the above exceptions, interviews (McGaurr 2015) and surveys (Hanusch 2011) designed to help scholars understand travel journalists' professional views and practices suggest relatively few think it is part of their role to highlight political problems. To date, I have attributed the tendency for relevant contemporary environmental conflict to be absent from travel journalism to shifting combinations of genre protocols, personal ideologies, insecure media work, employer expectations, and interactions with destination marketing organizations. However, as I aim to demonstrate in this chapter, a more nuanced explanation may sometimes be warranted, particularly when the conflict is about industrialized food production.

Case Study: The Bay of Fundy in New Brunswick

My case study draws on textual and contextual analyses of travel journalism features published between 2014 and 2020 about the Bay of Fundy in New Brunswick, a Canadian province where the native Atlantic salmon is an ecological, recreational, and First Nations asset in the wild but a source of environmental conflict when farmed. The analysis is based on websites, research reports, news articles, and interviews I conducted in 2015 with informants with a professional interest in how New Brunswick is represented: three environmentalists (Matt Abbott and Tracey Glynn from the Conservation Council of New Brunswick, and Andrew Holland, responsible for communications about New Brunswick for the Nature Conservancy of Canada); a scientific guide working for her family's wildlife cruise business (Nicole Leavitt); and a tourism public relations practitioner with Tourism New Brunswick (Margaret MacKenzie). This is not to suggest that the context obtained from these sources can fully account for a published journalism text, or how it is received (Fürsich 2009). Rather, it acknowledges that a multiplicity of factors can create or perpetuate "discursive holes" (Lester and Hutchins 2012, 664) in "soft" journalism that can be advantageous for corporations (Phillipov 2016).

While my principal aim in this chapter is to extend our understanding of the absence of conflict about industrialized food production in travel journalism, I also integrate elements of textual analysis to illustrate how this discourse plays out. In this, I am indebted to the example of Phillipov (2016), who took a similar approach when comparing a lifestyle television program and the marketing strategies of a supermarket to help demonstrate the potential consequences of texts that represent "food of 'known' and 'trustworthy' origin" (94) as desirable but fail to offer "a critique or exposé of the practices that produce the 'unknown' and 'untrustworthy'" (94).

New Brunswick, Tourism, and "The King of Game Fish"

New Brunswick is a 7.3-million-hectare Canadian province bordered to the west by the United States jurisdiction of Maine and along its south-western length by the Bay of Fundy. It is referred to by Canadians as both a Maritime Province (along with Nova Scotia and Prince Edward Island) and an Atlantic Province (along with Nova Scotia, Prince Edward Island, and the province of Newfoundland and Labrador). New Brunswick became part of the Canadian federation in 1867 following a long history of French and British occupation, which accounts for its official languages today being both English and French. It has a population of approximately 783,000. First Nations people have never ceded their lands, and the government acknowledges it has a duty to consult them on matters that may affect their aboriginal rights, which may include the right to fish, gather, and hunt on ancestral lands (Government of New Brunswick 2011).

For the New Brunswick Government, Atlantic salmon is an economic powerhouse (Government of New Brunswick n.d.) in a province that struggles to provide employment for its citizens. In 2020, it was among New Brunswick's top five seafood exports, behind lobster and crab, and ahead of herring and sardines (Government of New Brunswick 2021b). The New Brunswick Government says an important factor contributing to the success of salmon aquaculture in the province is "the pristine waters of the Bay of Fundy" (Government of New Brunswick n.d.). The Bay of Fundy is famous for the highest tides in the world and outdoor adventures such as viewing endangered North Atlantic right whales (Tourism New Brunswick 2021c). If you take a whale-watching tour from the seaside village of Saint Andrews beyond Passamaquoddy Bay and into the Bay of Fundy proper, or travel aboard a ferry from Blacks Harbour to the wildlife mecca of Grand Manon, or kayak around Deer Island, you are likely to see open-net salmon farms so abundant they have been incorporated into wildlife cruises. The family-owned New Brunswick company Cooke Aquaculture, which started in Blacks Harbour, is now among the biggest seafood businesses in the world. Cooke describes itself on its website as expanding from "a humble family aquaculture company with a single site" to a "global seafood leader" that has "recently embarked on an aggressive plan for growth, including acquisitions and an ongoing strategic search for development opportunities" (Cooke Aquaculture 2021a).

For Tourism New Brunswick, Atlantic salmon is "the king of the game fish. People come to New Brunswick from around the world in search of this prize catch and the fly-fishing experience of their lifetime on famous rivers like the Miramichi and the Restigouche" (Tourism New Brunswick 2021a). The Miramichi and Restigouche are far from the Bay of Fundy, but there was a time when sea-run Atlantic salmon thrived in the Fundy region. Today, any sea-run populations of wild Atlantic salmon in the rivers that empty into the bay are fighting for their survival, having suffered decades of environmental insult from pollution and dams, overfishing, changes in predator behavior, and interactions with farmed salmon (Government of Canada 2019a,b). There has been a moratorium on commercial fishing for Atlantic salmon in eastern Canada since 2000 (Government of Canada 2019c), and there is no open season for recreational fishing for wild sea-run Atlantic salmon in Bay of Fundy rivers (Government of New Brunswick 2021a). Many of the threats to wild salmon from aquaculture in New Brunswick stem from the fact that the farmed species is the same as the wild species, which means there is a risk that individuals escaping from fish farms will breed with wild salmon and diminish the wild salmon's genetic fitness to complete their breeding cycles in oceans and rivers (Morris et al. 2008). Another risk of salmon aquaculture is that it will spread disease (Atlantic Salmon Federation 2019) and sea lice (Godwin et al. 2020) to wild salmon. There are also reports of salmon aquaculture damaging New Brunswick's vital lobster fisheries. This happens because salmon farms use chemicals to manage sea lice; when illegal chemicals are used, as they have been on occasion, they can cause the deaths of lobsters and other marine life (Government of Canada 2013).

Lobster, fish, and other seafood from the bay are marketed by Tourism New Brunswick as major drawcards for visitors, and their attractions are represented as intimately connected with the province's "social and economic fabric" (Tourism New Brunswick 2021d): "Any coastal community you visit is bound to feature working fishing wharves, which serve as a hub for many fishing villages," writes Tourism New Brunswick, urging tourists to "chat with the fishermen aboard [their boat] and learn a little more about the fishing life" (Tourism New Brunswick 2021d).

A distinctive feature of the New Brunswick economy is the scale and pervasiveness of the Irving group of private companies, which has extensive holdings in oil, forestry, pulp, and paper and, for more than 80 years until early 2022, news media (Ali 2022; Poitras 2014). At the time this chapter was written, JK Irving's Brunswick News Inc. (BNI) still owned all three of the province's English-language dailies and six of its weekly newspapers (Ibrahim 2022). In mid-February 2022, when it was announced that Canadian media conglomerate Postmedia was to buy BNI, a professor of journalism and communications at St. Thomas University, New Brunswick, commented, "Over the years there's been ongoing and persistent concerns about the media concentration of ownership by a family that has such a strong influence on business affairs and economic life in the province" (Lee in Ali 2022). This suggests New Brunswick environmentalists wishing to publicize environmental problems associated with agribusinesses might have encountered challenges in gaining widespread provincial news coverage of their concerns. Indeed, a recent content analysis of news media in New Brunswick, Nova Scotia, and Newfoundland (Kraly, Weitzman, and Filgueira 2021) found considerably more articles discussing salmon aquaculture in positive tones (37 percent) and considerably fewer discussing it in negative tones (29 percent) in New Brunswick than in Nova Scotia (19 percent positive and 43 percent negative) or Newfoundland (20 percent positive and 41 percent negative). This finding was based on a New Brunswick sample of articles discussing salmon aquaculture of which 66 percent were from a BNI newspaper.

Excavating Discursive Holes

Travel journalism in national and international outlets offers potential for countering media deficiencies in the local and regional news markets. My detailed analysis begins by focusing in this section on five travel journalism articles about New Brunswick, each containing opportunities for critical engagement with the environmental impacts of salmon aquaculture and decreases in wild salmon. The first, written by Mike Unwin and published in the United Kingdom's *Independent* in 2014, reported on a province-wide trip hosted by Tourism New Brunswick (the article acknowledged the hosting). The second, written by Guy Wilkinson and published in the Australian edition of *Traveller* in 2015 (hosting by World Expeditions and the Canadian Tourism Commission acknowledged in the article), reported the author's experiences on an arduous three-day trek between Fundy National Park and Saint Martins. The third, written by Roy MacGregor and published in the travel section of Canada's *Globe and Mail* in 2017, explored the Saint John River, which empties into the Bay of Fundy at one of the province's largest cities, also called Saint John. The fourth, by Phoebe Smith, was published in Britain's *Wanderlust* in 2019 and was primarily concerned with whale-watching in the bay. The fifth, by Barbara Peck, appeared in the United States on the travel website *AFAR* in February 2020 and included a reference to "wilderness dining" on a beach in Saint Martins.

Enriched by stories of kayaking the Bay of Fundy and cracking lobsters in another part of the province, Unwin's article is perfectly aligned with Tourism New Brunswick's branding, delivering readers pristine salmon on a pebbly Fundy beach direct from the hands of a salty seafarer, albeit a kayaking guide rather than a fisherman. Thus, the purity of the salmon is established not by direct reference to its provenance but by the character of the guide:

> "Saw a leatherback turtle once," he added, tearing chunks from his home-baked loaf and portioning out slabs of salmon. Bruce is all you'd hope for in a Canadian kayaking guide: ragged beard, dry humour, eyes on the horizon. A bald eagle circled overhead as we listened to his stories.

There is no indication in the feature that wild Atlantic salmon are no longer plentiful in New Brunswick or any explanation of why their populations have declined. And although Unwin and his family kayak around Deer Island, he does not mention the salmon farms that dot that part of the bay.

The second feature (Wilkinson 2015) represents another success for Tourism New Brunswick because the travel journalist was enticed to New Brunswick by a new niche experience and subsequently produced a story with the potential to attract mass-market tourists who would spend money in the province during their holidays even if they never engaged in such an adventurous experience (MacKenzie, personal communication, June 1, 2015). The text celebrated eating in the outdoors as part of a guided and catered walk along the 64-kilometer Fundy Footpath. Having described a lobster boil on a beach and eating Atlantic salmon near the Little Salmon River – without noting that the river's name belies a current dearth of salmon in its waters – Wilkinson draws attention to the fact that logging, ship-building, and timber enterprises that occupied a site at Martin Head until the end of the Second World War had environmental impacts. This familiar strategy in ecotourism travel journalism uses references to historical environmental damage to enhance the credibility and cultural capital of the journalist but remains brand-aligned by conveying the pleasures of contemporary natural tourism experiences that function textually as testaments to a more enlightened present (McGaurr 2015). Salmon and lobster in Wilkinson's article are represented as rewards for the author's physical endurance, evidence of the destination's purity, and lures for future visitors:

> "Food tastes good in the woods, anyway," [our guide] says, "but if you feed people something a bit special, they're like, 'holy shit'. Sure, we could serve instant noodles and make more money, but that's not what we're about." His efforts don't disappoint. We begin with seared scallops wrapped in bacon, and the main course – fillets of Atlantic salmon on cedar wood with cracked pepper and maple syrup – would have Matt Preston [a judge on the television program *MasterChef Australia*] drooling on to his cravat.
>
> (Wilkinson 2015)

It is noteworthy, therefore, that foreign travel journalists Unwin and Wilkinson were in New Brunswick writing effusively about eating salmon and lobster after the deaths of hundreds of lobsters around Grand Manan and Deer Island from Cooke Aquaculture's use of an illegal pesticide in 2009 had been widely publicized (*CBC New Brunswick* 2010, 2013; Government of Canada 2013; Trotter 2013), having been vigorously communicated to the news media by the local environmental organization the Conservation Council of New Brunswick (Abbott, personal communication, May 29, 2015). The pesticide use resulted in one of the largest penalties ever imposed under the Canadian Fisheries Act (*CBC New Brunswick* 2013; Government of Canada 2013). This made the issue relevant to visitors, for whom lobster is a prime attraction promoted internationally by the tourism sector. Yet despite Unwin's account of penetrating a lobster's "formidable armour" and kayaking around Deer Island, and Wilkinson's willingness to discuss historic environmental degradation, they make no mention of the incident.

MacGregor's article entitled "Fishing For Answers" is different from those of Unwin and Wilkinson. From its opening statement that "diminishing fish populations imperil the future of those that depend on it," the story pulls fewer punches than most travel features about New Brunswick. The author describes past environmental abuse of the river, including by an Irving pulp mill, and quotes plain-speaking locals to drive home the consequences of the degradation:

> Mr. McCumber, the paddler, worked in the pulp and paper industry all over Canada, including the Saint John River Valley. He does not mince words when he says "the pulp mills killed the river. For generations you couldn't go near the river. People stayed away."
>
> (Wilkinson 2015)

In addition to giving voice to locals who are directly affected by environmental damage, MacGregor quotes WWF-Canada on calls for a hydroelectric dam to be dismantled, and references both WWF and the Conservation Council of New Brunswick on a proposal still current at the time of the article's publication to build a pipeline – Energy East – to carry crude oil from Alberta to Saint John. But even in this troubling account of a river now almost devoid of salmon that once swam in the Bay of Fundy as part of their breeding cycle, there is no mention of the aquaculture industry, or the fact that farmed salmon have sometimes been found in the river (Morris et al. 2008). Instead, the following optimistic paragraph appears immediately after the above quote from McCumber that people previously stayed away from the river because of the pulp mill pollution:

> But no longer. On a warm summer day, there are swimmers and kayakers, canoeists and motorboats all along the river. In those areas where it is allowed, they fish for striped bass and sturgeon and, yes, the Atlantic salmon that once made this the salmon river.
> (MacGregor 2017)

The year after MacGregor's article was published, an Irving pulp mill situated where the Saint John River meets the Bay of Fundy was fined $3.5 million dollars for dumping effluent into the river and placed on the Environmental Offenders Registry (MacDonald 2018). It was "one of the largest penalties ever imposed in Canada for an environmental violation" (MacDonald 2018), with a proportion directed towards research into the conservation of wild Atlantic salmon. In the MacGregor example, then, a genre-appropriate happy ending is delivered prematurely, diminishing the travel feature's contribution to the public sphere.

The fourth article (Smith 2019) was published in the year after Canada's Commissioner for the Environment and Sustainable Development released a report critical of government oversight of salmon aquaculture that drew attention to risks to wild fish from diseases and pesticides in fish farms and, specifically, the risks to wild Atlantic salmon from farmed fish that had escaped (Office of the Auditor General of Canada 2018; see also Holyoke 2019). Introducing readers to the Huntsman Marine Science Centre and Aquarium, the story refers to the Centre's research to develop "tests to determine the survival of salmon, a fish whose numbers have been severely depleted in recent years" (Smith 2019) but makes no mention of the burgeoning salmon farms in the bay. Nor does it refer to the possibility of aquaculture contributing to the deaths of wild salmon when it acknowledges their plight again and describes at length the efforts of a project to "restock local rivers with wild salmon – another of the region's native and endangered species" (Smith 2019). While the restocking project is not named in the article, it is almost certainly the Fundy Salmon Recovery Project, because the text includes a photo of, and quotes from, Kurt

Samways. Samways is a lead researcher on the Fundy Salmon Recovery Project – a partnership of, among others, the University of New Brunswick, Parks Canada, Fisheries and Oceans Canada, and Cooke Aquaculture (UNB Newsroom 2021).

The final article (Peck 2020) names "delicious seafood" in its first paragraph as one of New Brunswick's main attractions. In the Bay of Fundy, it recommends kayaking tours around Deer Island, "creative, market-fresh cuisine and local seafood like oysters and lobster" in Saint Andrews, "regional delicacies like lobster rolls and elk burger" in Saint John, and "a 'wilderness dining' experience on the beach by the caves, accompanied by stories about the region's culture and natural history" with Red Rock Adventure in Saint Martins (Peck 2020). An embedded link takes readers to Red Rock Adventure's website, which features culinary experiences such as an "Atlantic Salmon Beach BBQ" described with reference to the salmon's cultural and natural resonances:

> The Atlantic Salmon has been part of the Fundy's history since the beginning of time. Enjoy a beachside barbeque that celebrates the region through cuisine and the stories of our rich logging and shipbuilding history. As the salmon is cooked over and (sic) open fire, take in the sounds of the waves and wind coming from the Bay of Fundy.
>
> (Red Rock Adventure n.d.)

Obstacles to Criticism

Two factors especially seem to hinder widespread criticism of salmon farming in the region: the interconnectedness of local stakeholders and the consolidated news media market. Both appear to exert direct as well as subtle pressure to either ignore or downplay the environmental impacts of aquaculture.

Many in the Fundy region are likely to have worked across tourism, aquaculture, and/or commercial fishing, which means the environmental movement has little appetite for using its contacts in the tourism sector to raise awareness of the environmental impacts of salmon farming. Matt Abbott, an environmentalist with the Conservation Council of New Brunswick who held the title of "Fundy Baykeeper," was candid about the pressure to avoid criticism of aquaculture placed on tourism operators in Charlotte County, which takes in Saint Andrews in the Fundy inlet of Passamaquoddy Bay, and Grand Manan and Deer Island in the Bay of Fundy proper:

> It's hard to be critical of aquaculture in Charlotte County. It provides a lot of jobs. Tourism companies certainly don't want to be. They have to

show people salmon farms, they're everywhere. So they're going to be looking at them. They're going to be explaining to tourists what they are. They don't want bad press. It would be really hard to be critical of aquaculture from the boat deck. So there's that dynamic. Also everyone has someone in aquaculture. My wife works for the Aquaculture Association of Canada.
(M. Abbott, personal communication, May 29, 2015)

Biologist Nicole Leavitt exemplified the overlapping professional and personal identities of many people who live and work in the Bay of Fundy. In addition to being a scientist, she was a whale-watching guide in the family tourism business started by her father, a former fisherman. In her interview with me, Leavitt highlighted the iconic status of lobster but also linked aquaculture to local cultures and economies:

Fishing is huge here in the Bay of Fundy and one of the things that we're most famous for are lobsters ... [The lobster fishery] provides most of the jobs for the fishing communities that are along the coast of the Bay of Fundy. Now, aquaculture also has really in the last 35 years picked up steam in our area, and has really helped our economy, because we've seen such a decrease in our ground fisheries, things like haddock and cod ... [Aquaculture's] an important way of life here ... We like to incorporate it, again because it is an important part of our area, it's an important part of our economy here, and it's really played a vital role in our area over the past 35 years.
(N. Leavitt, personal communication, July 13, 2015)

Leavitt was not averse to taking a stand on environmental issues and had spoken out against the Energy East pipeline, but she was not opposed to aquaculture. She readily acknowledged that fish farms could diminish the visual amenity of hospitality businesses and may produce "a little pollution," but speaking from the perspective of a biologist she described aquaculture as a vital resource to feed the world's increasing population and called for continued scientific research to make it as environmentally responsible as possible (N. Leavitt, personal communication, July 13, 2015).

In addition to competing loyalties, the concentration of New Brunswick news media in the hands of the Irving company BNI hindered the public airing of environmental problems, according to the Conservation Council of New Brunswick. However, alternative avenues did exist in the *Saint Croix Courier* and *CBC New Brunswick*, as well as social media posts and websites produced by environmentalists, and also national and international news media such as Canada's *Globe and Mail*, and the *Bangor Daily News* in neighboring Maine, USA (M. Abbott, personal communication, May 29, 2015; T. Glynn, personal communication, May 29, 2015;

MacGregor 2017). The Conservation Council of New Brunswick saw this as a potentially effective way to alert both residents and international markets to its environmental concerns:

> A lot of people read the international newspapers or magazines and just knowing the control over the media in this province, it's hard to get our stories out there. So it's definitely, like, part of, I think, our campaigns to raise awareness and apply pressure.
> (T. Glynn, personal communication, May 29, 2015)

Although getting access to national and international news was challenging, it played an important role in environmental campaigns. As Abbott explains:

> We want national coverage on things, like on the illegal pesticide use, to touch on aquaculture for a second, and we weren't as successful at this as we wanted to be but it was very important, especially Boston, New York, other places that are the primary markets for the salmon produced here, we wanted them to know that there was flagrant and widespread illegal use of pesticides. It's really, really important that the markets for that product are aware of the practices going on here.
> (M. Abbott, personal communication, May 29, 2015)

One might expect recognition of the importance of national and international media to New Brunswick environmental campaigns would lead Abbott and other environmentalists to lobby tourism operators to speak out on environmental issues. In practice, he was willing to draw on his tourism networks when the campaign was about an oil pipeline but not when the issue was aquaculture, which he saw as too personally risky for people in the tourism industry, whom he considered friends and neighbors:

> I do expect to be able to get the tourism industry to take a stance of some sort on Energy East. I wouldn't even try on aquaculture. That would be too risky for them. I wouldn't try. It's too risky. I wouldn't ask that of my friends and neighbours. It's the nice thing about living in this small place. I've been to some of the people high up in Cooke's. I've been to their house, because I've been dropping things off or whatever. They've been to mine. I like that. I like that it's complicated. And it's the same thing—the tourism folks are really, really hard-working friends who are really dedicated to the region and everything else. There's that dynamic there. Sometimes it feels like New Brunswick is an example on aquaculture, but it's hard to be the agent of change on aquaculture because of the dynamic here.
> (M. Abbott, personal communication, May 29, 2015)

The year after my interview with Abbott, he won the transnational Gulf of Maine Council's Visionary Award in part for his long-term education and outreach on the issue of pesticide use in salmon aquaculture (Conservation Council of New Brunswick 2019). He was a campaigner with an acute appreciation of the cosmopolitical opportunities afforded by international media. Yet his loyalty to, and concern for, the networks that made him so successful as the Fundy Baykeeper were precisely the factors that would have deterred him from deploying them in attempts to access the cosmopolitical potential of travel journalism to advance the aquaculture campaign.

Reckoning with Discursive Alignments

While local environmental groups are struggling to publicize the problematic practices of farmed salmon, the "global seafood leader" Cooke Aquaculture has co-opted the discourse of sustainability in its marketing material without being challenged. Viewing the scrolling banner on the home page of the Cooke website in 2021, I was struck by its themes of environmental sustainability, lush tourism-style imagery, and alignment with Tourism New Brunswick's brand promises of seafood as an expression of local food culture, artisanal purity, seafaring traditions, trustworthy family enterprises, and an economy that nurtures its community. The website is not exclusively about salmon aquaculture or the Bay of Fundy, but its banner establishes an arresting visual and linguistic discourse for the broad sweep of Cooke's activities.

The first image is of the sun on the horizon along a stretch of calm water, a small boat motoring across the foreground, and a wharf with a distinctive blue shed in the distance. The text reads "Sustainable Growth. Sustainable Success. One of Canada's best-managed companies for 16 consecutive years" (Cooke Aquaculture 2021b), an accolade also celebrated (without reference to the number of years) on the Tourism New Brunswick website (Tourism New Brunswick 2021b). The second image is of a small fishing boat docked at a rustic wharf, with the caption "Some inherit land from their grandparents. We inherited the sea" (Cooke Aquaculture 2021b), a statement that seems to allude to inherited wealth and private custodianship of the ocean while ostensibly celebrating seafaring traditions and the trustworthiness of food sourced from local family-owned businesses. These tropes are evident in another seascape captioned, "It isn't just our life's work. It's our way of life" (Cooke Aquaculture 2021b) and in an image that appears to be seared salmon captioned, "It's not easy raising the best. Decades of experience just make it look that way" (Cooke Aquaculture 2021b). The final image is of snow-capped peaks at the water's edge, with the words, "The ocean called. They want us to keep up the good work" (Cooke Aquaculture 2021b). The ambiguity of photographs with no place attribution, together with linguistic text that invokes the universal "we" and "our," invites visitors to the website to invest Cooke agribusinesses with their own significance and meanings while calling to mind food discourses of purity, trustworthiness, and sustainability circulating in tourism marketing, environmental movement communications and, as we have seen, travel journalism about the Bay of Fundy.

Further down the Cooke home page are links to a long treatise on Cooke's "role as environmental stewards" (Cooke Aquaculture 2021c), its third-party environmental certification, and involvement in salmon research and conservation programs, including the Fundy Salmon Recovery Program (Cooke Aquaculture 2021c). The page entitled "No standards are higher than the ones we set for ourselves" (Cooke Aquaculture 2021d) is headed by a banner image of a man who could be described in the very words Unwin used to represent the kayaking guide who served him slabs of Atlantic salmon on a Fundy beach: "ragged beard, dry humour" (Unwin 2014), except the eyes of the man on the Cooke website are on us, not the horizon.

Conclusions

In a study of the relationship between insider and outsider media covering the coastal regions of another Atlantic Province, Newfoundland and Labrador, Stoddart and Graham (2016) found that images of environmental sustainability were used on most of the provincial websites they analyzed, while content about environmental problems and decline tended to be housed on the province's environmental websites rather than its tourism websites. Stoddart and Graham's content analysis of major newspapers in Canada, the United Kingdom, and the United States revealed "a relatively smooth process of translation from the image of the coastal environment articulated by tourism promoters and operators to the image enacted by outsider mass media" (Stoddart and Graham 2016, 39). It is not surprising, therefore, that the travel journalism analyzed in this Bay of Fundy case study demonstrates a similar alignment. What this chapter has added to existing knowledge is evidence that local loyalties and sympathies in the environmental movement should be considered when seeking to understand instances in which critiques of contested agribusinesses and current environmental damage are absent from travel journalism that covers regional food as a central point of attraction. This is particularly so for agribusinesses such as aquaculture that have been naturalized by the tourism sector as attractions in their own right. This case echoes other findings that, except when associated with "geotourism" (McGaurr 2015, 168; see also Stoddart and Nezhadhossein 2016), travel publications rarely critique tourism for its environmental impacts even when they cover environmental conflict in other sectors (McGaurr 2014, 2015; McGaurr and Lester 2018).

The analysis presented in this chapter has also demonstrated how, in the absence of critiques of New Brunswick aquaculture's chains of production in travel journalism, aquaculture's marketing may have been amplified by the genre's circulation of closely aligned tourism tropes. This is important knowledge for environmental organizations, which to date have tended to overlook the cosmopolitical potential of travel journalism even when they have seen qualified advantages in building relationships with the tourism sector. It is understandable that environmental organizations would be reluctant to mobilize tourism operators to raise environmental concerns with travel journalists if they believed there could be serious consequences for those operators. It does not follow, however, that the only path open to environmental organizations in these circumstances would be to ignore travel journalism. It is possible that a sufficiently well-crafted travel-journalism media strategy – even one that did not rely on tourism operators as spokespeople – could partially mitigate absent critiques of contested foodways in the genre, and draw attention to and underscore the importance of environmental victories. For example, in 2021, the Fundy Salmon Recovery Project recorded 100 wild Atlantic salmon – the largest number in more than 30 years – returning to Fundy National Park (Balintec 2021). This impressive result was the outcome of a large investment of time, money, passion, expertise, and co-operation to capture smolt in their native rivers, grow them into adults in a purpose-built facility on the Fundy island of Grand Manan, then release them back into their native rivers to complete their natural spawning cycle (Balintec 2021). But 100 individuals is a minuscule number compared to the huge populations that once swam in these waters. So, with this hard-won achievement comes perhaps the greatest pressure to date to monitor the health of surviving sea-run Atlantic salmon in the Bay of Fundy and protect them from every threat. By integrating travel and food journalism into their communication strategies, environmental stakeholders could utilize their reach beyond the region to get this important message across.

Acknowledgment

The New Brunswick fieldwork for this chapter was supported by a grant from the University of Tasmania's Institute for Social Change.

References

Ali, Adina. 2022. "Postmedia to Buy Irving's N.B. Newspaper Chain in 16.1M Cash and Share Deal." *Global News*. February 18, 2022. https://globalnews.ca/news/8630162/postmedia-buying-irvings-newspaper-chain-new-brunswick/.

Atlantic Salmon Federation. 2019. "Environment Commissioner Slams Feds Lack of Aquaculture Oversight." October 12, 2019. https://www.asf.ca/news-and-magazine/salmon-news/environment-commissioner-slams-feds-lack-of-aquaculture-oversight.

Balintec, Vanessa. 2021. "Number of Atlantic Salmon in Fundy National Park Rivers at 32-year High." *CBC New Brunswick*. October 15, 2021. https://www.cbc.ca/news/canada/new-brunswick/number-of-atlantic-salmon-in-fundy-national-park-reach-32-year-high-1.6210999.

Banjac, Sandra and Folker Hanusch. 2020. "Aspirational Lifestyle Journalism: The Impact of Social Class on Producers' and Audiences' Views in the Context of Socio-Economic Inequality." *Journalism*: 11–19. 10.1177/1464884920956823.

Becker, Elizabeth. 2008. "Lost in the Travel Pages: The Global Industry Hiding inside the Sunday Newspaper." Joan Shorenstein Center on the Press, Politics and Public Policy. Discussion paper series: D-45, https://shorensteincenter.org/lost-in-the-travel-pages-the-global-industry-hiding-inside-the-sunday-newspaper/.

Brett, David and Antonio Pinna. 2015. "Patterns, Fixedness and Variability: Using PoS-grams to Find Phraseologies in the Language of Travel Journalism." *Procedia – Social and Behavioral Sciences* 198:52–57.

CBC New Brunswick. 2010. "Illegal pesticide use probed in 4 N.B. sites." September 29, 2010. https://www.cbc.ca/news/canada/new-brunswick/illegal-pesticide-use-probed-in-4-n-b-sites-1.952089.

CBC New Brunswick. 2013. "Aquaculture Company on the Hook for $500K for Pesticide Use." April 26, 2013. https://www.cbc.ca/news/canada/new-brunswick/aquaculture-company-on-the-hook-for-500k-for-pesticide-use-1.1317105.

Cocking, Ben. 2020. *Travel Journalism and Travel Media: Identities, Places and Imaginings*. London: Palgrave Macmillan.

Conservation Council of New Brunswick. 2022. "Fundy Bay Keeper." https://www.conservationcouncil.ca/fundy-baykeeper/.

Cooke Aquaculture. 2021a. "The Cooke Story: From Small Family Company to Global Seafood Leader." https://www.cookeseafood.com/about-cooke/.

Cooke Aquaculture. 2021b. www.cookeseafood.com.

Cooke Aquaculture. 2021c. "Environment and Conservation." http://www.cookeseafood.com/sustainability/.

Cooke Aquaculture. 2021d. "Innovation." http://www.cookeseafood.com/innovation/.

Conservation Council of New Brunswick. 2019. "Ecoalert: Celebrating 50 Years." https://www.conservationcouncil.ca/celebrate-the-past-50-years-of-environmental-action-with-our-50th-anniversary-special-edition-ecoalert/.

Duffy, Andrew and Yang Yuhong Ashley. 2012. "Bread and Circuses: Food Meets Politics in the Singapore Media." *Journalism Practice* 6(1):59–74. 10.1080/17512786.2011.622892.

Fürsich, Elfriede. 2002. "Packaging Culture: The Potential and Limitations of Travel Programs on Global Television." *Communication Quarterly* 50(2):204–226. 10.1080/01463370209385657.

Fürsich, Elfriede. 2009. "In Defense of Textual Analysis: Restoring a Challenged Method of Journalism and Media Studies." *Journalism Studies* 10(2):238–252. 10.1080/14616700802374050.

Fürsich, Elfriede. 2012. "Lifestyle Journalism as Popular Journalism: Strategies for Evaluating its Public Role." *Journalism Practice* 6(1):12–25. 10.1080/17512786.2011.622894.

Godwin, Sean, Mark Fast, Anna Kuparinen, Kate Medcalf and Jeffrey Hutchings. 2020. "Increasing Temperatures Accentuate Negative Fitness Consequences of a Marine Parasite." *Scientific Reports* 10(18467). 10.1038/s41598-020-74948-3.

Government of Canada. 2013. "Kelly Cove Salmon Ordered to Pay $500,000 for Federal Fisheries Act Violations." https://www.canada.ca/en/environment-climate-change/services/environmental-enforcement/notifications/kelly-cove-salmon-fisheries-act-violations.html.

Government of Canada. 2019a. "Atlantic Salmon (Inner Bay of Fundy population)." https://www.dfo-mpo.gc.ca/species-especes/profiles-profils/salmon-atl-saumon-eng.html.

Government of Canada. 2019b. "Atlantic Salmon (Outer Bay of Fundy designatable unit)." https://www.dfo-mpo.gc.ca/species-especes/profiles-profils/atlanticsalmon-OBF-saumonatlantique-eng.html.

Government of Canada. 2019c. "Wild Atlantic Salmon Conservation: Implementation Plan 2019 to 2021." https://www.dfo-mpo.gc.ca/reports-rapports/regs/wildsalmon-conservation-saumonsauvage-eng.html.

Government of New Brunswick. 2011. "Government of New Brunswick Duty to Consult Policy." https://www2.gnb.ca/content/dam/gnb/Departments/aas-saa/pdf/en/DutytoConsultPolicy.pdf.

Government of New Brunswick. 2021a. "Fish 2021: A Part of Our Heritage." https://www2.gnb.ca/content/dam/gnb/Departments/nr-rn/pdf/en/Fish/Fish.pdf.

Government of New Brunswick. 2021b. "New Brunswick Agri-Food and Seafood Export Highlights 2020." https://www2.gnb.ca/content/dam/gnb/Departments/10/pdf/Publications/Aqu/ExportHighlightsforNewBrunswickAgrifoodandSeafood2020.pdf.

Government of New Brunswick. n.d. "Agriculture, Aquaculture and Fisheries: Salmon." https://www2.gnb.ca/content/gnb/en/departments/10/aquaculture/content/overview/salmon.html.

Hanitzsch, Thomas and Tim Vos. 2018. "Journalism Beyond Democracy: A New Look into Journalistic Roles in Political and Everyday Life." *Journalism* 19(2):146–164. 10.1177/1464884916673386.

Hanusch, Folker. 2011. "A Profile of Australian Travel Journalists' Professional Views and Ethical Standards." *Journalism* 13(1):1–19. http://jou.sagepub.com/content/early/2011/05/27/1464884911398338.

Hanusch, Folker. 2017. "'How Much Love Are You Going to Give This Brand?': Lifestyle Journalists on Commercial Influences in Their work." *Journalism* 18(2):141–158. 10.1177/1464884915608818.

Hanusch, Folker. 2019. "Journalistic Roles and Everyday Life: An Empirical Account of Lifestyle Journalists' Professional Views." *Journalism Studies* 20(2): 193–211. 10.1080/1461670X.2017.1370977.

Holyoke, John. 2019. "1,000 Farm-Raised Salmon Escape from Canadian Pen, Some Captured at New Brunswick Dam." September 12, 2019. *Bangor Daily News*. https://bangordailynews.com/2019/09/12/outdoors/1000-farm-raised-salmon-escape-from-canadian-pen-some-captured-at-new-brunswick-dam/.

Henry, Jacob. 2018. "Anthony Bourdain's Window into Africa." The Conversation. June 13, 2021. https://the conversation.com/anthony-bourdains-window-into-africa-98073

Ibrahim, Hadeel. 2022. "Irving-owned New Brunswick Newspapers to be Sold to Postmedia." *CBC New Brunswick*. February 18, 2022. https://www.cbc.ca/news/canada/new-brunswick/brunswick-news-sold-postmedia-1.6356427.

Kraly, Paul, Jenny Weitzman and Ramón Filgueira. 2021. "Understanding Factors Influencing Social Acceptability: Insights from Media Portrayal of Salmon Aquaculture in Atlantic Canada." *Aquaculture*. 10.1016/j.aquaculture.2021.737497.

Lester, Libby and Brett Hutchins. 2012. "Soft Journalism, Politics and Environmental Risk: An Australian Story." *Journalism* 13(5): 654–667. 10.1177/1464884 911421706.

MacDonald, Michelle. 2018. "Irving Pulp and Paper in New Brunswick Fined $3.5 Million for Dumping Effluent." *National Observer*. November 6, 2018. https://www.nationalobserver.com/2018/11/06/news/irving-pulp-and-paper-new-brunswick-fined-35-million-dumping-effluent.

MacGregor, Roy. 2017. "Fishing for Answers." *Globe and Mail*. August 27, 2017. https://www.theglobeandmail.com/life/travel/charting-the-future-of-canadas-historic-saint-johnriver/article36097707/.

McGaurr, Lyn. 2010. "Travel Journalism and Environmental Conflict: A Cosmopolitan Perspective." *Journalism Studies* 11(1):50–67 10.1080/14616700903068924.

McGaurr, Lyn. 2014. "Your Threat or Mine? Travel Journalists and Environmental Problems," In *Travel Journalism: Exploring Production, Impact and Culture*, edited by Folker Hanusch and Elfriede Fürsich, 211–248. Basingstoke: Palgrave Macmillan.

McGaurr, Lyn. 2015. *Environmental Communication and Travel Journalism: Consumerism, Conflict and Concern*. Abingdon: Routledge.

McGaurr, Lyn. 2016. "The Photography of Debate and Desire: Images, Environment and the Public Sphere." *Ethical Space* 13(2/3):16–33.

McGaurr, Lyn and Libby Lester. 2018. "See It before It's Too Late: Last Chance Travel Lists and Climate Change," In *Climate Change and the Media Volume 2*, edited by Benedetta Brevini and Justin Lewis, 123–140. New York: Peter Lang.

McGaurr, Lyn, Bruce Tranter, and Libby Lester. 2015. "Wilderness and the Media Politics of Place Branding." *Environmental Communication* 9(3):269–287. 10.1080/17524032.2014.919947.

Morris, Matthew, Dylan Fraser, Anthoney Heggelin, Frederick Whoriskey, Jonathan Carr, Shane O'Neil, and Jeffrey Hutchings. 2008. "Prevalence and Recurrence of Escaped Farmed Atlantic Salmon (Salmo Salar) in Eastern North American Rivers." *Canadian Journal of Fisheries and Aquatic Sciences* 65(12):2807–2826. 10.1139/F08-181.

National Geographic. 2015. "Geotourism." https://www.nationalgeographic.com/maps/topic/geotourism.

Office of the Auditor General of Canada. 2018. "2018 Spring Reports of the Commissioner of the Environment and Sustainable Development to the Parliament of Canada: Report 1: Salmon farming." https://www.oag-bvg.gc.ca/internet/English/parl_cesd_201804_01_e_42992.html.

Pan, Steve and Chris Ryan. 2008. "Tourism and Sense-Making: The Role of the Senses and Travel Journalism." *Journal of Travel and Tourism Marketing* 26(7):625–639. 10.1080/10548400903276897.

Peck, Barbara. February 20, 2020. "The Essential Guide to New Brunswick." *AFAR*. https://www.afar.com/magazine/the-best-things-to-do-in-new-brunswick.

Phillipov, Michelle. 2016. "The New Politics of Food: Television and the Media/Food Industries." *Media International Australia* 158(1):90–98. 10.1177/1329878X15627339.

Poitras, Jacques. 2014. *Irving Vs. Irving: Canada's Feuding Billionaires and the Stories They Won't Tell*. Toronto: Viking.

Red Rock Adventure. n.d. "Culinary: Taste Fundy! Discover Local Flavours." https://www.bayoffundyadventures.com/culinary.

Smith, Phoebe. 2019. "On the Tail: Whale Watching on the Bay of Fundy, Canada." *Wanderlust*. March 28, 2019. https://www.wanderlust.co.uk/content/whale-watching-bay-of-fundy/.

Stoddart, Mark and Paula Graham. 2016. "Nature, History and Culture as Tourism Attractors: The Double Translation of Insider and Outsider Media." *Nature and Culture* 11(1):22–43. 10.3167/nc.2016.110102.

Stoddart, Mark and Elahe Nezhadhossein. 2016. "Is Nature-Oriented Tourism a Proenvironmental Practice? Examining Tourism–Environmentalism Alignments through Discourse Networks and Intersectoral Relationships." *The Sociological Quarterly* 57:544–568. 10.1111/tsq.12148.

Tourism New Brunswick. 2021a. "Stories: Fishing in New Brunswick: What You Need to Know." https://tourismnewbrunswick.ca/story/fishing-new-brunswick-what-you-need-know.

Tourism New Brunswick. 2021b. "Village of Blacks Harbour." https://tourismnewbrunswick.ca/listing/village-blacks-harbour.

Tourism New Brunswick. 2021c. "Bay of Fundy: This is New Brunswick Nature in Its Grandest Setting." https://tourismnewbrunswick.ca/bay-fundy/

Tourism New Brunswick. 2021d. "Lobster and Seafood: A Taste of Coastal Living." https://tourismnewbrunswick.ca/lobster-and-seafood.

Trotter, Mike. 2013. "Cooke Aquaculture to Pay $490,000 after Illegal Pesticides Kill Lobsters in Canada." *Bangor Daily News*. April 27, 2013. https://bangordailynews.com/2013/04/27/news/cooke-aquaculture-to-pay-490k-after-illegal-pesticides-kill-lobsters-in-canada/.

UNB Newsroom. 2021. "N.B. Salmon Population Winning an Upstream Battle, UNB Research Suggests." https://blogs.unb.ca/newsroom/2021/10/nb-salmon-population-winning-an-upstream-battle-unb-research-suggests.php.

Unwin, Mike. 2014. "New Brunswick: It's Wild and Wonderful in This Corner of Canada." *Independent*. August 18, 2014. https://www.independent.co.uk/travel/americas/new-brunswick-it-s-wild-and-wonderful-corner-canada-9675876.html.

Wilkinson, Guy. 2015. "Trekking in Bay of Fundy, Canada: The Woods Best Left to Bear Grylls, until Now." *Traveller*. February 27, 2015. https://www.traveller.com.au/trekking-in-bay-of-fundy-canada-the-woods-best-left-to-bear-grylls-until-now-13ki4m.

4 Who Speaks and Are We Listening? Food Sovereign Voices in a Changing Climate

Alana Mann

When 37 leading scientists from 16 countries published the report *Food in the Anthropocene: EAT-Lancet Commission on Healthy and Sustainable Food Systems* (Willet et al. 2019), their call for healthier and more sustainable global food production and consumption was met with criticism from many sides. Along with a range of policies curtailing factory farming, food waste, and the mismanagement of land and water resources, the report recommended the adoption of a universal "healthy reference diet" that almost entirely eliminated meat. "Can we still eat Big Macs and avoid climate chaos?" wondered Agence France Presse, while *The Wall Street Journal* called out vegetarianism as "climate virtue signaling" and Joanna Blythman in *The Grocer* encouraged eaters to "resist the vegan putsch." The meat lobby launched a vigorous social media counter-campaign, #yes2meat, which soon outnumbered the EAT-Lancet tweets by ten to one (Garcia 2019).

Compared to this short-lived push-back through media, Anthony Green (2019) asked a more profound question in *Inside Development*: "Can the Eat-Lancet diet work for the Global South?" He noted that *Food in the Anthropocene* neglected issues that particularly affect poorer countries, including "how governments can ensure communities are still able to afford food if prices rise to reflect higher nutrition and sustainability standards—or what happens if they don't" (Green 2019). His statement raises an important point: dietary shifts by middle-class eaters in WEIRD (Western, educated, industrialized, rich, democratic) nations have little impact on the life chances of millions living with hunger, for indigenous peoples dispossessed of their homelands, or for those "making-do" in the "alternative-alternative food networks" of discount and dollar stores and food banks (Williams-Forson 2015, 4:03).

Green shifts the perspective to the different experiences of vulnerability to climate change that are being felt by marginalized populations around the world. These communities are on the frontline of the impacts of a fossil-fueled, *consumptagenic* food system that "encourages and rewards the exploitation of natural resources, excess production, and hyper-consumerism, and which results in climate change and health inequities" (Friel 2019, 136).

DOI: 10.4324/9781003283942-6

To tackle these wrongs in our food system demands that we pay "much more attention to the broader injustices that the cheap food dilemma rests on and perhaps less attention to what's on the menu" (Guthman 2011, 194). This approach requires a historical perspective that appreciates the evolution of global foodways from the colonial to the corporate food regime (McMichael 2009), an exploitative system sustained by the continuation of racialized land and labor relationships where hunger and obesity co-exist as a consequence of the overproduction of cheap food.

Yet explaining this moral, ethical, and cultural complexity is a challenge that media struggle to take on. This chapter considers how journalists and other content producers can contest classism and racism embedded within our food system through food justice approaches that "explore how power nuances the role of voice, storytelling, and positionality in narrations of food-related problems and their solutions" (Gordon and Hunt 2018, 14; Alkon and Agyeman 2011; Alkon et al. 2020). Moreover, drawing on Sabiha Ahmad Kahn's (2020) notion of "food sovereign voices," the chapter problematizes food media that only superficially amplify the voices of those who "act otherwise" (Fladvad 2019). Food media that privilege the voices and standpoints of frontline workers in fields, kitchens, food service, and processing lines can reveal the unequal power relations in food systems; however, they can also run the risk of reducing the autonomy of those voices in the media discourse. Despite the capacity of journalistic texts to contribute to our understanding of how capitalism operates on multiple levels, including the "personal, experiential, institutional, and structural" (Mosco 2008, 52), they often reproduce paternalistic framings of the "powerless" that prevail in food insecurity and climate change discourses. By focusing especially on indigenous voices and perspectives in this food discourse, this chapter provides suggestions on how to overcome this shortfall.

Climate, Food, and Media Coverage

Media coverage connecting food and climate has increased significantly since the Intergovernmental Panel on Climate Change (IPCC) (2007) released its report on climate change impacts, adaptation, and vulnerability (O'Neill et al. 2013; Schmidt, Ivanova, and Schafer 2013). Researchers have identified a range of contradictory and complementary media frames, ranging from an emphasis on technical aspects such as carbon sequestration to the need for massive foreign assistance to poor countries for adaptation (Boykoff and Roberts 2007). Contested frames, those demonstrating political dissension over climate change, are unsurprisingly prevalent in countries reliant on coal and gas exports, like Australia (O'Neill 2013). Despite the publication of the UN Food and Agriculture Organization (FAO)'s report *Livestock's Long Shadow* (2006), which identified animal agriculture as a significant source of greenhouse gas emissions, water pollutants, and soil erosion, researchers found that the correlation between livestock production and consumption and climate change remains a "media blind-spot" (Almiron and Zoppeddu 2015; Lahsen 2018). Núria Almiron even suggests that the "animal-based taboo" is a "neoliberal triumph" driven by the "political, social and economic elites with which the old media is interconnected" (Almiron 2020, 2). Advocating for a revision of journalistic ethics to "update moral boundaries" with "anthropocentric roots anchored in some Enlightenment ideals," Almiron urges us to tackle the "ideological roots of our activities" and promote "change based on principles, rather than upon pragmatic, self-serving concerns" (Almiron 2020, 3).

Despite the legacy media's previous lack of attention to the issue, the rising popularity of vegetarian and vegan diets in WEIRD nations demonstrates growing concern with human health, animal suffering, and the environmental impacts of factory farming including effluent runoff, antibiotic discharge, and land clearing for feed crops. The *Food in the Anthropocene* report, on the heels of Intergovernmental Panel on Climate Change (IPCC) data reporting that animal agriculture contributes 37 percent of global emissions (IPCC 2019), has promoted diet to "the latest front in the culture wars" (Anthony 2019). However, media coverage linking livestock and climate is infrequent and tends to rely on personal responsibility and frames that link environmental benefits to consumer purchases at the expense of arguments for policy reform and regulation, such as holding industrial meat corporations to account (Kristiansen, Painter, and Shea 2021).

In addition, popular media coverage, advertising or advocacy campaigns focused on our diets frequently overlook other forms of violence and discrimination embedded in our food systems. Problematic examples are PETA's "Are animals the new slaves?" exhibition; the Twitter campaign #AllLionsMatter, invoked after the much-publicized death of Cecil, the lion; or the 2014 publication of *Thug Kitchen*, a vegan recipe book written in "verbal blackface" by white authors. According to Jennifer Polish, all these examples highlight "the ways that white veganism often enacts upon the bodies of people of color the same thoughtless devaluation that they accuse others of when they call for people to recognize that animal lives do, in fact, matter" (Polish 2016, 386). Yet there is no universal veganism, any more than there is one way of being omnivorous. Greenebaum (2018, 682) advocates for a better version of vegan protest that is "anti-speciest, anti-racist, environmental, or health-centric"; one that enables vegans of color to use their veganism "as a tool to decolonize the body from a colonial diet that is killing the black community." As a "*counter*cuisine" veganism embraces a wide variety of meanings and interpretations, and like all social movements it experiences "regular negotiation of conflicts internal to the movement as well as those associated with outside entities in the wider social movement environment" (Wrenn 2019, 190). Media representations frequently fail to capture this complexity.

The (Media) Politics of Food Resistance

Discourses as Cultural Resistance

Food discourses wind through a "complex web of communication in which debates about citizenship, culture, identity, economics, and politics intertwine" (Lindenfeld 2011, 4). As a mediator of social relationships, a symbol of identity, and a marker of differences, food has great potential to unify (Sutton 2008, 159) but also to divide. As Baumann and Johnston explain, our personal foodscapes are "dynamic social construction(s) that relate food to specific places, people, and meanings" that embrace the "sociocultural mediatedness" and the "ecological connectedness" of food (Johnston and Baumann 2010, 2–3).

Within our foodscapes, discourses of responsibility, connectedness, and solidarity circulate between eaters and local producers that are forms of resistance, even "insurrection" (Nossiter 2019), against a global consumer culture. Resistance through food, throughout history, has included "spectacular public displays of starvation or as everyday actions, small gestures of rebellion located in (un)authorised or (in)appropriate spaces where they did not quite fit" (Cooks 2009, 94). Leda Cooks notes that in a "commodity-driven market" food becomes "a central and tangible trace of the dominant ordering of social relations" (Cooks 2009, 9). She argues:

> In the industrialized west, where food slips into image, into the imaginary, it becomes necessary for lifestyle, rather than sustaining life. As the means of producing food and the value assigned to its production are increasingly split off from consumption, food becomes less and less about its substance and the relation of that substance to subsistence, and becomes more available for signification. In a saturated capitalist economy that signification must be controlled by market forces precisely because of its importance to everyday life.
> (Cooks 2009, 95)

Food is both materially and symbolically powerful, not only because we depend on it for survival but because it is "no longer a widely (locally) accessible and equally produced resource" (Cooks 2009, 95).

Bočák's notion of "mediated foodscapes" establishes the constitutive role media play in this context (2019, 161). It implies dynamics beyond the "augmented distribution of culinary messages by (mass) media; it suggests the complete rearrangement of the foodscape by media" (Bočák 2019, 161). This includes defining "good" and "bad" food and messaging "degrees of hierarchy inclusion and exclusion boundaries and transaction across the boundaries" (Douglas 1972, 61). In these discursive sites of struggle our everyday food practices achieve political dimensions.

Models and Problems of (Western) Food Journalism

Immersive, longform journalism focused on the food industry is a potential outlet for a complex engagement with problematic foodway issues, a way of revealing "uncivilized truths" (Kautt 2019, 329). For example, in *Nickel-and-Dimed: On (Not) Getting By in America* (Ehrenreich 1999), journalist Barbara Ehrenreich documents her (short-) lived experience of the low-wage labor market in Key West, Florida. Unsurprisingly, she lands in the booming hospitality industry where positions abound for those "trainable, flexible, and with suitably humble expectation as to pay" (Ehrenreich 2021, 7). In the same vein, Tracie McMillan (2012) works undercover in the fields, kitchens, and supermarket aisles of the US to reveal the inequities that underpin the American diet.

The Covid-19 pandemic has put the media spotlight on "essential" but marginalized food workers, highlighting appalling working conditions in livestock processing plants, mainly in the United States but also in Australia (Dao, Green, and Huang 2021). A variety of documentary films, television series, and podcasts critique the industrial food system by following commodity chains (e.g., *Rotten* 2018) and interrogating injustices ranging from the murders and disappearances of UN Fisheries Observers (McVeigh 2020) to "food apartheid" in the planning and distribution of grocery stores in American cities (BBC 2021). These journalistic media texts counter lifestyle media content that often reinforces foodie culture, commodifies Otherness, and presents the home kitchen as "a form of empowerment without granting actual political or economic power to women" (Lindenfeld 2011, 15).

Nevertheless, the ability of documentary modes to give a voice to racialized and gendered subjects is contestable, particularly in biographic storytelling that focuses on individual triumphs and tragedies rather than systemic problems. The power of these cultural artifacts gives us fair warning that telling people's stories by sharing their cuisines can constitute "erasure through re-narration" (Grey and Newman 2018, 720), particularly when those narratives are co-opted by powerful actors who drown out, or co-opt, authentic voices. Writing in the US, Lorraine Chuen (2017) notes that the way White chefs and restaurateurs have built their reputations as "cultural authorities" on ethnic cuisine can be "dehumanizing" – even as it is profitable. White writers are paid to write recipes and are given platforms to share them. Accordingly, dishes are "prepared for the white gaze" and the "white palate," often lacking essential context. As Chuen asks:

> What remains of food, after it's been decontextualized? What are flavors without stories? What are recipes without histories? Why are people of color forgotten, over and over again, while their food (also: vocabulary, music, art, hair, clothing) are consumed and adopted?
> (Chuen 2017)

In Australia, Colin Ho and Nicholas Jordan (2018) note similarly that the national food media have been dominated by white people, including most leadership positions (such as head reviewers). They emphasize that diversity of journalistic staff generates more varied stories and ideas. Australian food writer Lee Tran Lam, for example, applies this idea in her edited collection *Diversity in Food Media: New Voices on Food* (2020).

Food Sovereign(ty) Voices

Articulating one's voice in the media can be a form of resistance against an economic system that strives to silence marginalized voices (Mann 2019). The concept of "voice" does more than value particular voices or acts of speaking; it values all human beings' ability to give an account of themselves; it values my and your status as "narratable" selves (Couldry 2010, 13; Butler 2005). In *Why Voice Matters,* Nick Couldry explains that "making voices matter is hard; it is even harder, amid the proliferation of new voices, to challenge the hidden forces and dislocation that prevent them mattering when it counts" (Couldry 2010, 50). He identifies "a contemporary crisis of voice" across not only political and economic, but also social and cultural, domains. He attributes this to the discourse of neoliberalism which "operates with a view of economic life that does not value voice and imposes that view of economic life onto politics, via a reductive view of politics as the implementing of market function" (Couldry 2010, 2). To deny the capacity to possess and share one's narrative is to "deny her potential for voice … a basic dimension of human life" (Couldry 2010, 7). Voice is a form of reflexive agency through which we "disclose ourselves as subjects" (Arendt 1958, 193) and make sense of our lives.

To overcome the deficiencies of voices in mainstream media narratives, Sabiha Ahmad Khan (2020) employs the concept of food sovereignty in arguing that "voice inheres in that which grates against a neoliberal understanding of food systems and the representational modes that operate within that sphere" (Khan 2020, 1). Her objective, as a documentary filmmaker, is to resist "medial frames of emergency" (Rangan 2017, 10) driven by the "humanitarian impulse" to cover "food sovereign voices" in alternative ways. This concept includes focusing on the "quotidian practices of social life" (Fladvad 2019, 11) and ways of "acting otherwise" (Fladvad 2019, 13) that characterize the food sovereignty movement.

The European Coordination of La Vía Campesina (part of a larger international grassroots peasant movement) describes food sovereignty as "a process of building social movements and empowering peoples to organize their societies in ways that transcend the neoliberal vision of a world of commodities, markets and selfish economic actors" (European Coordination Vía Campesina 2018, 1). Focused on "solidarity, not competition, and building a fairer world from the bottom up," the small-scale peasants, fisherfolk, agricultural workers, and landless peoples who formalized this concept in 1993 emphasize that peoples should have the right to define their own food and agricultural systems, prioritizing the needs of their families and communities above those of markets and corporations. Mark Tilzey describes food sovereignty as a "radical imaginary" and counter-narrative intent on "obstructing and reversing primitive accumulation and capitalist market dependence through the reappropriation of land and resources in both countryside and city as the basis for socially equitable, cooperative, and ecologically sustainable production, primarily of food, for family and community" (Tilzey 2021, 205). This reference to the city reflects how food sovereignty has evolved conceptually from a rural land reform movement to embrace urban food environments. Tornaghi and Dehaene, for example, make this connection:

> Agroecological urbanism, for instance, complements political agroecology – a combination of practices and approaches respectful of soil ecology and soil health, promoting biodiversity, recognising multispecies solidarities, cherishing horizontal knowledge reproduction and valuing people's knowledge and place/culturally sensitive practices.
> (Tornaghi and Dehaene 2021, 4)

These approaches can be applied to various food media. Food sovereign voices can be carried in texts like cookbooks and recipes that share intergenerational knowledge regarding traditional foods (Claasen and Chigeza 2019) and serve as "technologies of memory" (Kittler cited in Ayora-Diaz 2019, 115). Kathleen German's historic research on recipe exchange among concentration camp inmates, for example, illustrates the potentially forceful impact of cookbooks as "proclamations of identity [which] in the face of the denial of one's humanity become acts of resistance" (German 2011, 151).

Another model has been developed by Khan (2020, 4), who captures "intercultural food happenings" through an interactive documentary platform archiving food practices of community elders on the U.S.-Mexico border. She proposes "a conversational model of cataloguing and retrieving food memories of 'acting otherwise' that are specific to the region," initially focused on recipes but later extending to "a variety of food sovereign practices" (Khan 2020, 4). Users interact with "digitized embodied conversational agents" (Khan 2020, 4) – animated computer-generated characters that mimic face-to-face dialogue – scripted according to fieldwork interviews modeled on Meredith E. Abarca's idea of *charla culinarian* or culinary kitchen chats (Abarca 2007). This approach embraces a feminist methodology of "gathering women's stories through the lens of food" by providing a space to listen to "traditionally muted people" (Counihan cited in Abarca 2007, 189). Legitimizing different fields of knowledge, the work respects women as "grassroots theoreticians" whose culinary experiences "ground their knowledge, power, and personal, as well as collective, sense of agency" (Abarca 2007, 189). Through her documentaries, Khan seeks to capture the *sazón* or "the particular inflections of self-expression that pepper dishes made by a particular home cook" (Abarca 2006, 135), noting that this notion of "seasoning-as-voice" resonates with a definition of voice as the "sound of specific experiential encounters in civic life" (Watts 2001, 185).

Transforming Expert Voice in Indigenous Peoples' Food Stories

Socially grounded voice requires resources in the form of language and status. Celebrity chefs, as "cultural intermediaries" (Bourdieu 1984), have this in spades. Food media position these voices as cultural authorities, many of whom promote the "political morality of food" to make us better citizens (Matta 2019). Promoted on platforms such as the MAD symposia, chefs "produce themselves as intellectuals of food, eating and cooking" (Lee 2013, 211) and are leaders in promoting what Sam Grey and Lenore Newman (2018) refer to as "gastronomic multiculturalism." The accompanying enlightened food coverage, however, has its caveats. Peru, for example, has witnessed a "culinary revolution" manifested in gastro-tourism marketed as *concina novoandina*. As Raúl Matta criticizes, this "gastronomic boom" follows the "commercial logics of multiculturalism, which exploit difference and shape an exotic 'other' highly valuable in global markets" (Matta 2019, 197).

Yet gastronomic stardom can be particularly deleterious for Indigenous people. According to Grey and Newman, the "gentrification of Indigenous gastronomy keeps privilege intact" and represents a form of "culinary colonialism" (Grey and Newman 2018, 720). They even suggest that the "mindful withholding" of Indigenous foods might be the only way to protect them from the market. Australian Aboriginal Bunurong author and farmer Bruce Pascoe notes that where there is an opportunity to commercialize traditional foods, Indigenous people must retain ownership, "so large food companies don't put a brand on it and dispossess us once again" (Vernon 2019).

Australia's Indigenous "First Foods" sector is worth $AUD 20 million annually, yet profits to traditional owners account for only about 1 percent of that amount (Turner 2021). Indigenous food products, already viewed as novel, of good quality, and healthy, are highly marketable in a changing climate as they are adapted to native environments. It is now internationally recognized that "agricultural practices that include Indigenous and local knowledge can contribute to overcoming the combined challenges of climate change, food security, biodiversity conservation, and combating desertification and land degradation" (IPCC 2019, 29).

To those who grew up eating these now celebrated foods that required hard work to harvest and were at the center of ancient ceremonies, the idea that they are new culinary trends can be bewildering. In the US, Apache chef Nephi Craig argues: "Falsehoods of luxury built on the appropriation of Indigenous foodways is the equivalent of imperial slumming and often comical from an Indigenous person's perspective" (cited in Mihesuah 2019, 307). Instead, Craig suggests:

> If you want real Indigenous food advocacy speak from a point of community, mortality, healing, hurt, pain, violence, suicide, spiritual malady, unnatural death, and recovery. Come to ground zero and speak truths while offering solutions – not just speaking about Native foods from a disconnected professional level with a message that is designed to appeal to the colonial culinary elite (Native and non-Native) for the sake of making a name for one's self, company or organization.
>
> (cited in Mihesuah 2019, 309)

This raises the question of how the distinctiveness of Indigenous food sovereign voices can be accounted for in media coverage. For Indigenous people, food sovereignty includes the power to govern food systems, and steward bio-diversity in traditional ways, within a policy environment that guarantees secure and sustainable access to resources and the capacity to market crops (Argumedo and Pimbert 2005). Indigenous peoples face unique challenges related to food sovereignty in comparison with most small-scale farmers and participants in community-based food organizations. They seek interpretations that respect the rights of individuals and groups to identify the characteristics of their cultures and foodways. Dispossessed and already engaged in a long struggle for land rights, Indigenous peoples' movements, as Stevenhagen argues, "do not demand just *any* land, but rather *their* land. And they want control over their land and territories. Thus, closely linked to the concept of territory are the demands by organizations and movements of Indigenous people for autonomy and self-determination" (Grey and Patel 2015, 4). Indigenous participation and leadership are essential in policy-making processes that create effective, enabling legislation that recognizes these understandings. Accordingly, if the political platforms claiming to represent food sovereignty are to expand beyond the collection of rights attached to food production and consumption and build the broad coalitions necessary to transform societies, they must embrace the diverse food-generating practices and complex land-management strategies of Indigenous people (Mann 2021).

The "acts, deeds, and events" (Fladvad 2019, 8) that comprise Indigenous political autonomy can only be told by Indigenous food sovereign voices. These are scarce in our media. The Australian government report *When Inclusion Means Exclusion: Social Commentary and Indigenous Agency* (All Together Now 2021) reveals a preponderance of White Witnesses (McQuire 2019) writing on Indigenous issues. These voices are fixed on either "an 'us and them' dialogue or the focus on coming to terms with their responsibility to provide support and allyship for Indigenous people" (Thomas and Paradies 2021). The report found evidence of "surface level inclusion" in political debates and media, defined as "inclusion of Indigenous people through the absence of negative stereotypes, but excluding Indigenous authors, perspectives, historical and cultural contexts, and voices" (All Together Now 2021, 7). Moreover, media narratives often avoid topics including conflict and separation narratives, notably those that "challenge the status quo, which push for First Nations sovereignty, and which reject mainstream aspirations" (All Together Now 2021, 5). Rachel Hocking, a Warlpiri woman from the Tanami Desert, freelance journalist and former NITV presenter, describes well-intentioned but "hollow commentary" which has the gloss of inclusion and presents itself as "speaking authoritatively on Indigenous issues, without Indigenous input" (All Together Now 2021, 4).

Towards Better (Food) Media

Beyond adding more food sovereign voices, food media have a critical role to play in challenging the corporate power that dominates our food system. This means resisting the incorporation of a "personal responsibility frame" in media discourses about sustainability, localism, and organics that serves to "reproduce neo-liberal forms, spaces of governance, and mentalities" (Guthman 2008, 1171). In ignoring critical questions of difference including gender, race, and class, these discourses "miss the globe" and "the historical discontinuity of dispossession and disaster caused by empire" (DeLoughrey 2019, 2). This coverage limits possibilities for systemic and structural change, as Macarena Go'mez-Barris emphasizes, by failing to address the onslaught of a "colonial capitalism" intent on "discursively constructing racialized bodies within geographies of difference, systematically destroying through dispossession, enslavement, and then producing the planet as a corporate bioterritory" (Go'mez-Barris 2017, 4). Under this paradigm, those who grow food go hungry while those who never produced food thrive (De Souza 2019).

To confront this complexity, media practitioners must approach their work through the lens of food justice that reflects "antiracist and class-conscious principles, and foreground[s] the leadership of those most adversely affected by the industrial food system" (Povitz 2019, 240). This also includes diverse leadership and staff in food media. However, these calls for more complex media storytelling come at a time when many media are in distress given the decreasing number and profit margins of media outlets and the fact that many journalists themselves live in precarious work and life situations. For example, the South African journalist, food writer, and activist Ishay Govender-Ypma recalled a post of a local chef who complained that there were no local and "decent" food writers familiar with the international food scene. Govender-Ypma answered the chef by explaining that local freelancers do weeks of research for low word rates with zero expense accounts in a "volatile" industry (Govender-Ypma 2018). The dearth of trained and knowledgeable journalists able to produce the kind of narratives that this chapter advocates is part of the broader problem and needs to be addressed.

The repertoire of food media also has to be augmented by including issues of poverty and food insecurity. Ten years after writing *Nickel-and-Dimed*, Barbara Ehrenreich founded the Economic Hardship Reporting Project (EHRP), which aims to "change the national conversation around poverty and economic insecurity" by commissioning diverse formats of journalism that "puts a human face on financial instability" (Economic Hardship Reporting Project 2022). The EHRP found that less than 1 percent of news stories in US mainstream media outlets cover poverty. The organization tries to overcome this scarcity by developing staff diversity and inclusion. Its website proudly proclaims that 31 percent of its contributors are people of color and 68 percent are women (Economic Hardship Reporting Project 2022). In one of the stories supported by EHRP entitled "'It's not fair, not right': how America treats its black farmers," Weingarten describes decades of discriminatory lending practices and policies by banks and governments, and outright sabotage and violent harassment from local companies with a history of slavery under the plantation system of agriculture (farmers describe the United States Department of Agriculture (USDA) as "the last plantation") (Weingarten 2018). This article echoes what Ishay Govender-Ypma calls "the power and associated responsibility" that food writers bear in terms of "transforming the narrative of the land … beyond supporting the local farmers and presenting 'ethical,' seasonal, GMO-free produce, or even foraging" (Govender-Ypma 2018). The reporting strategies she suggests for South Africa can be taken as advice to food writers elsewhere:

> It means knowing the soil and the ancient stories that live there and giving priority to the often maligned, but rich and diverse food of black people. It asks that we empower the custodians of the dishes we replicate, dig deep to restore the food traditions we're at risk of losing, and present a unique, South African arc on the plate that ventures beyond Eurocentric aesthetics and flavors.
>
> (Govender-Ypma 2018)

In conclusion, even well-meaning journalists will need to self-reflectively challenge their established routines and recalibrate food media storytelling from the ground up. The inclusive concepts of food sovereignty and voice provide a new standard that respects diversity and highlights equality. By focusing on foodways in their totality and providing space for authentic voices, media are better situated to take on complex issues such as the relationship between food, people, and climate change. These are the stories and voices we need to hear.

References

Abarca, Meredith E. 2006. *Voices in the Kitchen: Views of Food and the World from Working-Class Mexican and Mexican-American Women*. College Station, TX: Texas A&M University Press.

Abarca, Meredith E. 2007. "Charlas Culinarias: Mexican Women Speak from Their Public Kitchens." *Food and Foodways* 15(3/4):183–212.

Alkon, Alison H., and Julian Agyeman. 2011. *Cultivating Food Justice: Race, Class, and Sustainability*. Cambridge, MA: MIT Press.

Alkon, Alison H., Sarah Bowen, Yuki Kato, and Kara Alexis Young. 2020. "Unequally Vulnerable: A Food Justice Approach to Racial Disparities in COVID-19 Cases." *Agriculture and Human Values* 37(1–2): 535–536.

Almiron, Núria. 2020. "The 'Animal-Based Food Taboo': Climate Change Denial and Deontological Codes in Journalism." *Frontiers in Communication*. 5:512956. 10.3389/fcomm.2020.512956.

Almiron, Núria and Milena Zoppeddu. 2015. "Eating Meat and Climate Change: The Media Blind Spot. A Study of Spanish and Italian Press Coverage." *Environmental Communication: A Journal of Nature and Culture* 9(3): 307–325.

All Together Now. 2021. *When Inclusion Means Exclusion: Social Commentary and Indigenous Agency*. Sydney, NSW: UTS, Australian Government.

Anthony, Andrew. 2019. March 17, 2019. "How Diet Became the Latest Front in the Culture Wars." The Observer https://www.theguardian.com/environment/2019/mar/17/how-dietlatest-front-culture-wars-eat-less-meat-lancet

Arendt, Hannah. 1958. *The Human Condition*. Chicago: Chicago University Press.

Argumedo, Alejandro and Michael Pimbert. 2005. *Traditional Resource Rights and Indigenous People in the Andes*. ANDES (Quechua- Aymara Association for Nature Conservation and Sustainable Development) and IIED (International Institute for Environment and Development). https://pubs.iied.org/14504iied.

Ayora-Diaz, Steffan I. 2019. "Technological Change and Contemporary Transformations in Yucatecan Cooking." In *Globalised Eating Cultures: Mediation and Mediatization*, edited by Jörg Dürrschmidt and York Kautt, 109–128. Cham, Switzerland: Palgrave Macmillan.

BBC. 2021. "America's 'Food Apartheid'." *The Food Chain*. May 2021. https://www.bbc.co.uk/programmes/w3ct1rfj.

Bočák, Michal. 2019. "Cooking the Past: Traditionalism in Czech Culinary Magazines." In *Globalised Eating Cultures: Mediation and Mediatization*, edited by Jörg Dürrschmidt and York Kautt, 157–179. Cham, Switzerland: Palgrave Macmillan.

Bourdieu, Pierre. 1984. *Distinction: A Social Critique of the Judgement of Taste*. Cambridge, Mass.: Harvard University Press.

Boykoff, Maxwell T., and J. Timmons Roberts. 2007. *Media Coverage of Climate Change: Current Trends, Strengths, Weaknesses*. Human Development Report Office Occasional Paper. Fighting Climate Change: Human Solidarity in a Divided World.UNDP. 2007/3.

Butler, Judith. 2005. *Giving an Account of Oneself*. New York: Fordham University Press.
Chuen, Lorraine. 2017. "Food, Race, and Power: Who Gets to Be an Authority on 'Ethnic' Cuisines." *Intersectional Analyst*, January 8, 2017. http://www.intersectionalanalyst.com/intersectional-analyst/2017/1/7/who-gets-to-be-an-authority-on-ethnic-cuisines.
Claasen, Nicole, and Shingairai Chigeza. 2019. "Traditional Food Knowledge in a Globalised World: Mediation and Mediatization Perceived by Tswana Women in South Africa." In *Globalised Eating Cultures: Mediation and Mediatization*, edited by Jörg Dürrschmidt and York Kautt, 129–155. Cham, Switzerland: Palgrave Macmillan.
Cooks, Leda. 2009. "You Are What You (Don't) Eat? Food, Identity, and Resistance." *Text and Performance Quarterly* 29(1):94–110.
Couldry, Nick. 2010. *Why Voice Matters: Culture and Politics After Neoliberalism*. London: Sage.
Cramer, Janet. M, Carlnita P. Greene, and Lynn M. Walters. 2011. *Food as Communication, Communication as Food*. New York: Peter Lang.
Dao, Andre, Michael Green, and Sherry Huang. 2021. "On the Chain." *The Monthly*. July: 26–40. https://www.themonthly.com.au/issue/2021/july/1625061600/andr-dao-michael-green-and-sherry-huang/chain#mtr
Day, Richard. 2000. *Multiculturalism and the History of Canadian Diversity*. Toronto: University of Toronto Press.
DeLoughrey, Elizabeth. 2019. *Allegories of the Anthropocene*. Durham, NC: Duke University Press.
De Solier, Isabella. 2019. "Ethnodelicious." In *Globalised Eating Cultures: Mediation and Mediatization*, edited by Jörg Dürrschmidt and York Kautt, 203–219. Cham, Switzerland: Palgrave Macmillan.
De Souza, Rebecca. T. 2019. *Feeding the Other: Whiteness, Privilege, and Neoliberal Stigma in Food Pantries*. Cambridge: MIT Press.
Douglas, Mary. 1972. "Deciphering a Meal." *Daedalus* no.101.1: 61–81.
Economic Hardship Reporting Project. 2022. Retrieved from https://economichardship.org/about-ehrp/.
Ehrenreich, Barbara. 1999. "Nickel-and-Dimed: On (Not) Getting By in America." *Harper's Magazine*, January 1999: 37–52
Ehrenreich, Barbara. 2021. *Had I Known: Collected Essays*. London: Granta Publications.
European Coordination Vía Campesina. 2018. *Food Sovereignty Now! A Guide to Food Sovereignty*. https://viacampesina.org/en/wp-content/uploads/sites/2/2018/02/Food-Sovereignty-A-guide-Low-Res-Vresion.pdf.
Food and Agriculture Organization (FAO) of the United Nations. 2006. "Livestock's Long Shadow. Environmental Issues and Options" [Writing Team: Steinfeld, H., Gerber, P., Wassenaar, T., Castel, V., Rosales, M., and de Haan, C.]. Rome: FAO.
Fladvad, Benno. 2019. "Diverse Citizenship? Food Sovereignty and the Power of Acting Otherwise." *Social Sciences* 8:331.
Friel, Sharon. 2019. *Climate Change and the People's Health*. Oxford: Oxford University Press.
Garcia, David, Victor Galaz, and Stefan Daume. 2019. "EATLancet vs. yes2meat: The Digital Backlash to the Planetary Health Diet." *The Lancet* 394: 2153–2154.

German, Kathleen M. 2011. "Memory, Identity, and Resistance: Recipes from the Women of Theresienstadt." In *Food as Communication, Communication as Food*, edited by Janet. M. Cramer, Carlnita P. Greene, and Lynn M. Walters, 137–154. New York: Peter Lang.

Go´mez-Barris, Macarena. 2017. *The Extractive Zone: Social Ecologies and Decolonial Perspectives*. Durham: Duke University Press.

Gordon, Constance and Kathleen Hunt. 2018. "Reform, Justice, and Sovereignty: A Food Systems Agenda for Environmental Communication." *Environmental Communications* 13(1):9–22.

Govender-Ypma, Ishay. 2018. "Why We Need to Democratise Food Writing in South Africa." *Sunday Times*. August 12, 2018. https://www.timeslive.co.za/sunday-times/lifestyle/food/2018-08-11-why-we-need-to-democratise-food-writing-in-sa/.

Green, Anthony. 2019. "Can the Eat-Lancet Diet Work for the Global South? *Inside Development*. June 25, 2019. https://www.devex.com/news/can-the-eat-lancet-diet-work-for-the-global-south-95168.

Greene, Carlnita P., and Janet M. Cramer. 2011. *Food as Communication/Communication as Food*. New York: Peter Lang.

Greenebaum, Jessica. 2018. "Vegans of Color: Managing Visible and Invisible Stigmas." *Food, Culture & Society* 21(5):680–697.

Grey, Sam, and Lenore Newman. 2018. "Beyond Culinary Colonialism: Indigenous Food Sovereignty, Liberal Multiculturalism, and the Control of Gastronomic Capital." *Agriculture and Human Values* 35:717–730.

Grey, Sam, and Raj Patel. 2015. "Food Sovereignty as Decolonisation: Some Contributions from Indigenous Movements to Food System and Development Politics." *Agriculture and Human Values* 32(3):431–444.

Guthman, Judith. 2008. "Bringing Good Food to Others: Investigating the Subjects of Alternative Food Practice." *Cultural Geographies* 15(4):431–447.

Guthman, Judith. 2011. *Weighing in: Obesity, Food Justice and the Limits of Capitalism*. Berkeley, CA: University of California Press.

Ho, Colin, and Nicholas Jordan. 2018. "Australians Love Asian Food, So Why Doesn't It Win as Many Awards as Italian?" *ABC News*. October 27, 2018. https://www.abc.net.au/news/2018-10-27/asian-food-fine-dining-good-food-guide-gourmet-traveller/10427934.

IPCC. 2019. *Climate Change and Land*. https://www.ipcc.ch/srccl/.

Josèe, Johnston and Baumann Shyon. 2010. *Foodies: Democracy and Distinction in the Gourmet Foodscape*. Abingdon: Routledge.

Jörg, Dürrschmidt and York Kautt. 2019. *Globalised Eating Cultures: Mediation and Mediatization*. Cham, Switzerland: Palgrave Macmillan.

Kautt, York. 2019. "Mediation and Global Foodscapes: A Conceptual Outline." In *Globalised Eating Cultures: Mediation and Mediatization*, edited by Jörg Dürrschmidt and York Kautt, 309–353. Cham, Switzerland: Palgrave Macmillan.

Khan, Sabiha Ahmad. 2020. "Mediating Food Sovereign Voices in Documentary Media." *Frontiers in Communication* 5, December 23, 2020. 10.3389/fcomm. 2020.553466

Kristiansen, Silje, James Painter, and Meghan Shea. 2021. "Animal Agriculture and Climate Change in the US and UK Elite Media: Volume, Responsibilities, Causes and Solutions." *Environmental Communication* 15(2):153–172.

Lahsen, Myanna. 2018. "Buffers against Inconvenient Knowledge: Brazilian Newspaper Representations of the Climate-Meat Link." *P2P & INOVAÇÃO*, Rio de Janeiro 4(1):59–84.

Lam, Lee Tran. 2020. *Diversity in Food Media New Voices on Food: Anthology No. 1*. SomeKind Press.

Lee, Nancy. 2013. *Celebrity Chefs: Class Mobility, Media, Masculinity*. PhD diss. University of Sydney, 2013.

Lindenfeld, Laura A. 2011. "Feast for Our Eyes: Viewing Films on Food through New Lenses." In *Food as Communication/Communication as Food*, edited by Carlnita P. Greene, and Janet M. Cramer, 3–12. New York: Peter Lang.

Mann, Alana. 2019. *Voice and Participation in Global Food Politics*. Abingdon: Routledge.

Mann, Alana. 2021. *Food in a Changing Climate*. Bingley: Emerald Publishing Ltd.

Matta, Raúl. 2019. "Celebrity Chefs and the Limits of Playing Politics from the Kitchen." In *Globalised Eating Cultures: Mediation and Mediatization*, edited by Jörg Dürrschmidt and York Kautt, 183–201. Cham, Switzerland: Palgrave Macmillan.

McMichael, Philip. 2009. "A Food Regime Genealogy." *The Journal of Peasant Studies* 36(1):139–169.

McMillan, Tracie. 2012. *The American Way of Eating: Undercover at Walmart, Applebee's, Farm Fields and the Dinner Table*. New York: Scribner.

McQuire, Amy. 2019. "Black and White Witness." *Meanjin Quarterly*, Winter 2019. https://meanjin.com.au/essays/black-and-white-witness/.

McVeigh, Karen. 2020. "Disappearances, Danger and Death: What Is Happening to UN Fisheries Observers?" *Guardian Online*. May 22. https://www.theguardian.com/environment/2020/may/22/disappearances-danger-and-death-what-is-happening-to-fishery-observers.

Mihesuah, Devon. A. 2019. "Nephi Craig: Life in Second Sight." In *Indigenous Food Sovereignty in the United States: Restoring Cultural Knowledge, Protecting Environments and Regaining Health*, edited by Devon A. Mihesuah and Elizabeth Hoover. Oklahoma: University of Oklahoma Press.

Mosco, Vincent. 1996. *The Political Economy Tradition of Communication: Rethinking and Renewal*. London: SAGE.

Mosco, Vincent. 2008. "Current Trends in the Political Economy of Communication." *Global Media Journal – Canadian Edition* 1(1):45–63.

Mukii, Ng'endo. 2018. "*National Geographic's* Photography Erased People. It's Too Late for an Apology." *Bright the Mag*. https://brightthemag.com/national-geographic-apology-too-late-ngendo-mukii-indigenous-taxidermy-animation-577503736beb.

Neff, Roni A., Iris L. Chan, and Katherine Clegg Smith. 2008. "Yesterday's Dinner, Tomorrow's Weather, Today's News? US Newspaper Coverage of Food System Contributions to Climate Change." *Public Health Nutrition* 12(7):1006–1014.

Netflix. 2018. *Rotten*. https://www.netflix.com/au/title/80146284.

Nikolić, Mona. 2019. "The Formation of a National Cuisine in Costa Rican Cookbooks and Its Impact on Regional Cuisines as Markers of Identity." In *Globalised Eating Cultures: Mediation and Mediatization*, edited by Jörg Dürrschmidt and York Kautt, 33–52. Cham, Switzerland: Palgrave Macmillan.

Nossiter, Jonathan. 2019. *Cultural Insurrection: A Manifesto for the Arts, Agriculture, and Natural Wine*. New York: Other Press.
O'Neill, Saffron. 2013. "Image Matters: Climate Change Imagery in US, UK and Australian Newspapers." *Geoforum* 49:10–19.
O'Neill, Saffron J., Maxwell Boykoff, Simon Niemeyer, and Sophie A. Day. 2013. "On the Use of Imagery for Climate Change Engagement." *Global Environmental Change* 23:413–421.
Polish, Jennifer. 2016. "Decolonizing Veganism: On Resisting Vegan Whiteness and Racism." In *Critical Perspectives on Veganism*, edited by Jodey Castricano and Rasmus R. Simonsen, 373–391. Cham, Switzerland: Palgrave.
Povitz, Lana Dee. 2019. *Stirrings: How Activist New Yorkers Ignited a Movement for Food Justice*. Chapel Hill: University of North Carolina Press.
Rangan, Pooja. 2017. *Immediations: The Humanitarian Impulse in Documentary*. Durham, NC: Duke University Press.
Schmidt, Andreas, Ana Ivanova, and Mike S. Schafer. 2013. "Media Attention for Climate Change around the World: A Comparative Analysis of Newspaper Coverage in 27 Countries." *Global Environmental Change* 23:1233–1248.
Sutton, David. 2008. "A Tale of Easter Ovens: Food and Collective Memory." *Social Research* 75(1):157–180.
Thomas, Amy, and Yin Paradies. 2021. "Included, but Still Marginalised: Indigenous Voices Still Missing in Media Stories on Indigenous Affairs." *The Conversation*. July 1, 2021. https://theconversation.com/included-but-still-marginalised-indigenous-voices-still-missing-in-media-stories-on-indigenous-affairs-163426.
Tilzey, Mark. 2021. "Peasant Counter-Hegemony Towards Post-Capitalist Food Sovereignty: Facing Rural and Urban Precarity." In *Resourcing an Agroecological Urbanism: Political, Transformational and Territorial Dimensions*, edited by Chiara Tornaghi and Michiel Dehaene, 202–219. Abingdon: Routledge.
Tornaghi, Chiara, and Michiel Dehaene. 2021. "Introduction: Embracing Political Agroecology, Transforming Sustainable Food Planning." In *Resourcing an Agroecological Urbanism: Political, Transformational and Territorial Dimensions*, edited by Chiara Tornaghi and Michiel Dehaene, 1–11. Abingdon: Routledge.
Turner, Alison. 2021. "Native Bush Foods: Who Really Profits?" *Eativity*. July 6, 2021. https://eativitynews.com/native-bush-foods-who-really-profits/.
Vernon, Clare. 2019. "In Conversation with Bruce Pascoe." *Greater Sydney Landcare Network, Inc.* March 20, 2019. https://greatersydneylandcare.org/in-conversation-with-bruce-pascoe/.
Watts, Eric K. 2001. "Voice" and "Voicelessness" in Rhetorical Studies. *Quarterly Journal of Speech* 87: 179–196.
Weingarten, Debbie. 2018. "It's Not Fair, Not Right": How America Treats Its Black Farmers." *The Guardian*, October 20, 2018. https://www.theguardian.com/world/2018/oct/30/america-black-farmers-louisiana-sugarcane.
Willet, Walter, Johan Rockström, Brent Loken, Marco Springmann, Tim Lang, Sonja Vermeulen, Tara Garnett, and Shenggen Fan. (2019). "Food in the Anthropocene: The EAT-Lancet Commission on Healthy Diets from Sustainable Food Systems." *The Lancet* 393(10170):447–492.

Williams-Forson, Psyche. (2015). *African-American Food Culture*. https://scalar.usc.edu/works/field-guides-to-food/psyche-williamsforson-african-american-food-culture-full?path=psyche-williams-forson-allvideo.

Wrenn, Corey Lee. 2019. "The Vegan Society and Social Movement Professionalization 1944–2017." *Food and Foodways* 27(3):190–210.

Part II
Raising Questions of Legitimacy, Power, and Good Citizenship

5 From Bad Boys to Heroes: Culinary Philanthropy and Good Citizenship in the Age of COVID-19

Kathleen LeBesco and Peter Naccarato

The impact of the COVID-19 pandemic has been devastating for the food industry and has had severe economic consequences across the food chain, from farmers and manufacturers to distributors and retailers. At the same time, consumers have struggled to balance the cost of food with other expenses while facing rising unemployment, health concerns, and additional stresses on their professional and personal lives. In this chapter, we focus specifically on the pandemic's impact on celebrity chefs, from their restaurants and other business ventures to their public personas and cultural status. We consider how journalistic narratives about celebrity chefs have shaped the public's understanding of how they have responded and adapted to this crisis. We also discuss how these narratives have influenced consumer behavior. We define "journalistic narratives" broadly, and throughout the chapter we draw on a range of examples from television, radio, magazines, newspapers, and other distribution platforms. We do so to understand the prevalence and persistence of representations of culinary philanthropy across media that work to reinforce hegemonic masculinities that have long dominated the restaurant business and associated industries.

In our analysis, we introduce the concept of "culinary philanthropy" to illuminate how journalistic narratives represent chefs and consumers in ways that reaffirm their identities as good citizens through their food-related practices and choices. However, we critique such framing to the extent that such philanthropic posturing serves to protect rather than challenge existing power dynamics and to reinforce capitalist values and traditional gender ideologies. We conclude by considering a counter-narrative that is inflected by a feminist ethics of care and speculate about whether such a perspective could influence journalistic narratives about celebrity chefs and their work in ways that could potentially disrupt a food system that incentivizes profit and perpetuates inequality.

From Bad Boys to Heroes: Shifting Pathways to Culinary Capital

Our previous work explores the concept of "culinary capital," arguing that "certain food practices give people a sense of distinction within their communities," which contributes to "the work of creating and sustaining a sense of Self" (Naccarato and LeBesco 2012, 1–2). Informed by the work of Pierre Bourdieu (1984), we identify culinary capital as a marker of social status. But as recognized by Josée Johnston and Shyon Baumann (2010), the ways in which such distinction is conferred are fluid. Rather than identifying a list of stable food practices that inherently have the power to confer culinary capital, we consider how specific practices are invested with the power to do so within specific socio-economic circumstances. A food practice that may bestow culinary capital at one historical moment or within one cultural context may not do so as social conditions change. Within this context, we examine how the COVID-19 pandemic has accelerated a shift in how journalistic narratives represent celebrity chefs and consumers in ways that allow them to access culinary capital while simultaneously reframing these representations to correspond to changing cultural values and priorities.

Regarding celebrity chefs, the COVID-19 pandemic has accelerated a transition in journalistic narratives away from the iconic figure of the "culinary bad boy," toward images of the "culinary hero." The roots of the former can be traced to the publication of Anthony Bourdain's *Kitchen Confidential: Adventures in the Culinary Underbelly* in 2000 and the success of Gordon Ramsay's early forays into television, including his two British series, *Ramsay's Kitchen Nightmares* and *Hell's Kitchen*, both of which premiered in 2004, the US versions of *Hell's Kitchen*, which premiered in 2005, and *Kitchen Nightmares*, which premiered in 2007. The quintessential "bad boy chef," Bourdain achieved celebrity status by launching unapologetic attacks on other celebrity chefs while Ramsay became the poster child for outrageous, foul-mouthed behavior in the kitchen. Given their success, it was inevitable that others would adopt this "bad boy" persona, which is characterized by a sense of narcissism, selfishness, over-confidence, unpredictability, and a healthy dose of disdain for the rules, culinary and otherwise.

Over the last several years, however, this much-hyped image of the chef has begun to lose its currency. Ashley Stevens, deputy food editor for Salon.com, suggests that media attention to the bad boy chef began to wane around 2017, in part owing to the #metoo movement and associated scrutiny of alleged sexual misconduct by chefs, including Johnny Luzzini, John Besh, Ken Friedman, and Mario Batali. She also notes a transition toward representations that "show vulnerability on the part of these chefs, and efforts to change" (Stevens 2020). In his 2018 article, Branden Klassen, managing editor of Kwantlen Polytechnic University's student-run publication *The Runner*, offers a similar timeline for the start of this transition, noting that "Just last year, Bourdain expressed regret for his own complacency in—and even glorification of—toxic elements of kitchen culture, namely the unchecked sexism of the back of house" (Klassen 2018). More recent analyses of this transition link it to a broader pushback against "the power of the chef-auteur as an idea," which Tejal Rao, James Beard award-winning restaurant critic for the *New York Times*, argues "is fading ... as restaurant workers organize and speak up about abusive workplaces, toxic bosses and inequities in pay and benefits" (Rao 2020). Rao goes on to consider how this process has been accelerated by the COVID-19 pandemic, which "has exposed the fragility and inequity of the restaurant industry, disproportionately affecting Black people, people of color, restaurant workers and those who keep the food chain running in the nation's factories and farms" (Rao 2020). Similarly, Esther Tseng, a Los Angeles-based freelance food writer, explains that the militaristic, top-down chain of command that permeates restaurant kitchens makes them particularly vulnerable to exploitation and abuses of power. She points out that the industry is characterized by widespread labor violations as well as racial and gender discrimination, noting that "there needs to be active policy changes and vehicles created for accountability across the industry in order to make it more equitable" (Tseng 2020).

Although media celebration of the bad boy chef has faltered over the past few years, this has not marked the end of media celebration of the chef more broadly. Instead, we argue that we are seeing a shift in the values, attitudes, and attributes identified in journalistic narratives as marking chefs as worthy of recognition and respect. In many of these narratives, this manifests as a reorientation of the celebrity chef from bad boy to hero. While the protagonists of such narratives remain privileged white male chefs, they are no longer framed as tough and aggressive bad boys but instead are depicted as admirable and courageous heroes who direct their energies towards protecting the vulnerable and aiding those who are suffering. Even as this reorientation brings the image of the celebrity chef more in line with contemporary critiques of toxic masculinity, it is still firmly embedded in and works to reinforce traditionally masculine, heteronormative, white privilege in and beyond the food and media industries. As we argue in our conclusion, a more impactful intervention against such ideologies requires a different type of reframing, one that goes beyond the hero trope and adopts a moral and ethical framework of care.

While the transition from bad boy to hero began before COVID-19, it has accelerated during the pandemic, which has provided journalists with countless examples of the heroic efforts of chefs and restaurateurs in the face of this crisis. For example, though never framed as a "bad boy," chef José Andrés was already recognized for launching his nonprofit World Central Kitchen in the aftermath of the 2010 earthquake in Haiti and then gaining wider visibility for his work in Puerto Rico after Hurricane Maria in 2017. He has recently emerged as the quintessential culinary hero as narratives about his NGO have focused on its work supporting restaurants, food industry workers, and neighborhoods that are impacted by the pandemic. This work includes collaboration with Eric Ripert, chef and co-owner of New York City's high-end restaurant Le Bernardin, to feed the City's frontline medical workers. The media have likewise celebrated the quintessential "dude" chef Guy Fieri's partnership with the National Restaurant Association Educational Foundation to raise money for the Restaurant Employee Relief Fund to support people in the food industry who have been negatively impacted by COVID-19.

However, as we discuss in detail below, when such heroic narratives are framed through the lens of culinary philanthropy, they merely shift the terms through which chefs attain their celebrity status and retain their culinary capital. Such narratives reinforce rather than challenge class and gender ideologies that have shaped the restaurant industry and determined who is most valued within it.

The Culinary Philanthropist as Masculine Hero

There is little doubt that Americans have been looking for heroes during the pandemic and the media have provided them, with local and national news outlets celebrating the heroic efforts of healthcare providers, first responders, essential workers, and other community members who have risen to the crisis. Within the food industry, such heroic narratives often focus on chefs and restaurateurs who have found ways to sustain their businesses while supporting their local communities. Many of them do so by embracing what we are calling "culinary philanthropy" as they direct their resources and talents towards helping those in need. Narratives about such culinary philanthropists do celebrate the heroic efforts of chefs and restaurateurs in the face of the pandemic, but they do not seem particularly interested in addressing the larger inequalities across their industry. Instead, despite the "feel-good" nature of these narratives and their tribute to the chefs and restaurateurs on whom they are typically centered, they generally serve to maintain the status quo vis-a-vis the power of the celebrity chef, just shifting the terms by which this celebrity is achieved. Ultimately, we conclude that narratives that herald the work of "culinary philanthropists" serve to repackage the class and gender ideologies that are reflected in more familiar routes to culinary capital.

Narratives praising culinary philanthropy in response to the COVID-19 pandemic can be found across journalism. For example, in their article for *Forbes* magazine, Michael Kaufman, Lena Goldberg, and Jill Avery note that "amidst their own pain, restaurateurs are helping others in their communities by lending their physical spaces and staff" (Kaufman, Goldberg, and Avery 2020). They cite award-winning chef and restaurateur Thomas Keller, whose Yountville, California restaurant *ad hoc* delivers food to the homebound elderly, provides inexpensive, three-course meals for the unemployed, and hosts a small food bank. The *Forbes* article also profiles the owners of New York City's three-Michelin-starred restaurant Eleven Madison Park, who have teamed up with the nonprofit Rethink Food to prepare 3,000 meals daily for community members facing hunger.

Such narratives are certainly not unique. In her piece for National Public Radio, business correspondent Alina Selyuk tells the story of Mark Bucher, co-founder of the Washington, DC steak-and-fries chain Medium Rare, who set up free-food refrigerators for families with children and complimentary Thanksgiving dinner deliveries for people over 70 who were at home alone for the holiday. Selyuk explains, "Bucher expected maybe a couple hundred orders around the District. Instead, he expects to top 3,000" (Selyuk 2020). For her story in *Harper's Bazaar*, Jaclyn Alexandra Cohen celebrates the fact that "Five-star kitchens are opening up shop and scaling up their operations to feed hundreds of hospital employees, and boxes of gourmet meals and fresh produce are being dropped off to those hungry, in need, and doing essential work across the country" (Cohen 2020). In addition to Eleven Madison Park, Cohen profiles Chef Marcus Samuelsson's Red Rooster in Harlem, Daniel Teran's The Wheelhouse, and Millie's Cuban Café in Bushwick, Brooklyn, restaurants that are preparing and distributing meals in their local communities.

While such narratives of culinary philanthropy tug at readers' heartstrings, they also serve to highlight the exalted status of celebrity chefs and restaurateurs by intertwining familiar heroic tropes into their narratives. DeDauw and Connell have identified a "lone wolf" narrative in mainstream media depictions of heroes. As they explain, this hero "often exist[s] as the sole arbiter of power and protection" and "promotes an ethics of self-reliance that casts the non-hero civilians (usually white women, people of color, disabled people, LGBTQIA+ identities, and other historically marginalized groups) as victims who can only be protected by the overwhelming might and masculinity of the hero" (DeDauw and Connell 2020, 6).

Thus, even as media have shifted from depicting celebrity chefs as bad boys to celebrating them as heroes, and as journalistic narratives of their actions during the pandemic offer culinary philanthropy as a new pathway for attaining culinary capital, we note that such narratives remain entrenched in familiar capitalist imperatives and codes of masculinity. As such, these narratives align with broader changes in the cultural representations of cooking—both professional and domestic—including the class and gender ideologies that inform them.

In our previous work, we explore how the range of cooking-related programming available on the Food Network reflects such ideological shifts, concluding that the network's ability to adapt its programming to ever-changing discourses of gender, race, and class is likely one explanation for its longevity and popularity (Naccarato and LeBesco 2012, 66). The same seems true for the changing representations of celebrity chefs from bad boys to heroes. As Pascual Soler notes, the "chef-as-hero" trope is one way to "control the feminizing power of cooking" and to defuse contemporary challenges to masculinity in professional and private kitchens (2018, 49). She writes, "Because masculinist ideology is deeply inhered in the heroic, ... heroism smooths masculine insecurities in the kitchen, putting cooking men in their true place" (2018, 35).

Holt and Thompson provide additional insight into how the trope of the chef-hero fits into American culture's idealization of the "man-of-action hero," arguing that this figure "resolves the stigmas of America's two antithetical masculinity models" (Holt and Thompson 2004, 429). As they explain:

> Successful responsible men, breadwinners, will always be haunted by the stigma of conformity, while the successful rebel is equally troubled by his inability to take responsibility and work on behalf of others. This ideological contradiction calls for an idealized figure who is rewarded for skills and talents without being compromised or constrained by institutional hierarchies and requirements. He must be adventurous, exciting, potent, and untamed, while also contributing to the greater social good. He must be perpetually youthful, dynamic, and iconoclastic, while at the same time fulfill the duties of a mature patriarch. He must continually defy the social status quo, while he enjoys a considerable degree of status and respect. He must be an unreconstructed risk taker, be dangerous, and yet be utterly indispensable to the integrity and functioning of the social order.
>
> (Holt and Thompson 2004, 429)

This is especially true at a time when public distrust of government is at a record high. At such a moment, the public seems especially receptive to media accounts of celebrity chefs that exemplify what Nimmo and Combs view as the redemptive nature of the modern hero whose story can "help restore the Edenic vision of the United States" (1980, quoted in McLennan 1994, 114). While Nimmo and Combs situate their analysis within the context of Watergate and the Vietnam War, it seems applicable to the pandemic as well. These chef-heroes remind us of pre-pandemic times as we take succor from their stories, celebrate them for helping those in need, and see their triumph in the face of crisis.

At the same time, media accounts of culinary heroism that privilege such masculine attributes are not limited to stories about male-identified chefs but are used to applaud the fortitude, ingenuity, and business acumen displayed by chefs regardless of their sex or gender. Regardless of their specific subject, such narratives of heroic efforts to save businesses and support employees and the local community are gendered in ways that reinforce familiar and highly traditional masculinities, lauding chefs as heroes for demonstrating a rugged individualism that sets them apart from the masses while also leading the types of communal efforts that are necessary to combat the hardships posed by the pandemic. Such representations align with what Jeffery S. McMullen describes as the modern entrepreneur, a figure "deeply rooted in a narrative of mythological heroism," but that also acknowledges the fact that "it takes a village to innovate, and entrepreneurship is considered a team sport" (McMullen 2017, 258).

Such framing is present in the journalistic narratives of culinary philanthropy and culinary heroism that we discuss in detail in the next section. Moreover, this version of the chef-hero reflects another important shift, namely one in which "being a chef meant only cooking food for others" to the more recent expectation that chefs "must opine on cultural and policy questions, understand complex sustainability and nutrition issues, take stances in their restaurants and through direct political action, and be keenly aware of societal shifts that influence their customers' values" (McBride and Flore 2019, 1). As McBride and Flore explain, today's chef is expected to "address social, political and environmental issues through their preferred form of artistic expression—food" (McBride and Flore 2019, 3). Such framing is useful for understanding media representations of celebrity chefs within the context of the COVID-19 pandemic. Such accounts often highlight how chefs like José Andrés and Guy Fieri leverage their celebrity status to do more than feed the hungry or support restaurant workers negatively impacted by the pandemic; rather, they also seek to redirect the work of government agencies, influence public policy, and change laws. In doing so, these narratives provide a glimpse of how celebrity chefs can potentially do more than engage in philanthropic activities that do little to challenge the structural inequalities that make them necessary in the first place, particularly in a time of crisis. As such, they exemplify the type of alternative interventions that we call for at the end of the chapter, namely ones that could do more than alleviate short-term suffering but rather, could promote systemic changes aimed at eradicating such inequalities.

Heroic Narratives across the Mediascape

Throughout the COVID-19 pandemic, the media have covered the virus's global devastation; yet, they have also produced feel-good narratives aimed at lifting the spirits of beleaguered audiences. This is certainly true when it comes to coverage that reveres the heroic efforts of chefs/restaurateurs to save their businesses and support their employees and their local communities. For example, in his 2020 piece published in the *Washingtonian* titled "The Heroic Story of How José Andrés' Charity Feeds 250,000 People a Day in a Pandemic," Benjamin Wofford describes Andrés as "a wunderkind of humanitarian work." He tells the story of Andrés' transformation from "the elite chef behind some of Washington's priciest meals" into "the nation's humanitarian in chief." In recounting the evolution of World Central Kitchen and the scope of its work, Wofford quotes CEO Nate Mook following his recent visits to New York, Chicago, and the Navajo Nation. Referring to people in Queens who started lining up at 3 a.m. and waited up to nine hours for their meals, Mook asks, "How long can World Central Kitchen keep doing what it's doing, and what happens when we can't. ... If we're their only source of food right now and we stop serving food—like, what happens?" With its focus on Andrés and Mook as the heroic forces behind the work of World Central Kitchen who come to the rescue of the victims of natural disasters, pandemics, and other crises, this article is emblematic of the chef-as-hero trope that shapes numerous similar narratives; yet, it also points to the limitations of philanthropy alone and of journalistic narratives that celebrate this approach to solving social problems without addressing systemic, sustainable government solutions as well.

The admiration of culinary philanthropy and the chef-as-hero is also evident in journalistic accounts of Guy Fieri's role in launching the Restaurant Employee Relief Fund in partnership with the National Restaurant Association in March 2020. Notable headlines include "How Guy Fieri Has Become A Food Industry Hero During The Pandemic" (Behr 2021), "The Hero of the Pandemic: Guy Fieri" (Gastromasa 2021), "20 Reasons Why Guy Fieri Is The Hero We Need Right Now" (Rennie 2020), and "Guy Fieri, the Fundraiser of Flavortown" (Krader 2020). These stories focus on Fieri's unique ability to raise money from some of the country's largest companies, his success in providing needed relief when government agencies have failed to do so, and his use of his celebrity status to give voice to those in the restaurant industry who are struggling in the face of the pandemic. This was particularly evident in three special episodes of Fieri's wildly popular Food Network show, *Diners, Drive-Ins, and Dives* in which he revisited chefs from previous episodes to see how they were getting through the pandemic (Pomranz 2020). Clearly, such programs, along with news and feature stories that highlight Fieri's work during the pandemic, position him as a singular force who has the power (and thus wins the prestige) to come to the rescue of those in need. Fieri's commitment to equitable transformation of the restaurant industry is, however, questionable, as he has suggested that a key problem facing the industry post-COVID is not structural inequity, but rather restaurant workers refusing to return to work because they have become accustomed to government handouts (Swisher 2021). Moreover, his preferred solution to ensuring fair pay for restaurant workers, instead of increased government regulation, is a "gigantic philanthropist" who would "save the restaurant businesses that don't have the ability" to save themselves (Swisher 2021).

Critiques of structural inequities are either muted or entirely absent in the many, many media accounts that celebrate Fieri, including those that highlight his role as Executive Producer of the Food Network documentary *Restaurant Hustle 2020: All on the Line*, which follows four chef/restaurateurs—Maneet Chauhan, Antonia Lofaso, Christian Petroni, and Marcus Samuelsson—as they struggle to save their restaurants and support their employees and local communities in the wake of COVID-19. In a voiceover, Fieri expresses anger at the impact of the pandemic on the restaurant industry and the havoc wrought on his "brothers and sisters" who are losing their jobs. He also expresses his determination to help, both by raising money for restaurant workers by launching the Restaurant Employee Relief Fund and by documenting how the pandemic is impacting his industry. Like Fieri, the four chefs around whom the rest of the documentary is framed emphasize their sense of responsibility for the people who helped them build their restaurants—their employees and loyal customers alike.

As each of the four chefs/restaurateurs tells their stories, two themes emerge. First is their commitment to their businesses. They each note the blood, sweat, and tears that they put into building their restaurants, the sacrifices they've made to sustain them, and their focus on preventing what took years (even decades) to build from collapsing. Second is their obligation to others, primarily their workers who helped them build their businesses, but also the broader public as they reflect on their role in feeding their neighbors at a time of crisis. These themes are intertwined as each chef/restaurateur shares their approach to saving their businesses while helping their employees and their local community.

For Christian Petroni, culinary philanthropy in aid of his business and the broader public took the form of Pies for the People, a program that allowed individuals to visit his restaurant's website and buy a pizza to send to someone in need. As he describes the program, viewers follow him to Bridgeport Hospital, where he delivers 100 donated pizzas. For Maneet Chauhan, the focus was on restarting her business and bringing back as many employees as possible. To do so, she and her husband launched curbside pickup at one of their restaurants. Noting the appreciation expressed by customers who thanked them for reopening and cooking for them, Chauhan expresses pride in their accomplishment and explains that she and her husband have always been fighters, which is what allowed them to build their successful business in the first place and what has motivated them to preserve it through this crisis.

Antonia Lofaso's story focused on how she helped her community by securing permission from the city of Los Angeles to transform each of her restaurants into markets that sold pre-cooked food as well as kitchen essentials. As she explains, this provided an important service to her community since supplies in supermarkets were scarce and people were hesitant to go to them. Similarly, Marcus Samuelsson described how he went from feeling helpless to empowered as he and other restaurateurs in Harlem transformed their restaurants into community kitchens. In doing so, they relied on the inherent strength and resiliency of the Harlem community, with Samuelsson paying special tribute to his own staff, whom he describes as the "true" heroes. At the same time, he notes that he is the "captain of the ship," and his staff looks to him for security for themselves and their families.

Taken collectively, these four narratives underscore the inherent tensions of culinary philanthropy. On the one hand, these chefs/restaurateurs are lauded for their dedication to their communities and their tireless efforts to help others in the face of the pandemic. In this way, they emulate the characteristics of the modern-day hero described by DeDauw and Connell as they redirect those energies that allowed them to build successful businesses in the first place towards helping those who can't help themselves, including their own employees and the members of their local communities who presumably lack the resources (and perhaps the wherewithal) to come to their own aid.

At the same time, such philanthropic intentions mask the capitalist imperative that also motivates them. This financial undercurrent rises to the surface at several points throughout *Restaurant Hustle 2020: All on the Line*, particularly when the profit motive behind what is framed as charitable works is revealed. For example, Antonia Lofaso is jubilant when she talks about getting approval to sell alcohol in addition to groceries in her restaurant markets since the profit margins on alcohol are considerably higher than on food. Lofaso is also the most transparent in connecting community support to making money, including when she develops a plan to sell takeout Easter and Passover dinners as a way to both make money and serve the community. Given the potential success of this program, she notes that even when things get back to normal, she's going to continue it because it provides a reliable new revenue stream. Christian Petroni also finds new business opportunities in his philanthropic endeavors, developing a series of pre-packaged, restaurant-quality food that customers can purchase in supermarkets and finish in their own ovens. For Maneet Chauhan and her husband, the new revenue stream comes from introducing "socially distanced" drive-through pick-up at their HOP Strings Craft Brewery. Thus, while on the surface these stories celebrate the generosity and care of their protagonists, they also reveal the profit motive that lies just beneath the surface. As such, they reflect both the role of culinary philanthropy in bestowing heroic status on chefs and restaurateurs who have "risen to the occasion" in the face of the pandemic and the limitations of this model in terms of challenging the structural inequities that make such philanthropic interventions necessary in the first place. Rather than promoting government actions aimed at leveling the economic playing field, traditional models of philanthropy seek to maintain the status quo while presenting the capitalist class as the solution to such inequalities rather than being deeply implicated in them. In doing so, they sidestep broader questions about how capitalist economies can promote equity and fairness and whether there are alternative models of philanthropy that could contribute to this effort.

Doing Your Part: Heroic Consumption, Good Citizenship, and an Ethics of Care

While media have played an important role in conferring heroic status upon chefs and restaurateurs, they have also directed calls to action toward consumers, urging them to make their own claims to heroism as they make food-related decisions in the face of the pandemic. Historically, the United States has often called upon its citizens to change their food practices during times of crisis, most notably encouraging them to plant victory gardens and willingly ration valued food items such as butter and coffee during times of war. This has also been the case during COVID-19. From preparing for potential food shortages to supporting local businesses, consumers have been told that they have a role to play in getting the country through the pandemic. And as they fulfill this role, they are lauded as good citizens and rewarded with the culinary capital that comes with this status.

As with the shifting depiction of celebrity chefs discussed above, journalistic narratives have played an equally important role in shaping the messaging to the would-be consumer-hero. This is especially true across lifestyle publications, which have circulated countless narratives about how consumers could do their part to support the struggling restaurant industry. For example, just weeks into the escalation of COVID-19 cases in the United States, *Food and Wine* offered "12 ways to support local restaurants without leaving home" (Friend 2020) while *Saveur* advised on "How to help your favorite restaurants through the COVID closures" (Hirschorn 2020). *Bon Appetit* asked, "Feeling helpless? Here are several ways to help your favorite restaurants—and their staff—get through this unprecedented time" before going on to list a number of methods, from donating to industry-focused nonprofits and organizations that feed front-line workers to buying merchandise and gift cards directly from restaurants. The article acknowledged that "it will take more than buying a T-shirt to save the restaurant industry" and encouraged all readers, even those who can't provide financial support, to "contact your elected officials and tell them not to forget about the restaurant industry" (Fegan 2020).

Many other lifestyle media sources acknowledged that, in the face of an inadequate government response, the onus was now on individual consumers to pitch in, as when a contributor to Eater.com wrote, "That feeling of helplessness we as restaurant lovers all feel is likely a mix of frustration that the federal government is still failing to provide any meaningful aid to small business owners, coupled with the nagging knowledge that our weekly $25 take-out order of khao soi and pad see ew is likely a drop in the bucket in terms of what that restaurant really needs to survive" (DeJesus 2020). Readers were frequently described as feeling helpless, reflecting a mix of social outrage and individual impotence as we were invited to make singular gestures in the face of seemingly insurmountable challenges. To wit, the Eater.com piece continued, "In a time when our social media feeds are full of new menus, new pivots, new appeals for support, my new to-do list [of ways to help the restaurant industry] is a way to concentrate all that energy into something that feels slightly less paralyzing to me as a consumer" (DeJesus 2020). These examples demonstrate how lifestyle media frame culinary philanthropy as empowering and helpful not to just the restaurant industry, but also to the eater-citizen.

Clearly, not just celebrity chefs and restaurateurs are framed as philanthropists; media audiences, as would-be consumers, are also hailed loudly and often to support their struggling fellow citizens by supporting the restaurant industry. In this imaginary, homebound citizens are exhorted to engage in a heroic quest (Vander Veen 1994) via shopping at restaurants, ordering takeout, and tipping generously, helping to keep economic collapse at bay. Consumer sentiment during the pandemic maps perfectly onto what sociologist Colin Campbell has described as the mindset of romantic consumption, marked by "dissatisfaction with the contemporary world, a restless anxiety in the face of life, a preference for the strange and curious, a penchant for reverie and dreaming, a leaning to mysticism, and a celebration of the irrational" (Campbell 1987, 181). Revolt, escape, melancholy, fantasy, restless anxiety—how better to describe the emotional landscape of COVID-19?

Journalistic narratives in this era allow consumers to reframe their food-related practices to focus less on how they can be used to maintain social and class distinctions and the status that comes with them, and more on how they can sustain romantic visions of heroism, saving self and others in a time of crisis. Campbell says it best, "In struggling to cope with the necessity of making trade-offs between need and pleasure, whilst seeking to reconcile their Bohemian and bourgeois selves, modern individuals inhabit not just an 'iron cage' of economic necessity, but a castle of romantic dreams, striving through their conduct to turn one into the other" (1987, 227).

The question, in this context, concerns the moral status of consumption. Is the aspiration to heroic philanthropy that is touted in journalistic narratives naive? Campbell critiques theories of consumption that position consumers as driven by greed or envy, and instead focuses on what he calls the "idealistic dimension" of modern consumption (1997, 139). Similarly, Robert Lane (1997) describes two motives for consumption—affiliative and materialistic—and COVID-era exhortations to "support your favorite restaurant" are less about the food (materialistic) and more about connecting with community (affiliative) like a friend who provides support.

Indeed, lifestyle media have hailed citizen-consumers to act out in ways large and small upon the landscape of inequality and detachment wrought by the COVID-19 pandemic—to embody what psychologist Carol Gilligan describes as the moral injunction to not turn away from someone in need by demonstrating an ethic of care (Gilligan 1987, 20). Long celebrated as feminine, this moral stance has been roundly critiqued by feminists concerned with the degree to which it compromises caregiver autonomy. Nonetheless, because such an ethic of care suggests that personal relationships should epitomize all moral relations (Clement 2018, 7), it stands to interrupt the masculinized narrative of heroism discussed earlier. It would be cynical to imagine that the recent visibility of the ethic of care, called for on the part of citizen-consumers and touted by celebrity chefs, is a mere exercise in good optics in the wake of #metoo-era reckonings with sexism. The ethic of care may instead be a tool that allows for genuine interventions that can lead to truly equitable social institutions. Arguably, it is this type of intervention that seems to inform the work of José Andrés and World Central Kitchen as they promote systemic changes in the hope of addressing—and ultimately eliminating—underlying structural inequalities. But such motivations and intentions are often lost—intentionally or unintentionally—in media accounts that frame this work through the more capitalist-friendly language of culinary philanthropy.

Conclusion

In the end, we face a few key questions: Are the actions of chef/restaurateurs and heroic consumer citizens in response to the COVID-19 pandemic merely a new spin on familiar capitalist imperatives during times of crisis—think, for example of how shopping was framed as "not letting the terrorists win" after 9/11—or are they morally important exercises? Have journalistic narratives participated in allowing chef/restaurateurs and consumers to shift the terms by which they sustain class and gender ideologies in pursuit of culinary capital, or have they promoted a more fundamental rethinking of the culinary landscape, one that began before the COVID-19 pandemic but has been accelerated because of it? Perhaps it is both: this framing surely supports—and justifies—the lifestyle imperatives of white middle-class liberalism, while it encourages individual interventions in a catastrophic economic situation. The motives of chef/restaurateurs and consumers alike may be noble, but what gets largely lost in the media messaging about individuals motivated by an ethic of care is the necessity of structural changes that would promote a more equitable playing field within the framework of a "new normal" while also providing the social safety net that is vital for future crises.

References

Behr, Felix. 2021. "How Guy Fieri Has Become a Food Industry Hero During the Pandemic." *Mashed*, January 14, 2021. https://www.mashed.com/312991/how-guy-fieri-has-become-a-food-industry-hero-during-the-pandemic/#:~:text=However%2C%20Guy%20Fieri%20has%20put,Employee%20Relief%20Fund%20(RERF).
Bourdieu, Pierre. 1984. *Distinction: A Social Critique of the Judgement of Taste*. Translated by Richard Nice. Cambridge, MA: Harvard University Press.
Campbell, Colin. 1987. *The Romantic Ethic and the Spirit of Modern Consumerism*. New York: Blackwell.

Campbell, Colin. 1997. "Consuming Goods and the Good of Consuming." In *Ethics of Consumption: The Good Life, Justice, and Global Stewardship*, edited by David A. Crocker and Toby Linden, 139–154. Lanham, MD: Rowman and Littlefield.

Clement, Grace. (1996) 2018. *Care, Autonomy, and Justice: Feminism and the Ethic of Care*. Reprint, New York: Routledge.

Cohen, Jaclyn Alexandra. 2020. "How Top Chefs & Restaurants Are Helping to Feed Those Across NYC During the COVID-19 Pandemic." *Harper's Bazaar*, April 17, 2020. https://www.harpersbazaar.com/culture/travel-dining/a32157366/food-restaurant-donations-covid-19/.

DeDauw, Esther and Daniel J. Connell. 2020. "Introduction: The Subaltern and the Hegemonic." In *Toxic Masculinity: Mapping the Monstrous in our Heroes*, edited by Esther DeDauw and Daniel J. Connell, 3–18. Jackson, MS: University Press of Mississippi.

DeJesus, Erin. 2020. "Overwhelmed by How to Help the Restaurant Industry? Make a List." *Eater*. https://www.eater.com/21578524/how-to-help-the-restaurant-industry-make-a-list-start-ordering. Posted 20 November 2020; accessed 11 December 2020.

Fegan, Mackenzie Chung. 2020. "How to Support Restaurants and Their Workers Right Now." *Bon Appetit*, September 30, 2020. https://www.bonappetit.com/story/how-to-support-restaurants.

Friend, Nina. 2020. "12 Ways to Support Local Restaurants Without Leaving Home." *Food and Wine*, March 17, 2020. https://www.foodandwine.com/news/support-restaurants-coronavirus.

Gastromasa. 2021. "The Hero of the Pandemic: Guy Fieri." *Gastromasa*, March 10, 2021. https://en.gastromasa.com/the-hero-of-the-pandemic-guy-fieri/.

Gilligan, Carol. 1987. "Moral Orientation and Moral Development." In *Women and Moral Theory*, edited by Eva Feder Kittay and Diana T. Meyers, 19–36. Totowa, NJ: Rowman and Littlefield.

Hirschorn, Anna. 2020. "How to Help Your Favorite Restaurants through the COVID Closures." *Saveur*, March 24, 2020. https://www.saveur.com/story/lifestyle/help-your-favorite-restaurants-through-covid-closures/.

Holt, Douglas B., and Craig Thompson. 2004. "Man-of-Action Heroes: The Pursuit of Heroic Masculinity in Everyday Consumption." *Journal of Consumer Research* 31(2):425–440.

Johnston, Josée, and Shyon Bauman. 2010. *Foodies: Democracy and Distinction in the Gourmet Foodscape*. New York: Routledge.

Kaufman, Michael S., Lena G. Goldberg, and Jill Avery. 2020. "Restaurant Revolution: How the Industry is Fighting to Stay Alive." *Forbes*, August 10, 2020. https://www.forbes.com/sites/hbsworkingknowledge/2020/08/10/restaurant-revolution-how-the-industry-is-fighting-to-stay-alive/?sh=1c503a25f1eb.

Klassen, Braden. 2018. "Kitchen Culture Serves Up Toxicity for Employees." *The Runner*, August 2, 2018. https://runnermag.ca/2018/08/kitchen-culture-serves-up-toxicity-for-employees/.

Krader, Kate. 2020. "Guy Fieri, the Fundraiser of Flavortown." *Bloomberg Bussinessweek*, December 3, 2020. https://www.bloomberg.com/news/articles/2020-12-03/guy-fieri-flavortown-mayor-raises-21-5-million-for-workers-bloomberg-50-2020.

Lane, Robert E. 1997. "The Road Not Taken: Friendship, Consumerism, and Happiness." In *Ethics of Consumption: The Good Life, Justice, and Global Stewardship*, edited by David A. Crocker and Toby Linden, 218–248. Lanham, MD: Rowman and Littlefield.

McBride, Anne E. and Flore, Roberto. 2019. "The Changing Role of the Chef: A Dialogue." *International Journal of Gastronomy and Food Science* 17 (October):100157. 10.1016/j.ijgfs.2019.100157.

McLennan, David B. 1994. "Autobiography, Cultural Mythology and the Modern Hero." In *American Heroes in a Media Age*, edited by Susan J. Drucker and Robert S. Cathcart, 111–133. Cresskill, NJ: Hampton Press.

McMullen, Jeffery S. 2017. "Are We Confounding Heroism and Individualism? Entrepreneurs May Not Be Lone Rangers, But They Are Heroic Nonetheless." *Business Horizons* (60):257–259.

Naccarato, Peter, and Kathleen LeBesco. 2012. *Culinary Capital*. Oxford: Berg.

Pascual Soler, Nieves. 2018. *Food and Masculinity in Contemporary Autobiographies*. London: Palgrave Macmillan.

Pomranz, Michael. 2020. "Guy Fieri Is Hosting a Special 'Takeout' Edition of 'Diners, Drive-Ins and Dives.'" *Food & Wine*, April 16, 2020. https://www.foodandwine.com/news/guy-fieri-diners-drive-ins-and-dives-takeout-edition-coronavirus.

Rao, Tejal. 2020. "Twilight of the Imperial Chef." *The New York Times*, August 4, 2020. https://www.nytimes.com/2020/08/04/dining/chef-restaurant-culture.html.

Rennie, Mark. 2020. "20 Reasons Why Guy Fieri Is the Hero We Need Right Now." *Ranker*, May 12, 2020. https://www.ranker.com/list/guy-fieri-king-tweets/mrennie.

Selyuk, Alina. 2020. "Restaurants Reinvent Themselves for Thanksgiving and Beyond: 'You Just Pivot.'" *NPR.com*, November 26, 2020. https://www.npr.org/2020/11/26/938590231/restaurants-reinvent-themselves-for-thanksgiving-and-beyond-you-just-pivot.

Stevens, Ashlie D. 2020. "'Best American Food Writing' Spotlights Kitchen Abuse and the Curious Reformation of Bad-Boy Chefs." *Salon.com*, December 11, 2020. https://www.salon.com/2020/12/10/best-american-food-writing-j-kenji-lopez-alt-restaurant-chefs/.

Swisher, Kara (Host). 2021. "Guy Fieri Has a Reminder for America." Interview of Guy Fieri. *NewYorkTimes.com*, June 28, 2021. https://www.nytimes.com/2021/06/28/opinion/sway-kara-swisher-guy-fieri.html?showTranscript=1.

Tseng, Esther. 2020. "Toxic Kitchen Culture: Reform is Sorely Needed in 2020." *Shondaland*, July 29, 2020. https://www.shondaland.com/live/travel-food/a33447650/toxic-kitchen-culture-reform-is-sorely-needed-in-2020/.

Vander Veen, Steve. 1994. "The Heroes of Consumption and the Consumption of Heroes." In *Advances in Consumer Research* (21), edited by Chris T. Allen and Deborah Roedder John, 331. Provo, UT: Association for Consumer Research.

Wofford, Benjamin. 2020. "The Heroic Story of How Jose Andres' Charity Feeds 250,000 People a Day in a Pandemic." *Washingtonian*, July 19, 2020. https://www.washingtonian.com/2020/07/19/world-central-kitchen-jose-andres-how-you-feed-250000-people-pandemic/.

6 Cooking in the Time of Corona: The Politicized Domesticity of Food Journalism in *The New York Times*

Elfriede Fürsich

When the COVID-19 pandemic brought public life in the United States to a halt in mid-March 2020, not only did people quickly have to rearrange their daily schedules, work routines, and family lives, but many news and lifestyle media outlets also had to adjust to the new reality. *The New York Times (NYT)*, for example, stopped its famed weekend "Travel" section and produced instead an "At Home" section that gave readers tips on how to keep themselves busy, entertained, and mentally strong in the many hours in lockdown. The Wednesday "Food" print section continued to be produced but, as this chapter will illustrate, underwent significant changes. The food journalists who produced content across several print and online platforms such as the popular *NYT Cooking* subscription service, including an App and YouTube channel, soon realized the importance of their beat for their readers and users. As the assistant managing editor in charge of culture and lifestyle coverage, Sam Sifton, explained: "If you're looking for glimmers of grace and goodness amid [the pandemic], start in the kitchen" (*The New York Times Company* 2021).

This chapter examines how food journalism responded during the months when most states imposed social distancing measures and people found themselves spending more and more time at home. Analyzing the Wednesday food section of *The New York Times*, I highlight how food journalists profoundly changed their agendas and topics to connect to their readers beyond explaining how to cook specific recipes. Their writing negotiated issues such as belonging and risk while transforming the political relevance and cultural assumptions of food coverage. In particular, I argue that food journalism expressed a new type of politicized domesticity that integrated and transcended neoliberal governmentality and focused on individual responsibility and consumer engagement towards a more holistic ideological position.

Pandemic as a Media Event

In times of national crisis such as a pandemic, the media play an extraordinary role that goes beyond the typical functions of providing

DOI: 10.4324/9781003283942-9

information and entertainment. Disasters of major consequences can be anthropologically explained as liminoid experiences (Turner 1977) that are marked by a rupture and suspension of everyday practices followed by a phase of flexibility that can lead to the formation of new routines. The media accompany audiences through all phases of such extraordinary times and in the process they, too, experience and must respond to profound disruptions.

Unsettling events that force media to take a "time-out" from ordinary business – a pause that can help "integrate societies in a collective heartbeat" (Dayan and Katz 1992, 9) – can be understood as "media events" or rituals that dislodge media from their everyday professional routines and narratives. While the concepts of "media events" and "ritual" have most often been applied by scholars to highly unusual and significant short-term events that are "created with the media in mind" such as presidential funerals, royal weddings, the Olympics, or even the Watergate hearings (Dayan and Katz 1992), the unforeseen and abrupt upheaval of the private and public spheres worldwide caused by the pandemic and the new media routines that emerged in its wake, allow for such a designation. Audiences began to look to their media to provide not only much-needed information and entertainment but also for interpretation, release from tension, and reinforcement of social solidarity; and many media outlets did their best to meet these new demands. As they did so, they fortified their legitimacy, authority, and relevance to public and private life. As Nick Couldry has argued, the concept of media rituals can be used to "explain the media's role in ordering our lives, and organising social space [during] times when our attention to media seems more than casual, even necessary, and when the media appears to stand in for something essential about our lives together as social beings" (Couldry 2002, 1). This chapter seeks to illuminate this process during the COVID-19 pandemic as one of the most disruptive media events of our time.

Domesticity and Media – The Political Dimension of Home

Unquestionably, the pandemic has had a profound impact on domestic life, and media have stepped in to provide audiences with frameworks that they can use to control the chaos in their everyday lives in new ways as they work to maintain relationships, refine family roles, create productive learning and working environments at home, and find opportunities for leisure. These tasks connect to the established service functions that media, especially lifestyle journalism, have historically performed. Scholars have investigated how in the process of performing these roles, media and media technologies represent the structure of everyday life and produce domesticity. They have also analyzed the social, cultural, and political implications of these representations. Classic work by David Morley (Morley 1986) and more recent work by Maggie Andrews (Andrews 2012) explain how the media create and maintain gendered spheres and provide specific scripts on how work and leisure are divided and valued. They and others have also interrogated how media content represents domesticity. For example, research on contemporary home improvement shows and lifestyle television, in general, has illustrated that these programs often represent a domesticity in which traditional gender roles seem to have been dissolved; in their place, these programs construct and glamorize a private commodified perfectionism that ties into neoliberal ideologies of self-optimization (Gorman-Murray 2006; Ouellette 2016; Spigel 2001).

This media representation and structuring is political, not only in the feminist sense that "the personal is political." Maureen Ryan termed this unique relationship between the media and domesticity the "politics of ordinariness" and emphasized the social dimension of this effort. The work performed by lifestyle media is to "transform ordinariness into something richly inviting, even transcendent. Most of all, they tie ordinariness and consumption to ideas about social life and authentic social relations with others" (Ryan 2018, 9–10).

Adopting this social and political notion of ordinariness, this chapter interrogates how the food section narrated, structured, and transcended the everyday lives of its readers at a time of crisis. The question guiding this chapter is: how did the Food section negotiate this unique time of food supply problems and economic upheaval in private households, the food industries, and culinary professions? How did the coverage position the readers, the food writers, and other stakeholders in relation to each other and to wider political, social, and economic systems?

Food Sections and Lifestyle Journalism

The New York Times not only survived but thrived during the pandemic. Its subscriptions, especially to its digital editions and apps, increased tremendously. This upward trend that started during the early days of the Trump administration intensified exponentially during the pandemic. While the *New York Times*' established reputation as a credible and reliable news brand was unquestionably a major factor in this rise, its food journalism emerged as a significant driver of the subscription gains. A published corporate report summarized this success:

> People from around the world turned to *NYT Cooking* in record numbers for recipes, advice and inspiration that made their time in the kitchen easier and more enjoyable … . In 2020, *Cooking* attracted 113 million users to its recipes, guides and collections, an increase of over 40 percent compared to 2019.
>
> (*The New York Times Company* 2021)

While these numbers refer to the Cooking App, it can be deduced that *The New York Times* digital and print food sections became vital in sustaining and expanding reader loyalty as well. For this chapter, I analyzed print editions of the *New York Times* Food section that is published every Wednesday, as well as other food content. The classic Wednesday section remains a flagship outlet, even as many articles in the Food section are published online and are used across various platforms before and after they are printed in the paper. I included all sections from four months starting from April 1, 2020, when the first lockdowns went into effect across the US, through August 26, 2020, when it seemed that the first COVID-19 wave was easing and there was some hope for improvement. This first crisis phase of the pandemic was characterized by major life, work, and school upheavals, a strong fear of infection, and a general state of emergency because no vaccinations or anti-viral medications had been developed. Along with the main food section, I also monitored the *NYT* Cooking App, the weekly *New York Times Magazine* food section called Eat, and the newly created "At Home" that replaced the Sunday Travel section.

Themes of Coverage

Throughout the period under investigation, the food section offered a lively and multifaceted coverage of food-related content. Well-known writers (e.g., Melissa Clark) produced their regular columns in addition to well-researched articles that took a more in-depth look at food-related issues. While a cursory glance at this section may have overlooked changes, more careful attention would have noticed more illustrations, negative space, and more full-page introductions, all of which suggested more profound, foundational changes to the coverage of food. A close analysis of the articles confirmed a subtle but meaningful reorientation. Three central themes emerged in the coverage that I call coping, struggling, and sustaining.

Coping

The first dominant theme of the coverage related to coping strategies. It reflected the fact that users and journalists had to adjust to spending most waking hours at home. Articles reassured readers that their home could provide refuge, and the right food supplies and cooking strategies could make eating at home not only nourishing but also delicious and enjoyable, thereby easing the sense of loss at not being able to go to restaurants, bars, and coffee shops. Since public eating and drinking establishments were no longer safely accessible, the home became the new arena for celebrating food. If earlier food sections often balanced efficiency with leisure (for example, by providing recipes for quick meals under 30 minutes for weekdays alongside recipes for sophisticated weekend and holiday cooking), now writers focused on creative cooking in the face of restricted supplies. For example, David Tanis, in his article "Sailing the Mediterranean," reassured his readers that

"We may be anchored at home, but our pantries are a way to travel the world (Tanis 8 April 2020, D1).

Yet as the pandemic dragged on, even initially reassuring coping strategies such as baking with family members began to fall short. By August 5, 2020, it takes a blueberry Bundt cake drizzled with a shockingly pink glaze to "Pull you out of your baking rut." As renowned food writer Melissa Clark explains: "The charm of a Bundt cake lies in its fanciness, which, if your family has become as complacent on the homemade baked goods front as mine, might be just the thing to jolt them out of their doldrums" (Clark 8 April 2020, D3). Enthusiastic pandemic cooks and writers had to acknowledge that not every person found respite by cooking or baking. Complemented by a number of illustrations on the "pressures of pandemic cooking" by illustrator Jessica Olien, Priya Krishna, in an article on June 3, 2020, titled "Quarantine Exposes Hapless Home Cooks," sympathetically acknowledges the failure, annoyance, and online squabbles of people who don't like or are not good at cooking: "[F]or all the home cooks who are embracing the art as a therapeutic escape or mode of entertainment, there are as many others who are left cold, or confounded, by the sight of a stove" (Krishna 3 June 2020, D8).

Closely related to this advice for "coping-by-cooking" were tips on how to make cooking at home a social rather than an individual task by inviting children, other family members, and even friends to take part. While pre-pandemic food writing often focused on ways to use cooking to impress friends, improve nutrition, and practice politics and ethics of sustainability, pandemic food writing was more about "making do". It was about making the most of what we still had, and valuing time spent with family even as increased and forced "togetherness" led in many instances to increased tension. A typical example is an article by Eric Asimov, "Taking Comfort in a Familiar Wine" (Asimov 1 April 2020, D7). Its subheading provides a meta-discourse on coping with the frustration, anxiety, and intense grief caused by losing loved ones and precious aspects of everyday life to the virus: "In times of fear, we find solace in things that conjure up memories and emotions" (D7). Before introducing specific wines, Asimov refers to his family as a way to connect to readers: "Like so many others, my wife and I have been self-isolating in our apartment, doing our best to stay close to our loved ones from afar, and cooking the foods that we find most comforting" (D7).

Finally, pandemic food coverage stressed the importance of adaptability and helped readers develop an attitude of flexibility that, while focused on the kitchen, was equally essential and could be applied to other aspects of domestic and professional, public and private life. In "My Seder Menu," Alison Roman helped readers figure out how to honor Passover, the first major holiday in the early months of COVID-19, despite pandemic deprivations. Her article, accompanied by an almost full-page illustration of a matzo ball soup, is steeped in connotations of comforting family, community, and tradition. In what is highly unusual for lifestyle journalists, she gives readers a glimpse behind the scenes of the difficult production process of this article. She discloses that she worked for weeks on a traditional article with upbeat descriptions of various recipes that embrace and transform traditions. But when the pandemic hit, she felt that writing "a piece on how to enthusiastically cook fancy cuts of meat for many of your friends and family ... suddenly seemed not only insensitive but nearly impossible. So things here have shifted a bit: The tone is different and the scope scaled back, but Passover is still on the calendar" (Roman 2020, D1). Along with other authors, Roman appeals to the readers' flexibility, resourcefulness, and resilience in challenging times.

Journalists' calls for adaptability became a standard mechanism for coping, not only for their audiences but also for themselves. This situation led to some drastic journalistic adjustments. For example, Melissa Clark in her weekly column "A Good Appetite" does the opposite of what most recipe writers are expected to do – instead of presenting an authoritative, prescriptive set of ingredients and instructions, she encourages her audience to change her recipes, even radically. In "Here's a Salad That's Negotiable" (Clark 8 April 2020, D3), Clark offers a recipe for an asparagus salad that she had developed before Covid-19, along with many suggestions for how to improvise on the ingredients when the ones she suggested were not readily available. Even the subtitle urges readers to improvise with what they have on hand: "Change the nuts and cheese. Even the asparagus can go." Reflecting on this radical approach for substitutions, she concludes: "Does it feel strange to give a recipe for asparagus salad and then write that the asparagus is negotiable? Maybe. But it's also practical and, I hope, helpful. Then, when you do get your hands on some gorgeous, purple-tipped asparagus, this recipe will be here, waiting for you" (Clark 8 April 2020, D3).

Struggling

The second major theme of pandemic food writing was the acknowledgment of struggles, especially those relating to work-life balance while having all family members at home or while being alone and relying on virtual communities. This coverage is marked by a distinctive sense of loss: loss of friends and loved ones, loss of social and festive gatherings, and loss of public eating and drinking establishments. The emotional dimensions in these stories are similar to those expressed in the stories that emphasized coping strategies, but now they are much darker. For example, on June 17, 2020, the first page of the food section was dominated by a striking hand-drawn illustration of the inside of a restaurant depicting a bar, a busy cook, and a number of tables occupied by people happily eating and talking. Only the bottom of the page was taken up by the headline, "More Than a Meal," and a short statement: "When restaurants closed this spring, we didn't just lose a place to be fed. We lost a theater of experience. Here, several renowned writers recount some of their most memorable meals out" ("More Than" 17 June 2020, D1). Three pages of the section were devoted to these nostalgic recollections of bygone restaurant visits enjoyed in more carefree times.

What is significant here is that in addition to writing about cooking at home, writers in the sections I analyzed started to broaden their coverage to include the pandemic-related economic problems of food businesses and services. Articles increasingly covered small culinary businesses and individually owned restaurants, such as craft brewers and family-run wineries. One article, featuring a startling photograph of the staff of an Atlanta steak house wearing masks and facing the camera directly under the headline "The New Faces of Restaurant Hospitality" by Kim Stevenson, tells readers that "[a]s dining rooms reopen, owners are trying to reduce risks and reassure customers" (Severson 20 May 2020, D1). Another article, (Severson 24 June 2020, D1) "Ballpark Peanuts, A Classic Pleasure, Are Benched For the Season," laments the disappearance of peanuts at stadiums during baseball games and at the same time explores the impact of pandemic restrictions on peanut farmers. This attention to the economic underpinnings of various culinary pleasures increased throughout the examined timeframe. For example, Clay Risen in "Craft Distillers' Boom Goes Bust" reviews the state of the craft brewing and distilling market by highlighting the distinctive challenges that the industry was facing, especially those new to the business:

> [T]he one-two punch of shuttered bars and mass unemployment has hit craft distilling especially hard. ... How can a sector that relies so heavily on bars, tasting rooms and face-to-face sales ... move forward in an economy defined by social distancing and thinner wallets?
> (Risen 29 April 2020, D5)

Despite a few references to the whole industry, the focus of that story, like many others in the Food section, remains trained on the individual distiller and small operations. Articles that highlight the broader impact of the pandemic on large-scale and industrial food production and distribution remain in the Business section. This editorial positioning demonstrates that the *New York Times* Food section continued to engage in a discourse of "elite authenticity," which Gwynne Mapes documented in the pre-pandemic food section (Mapes 2018). She identified two rhetorical strategies which continue to frame most stories: first, the "Pioneer Spirit [with] a celebration of innovation, personal labor and adventurousness" and second, "Locality/ Sustainability [with] consistent references to responsible sourcing of ingredients and/or environments and community practices" (Mapes 2018, 271). Mapes connects these and similar strategies to a neoliberal ideology that explains individual success as a process of elite self-optimization and avoids addressing systemic power structures that can enable or restrict the success of individuals, such as labor or market inequalities. The continuous focus on smaller stakeholders in the food industry along with an overall focus on home and private domesticity in the analyzed material support Mapes' findings. However, the pandemic also opened up ways of restructuring journalistic routines that, I argue, transcend the neoliberal tilt of earlier coverage. This change plays out in another theme that I call "Sustaining."

Sustaining

The theme of "sustaining" emerges later in the pandemic cycle and is enacted in the dimensions of home and professional food production. It starts to appear in articles about coping with scarcity. While writers at first focused on the need for individuals to be creatively and resiliently flexible, they soon began to connect individual and small-scale frustrations (such as scarcity of ingredients in local grocery stores) to structural problems in complex national and international foodways. The early emphasis on "making do" out of necessity is developed into reflections on potentially better ways of "making do" in a wider social, political, and economic context. References to memory and the past are less emotional and nostalgic but more concretely didactical – it's about learning from the past or past mistakes. The focus now is simultaneously inward and, more importantly, outward. An article, "Good Wine Leads Back to Nature" by Eric Asimov, oscillates in this fashion. He begins with a first-person experiential narrative common in lifestyle journalism:

> [N]othing in wine has affected me so profoundly as observing the intimate relationship that enlightened farmers have with the land ... . [It has influenced] many important facets of my life, from the foods and wines I buy to the clothes I wear to how I think about climate change and political issues.
>
> (Asimov 22 July 2020, D7)

But then Asimov quickly expands his self-reflection in significant and outward-focused ways. He does not simply reiterate a yearning for past methods and small (but elite) producers; instead, he begins to critically reflect on the complexity of food production and foodways, including the problems created by monocultures which he describes as concessions for financial gain and the benefits of innovative regenerative agriculture. He elaborates on the complexities of sustainable ecosystems by connecting wine production to soil consistency, biodiversity, water supplies, and air quality while warning that even minor modifications can have potentially unintended consequences.

During the first phase of the pandemic, food journalists expanded and deepened their coverage of the environmental impacts of food production methods as well as unfair labor practices, and hostile working environments in the food industries. Journalists also began turning away from stories that cultivated an exploitative "fascination with foods/environments associated with 'the poor': the working class, immigrants, rural areas" as a sign of "lowbrow appreciation" (Mapes 2018, 276–77) and began diversifying the sources and perspectives that they centered in their stories. An early example is an article prominently positioned on the first page of the Food section: "In a Rising Food Crisis, Drawing On Survival Skills: As the pandemic limits supplies, many Native Americans are turning to canning, dehydrating and seed saving" (Krishna 15 April 2020, D1). Instead of framing Native American food production in a nostalgic, aesthetic, or (pseudo-) spiritual way to provide relief and entertainment to urban dwellers, this article concretely connects the pandemic food scarcity problems to long-established food deserts on Reservations, and to poverty, environmental pollution, and government overreach. The focus is on the self-sustaining and pro-active methods of the members of several tribes. The past is not treated as an embellished trove to be plundered but as a problematic and brutal precursor. A significant statement by a tribal chairman of the Turtle Mountain Band of Chippewa even became the "Quote of the Day" in the paper:

> "You're forced to stay in a specific area, you're told to trust the government, you're told food will be scarce—welcome to 1700s Native nation." —JAMIE AZURE ... on how Native Americans are looking to their forebears for strategies to cope with food shortages during the coronavirus crisis.
>
> ("Quote" 15 April 2020, 3)

Instead of looking to the past as a coping mechanism for current problems, the coverage emphasizes contemporary experimenation and innovation. For example, the article "'Thinking Like a Sturgeon'" highlights the long-term pre-pandemic entrepreneurial strategies of the Native American conservationist Donella C. Miller: "Patient conservation efforts by the Yakama Nation have preserved the Columbian River and nurtured its fish. Now those long-term investments are reaping a healthy ecosystem and lucrative caviar" (D1). Many articles covering both personal experiences with food as well as more complex issues of foodways shifted to asking what readers can learn from the struggles during and responses to the pandemic that can make food consumption and production more sustainable in the future – as we face large-scale disruptions in years to come.

Ideological Spectrum: Neoliberal versus Holistic Positions

Giving attention to the underlying cultural assumptions of food writing during the pandemic, two distinct yet related ideological positions emerge. Much of the coverage is still shaped by a rhetoric of neo-liberal "elite authenticity" that was diagnosed and criticized by Mapes in her analysis of pre-pandemic editions of the *New York Times* food section (Mapes 2018). This neoliberal ideological position is shored up by an inward focus on the home and individual coping strategies. The problems of the pandemic are reduced to personal challenges to be managed with individual creativity and resilience, rather than as collective problems requiring systemic government and corporate solutions. This framing is constructed using rhetorical strategies commonly used in lifestyle journalism. First, the stories are written in the first-person voice of a good friend to affectively connect the writer to the audience, and to offer trustworthy, authentic advice on how to respond as individuals to complex problems by "making do" rather than working for change. Similarly, modifications in the graphic design of these stories, which relied on full-page illustrations or photographs surrounded by generous amounts of white space play into an aesthetic of aloof minimalism, detached from the messy sociopolitical context – an aesthetic that resonates with the neoliberal stance. Finally, these stories draw heavily on nostalgia for a less complicated past. In this, the coverage follows other lifestyle content. Lifestyle media's ideology in general, as Laurie Ouellette observed, is linked to "the rising currency of self-help in neoliberal societies that embrace the market-place as a model of self-hood and social relations, and with new strategies for governing citizens that emphasize individual choice, personal responsibility and self-empowerment" (Ouellette, 2016a, 4).

But the liminoid aspect of the global pandemic challenged food journalism and offered opportunities for reflection, innovation, and restructuring of routines that moved away from neoliberalism towards a more holistic ideological position. The disruptions of the pandemic freed journalists from having to adhere to previously established genre conventions. This rupture happened at a time when recent social upheavals such as #metoo, #blacklivesmatter, and global protests against climate change inaction had already or were about to provoke a re-evaluation of core tenets of the food and media industries. Suddenly, experimentation and innovation became not only possible but necessary.

For this more holistic ideological position to be realized, however, several significant changes in food writing had to occur. Attention had to shift from an inward orientation to an outward one; the problems of the pandemic had to be defined as systemic and they had to be contextualized in relation to global foodways, environments, and economies; and desirable solutions had to be framed as achievable, sustainable, political, and collective. Also, instead of looking backward and lamenting the loss of a seemingly perfect past, the perspective had to turn toward a hopeful future that could be created collectively, including the experiences and knowledge of undervalued, under-represented, and exploited groups.

Importantly, these changes always required a significant repositioning of the writer in the articles. The authors had to take a step back and tone down the didactic, elite, expert voice of food writing (Fürsich 2013) or the somewhat self-indulgent commiseration that marked much food writing in the early months of the pandemic. The authoritative voice of the expert-writer had to be de-centered and replaced with individuals traditionally marginalized in food media, quoted extensively and as voices of authority and valuable experience and knowledge.

An example of an article grounded in the holistic rather than neoliberal position was published on August 19, 2020, under the headline "Spreading the Awareness of Inequity" (Severson 19 August 2020, D1, D7). The article covered the online scandal that erupted after Jessica Koslow, founder of the trendy Los Angeles restaurant Sqirl and an expert jam maker, was accused of running an unsanitary kitchen and selling jam that had been covered in mold. The scandal over these allegations of unsanitary food production and mistreated workers who were ordered to scrape the mold off the jam became an opportunity in the article for a group of African-American preservers and food policy advocates to speak out against the unequal acknowledgment and appreciation of people of color as craft food entrepreneurs and to tell the story of preserving from their perspective. The article explains how food preservation traditionally has been an expression of independence and self-reliance in Black communities by avoiding a reliance on inequitable food supplies.

However, the women quoted in the article refuse to be reduced to speaking only about a painful past and instead emphasize their contemporary expertise and professionalism. For example, a jam company owner explained that jam preserving as a survival strategy can "be a burden for Black jammers, locking them into a role white investors and customers expect them to play" (D7). She argues,

> In no way are we trying to hide culture or get around it, but it's important to start seeing things outside of that 'I started my jam because my grandmother was a slave. … No. I started it because I am a foodie and I went to culinary school. (D7)

By including long direct quotations from food activists and jam makers who complicate the relationship between history, race, and economics in the craft food movement, the article forcefully breaks problematic binaries in food writing that have often positioned contemporary food production by people of color as pre-modern nostalgic endeavors outside the professional realm (Fürsich 2013).

Popular Journalism, Public Quality, and a Politicized Domesticity

The narrative changes in the *New York Times* Food section played out against a backdrop of ongoing crises and calls for change in food media that elite producers had to take seriously in order to maintain their legitimacy, relevance, and economic viability. But the existential and liminoid experience of a global pandemic accelerated the transformation and provided strong incentives for changing entrenched routines. Analyzing the first phase of food writing during the abrupt fallout from Covid-19, I argue that these events forced on the food section staff and writers a pause to re-evaluate their roles and practices. This rupture ultimately catalyzed and intensified projects that engaged with new voices and sources in the context of food writing and lifestyle content.

Following a strategy for a "critical evaluation of lifestyle journalism's democratic role against the background of contemporary social change" (Fürsich 2012, 23), this examination of the political relevance of the *New York Times* Food section remains complex. The fact that these articles are using the genre conventions of lifestyle journalism makes them especially appropriate in this time of crisis as they engage with "journalism of the ordinary," inspire the interactive engagement of audiences (as the lively comment section in food online platforms attest to), and as they offer coping strategies in the absence of effective solutions. These aspects represent relevant and productive elements of what John Fiske called "popular journalism" that has civic and political value (Fiske 1989). The coverage reached what Irene Costera Meijer defined as "public quality" (Meijer 2003; 2005) in several dimensions: the food section writers provided practical help, reassurance, and support to their readers in a time of existential crisis that was accessible. Moreover, the section employed various editorial elements from traditional food writing (recipes, reviews, profiles) but also embraced newly trending subjects such as diversity, sexism, and environmentalism (a move that was often driven by external forces, such as viral campaigns and online competition from new food sites), and a frank, meta-discursive reevaluation of journalists' roles (see also, "What Does a Dining Critic Do Now?" 28 April 2020). In addition, the writers eventually abandoned a nostalgic longing for food and dining in pre-pandemic times for a more productive engagement with what we can learn from the pandemic to build a better future. The political relevance of articles in the sections I examined is the most persuasive when writers move beyond addressing audiences as efficient self-optimizers. Maybe it took a crisis as severe as a global pandemic that was beyond quick solutions to undermine the didactic tone of service journalism and the common lifestyle media trope of the "Entrepreneurs of the Self" (Ouellette, 2016a, 80). Moreover, introducing the decidedly innocuous "At Home" section in the *New York Times* diverted the typical small "hacks" approach to major problems that is often criticized in lifestyle media in general.

A cursory review of the Food section after the initial phase of the pandemic ended suggests to me that the politicization of the food section will endure. For example, an article one year later in May 2021 (during yet another Covid-19 wave) headlined "Using Food As a Policy Platform, Not a Prop" (Wharton 5 May 2021, D1) covered the labor policy initiatives of a New York state senator not as a "feel-good" feature but as a story about the senator's conflicts with constituents – a topic and angle that traditionally would have landed this article on the politics desk. This article explains how "State Senator Jessica Ramos speaks up for street vendors, farmworkers and restaurants" (D1). While stories published in food sections that directly cover public institutions such as governments and unions continue to be scattered, they are not as rare as they once were. This type of reporting by the *New York Times* as a powerful, agenda-setting food journalism institution should not be downplayed. It may hint at an emerging re-evaluation of readership and citizenship beyond the neoliberal project that only allows for presenting "democracy and self-government in profitable, privatized and personalized terms" (Ouellette, 2016a).

Overall, in order for food media to remain politically relevant in the time of Covid-19, the concept of domesticity in food writing had to be transformed. While scholars often criticize the gendered conservatism of media genres, especially in lifestyle media focused on the home, this analysis illustrates that domesticity is a more flexible and complex category than might be expected. The pandemic literally constrained journalists and their audiences to their homes, often exacerbating existing conflicts based on domestic gender roles and inequality. However, the desolation of the pandemic world and the need to address it also allowed for what Maud Ceuterick called the "affirmative politics" of the pandemic-enforced domesticity (Ceuterick 2020). In the case of the *New York Times* Food section, the pandemic as a liminoid media event connected to systemic and existential "pauses" that presented openings for different perspectives on and from domestic spaces. This domesticity was politicized; it could be activated as a familiar (and maybe safe) platform from which to reconsider the wider contextual factors of a world in crisis and reimagine a more equitable future beyond our own four walls.

References

Andrews, Maggie. 2012. *Domesticating the Airwaves: Broadcasting, Domesticity and Femininity*. 1st ed. London: Continuum International Publishing Group. 10.5040/9781350048294.

Asimov, Eric. 2020 "Taking Comfort in a Familiar Wine." Food. *New York Times*, April 1, 2020: D7.

Asimov, Eric. 2020. "The Pour: Good Wine Leads Back to Nature." Food. *New York Times*, July 22, 2020: D7.

Ceuterick, Maud. 2020. "An Affirmative Look at a Domesticity in Crisis: Women, Humour and Domestic Labour during the COVID-19 Pandemic." *Feminist Media Studies* 20 (6):896–901. 10.1080/14680777.2020.1789396.

Clark, Melissa. 2020 "Here's a Salad That's Negotiable." Food. *New York Times*, April 8, 2020: D3.

Couldry, Nick. 2002. *Media Rituals: A Critical Approach*. London: Routledge. 10.4324/9780203986608.

Dayan, Daniel, and Elihu Katz. 1992. *Media Events the Live Broadcasting of History*. Cambridge, MA: Harvard University Press. 10.4159/9780674030305.

Fiske, John. 1989. *Reading the Popular*. Boston: Unwin Hyman.

Fürsich, Elfriede. 2012. "Lifestyle Journalism as Popular Journalism: Strategies for Evaluating Its Public Role." *Journalism Practice* 6 (1):12–25. 10.1080/17512786.2011.622894.

Fürsich, Elfriede. 2013. "Analyzing Text: The Cultural Discourse in Ethnic Food Reviews." In *The International Encyclopedia of Media Studies*, edited by Angharad N. Valdivia, 338–357. John Wiley & Sons. 10.1002/9781444361506.wbiems186.

Gorman-Murray, Andrew. 2006. "Queering Home or Domesticating Deviance?: Interrogating Gay Domesticity through Lifestyle Television." *International Journal of Cultural Studies* 9 (2):227–247. 10.1177/1367877906064032.

Krishna, Priya. 2020. "In a Rising Food Crisis, Drawing On Survival Skills." Food. *New York Times*, April 15, 2020: D1,7.

Krishna, Priya. 2020. "Quarantine and the Hapless Home Cook." Food. *New York Times*, June 3, 2020: D1, 8.

Mapes, Gwynne. 2018. "(De)Constructing Distinction: Class Inequality and Elite Authenticity in Mediatized Food Discourse." *Journal of Sociolinguistics* 22 (3):265–287. 10.1111/josl.12285.

Meijer, Irene Costera. 2003. "What Is Quality Television News? A Plea for Extending the Professional Repertoire of Newsmakers." *Journalism Studies* 4 (1):15. 10.1080/14616700306496.

Meijer, Irene Costera. 2005. "Impact or Content?: Ratings vs Quality in Public Broadcasting." *European Journal of Communication (London)* 20 (1):27–53. 10.1177/0267323105049632.

Morley, David. 1986. *Family Television: Cultural Power and Domestic Leisure*. Comedia Series; No. 37. London: Comedia Pub. Group.

"More Than a Meal." 2020. Food. *New York Times,* June 17, 2020: D1, 4-6

Nierenberg, Amelia. 2020. "'Thinking Like a Sturgeon'." Food. *New York Times*, June 3, 2020: D1,7.

Nierenberg, Amelia. 2020. "For the Navajo, A Fight for Better Food." Food. *New York Times*, August 5, 2020: D7.

Ouellette, Laurie. 2016 *Lifestyle TV*. Routledge Television Guidebooks. New York, NY: Routledge.

"Quote of the Day." *New York Times*, April 15, 2020, 3.

Risen, Clay. 2020. "Craft Distillers' Boom Goes Bust. Food. *New York Times*, April 29, 2020: D5.

Roman, Alison. 2020 "My Seder Menu." Food. *New York Times*, April 1, 2020: D1, D4, D5.

Ryan, Maureen E. 2018. *Lifestyle Media in American Culture: Gender, Class, and the Politics of Ordinariness*. 1st ed. Routledge Research in Gender, Sexuality, and Media. Milton: Routledge. 10.4324/9781315464978.

Severson, Kim. 2020. "Ballpark Peanuts, A Classic Pleasure, Are Benched for the Season." Food. *New York Times*, June 24, 2020: D1, 8.

Severson, Kim. 2020. "Spreading Awareness of Inequity." Food. *New York Times*, August 19, 2020: D1,7.

Severson, Kim. 2020. "The New Faces of Restaurant Hospitality." Food. *New York Times*, May 20, 2020: D1, 5.

Spigel, Lynn. 2001. "Media Homes: Then and Now." *International Journal of Cultural Studies* 4 (4):385–411. 10.1177/136787790100400402.

Tanis, David. 2020. "Sailing the Mediterranean." Food. *New York Times*, April 8, 2020: D1, 2.

The New York Times Company. 2021. "Record Number of Home Cooks Find Joy and Inspiration with NYT Cooking." January 13, 2021. https://www.nytco.com/press/record-number-of-home-cooks-find-joy-and-inspiration-with-nyt-cooking/.

Turner, Victor W. 1977. *The Ritual Process: Structure and Anti-Structure*. Symbol, Myth, and Ritual Series. Ithaca, N.Y: Cornell University Press.

Turner, Victor. 1974. "Liminal to Liminoid, in Play, Flow, and Ritual: An Essay in Comparative Symbology." *Rice Institute Pamphlet - Rice University Studies* 60(3). https://scholarship.rice.edu/handle/1911/63159.

"What Does a Dining Critic Do Now?" Inside The Times. *New York Times*, April 28, 2020: 2.

Wharton, Rachel. 2021. "Using Food As a Policy Platform, Not a Prop." Food. *New York Times*, May 5, 2021: D1,7.

7 Paleo and Pain Free: Reporting on Scandals of Food Celebrities

Katherine Kirkwood

The impact of the growth of lifestyle media—particularly food media—over the past 30 years has been well documented (see for example Lewis 2008a; 2008b; Ouellette and Hay 2008; Rousseau 2012). As Ouellette and Hay assert, food media form part of a "circuit of cultural technologies for shaping and guiding conduct" (Ouellette and Hay 2008,117). These lifestyle media texts are designed to perform a governing function that encourages audiences to engage with middle-class tastes and modes of consumption.

Looking at food media more specifically, many of these cookbooks, television programs, and social media accounts are fronted by charismatic chefs, cooks, or notable personalities. In the late 20th and into the early 21st centuries, some of these figures have become global opinion leaders who are elevated to celebrity status, with journalists reporting on their activities in the same way they would cover politicians or royalty. For instance, Jamie Oliver was photographed alongside then British Prime Minister Tony Blair presenting his *Feed Me Better* petition in the aftermath of his *Jamie's School Dinners* TV series (Hinscliff and Hill 2005), and in another instance moving from his north London home to "a £6 million 16th century mansion in one of the UK's most picturesque villages, Finchingfield, Essex" (Fillingham 2019). This type of reporting demonstrates that celebrity chefs and other food media personalities are central in lifestyle and entertainment journalism, and even in "hard" news as they wield power to effect meaningful food-related social and political change. Coverage of these figures also offers examples of the "tabloidization" of hard news, bringing to these reports entertainment, emotional engagement, and drama. But regardless of whether these figures are depicted as political, lifestyle, entertainment, tabloid, or hybrid subjects, the veracity of the messages they disseminate, especially claims about food, health, and nutrition, needs to be more vigorously interrogated by journalists since, if left unchecked, erroneous claims can be dangerous to the health of audiences.

This chapter evaluates the limitations of celebrity lifestyle expertise by analyzing the trajectories of the public lives of two controversial Australian food personalities, Pete Evans and Belle Gibson. Evans was a celebrity chef who had published 15 cookbooks since 2014 with Pan Macmillan (Wilson 2020) and

DOI: 10.4324/9781003283942-10

owned the world-renowned pizza restaurant, Hugos. Most notably, Evans served as a judge on the Australian Seven Network's reality television cooking competition *My Kitchen Rules* from the program's inception in 2010 until May 2020 when the network did not renew his contract (Blackiston 2020). Belle Gibson, meanwhile, was a social media influencer who established her Instagram identity in 2013 under the handle @healing_belle and soon attracted more than 300,000 followers (Price, H. 2021). Her claims to have beaten brain cancer by eschewing traditional medicine and pursuing a regimen of clean eating and alternative therapies generated an outpouring of public sympathy and attention in mainstream media outlets. Subsequently, Gibson developed *The Whole Pantry,* a cookbook published by Penguin, and a smartphone app that was so successful Apple wanted to integrate it into its smartwatch, which was released in 2015 (Donelly and Toscano 2017).

Today, both figures are widely derided. Evans's downfall was precipitated by a steady shift from easy-going television chef to fanatical advocate for fad diets, conspiracy theories, and alt-right ideology. By February 2021, Evans had lost most of his mainstream commercial and media agreements and was banned from both Facebook and Instagram (AAP 2021). At the time, he had approximately 1.5 million followers on Facebook and 278,000 on Instagram (BBC 2021). Gibson was similarly discredited when journalists Beau Donelly and Nick Toscano exposed her as a fraud in March 2015. Not only did they find evidence that Gibson's pledges to donate a percentage of cookbook and app sales to charity were false, but they also revealed that Gibson never had cancer. Consumer Affairs Victoria brought a civil case against her, which resulted in Gibson receiving fines totaling AUD 410,000 for five offenses related to The Australian Consumer Law Act (Percy 2017).

Gibson and Evans found their fame and subsequent infamy in different ways, but they are linked by three key dynamics. First, they both enjoyed a presence in mainstream media that lent credibility to their claims; second, both told dramatic and emotional stories that attracted a large audience; and third, their messages made health claims targeting vulnerable communities, including people living with cancer and other chronic illnesses. This chapter explores these three dynamics through analysis of online news stories and other media texts produced by or about Gibson and Evans. In relation to Gibson, key texts this chapter draws on include *The Woman Who Fooled the World: Belle Gibson's Cancer Con and the Darkness at the Heart of the Wellness Industry* (2017), which was written by Beau Donelly and Nick Toscano, the journalists who originally exposed Gibson's deceit.- Furthermore, I cite a 2021 BBC-commissioned documentary, *Bad Influencer: The Great Insta Con,* which chronicled Gibson's story from awkward Brisbane teenager, to influencer, to social pariah. Evans's 2017 documentary *The Magic Pill,* which asserted that following the Ketogenic diet (a close relation to the Paleolithic diet Evans is famous for promoting) would improve the lives of people living with chronic health conditions such as asthma, autism, and even cancer, as well as his appearance on a June 2020 episode of *60 Minutes* Australia about COVID-19 conspiracy theories, underpin my analysis of his career trajectory.

In examining Gibson and Evans's respective roles in the food mediascape, I make an argument that sits at the intersection of concurrent changes in food media and journalism. In relation to food media, it must be acknowledged that the individuals who have platforms or 'a voice' in the food mediascape have diversified due to the participatory nature of Web 2.0 technologies. Although the power of these platforms has been recognized for the past 20 years, the real implications of such power are still far from being understood. Relatedly, in journalism, the impact of tabloidization on the industry has been much criticized (Johansson 2008). Indeed, reporting on food could be considered part of the incursion of softer news into traditional journalism's territory and vice versa. Through these case studies, I argue that Gibson and Evans's views have serious and very real consequences for their fans and audiences of the culinary and health approaches they advocate in their own media and in the different kinds of journalism produced about them.

Locating Food Media and Journalism

There is a commonality between perceptions of food, food media texts, and tabloid news: all traditionally have been coded as feminine. Food has been perceived as feminine because the work connected to food—shopping, cooking, and cleaning—has been associated with the domestic or private sphere, and therefore as belonging to women's domain (Beardsworth and Keil 1997; De Vault 1991; Koch 2012; Mennell, Murcott, and van Otterloo 1992). This view overlooks both the fundamentality of food to maintaining life and the "enormous amounts of human energy, ingenuity and co-operative effort [that] are devoted to the processes involved in the production, distribution and preparation of food" (Beardsworth and Keil 1997, 2). Second, clear distinctions have been drawn between the ways women engage with food, defined primarily as the day-to-day work of feeding families, and the ways men engage with food, defined as weekend BBQ or outdoor adventure cooking, occasional helpmate cooking in the home kitchen, or as a creative and professional pursuit (Cairns, Johnston, and Baumann 2010). Like food, food media texts have also been coded as feminine because of their connection to the private sphere and because of their production and distribution primarily in magazines and television, which historically have been associated with women and their domestic concerns and entertainment pastimes, in contrast to newspapers, news magazines, and news programming, which historically have been associated with men and their serious public, political, and economic concerns.

Since James Beard's *I Love to Eat*, the first stand-alone cooking show to be aired on television in the United States (August 1946 to May 1947), food television has combined information and entertainment in the format of how-to programs, travelogues, and more recently reality television competitions (Collins 2009). Outside of television, food has been treated primarily as lifestyle, "news you can use" journalism, with political, economic, and environmental food issues being dealt with by "hard news" journalists. Only recently have hybrid narratives emerged that combine the two, for example in later episodes of Anthony Bourdain's *No Reservations* on CNN where he talked about war, drug addiction, and other violence, in Andrew Zimmern's *What's Eating America* on MSNBC where he explored contemporary challenges in immigration and voting rights through food, and in digital outlets like Eater.com, which publishes both food news and lifestyle journalism side-by-side on its site.

Food media have also been instrumental in the rise of the celebrity chef, a figure that emerged in the late 1980s and early 1990s (Collins 2009; Hansen 2008). Before this, valorization of professional chefs was more commonly ascribed through praise from industry channels like Michelin stars or from cooking for notable members of society or distinguished restaurants (Collins 2009; Hansen 2008). Now, being photogenic, charismatic, and adept at engaging an audience have become important skills for chefs who wish to add food media (news, lifestyle, television, and social media) to their portfolios, an option that has been made increasingly available since the 1990s.

However, it would be naive—and even dangerous—to dismiss even the most seemingly innocuous stories relating to personalities such as Gibson and Evans as inconsequential. Although their rise to prominence comes as part of the celebrification of media (Turner 2016), celebrity television chefs and social media influencers have gained authority among their followers. Even a decade ago, the American Dietetic Association (ADA) (2011) reported that although 71 percent of respondents to its 2011 survey thought that registered dieticians and nutritionists were "'very credible' sources of nutrition information," followed by doctors with 64 percent, the convenience in accessing information in the media meant that 67 percent of respondents received most of their nutrition information from television, followed by 41 percent citing magazines and 40 percent accessing information primarily via the Internet. Contois and Day point to this survey's findings as highlighting "the significant influence of media and popular culture—what can be called broadly the consumer culture—upon food and public health" (Contois and Day 2018, 16).

This influence can be both problematic and constructive. In exploring the intersection between journalism, politics, and entertainment, Harrington (2017) argues that elements of tabloidization whereby news and entertainment become blurred may provide the antidote to some of journalism's shortcomings. When looking at health edutainment, for example, Lindsey-Warren explains that health messages from the Centers for Disease Control and Prevention or pharmaceutical companies leave many in their audience feeling "uninspired and even numb to taking action towards healthier regiments" (Lindsey-Warren 2017, 60) because they hinge on conveying fear and are delivered in alienating forms. She emphasizes the importance of storytelling in this genre, arguing that in order for information to be received and acted upon, it needs to be packaged in narrative forms that employ "engaging/realistic story & plotlines," as well as "authentic/credible characters, educational health messages with values, relevant and empowering tone of voice, and credible production values & source of delivery channel" (Lindsey-Warren 2017, 65).

Although the confluence of health education and entertainment may have productive outcomes, the advent of Web 2.0 and its participatory functions means that published information is often not vetted by experts. In relation to the ADA's (2011) finding that 40 percent of respondents used the Internet as their primary source of nutrition information, ADA spokesperson Jeannie Gazzaniga-Moloo stated that, "Unfortunately, there is less editorial oversight when it comes to the content found on websites and blogs, which leaves room on the internet for the spread of misinformation about nutrition and health" (ADA 2011, 1).

While food-as-entertainment continues to be popular, the formula for how to tell stories about food in entertainment media is expanding, allowing for more "serious" narratives to emerge. In investigating the views and habits of Australian foodies, Isabelle de Solier found that people whose lives were geared to the pursuit of food saw it as "a necessity not a luxury, a need not a want" (de Solier 2013, 15). For example, de Solier interviewed a couple named John and Elena who canceled their subscription to a Melbourne broadsheet newspaper when the weekly food lift-out *Epicure* was incorporated into the newspaper's "Style" section. The couple lamented that food was conflated with fashion rather than being recognized for fulfilling a basic human need (de Solier 2013, 15). Similarly, in examining foodies' television habits de Solier (2008) found that they tended to prefer programs fronted by chefs such as Rick Stein, Kylie Kwong, or Maggie Beer who explored food and culture rather than programs hosted by culinary celebrities such as Jamie Oliver and Nigella Lawson who showcased their private lives and professional brands (de Solier 2008).

Navigating Legitimacy

Pete Evans

Evans and Gibson's relationships with mainstream media affected their trajectories in public life in different ways. Evans mobilized his public profile in his 2017 feature-length documentary *The Magic Pill*, which promoted a ketogenic diet. Evans's status as an outspoken advocate for that diet had been established as early as November 2012 when he was featured in the "My Day on a Plate" profile for *Sunday Life,* a weekend newspaper lifestyle lift-out, in which he encouraged readers to eat meals such as "sprouted millet, sorghum, chia and buckwheat bread, with liver paté, avocado, cultured vegetables, plus ginger and liqorice root tea" (Lees 2012). What gained most media attention and ridicule, however, was his advice to eat activated almonds—almonds that have been soaked in water to ostensibly increase nutritional value and decrease digestive distress. He was pilloried on Twitter with @thecyclingcook tweeting "'Activating your almonds'-- Aussie slang for being a wanker #activatedalmonds" (Starke 2012).

From then on, Evans was considered by many to be eccentric, but still maintained a media profile, continuing as a judge on *My Kitchen Rules* and later starring in *The Magic Pill*, which appeared to be yet another entry in the genre I call Food System Exposés (FSEs) (Kirkwood 2021). This genre encompasses documentary films, non-fiction books, and other media that interrogate various aspects of industrialized food systems, including their health and environmental impacts. Some of the points the documentary makes—that processed foods are harmful, that products labeled "low fat" are not necessarily healthy, and that the interests of food industries don't always align with public health interests—have been explored in other FSEs including *Super Size Me* (2004), *Food Inc.* (2008), and *That Sugar Film* (2014). However, the claims *The Magic Pill* makes for the diet it advocates went too far.

Criticism of *The Magic Pill* was directed at its advocacy for a high-fat diet that excluded grains, legumes, and dairy, and its claims that such a diet had fast-acting positive outcomes for people living with significant health conditions including autism, asthma, diabetes, and cancer. For example, the documentary features five-year-old Abigail Dudley who lives with autism, digestive distress, an inability to speak, and seizures that often number close to 50 a day. Her father Barry appears on camera, explaining how Abigail refused to eat most foods, except Goldfish crackers, Doritos, chicken nuggets, macaroni and cheese, and SpaghettiOs. He laments having to give his daughter strong anti-convulsant drugs that cost more than $300 a month after insurance, as he empties the contents of one of the capsules into a sippy cup of apple juice. He then recalls how after Abigail refused to eat any food for five days, he and his wife Lauren switched to a high-fat diet restricted to meat and vegetables. Abigail slowly embraced the new diet and after five weeks was reported to be calm, able to say basic words, and have improved digestion and fewer seizures.

However, the then-president of the Australian Medical Association (AMA) Dr. Michael Gannon asserted that the idea that such a diet could change Abigail's behavior so quickly was "patently ridiculous" (Price, A. 2017). A year later, Dr. Tony Bartone, who followed Dr. Gannon as AMA President, said Evans's expertise was in the kitchen, and people needed to turn to health professionals like general practitioners for health advice (Carmody 2018). He urged Netflix to stop streaming *The Magic Pill*, acknowledging the role that media can play in the dissemination of accurate—and dangerous—health information: "All forms of media have to take a responsible attitude when trying to spread a message of wellness ... Netflix should do the responsible thing. They shouldn't screen it [*The Magic Pill*]. The risk of information ... is too great" (Carmody 2018).

The Magic Pill followed many of the tropes and high production values of other prominent FSE texts, but, as Dr. Bartone's comment in *The Courier Mail* suggests, Evans's status as a celebrity chef may also have played a role in influencing audiences to follow his advice. But rather than restricting his lifestyle-oriented advice to cooking, Evans's documentary offers advice about how to manage serious health conditions, advice that has been repeatedly challenged by scientists and doctors.

Belle Gibson

In the 18 months during which Belle Gibson enjoyed a large following, her story was disseminated by journalists, television producers, publishers, and tech giants. She appeared on the breakfast television show *Sunrise*, was profiled as *The Most Inspiring Woman You've Met This Year* in *Elle*, and received a Fun Fearless Female award from *Cosmopolitan*. She signed commercial agreements with Penguin and Apple for the publication and development of her *The Whole Pantry* cookbook and app (Donelly and Toscano 2017). But in the aftermath of Donelly and Toscano's (2015) expose, the institutions and publications that perpetuated and legitimized her story came into question almost as much as Gibson herself. In a 2022 episode of their podcast *Maintenance Phase*, journalist Michael Hobbes and author Aubrey Gordon questioned the mainstream media's role in letting Gibson become so prominent and influential. Hobbes asked if Gibson's conduct in lying about her cancer diagnosis and charity contributions was so "fucking obvious, why are you putting her on TV? ... Why were you giving her awards? Why were you not checking this stuff?" (Gordon and Hobbes 2022). They explained why media organizations should not take claims like Gibson's at face value: "[W]hen you are writing for a popular audience, you are duty bound to get it right. The core argument here is, it's popular media, so, what does it matter? No. What we need to be focusing on here is, it's going out on the biggest platform to the widest audience" (Gordon and Hobbes 2022, 43/48).

Evidently, audiences *did* put faith in these media organizations, believing that they had done their due diligence in vetting Gibson's health advice. As Kylie Wyllie, a cancer survivor who appeared in the documentary *Bad Influencer*, stated:

> You didn't even for a second question her because of who supported it, who was backing her. It wasn't just Apple. It was Penguin Books. It was *Cosmopolitan* that had, you know, endorsed her. So I wouldn't have thought it was ever my responsibility to fact check her.
>
> (Wyllie quoted in Desai 2021, 42–43)

Although some organizations, like *Elle Australia* (2015) did issue *mea culpas*, admitting they had dismissed an anonymous e-mail warning them of Gibson's deception as a "bunch of lies," other organizations were not as concerned. Journalist Richard Guilliatt, who had investigated Gibson's claims and appeared on *Bad Influencer,* described how flippant Penguin and Apple had been:

> The biggest publishing company in the world and the biggest computer company in the world had apparently completely failed to do any due diligence on her claims. I mean Penguin admitted to me that they didn't really do any proper fact checking on her medical history. And Apple, when I finally got someone to talk to me, effectively said, well they didn't care about the questions that were being raised about her cancer claim as long as her app worked.
>
> (Desai 2021, 43.47)

Sensational Narratives and Endearing Personalities

Gibson and Evans both epitomize tabloidization as their stories were sensational, dramatic, emotional—and went largely unchecked. They occupied the headlines for vastly different reasons, however. Gibson courted public sympathy as a single mother with her odds-defying battle against brain cancer that had given hope to others, while Evans continued to slip into disrepute, prompting mockery whenever he publicized another controversial approach to health and well-being. Although Gibson and Evans's personas and actions have prompted ongoing interest and scandal in the press, journalists' dismantling of their legitimacy was important in preventing the ongoing spread of misinformation. As this section will highlight, however, in some instances, media outlets were not adequately critical.

Part of what made Gibson's story so remarkable is that she looked vital and well despite the serious illness she claimed to have. In Gibson's February 2014 appearance on Australian breakfast television program *Sunrise,* host Samantha Armytage commented that "for a person living with brain cancer, might I add, you look incredibly healthy" (Sunrise/Seven News 2014). Her appearance, which seemed to give credence to her claims and fueled her popularity, also led partially to her undoing. Journalist Richard Guilliatt saw Gibson's vibrance differently. He commented to his editor, "'look, there's something that just doesn't add up.' I mean, she's claiming that she's got this malignant brain tumor and four other cancers, and she looks like a million dollars" (Desai 2021, 21.33).

In January 2018, after Gibson's deception was uncovered, BBC journalist Kasia Madera interviewed Beau Donnelly and nutritionist Pixie Turner on BBC World News. Madera asked if Gibson's purported brain cancer generated more empathy and interest than that garnered by other similar influencers. Turner's response indicates how powerful Gibson's cancer claims were in heightening her appeal:

> I think so, ... it was definitely something that made her more appealing to listen to because she had this amazing story and that's what made her stand out over a lot of people. She had this sort of compelling narrative that made people much more drawn to her than they would [be to] someone who was simply saying, 'just eat well and you'll live longer'.
>
> (Madera 2018, 3.44)

Even for someone like Turner who is formally educated in nutrition, the allure of a story like Gibson's was irresistible.

In contrast to Gibson, Evans's popularity did not ride on an inspiring personal story, but rather on the spectacle of his promotion of discredited health and nutrition products and practices and COVID-19 conspiracy theories. In April 2020, the Therapeutic Goods Administration (TGA), part of Australia's Department of Health, fined Evans AUD 25,000 for promoting an AUD 15,000 "Bio Charger" lamp via a Facebook Live video that he claimed could be used to combat COVID-19 (Hayes 2020; Therapeutic Goods Administration 2021a). A month later, the TGA issued another nearly AUD 80,000 in fines to Evans for continuing to promote the BioCharger and other devices purported to improve health and well-being that were not approved by the TGA (Therapeutic Goods Administration 2021b).

60 Minutes Australia capitalized on Evans's notoriety by interviewing him as part of its "Mad as Hell" story, which aired on 7 June 2020. Journalist Liz Hayes's (2020, 2.00) segment about those who believed COVID-19 "is nothing more than a sinister plot to control their lives" featured an interview with Evans as well as with anti-lockdown protest leader Fanos Panayides. Their conspiracy theories offered their followers someone to blame for the chaos of the pandemic, while dismissing it as a serious concern. As Nichols argues, such theories can be powerfully persuasive and comforting when people are faced with a dilemma that can only be solved by imagining "a world in which our troubles are the fault of powerful people who had it within their power to avert such misery. ... it is the result of some larger malfeasance by industry or government" (Nichols 2017, 58).

While showing footage of Evans's more mainstream work on *My Kitchen Rules,* Hayes's (2020, 8.30) in a voiceover noted that:

> [f]or a long time now celebrity chef Pete Evans has straddled two very different worlds. To the more than the million and a half people who follow him on social media, he's 'Paleo Pete,' promoting a diet of low carbs, served with a side dish of what he calls 'expanded consciousness,' with a dollop of conspiracy.

When Hayes asked Evans about his views on COVID-19, he replied that he believed the virus was real, but he would not get a vaccine when one became available unless it "was proved to be 100 percent safe for every single man, woman, and child on the face of the planet" (Hayes 2020, 13.35). Evans also relied on emotional appeals, crying as he recounted asking his mother if he and his children could give her a hug, but ended by harnessing the powerful appeal of conspiracy as he looked directly into the camera and said, "If I disappear or have a frickin weird accident, it wasn't an accident, OK?" (Hayes 2020, 22.07).

In different ways, Evans and Gibson's narratives and personalities solicited sympathy and awe, mockery and outrage. They promoted themselves by strategically harnessing emotional stories that exploited hope and fear, and they were helped in their efforts by positive coverage in news, magazines, and other media. Eventually, their deceptions and misleading, even dangerous, claims were covered in the news, but by then much damage had already been done.

Vulnerable Communities

One of the functions of lifestyle media is to provide in an engaging and often entertaining way advice and information that audiences can act upon. What makes Gibson and Evans's stories different from most other food lifestyle and social media influencers is their claim that following their approach to health and nutrition would benefit people living with cancer and chronic health conditions, or—in Evans's case—those who were afraid of contracting COVID-19. More specifically, Gibson claimed to have staved off brain cancer by stopping conventional treatment and relying instead on diet and natural therapies that she promoted and profited from through *The Whole Pantry* app and cookbook. This influenced people living with cancer and other chronic illnesses, such as Maxine Ali and Kylie Wyllie, to change their approaches to treatment, to the detriment of their health. Similarly, through media content like *The Magic Pill*, Evans depicted families claiming to have alleviated or cured symptoms of asthma, autism, and cancer by following a keto diet. In time, these claims were questioned and discredited by news journalists, Gibson's *The Whole Pantry* app and cookbook were removed from sale, and Netflix dropped *The Magic Pill*, but that does not diminish the influence they exerted in the time they enjoyed legitimacy and public respect.

In explaining why they felt so let down by the false claims they encountered—particularly in Gibson's case—individuals who spoke to journalists referred consistently to media platforms that gave people like Gibson widespread visibility and a veneer of legitimacy, and that enabled them to offer false hope to people who had little else left to sustain them. For example, as *60 Minutes* journalist Tara Brown noted,

She was feeding into this sort of conspiracy that modern medicine will fail you, that there is another way. For people who are really, really sick, for people who are dying anyway, offers them some hope, but her way was based on nothing. I mean it was based on taking recipes off the internet and making them her own. It was about—it was talking about the hope of lemons. It just wasn't based on anything.

(Brown, *60 Minutes Australia* 2020, 6.15)

For some who bought Gibson's app or cookbook chasing false hope, Gibson's deceit felt personal. Maxine Ali explained how trying to live with ulcerative colitis and following Gibson's "clean eating" approach resulted in her going through cycles of binge eating, losing her period, feeling run down—and feeling like a failure because her life did not live up to the image that Gibson projected:

I definitely think that there was a frustration that I was doing everything. I was following all the rules. I had books that all these wellness influencers were selling that would help me transform my life and my life didn't look like that. It didn't look that glamorous, or exciting. I just felt like a complete failure.

(Desai 2021, 27.52)

In trying to assign responsibility, Ali looked beyond Gibson to the people and institutions that enabled Gibson to propagate false hope:

I don't feel anger towards Belle in the same way that I do towards the [wellness] industry as a whole. I feel angry at social media for creating this space where misinformation can spread unchecked. I feel angry at the publishers who gave Belle a platform to profit from people's vulnerability.

(Desai 2021, 43.04)

Cancer survivor Kylie Wyllie expressed similar frustrations:

She [Gibson] was saying that what she was doing was curing her cancer. It was making it better. And I had her there to look at. I had her on my phone, and she was in the magazines, and she was on the news, and she was being reported [on] so, I trusted her. I trusted everybody that supported her.

(Desai 2021, 17.34)

Along with the very sick, Evans and Gibson wanted to extend their reach to the very young, and to their parents as well. Evans made headlines in 2015 just before the scheduled publication of a cookbook authored with food blogger and actress Charlotte Carr and nutritionist Helen Padarin. The book, *Bubba*

Yum Yum: The Paleo Way for New Mums, Babies, and Toddlers, drew criticism from experts including then-president of the Public Health Association of Australia Heather Yeatman, who stated that a bone broth recipe in the book contained "10 times the maximum safe daily intake of vitamin A for babies" (Davey 2015). She claimed, "there's a very real possibility that a baby may die if this book goes ahead" (Davey 2015). After this criticism, the trio resorted to self-publishing the book online and in print (Malpass 2015).

Gibson also reached out to Joshua Schwarz, who in 2013 at age five was diagnosed with inoperable brain cancer. Gibson invited the boy and his parents to her son's birthday party, asked friends to cook meals for them, and pledged to raise and donate money for Joshua's care, a pledge that never materialized (Donelly and Toscano 2017). After Gibson's fraud was exposed, the family was met with distrust from their community, who in light of the family's association with the discredited influencer, questioned Joshua's diagnosis, a distrust that increased when the boy defied his doctors' prognosis that he had only four months to live (Donelly and Toscano 2017). Joshua eventually succumbed to the cancer in 2017 at age nine (Douglas 2017; Donelly and Toscano 2017).

Gibson also targeted those who wanted to help others. A key example of this was *The Whole Pantry* app launch in December 2013, which Gibson leveraged as a fundraiser, asking supporters to buy virtual tickets to support various causes including the Asylum Seeker Resource Centre, the Birthing Kit Foundation, and the family of Joshua Schwarz (Donelly and Toscano 2017). Gibson's speech at the launch elicited emotional responses from supporters. Yoga teacher Monica Aurora told Donelly and Toscano, "there were people up at the front fully crying and donating all this money" (Donelly and Toscano 2017, 45). Attendees of a networking event called Fierce Women recounted similar reactions "where the whole room was crying" and were persuaded by Gibson's story (Donelly and Toscano 2017, 49).

While Gibson had convinced these people and many others of her story, her soliciting of money under the pretense of donating it to charities and people in need proved to be her undoing. Donelly and Toscano began investigating her finances; and the Federal Court fined Gibson in response to Consumer Affairs Victoria's civil case for her fraudulent pledges to donate money from events and sales related to *The Whole Pantry,* specifically mentioning pledges made to the Schwarz family.

The false hopes, conspiracy theories, and fear mongering that Evans and Gibson peddled so successfully and for so long demonstrate the serious consequences that lifestyle and social media personalities can have on the lives and well-being of their followers if their claims go unchecked. These two figures enjoyed public adoration and profited from, or sought to profit from, people fighting cancer, people living with chronic illnesses, people who wanted to raise funds for charity, and people who feared COVID-19. It took the investigative journalism of Donelly and Toscano, as well as Richard Guilliatt, to expose Gibson. And in Evans's case, it took fines and rebukes from the TGA and the AMA; severed ties with television network Seven and Ten, publisher Pan Macmillan, and other commercial partners; and bans on Evans's Facebook and Instagram accounts, to stem the flow of dangerous misinformation, at least in more mainstream media outlets.

Conclusions

The cases of Pete Evans and Belle Gibson demonstrate that journalists can and should regularly investigate claims made by food media personalities and social media influencers. This chapter articulates three key reasons why figures such as Gibson and Evans need to be viewed as subjects requiring scrutiny. First, although they were ultimately discredited, they were able to spread harmful messages to vast audiences for a long time. This was enabled by Gibson and Evans's relationship with mainstream media, which allowed them to leverage their ideas with a sense of legitimacy. Evans's standing as a celebrity chef on *My Kitchen Rules* made him a household name with a large following. Furthermore, the high production values of *The Magic Pill* documentary and its adherence to the tropes of the Food System Exposé genre also gave Evans's views an air of legitimacy. Meanwhile Gibson's emergence on social media subsequently propelled her to mainstream popularity through profile pieces in magazines, appearances on breakfast television, and most importantly, deals with publisher Penguin and tech giant Apple for *The Whole Pantry*. Second, both Gibson and Evans were able to hold the attention of audiences because they had sensational narratives; Gibson with her inspiring story of ostensibly overcoming adversity through adopting alternative approaches to treating cancer, and Evans with his skepticism of mainstream science and belief in conspiracy theories, particularly around COVID-19. Lastly, unlike other lifestyle celebrities or influencers, Gibson and Evans's messages targeted vulnerable people living with severe or chronic illnesses, who were scared and searching for hope. The fines leveled at Evans for his promotion of the BioCharger lamp and the distress of people like Maxine Ali who felt like a failure for not feeling better after following Gibson's advice highlight the severity of these fraudulent claims. In focusing on Gibson and Evans, this chapter has made a case for why food media influencers need to be treated by journalists not only as entertaining celebrities, but also as authority figures with real power to influence the health and well-being of their followers, which, as in the case of Gibson and Evans, can number in the hundreds of thousands, even millions.

References

AAP. 2021. "Facebook Deletes Pete Evans's Instagram Account over Repeated Coronavirus and Vaccine Misinformation." *ABC News*, February 17, 2021. https://www.abc.net.au/news/2021-02-17/pete-evans-facebook-deletes-chefs-instagram-account-coronavirus/13164812.

American Dietetic Association. 2011. "Where Did You Hear That? Do You Believe It? American Dietetic Association Survey reveals popularity and perceived credibility of sources of nutrition information." Accessed December 20, 2021. https://www.eatrightpro.org/~/media/eatrightpro%20files/media/trends%20and%20reviews/nutrition%20and%20you/where_did_you_hear_that_ada_trends_2011.ashx.

Australian Good Food guide. n.d. Pete Evans. https://www.agfg.com.au/chef/pete-evans.

Baker, Stephanie Alice and Chris Rojek. 2020. "The Belle Gibson Scandal: The Rise of Lifestyle Gurus in Low-Trust Societies." *Journal of Sociology* 56(3):388–404. 10.1177/1440783319846188.

BBC. 2021. "Pete Evans: Instagram Ban for Australian Chef over Conspiracy Theories." February 21, 2021. https://www.bbc.com/news/world-australia-56095218.

Beardsworth, Alan and Teresa Keil. 1997. *Sociology on the Menu: An Invitation to the Study of Food and Society.* London: Routledge.

Blackiston, Hannah. 2020. "Seven Ends Relationship with Controversial TV Chef Pete Evans." *Mumbrella*, May 8, 2020. https://mumbrella.com.au/seven-ends-relationship-with-controversial-tv-chef-pete-evans-627524.

Brown, Tara (Reporter). 2015. The Whole Hoax [News Story]. In Stephen Taylor & Alice Dalley (Producers), *60 Minutes*. June 28, 2015. Nine Network. https://www.youtube.com/watch?v=tCN2Uvyz72k.

Cairns, Kate, Josée Johnston and Shyon Baumann. 2010. "Caring About Food: Doing Gender in the Foodie Kitchen." *Gender and Society* 24(5):591–615. http://www.jstor.org/stable/25741206.

Carmody, Broede. 2018. "Netflix Urged to Pull Pete Evans Documentary." *Sydney Morning Herald*, June 1, 2018. https://www.smh.com.au/entertainment/tv-and-radio/netflix-urged-to-pull-pete-evans-documentary-20180531-p4zim2.html.

Collins, Kathleen. 2009. *Watching What We Eat: The Evolution of Television Cooking Shows.* New York: Continuum.

Contois, Emily and Anastasia Day. 2018. "The History of Food and Public Health." In *Food and Public Health: A Practical Introduction*, edited by Allison Karpyn, 1–30. New York: Oxford University Press.

Davey, Melissa. 2015. "Pete Evans Paleo for Kids Cookbook Put on Hold amid Health Concerns." *The Guardian*. March 12, 2015. https://www.theguardian.com/australia-news/2015/mar/12/pete-evans-paleo-for-kids-cookbook-put-on-hold-amid-health-concerns.

Davey, Melissa. 2019. "Cancer Con Artist Belle Gibson Quizzed over Failure to Pay $410,000 Fine." *The Guardian*, May 14, 2019. https://www.theguardian.com/australia-news/2019/may/14/cancer-con-artist-belle-gibson-to-have-bank-statements-examined-after-failure-to-pay-410000-fine.

Desai, Ziyaad. (Director). 2021. *Bad Influencer: The Greatest Insta Con* [Film]. Minnow Films.

de Solier, Isabelle. 2008. "Foodie Makeovers: Public Service Television and Lifestyle Guidance." In *Exposing Lifestyle Television: The Big Reveal*, edited by Gareth Palmer, 65–81. Aldershot: Ashgate.

de Solier, Isabelle. 2013. "Making the Self in a Material World: Food and Moralities of Consumption." *Cultural Studies Review* 19(1):9–27.

De Vault, Marjorie. 1991. *Feeding the Family: The Social Organisation of Caring as Gendered Work.* Chicago: University of Chicago Press.

Donelly, Beau and Nick Toscano. 2015. "Charity Money Promised by 'Inspirational' Health App Developer Belle Gibson Not Handed over." *Sydney Morning Herald*. March 8, 2015. https://www.smh.com.au/technology/charity-money-promised-by-inspirational-health-app-developer-belle-gibson-not-handed-over-20150306-13xgqk.html.

Donelly, Beau and Nick Toscano. 2017. *The Woman Who Fooled the World: Belle Gibson's Cancer Con*. Brunswick, Victoria: Scribe Publications. https://qut.primo.exlibrisgroup.com/permalink/61QUT_INST/1g7tbfa/alma991006508739-704001.

Douglas, Peter. 2017. "Josh's Brave Fight Ends." *Ranges Trader*. January 27, 2017. https://rangestrader.mailcommunity.com.au/mail/2017-01-27/joshs-brave-fight-ends/.

Elle Australia. 2015. "What We Know about Belle Gibson." *Elle Australia*, March 13, 2015. https://www.elle.com.au/news/what-we-know-about-belle-gibson-5919.

Fillingham, Hanna. 2019. Jamie Oliver and His Family Prepare to Move House. *HELLO! Magazine*, June 30, 2019. https://www.hellomagazine.com/homes/2019063074782/jamie-oliver-wife-jools-children-move-home-essex/.

Gordon, Aubrey and Michael Hobbes. 2022. "'Illness Influencer' Belle Gibson." *Maintenance Phase*, Feb 1, 2022. [Podcast].

Hansen, Signe. 2008. "Society of the Appetite: Celebrity Chefs Deliver Consumers." *Food Culture and Society* 11(1):49–67. 10.2752/155280108X276050.

Hanusch, Folker. 2013. "Broadening the Focus: The Case for Lifestyle Journalism as a Field of Scholarly Inquiry." In *Lifestyle Journalism*, edited by Folker Hanusch, 1–11. Abingdon: Routledge.

Harrington, Stephen. 2008. "Popular News in the Twenty-First Century: Time for a New Critical Approach?" *Journalism: Theory, Practice and Criticism* 9(3):266–284. 10.1177/1464884907089008.

Harrington, Stephen. 2017. "What if 'Journalism' Is the *Problem?*: Entertainment and the 'De-mediatization' of Politics." In *Entertainment Industries: How Do We Assess Entertainment and Why Does It Matter?*, edited by Stephen Harrington, 165–178. London: Palgrave Macmillan.

Hayes, Liz (Reporter). 2020. Mad as Hell [News Story]. In Garry McNab (Producer), *60 Minutes*, Nine Network. June 6, 2020. https://search.informit-org.ezp01.library.qut.edu.au/doi/10.3316/edutv.5286926.

Hinscliff, Gaby and Amelia Hill. 2005. "Blair Acts on Jamie's Plan for Schools." *The Guardian*, March 20, 2005. https://www.theguardian.com/society/2005/mar/20/childrensservices.food.

Johansson, Sofia. 2008. "Gossip, Sport and Pretty Girls: What Does 'Trivial Journalism Mean to Tabloid Newspaper Readers?'" *Journalism Practice* 2(3):402–413. 10.1080/17512780802281131.

Kirkwood, Katherine. 2021. *"SuperFood Me: Negotiating Australia's Post-Gourmet Food Culture"* PhD diss., QUT ePrints. https://eprints.qut.edu.au/208209/.

Koch, Shelley L. 2012. *A Theory of Grocery Shopping: Food, Choice and Conflict*. Oxford: Berg.

Lees, Philippa. 2012. The Pete Evans Diet Decoder. https://kitchen.nine.com.au/healthy/the-pete-evans-diet-decoder/0fcf035f-84f5-4238-a3e3-b4d047128fc0.

Lewis, Tania. 2008a. "Changing Rooms, Biggest Losers and Backyard Blitzes: A History of Makeover Television in the United Kingdom, United States and Australia." *Continuum* 22(4):447–458. 10.1080/10304310802189949.

Lewis, Tania. 2008b. *Smart Living: Lifestyle Media and Popular Expertise*. New York: Peter Lang.

Lindsey-Warren, Tyrha M. 2017. "Entertainment for the Mind, Body and Spirit." In *Entertainment Values: How Do We Assess Entertainment and Why Does It Matter?*, edited by Stephen Harrington, 59–69. London: Palgrave Macmillan.

Madera, Kasia. 2018. *Beau Donelly & Pixie Turner Talking to Kasia Madera about Belle Gibson* [Video]. YouTube. https://www.youtube.com/watch?v=nKT5bqHwwdY.

Malpass, Luke. 2015. "Chef Pete Evans to Self-Publish Baby Paleo Book." *Sydney Morning Herald*. March 17, 2015. https://www.smh.com.au/national/pete-evans-paleo-book-for-babies-dumped-20150316-1m0805.html.

Mennell, Stephen, Anne Murcott, and Anneke H. van Otterloo. 1992. *The Sociology of Food: Eating, Diet and Culture*. London: SAGE.

Nichols, Tom. 2017. *The Death of Expertise: The Campaign against Established Knowledge and Why It Matters*. New York: Oxford University Press.

Ouellette, Laurie and James Hay. 2008. *Better Living through Reality TV: Television and Post-Welfare Citizenship*. Malden, MA: Blackwell Publishing.

Percy, Karen. 2017. "Belle Gibson, Fake Wellness Blogger, Fined $410,000 over False Cancer Claims." *ABC News*, September 28, 2017. https://www.abc.net.au/news/2017-09-28/disgraced-wellness-blogger-belle-gibson-fined/8995500.

Price, Amy. 2017. "Pete Evans' Documentary about the Benefits of the Paleo Diet Has Been Slammed." *The Courier Mail*, August 2, 2017. https://www.couriermail.com.au/lifestyle/food/qld-taste/pete-evans-documentary-about-the-benefits-of-the-paleo-diet-has-been-slammed/news-story/53581c96d5ecc7a927b2189d745c9376.

Price, Hannah. 2021. "Belle Gibson: The Influencer Who Lied about Having Cancer." *BBC Three*. July 9, 2021. https://www.bbc.co.uk/bbcthree/article/b2538e04-87f5-4af5-bd6f-f6cf88b488c4.

Rojek, Chris. 2001. *Celebrity*. London: Reaktion Books.

Rousseau, Signe. 2012. *Food Media: Celebrity Chefs and the Politics of Everyday Interference*. London: Bloomsbury.

Senft, Theresa M. 2013. "Microcelebrity and the Branded Self." In *A Companion to New Media Dynamics*, edited by John Hartley, Jean Burgess and Axel Bruns, 346–354. Malden, MA: John Wiley & Sons.

Sunrise/Seven News. 2014. Belle Gibson Talks about Creating the World's First Health, Wellness and Lifestyle App. [Video]. https://www.news.com.au/lifestyle/health/health-problems/belle-gibson-cancer-confession-sparks-fury/news-story/f36ec9dbd6db79c6c8c97da162fe3444.

Starke, Petra. 2012. "Social Media Buzzing with Talk of Activated Almonds." *news.com.au*. November 5, 2012. https://www.news.com.au/lifestyle/food/activated-almonds-line-lights-up-twittersphere/news-story/34f25c3167e842b8e389486d11-53c201.

Therapeutic Goods Administration. 2020a. "Pete Evans' Company Fined for Alleged COVID-19 Advertising Breaches." https://www.tga.gov.au/media-release/pete-evans-company-fined-alleged-covid-19-advertising-breaches.

Therapeutic Goods Administration. 2020b. "Peter Evans Chef Pty Ltd Fined $79,920 for Alleged Unlawful Advertising." https://www.tga.gov.au/media-release/peter-evans-chef-pty-ltd-fined-79920-alleged-unlawful-advertising.

Turner, Graeme. 2016. *Re-inventing the Media*. Abingdon: Routledge.

Wilson, Cam. 2020. "Pete Evans' Publisher Says It Is 'Finalising' Its Relationship with the High-Profile Conspiracy Theorist amid His Increasingly Extreme Social Media Posts." *Business Insider Australia*. November 16, 2020. https://www.businessinsider.com.au/pete-evans-pan-macmillan-finalising-relationship-conspiracy-theories-2020-11.

60 Minutes Australia. 2020. *What It Was Like to Interview "Cancer Fraudster" Belle Gibson | 60 Minutes Australia* [Video]. YouTube. https://www.youtube.com/watch?v=jRtnPFosuEg.

Part III
Negotiating Regional, National, and Global Identities

8 Of Clay Stoves and Cooking Pots: "Village Food" Videos and Gastro-Politics in Contemporary India

Sumana Kasturi

A slight woman walks through the woods with her sickle and basket. The light filters through the leaves overhead as she delicately snips off long tendrils of pumpkin vines and forages for wild mushrooms. Under the thatched roof of a tiny veranda, she cooks the mushrooms and pumpkin leaves in a wide iron *kadai* and serves it on a flat metal plate, some version of which is used in homes across India. The dish might seem like something served at a high-end restaurant, but is in fact the lunchtime fare of a tribal woman in rural Bengal. The YouTube video depicting this scene has attracted 1.1 million views on a channel with nearly 700,000 subscribers.

This chapter examines a trend in Indian food media called "village food" that has emerged as a popular category on YouTube. The category comprises videos from across India of people cooking traditional recipes on clay stoves and wood fires in village settings. The 106-year-old great-grandmother, the tribal woman, the village housewife, and the feisty grandfather and his grandsons, are some of those cooking for their families or for charity on video, as they showcase their skills and local specialties garnering views in the thousands and even millions.

In this chapter, I offer an introduction to food traditions and contemporary gastro-politics in India. I examine how globalization and migration expand the range of understandings of "Indian food" and conversely work to create both a national cuisine and greater visibility for regional food cultures. I then discuss the role of social media platforms that allow ordinary people to participate in online food cultures to create alternative culinary publics to those represented in legacy media. Finally, I analyze a sample of YouTube "village cooking" channels to contextually and theoretically situate them within the Indian foodscape. Steeped in the everyday rituals of village life and generational domesticity, these YouTubers offer an alternative to urban food consumption patterns, focusing on local foods, simple tools of preparation, and ancient methods of cooking. I argue that these village chefs provide a grounding counterpoint to the spectacle of celebrity cooking and form a valuable archive of culinary practices with cultural, ecological, and political implications for contemporary food discourse.

DOI: 10.4324/9781003283942-12

Food and Foodways of India

The foodways of India have been the subject of academic study and popular interest for decades. In South Asia, food plays a strong affective and symbolic role, especially given the regional, religious, and caste-specific norms that control everyday food practices. While this is common in many cultures, it becomes particularly contentious and deep-rooted in historically agrarian societies such as India (and South Asia in general) where grain, and by extension, all food, holds a deep social, economic, and religious significance. Thus food – its production, preparation, and consumption – becomes both the commodity of economic stratification, as well as the symbol of social stratification.

Khare (2012) has noted that traditional Indian approaches to food locate food distribution and sharing patterns within frameworks of spirituality and religion, health and ecology, and caste and kinship. While previous anthropological studies have taken a caste-focused approach (Dumont 1970; Marriott 1968), Khare suggests that a true understanding of Indian foodways requires us to look beyond this framework, and he has shown that material cultures and food practices are governed as much by regional practices and universal value systems as by caste-based rules. He notes that ecological factors such as rain or drought, as well as economic and political changes, result in a social life that is dynamic rather than static, forcing the population to reconfigure consumption patterns based on scarcity or abundance. Most importantly, he found that certain common or everyday rules and values of eating, sharing, and feeding – *sahaj dharma* – were often more strongly implicated in food consumption patterns than caste-based rules alone (Khare 2012, 245). Thus, he argues that caste rules are only one factor in determining foodways, showing how regional, linguistic, and religious-ritualistic-philosophical affinities can also play a role.

It is traditional in Hindu communities to offer food to the gods first before serving it to one's self or others (called *prasadam*), thus blessing the food. This hierarchy between man and god is further established along a food chain that governs who is in a position to offer food, and who is in a position to accept that food. These rules are further complicated by the gendered nature of *all* food-based transactions. No matter their position in the caste and class hierarchy, urban or rural, of different regional and religious dispositions, women tend to bear the burden of producing, procuring, and preparing food, especially in the domestic environment (Katrak 2014, 263–266).

This underlying logic, along with a highly stratified and elaborate system of rules and conventions, regulates a hierarchy of foods, cuisines, and castes that continues to pervade Indian eating habits at various levels of society. Appadurai (1981) argues that beliefs about food in India, especially among Hindu communities, encode a complex set of socio-economic and cultural propositions imbued with "moral and cosmological meanings" (Appadurai

1981). The gods and men come together to produce food, the former by bestowing rainfall and appropriate ecological conditions, and the latter by their labor. Appadurai also explains how in this highly contentious, socio-religious context, food can serve two diametrically opposed functions: on the one hand it can serve to signify a social relation of equality, intimacy, and solidarity; on the other hand, it can serve to reinforce or create a hierarchy of rank, distance, and segmentation. The semiotic outcome of these food-related social interactions depends on the particular food, the actors involved, and the context and audience of their interactions (Appadurai 1981, 495–496). In the ensuing section, we will see how these opposing factors play out in a contemporary food landscape.

Gastro-Politics in Contemporary India

Food evokes strong emotions and contributes to our sense of belonging and rootedness, nostalgia, and identity. It therefore has semiotic power that can be deployed in positive and negative ways to evoke a range of visceral emotions. Thus, food has often been used by astute public figures to stir up emotions and to intensify feelings of inclusion and exclusion.

Gastro-politics can be defined as "conflict or competition over specific cultural or economic resources as it emerges in social transactions around food" and can arise "when food is manipulated to carry messages between actors who, though they share the fundamental meanings of the system, are engaged in a struggle over the particular syntagmatic chain of food events in which they are involved" (Appadurai 1981, 494–497). The growing, cooking, sharing, and consuming of food simultaneously represents the most banal, yet also some of the most intimate and affective aspects of our everyday lives. Food and food habits act as powerful semiotic symbols within the Indian social context, and cultural battles over food continue to animate the Indian public sphere (e.g., Sanghvi 2019). Recent events have highlighted politically motivated cultural struggles over issues such as vegetarianism, the consumption of beef, and the construction of popular foods such as biryani (a spicy rice and meat dish) as un-Indian (Trivedi 2020). The scattered and seemingly innocuous reports about food-related events in Indian media – print, television, and social media – create an overarching narrative of a national cuisine, and a homogeneity of food consumption that is belied by research that shows a wide diversity of food practices even within specific regional, caste, or faith-based social groups (e.g., Natrajan and Jacob 2018, 54).

For example, India has a historically long tradition of vegetarianism, related especially to practitioners of Hinduism and Jainism, and vegetarian food is widely available across the country. Within the country, it has moral-ethical implications, while for the non-Indian, the practice of vegetarianism (along with other Indian cultural traditions such as yoga and meditation) has gained greater visibility and popularity in recent decades and has largely health-related (and some ethical) associations. As such, vegetarianism is widely associated with India and accepted as a customary dietary practice all over the country.

Nevertheless, statistically, vegetarianism is a food culture largely restricted to certain upper castes. An analysis of large-scale survey data (including government surveys) to study food habits in India found that while government data showed that less than 25 percent of Indians are vegetarian, other estimates indicated the percentage of vegetarians as closer to 20 percent as Indians tend to under-report meat-eating (Natrajan and Jacob 2018, 62). Yet, vegetarianism in India is often conflated with national identity (Biswas 2018). Whereas being vegetarian is associated with ethical eating practices and animal rights issues, and therefore considered a liberal cause in the West, the association of vegetarianism with dominant caste practices, and the cultural politics that denigrate meat-eaters have made the matter a conservative issue in India (Sathyamala 2019, 879).

Another instance of gastro-politics is the public rhetoric over beef-eating. While beef is considered taboo for Hindus, India has always had beef eaters among certain Hindu caste groups, Dalits, and those of other faiths. The above-cited study found that according to government surveys the extent and prevalence of beef-eating among communities was higher than that suggested by stereotypes and public claims by political and religious figures. Further, it was found that meat-eating habits were significantly gendered within social and regional groups, making generalized claims about food habits even more problematic (Natrajan and Jacob 2018, 55). Socio-political agendas that seek to elevate dominant caste narratives and alienate or segregate non-Hindus, Dalits, and tribal groups, have turned beef consumption into a weapon. Despite there being no constitutional stipulations regarding food choices, there have been reports of vigilante groups violently attacking individuals, households, and businesses they suspect of selling or consuming the meat. Media-reported incidents include harassment, social discrimination, beatings, and even a lynching, while observers believe that many more instances go unreported. In recent years, 30 Indian states have instituted a ban on the transport, export, sale, and consumption of beef that has been called out as discriminatory (Mangaldas 2017).

Other food battles periodically enter the public discourse, such as the origins and implications of the popular rice dish biryani. Historically, the dish has been served at weddings, political rallies, and other contexts where large numbers of people need to be fed, as the combination of rice, meat, and vegetables is tasty and convenient to cook and serve to crowds. Recently, the dish has been reframed in some media outlets as un-Indian and anti-national, and it has been used to criticize participants in events such as the Shaheen Bagh protests in Delhi (December 15, 2019–March 24, 2020) and the farmers' protests in North India (September 2020–November 2021) (Joshi 2020; Zargar 2021).

Even as Indian "peasant food" has achieved a level of global visibility and legitimacy (e.g., Pillai 2021), gastro-politics in India continue to roil in places as diverse as college campuses and office cafeterias. The pitched battles over foodways and the tacit approval by authorities of the imposition of dominant food cultures symbolize an exercise of power, and a conscious deployment of food's semiotic ability to enhance segmentation and emphasize social rank, thereby conveying distance and exclusion.

Social Media and Online Food Cultures

The enormous popularity and accessibility of social media platforms have created a great deal of academic interest in the role of digitality in our everyday lives. Digital media play a role in our engagement with everything from politics to personal relationships, from the nature of work to the value of parenting, from social justice and activism to consumption practices and lifestyle choices. Bruns notes that "there can be little doubt that social media are having a profound impact on social processes, from political debate to everyday communication and from the media ecology to the national economy" (Bruns 2015, 2).

As digital interactions have colonized our everyday routines, perhaps the most visible aspect is in the realm of food. The proliferation of online grocery and restaurant delivery services, the plethora of cooking instructions from professional chefs and home cooks via videos and blogs, and the emergence of online food activism offer glimpses into the myriad ways in which the digital has transformed our everyday relationship with food (Lupton 2020, 1–16). Niche food blogs, stylized Instagram photos, pithy Twitter quotes, and food videos from the sophisticated to the amateur, apps that connect us to the farmer, the grocer, and the activist – social media platforms and their "producers" (Bruns 2008, 2–3) are at the center of it all.

Scholars have observed the connection of food consumption patterns and the emergence of "foodie culture" to other transnational lifestyles and consumer choices (Amit 2007; Raman and Kasturi 2016), and the digital has played a key role in the growth of this phenomenon. Tania Lewis notes the growing participation of non-professionals and amateurs in online food cultures and sounds the call to pay attention to the "cultural economies of participation" (Lewis 2018, 213). Research has also documented the rise of digital food activism (Schneider et al. 2018) and the greater visibility of environmental, animal rights, and anti-corporate viewpoints that were previously at the margins of mainstream discourse (Phillipov and Kirkwood 2018). Simultaneously, the entrance of food corporations and agri-businesses into the digital food domain as well as the increasing monetization of digital food content has been analyzed (Goodman and Jaworska 2020; Lewis and Phillipov 2018). Where some studies have considered digital food media as culinary artifacts that share essential cultural knowledge, such as "home cooking" food blogs (Kasturi 2019) and "Asian Aunty" food videos (Seid 2018), others have examined digital food media to identify potential sources of bias and consequent misinformation (Steils and Obaidalahe 2020).

Indian Food Media and Digital Foodscapes

In India, a surprise appearance by opposition politician Rahul Gandhi on the popular Village Cooking Channel showed him cooking and eating a "Mushroom Biryani" with the villagers. The dish was likely chosen as a popular, and uncontroversial version of the spiced rice beloved across India, and boosted both the channel's and the politician's ratings. The video went viral and helped the channel earn the coveted Diamond Creator Award from YouTube in July 2021 for reaching 10 million subscribers.

Traditional food media in India tend to be occupied by those who have the social and economic capital to set themselves up as experts in the field. While cookbooks are produced by a range of writers from different regions and faiths, their authors tend to be from upper-class backgrounds (Appadurai 1988, 5–7). Indian television has not historically had the kind of dedicated space for food programming that is so popular in many other countries, but there has been a gradual increase over the past 20 years in television shows that center on food, including food and travel shows, recipe shows with celebrity chefs (largely male), cooking segments on "women's shows," and most recently MasterChef-style game shows. So it is no surprise that the ease of access to social media platforms has resulted in an explosion of food content from India. An important component among the wide array of digital food media are food videos, thousands of which are uploaded by users onto video-sharing platforms such as YouTube every day. However here, too, class and caste privilege often dominate, as a majority of content producers tend to be upper caste men and women from largely urban, middle, and upper-class backgrounds. This is in keeping with findings from other parts of the world where studies have found that social media influencers and food celebrities tend to be from privileged backgrounds (Perrier and Swan 2020, 129; Goodman and Jaworska 2020, 183).

Over the last few years, increased Internet expansion into rural areas as well as greater access to smartphones has allowed a previously marginalized section of Indians to access social media and consume the varied user-generated content it has to offer. In turn, this greater exposure along with the increasing accessibility and affordability of technology and internet connections has allowed a new class of people to tell their stories and share their own content.

The Visual and Narrative Vocabulary of Village Food Videos

Deftly weaving bucolic rural settings, local and unusual ingredients, and an upbeat presentation style, the village food video seems determined to bring Indian "village cooking" out from the shadows and into the light of a global audience. These videos have developed a unique visual vocabulary, one that stands apart from the more mainstream celebrity chef videos, amateur home cooking videos, street food, and mukbang (eating) videos that have tended to dominate the food video world thus far.

In one popular video released in 2017, then 106-year-old Mastannamma – perhaps the world's oldest YouTuber (Schultz 2018) – shows off a giant emerald-colored egg. The camera follows her movements as she prepares her ingredients, slicing onions and green chillies on her *katti peeta* and cracking the emu egg into the *kadai*. She proceeds to cook as she chats with her grandson about her precious emu and her recent birthday party. Since her debut at age 105 on YouTube, she has become famous and has received greetings from all over the world. The 15-minute video is simple, unassuming, and seemingly unrehearsed. The locale is rustic and the participants (Mastannamma, her daughter, and her grandson) seem completely at ease in their environment. The mood is quiet and intimate, a family meal enjoyed under the shade of a tree. The cameraperson changes angles a few times, but there is no attempt to "dress up" the participants, the props, the production value, or the location. The video, released in 2017, has since attracted more than 3.3 million views and 2,500 comments.

In another video, "Grandpa" Narayan Reddy of *Grandpa Kitchen* smiles widely as he shows his viewers how to make "traditional mutton biryani," a regional specialty made with goat meat and rice. The production values are simple, yet professional, with a Steadicam following the action in candid camera style. In contrast to Mastannamma's videos, the mood here is celebratory and expansive. Grandpa cooks huge cauldrons of food, which his grandsons serve to the poor, or to children from a nearby orphanage. Where Mastanamma's videos have the atmosphere of an intimate family meal, Grandpa's videos have the upbeat vibe of a celebration, a feast. Clearly, his viewers are enjoying the feasting: some of his videos have 30 million views to date. Goodman and Jaworska posit that social media influencers contribute to building a set of norms and practices that emerge not from a single elevated authority but from the "decentralized interactions of agents" (2020, 184). This is evident in these village food videos, allowing us to identify a set of visual and narrative markers that indicate the recurring tropes and themes of this genre.

For the study on which this chapter is based, I selected an initial sample of 50 village food videos from different channels and in different languages for a preliminary analysis in order to draw out a general framework of tropes and narrative elements. Next, I selected five channels (Grandpa Kitchen, Village Cooking – Kerala, Anitaji ka Kitchen, Nawabs Kitchen, and Village Cooking Review/Tribal Foods) for deeper textual analysis to identify some of the dominant themes that played out in these alternate food narratives (Table 8.1).

The initial analysis revealed six basic recurring tropes. Each trope included a set of elements that together created a visual vocabulary that familiar viewers could recognize. While some elements were universal to all the videos, others appeared in particular combinations. The six tropes

Table 8.1 Particulars of Sample "Village Food Channels"

YouTube channels	Tropes	Language	Statistics (average numbers for views and comments on popular videos)	Other platforms
Grandpa Kitchen	Rural setting; Grandfather character; Spectacle cooking; feeding the poor	Telugu and English	9.23 million subscribers, between 3 and 30 million views, 1000–2500 comments	Facebook and Patreon
Village Cooking – Kerala	Grandmother character; Rural setting; Family meal	Malayalam	744,000 subscribers, between 1 and 2 million views, 1000–2000 comments	Website, Facebook, Instagram, and Pinterest
Anitaji ka Kitchen	Homemaker/ mother; rural setting; family meal	Hindi	396,000 subscribers, 1–2 million views, 1000–1500 comments	YouTube "life vlog," Facebook, and Instagram
Nawabs Kitchen	Young father; rural setting; Spectacle cooking; feeding the poor	Urdu and English	2.37 million subscribers, 5–12 million views, 8000–13,000 comments	Website, Facebook, Twitter, Instagram, and Patreon
Village Cooking Review (Tribal foods)	Rural, intimate, features mainly women	Bengali	597,000 subscribers, 1M–2M views on select videos, 300–500 comments	None

include rural village settings, traditional methods using local ingredients, grandmother trope, grandfather trope, spectacle cooking, and intimate home cooking.

Rural Village Setting

The "rural village" setting was universal and vital to every video, since it acts as the identifying visual marker for this genre. The videos are often shot in a courtyard, backyard, or verandas of small houses – ranging from mud huts to simple brick-and-mortar dwellings. Backdrops vary from lush fields to shady groves. The central actor may walk through a field, a vegetable garden, or forage in the woods or ponds. There may be more than one participant in the video, helping the main actor with collecting and preparing ingredients, and then sharing the food after it's cooked. The participants are dressed in their everyday clothes; no artfully arranged backdrops, stylish costumes, make-up, or props, which have become ubiquitous on social media, are visible. The setting appears humble and authentic, lacking artifice or theatricality. It provides an appropriate and comforting backdrop for unassuming local dishes made with locally available, honest ingredients.

Traditional Methods and Local Ingredients

Many of the videos present indigenous, regional dishes made with locally available, unprocessed ingredients. Purple eggplants, bright green chillies, and whole fish, as well as hyper-local ingredients such as snails and eels, morel mushrooms and quail eggs, are all featured in these videos. The actors take their time preparing the ingredients – washing the vegetables, scaling the fish, chopping large quantities of onions, tomatoes, and chillies. The food is usually cooked on a wood fire using small clay or iron stoves or a large campfire. The cooking implements are basic: a *katti peeta*, wooden spoons, battered metal pots, and *kadais*. This cooking is traditional and nostalgic – tapping into the worldwide comforting appeal of the cooking of "our grandmothers."

The Grandmother

The village grandmother trope seems to have emerged from the global fascination with "grandma's cooking" videos – from Mexico to Italy, from Illinois to Andhra Pradesh. These women share traditional and old family recipes and have become a hugely popular trope of food videos. The Indian grandmothers range from the feisty village great-grandmother and the tribal elder to the quietly elegant small town "grannies" from Punjab, Kerala, or Gujarat. Their settings are scattered around the country, their circumstances are varied, and their cooking repertoires are wide. Most "grandmother videos" tend to feature family meals rather than charity cooking.

The Grandfather

The grandfather trope is distinctly different from the grandmother trope in this YouTube vertical, but just as popular. The videos feature a smiling and often flamboyant older man as the master cook, assisted by sons or grandsons. Preparing, cooking, and serving is usually an all-male effort. Other features are the enormous quantities of food prepared, and the charitable giving. The food is served to the poor, usually children at an orphanage or local school.

Spectacle Cooking

In this trope, the emphasis is on quantity, and the recipe becomes secondary. Sometimes the name of an ingredient being used may be superimposed on the screen; at other times, the cook may use either his native language or very simple English to give brief, one-sentence explanations. Enormous amounts of the chosen dish are cooked, and a key part of the appeal of the video is the performance of this large-scale cooking process – tubs full of vegetables, huge platters of glistening meats, sometimes a whole goat, or a large fish. These videos always have at least three actors to prepare and cook the food on large campfire-style wood fires, and in enormous pots and pans. The scale of cooking is that of a feast and the mood is similarly upbeat, and often boisterous. Spectacle cooking is also accompanied by "feeding the poor," a form of charitable giving that is traditional in India.

Intimate Home Cooking

In contrast to spectacle cooking, this trope takes a more intimate approach. The dishes cooked may be elaborate and require multiple steps of preparation, or they may be very simple and focus on putting together an everyday family meal. The quantities cooked are small, meant for four or five family members. Here too, the ingredients are local, the implements are basic, and the housewife or young farmer walks through gardens and backyards picking vegetables to cook for their families. Sometimes the actor – a man or woman – may look into the camera and talk directly to the viewer, but just as often, the camera takes a fly-on-the-wall approach and simply follows the actors as they go about their tasks. There are more close-up shots than in videos featuring spectacle cooking, and the video conveys an overall sense of quiet and calm.

Creating Subaltern Culinary Counterpublics

With their rural, idealized settings, candid camera visuals, and quirky village characters, the "village food" videos convey an immediacy and authenticity that is hard to resist. Where food blogs by suburban women from India and the diaspora contribute to a narrative that promotes Indian cooking as a global haute cuisine (Hegde 2014) and transnational practice (Kasturi 2019), and home-cooking and chef videos perform a similar function, these village food videos take the narrative in a different direction altogether, creating counterpublics that open up the public sphere to marginalized groups and enabling the dissemination of alternative discourses.

In her critique of the Habermasian notion of the public sphere, Nancy Fraser argues that in a stratified society, equality of participation in the public sphere is impossible as dominant groups will have a greater advantage, and that "a plurality of competing publics (will) better promote the ideal of participatory parity" (Fraser 1990, 66). This allows a multiplicity of voices and stories to occupy the public sphere, jostling for space with more dominant mainstream voices and providing greater opportunity for a more equitable public sphere. She coins the term "subaltern counterpublics" to describe the multiple counterpublics formed by marginalized social groups that may "invent and circulate counter discourses to formulate oppositional interpretations of their identities, interests, and needs" (1990, 67). By creating alternate or oppositional spaces for discourse, these subaltern counterpublics elicit challenges to and allow for ruptures in the dominant narrative. This concept has been extended to the specificities of oppression within Indian society to describe digital Dalit counterpublics that have permitted oppressed castes to defy dominant caste narratives and create oppositional narratives that resist caste-based discrimination (Thakur 2020, 360–361; Vrikki and Malik 2019, 273).

In sharing their local food practices through the particularized vocabulary of the village food videos described in this chapter, I argue that the "village food" YouTube videos play an important role in countering the exclusionary food narratives circulating in the Indian public sphere and act as culinary subaltern counterpublics. Several themes emerge from the analysis.

Nostalgia and Authenticity

One of the recurring themes that Indian digital foodscapes evoke is that of nostalgia, recalling memories of family, home, and a sense of rootedness. Indian food blogs build this connection through storytelling, photos, and recipes (Kasturi 2019, 141–144), while the village food videos convey this through their village settings, the actors (grandparents, housewives, tribal women, or farmers), and the dishes they cook. We see the rural housewife walking through her vegetable garden as she ponders what she will cook for her family that day, the tribal women searching for snails in the pond, and the village grandmother and grandfather presiding over lunch with family members.

The trope of the grandmother and grandfather also work in a similar way, emphasizing a connection to home and childhood, and making the viewer feel connected to the elderly person on the screen. The setting and the protagonist elicit warm feelings of home and family, and a nostalgia for a time or an experience that may be real or imagined. The grandmother videos allow us to experience these feelings vicariously while turning these humble grandmas into YouTube stars. Perhaps as a reminder of lost days with our own grandmothers, or perhaps as a way to connect with something that feels warm and caring, these videos garner thousands of views from across the world. Khare notes how globalization, migration, and modernity have rekindled an interest in food, health, and the quality of life, deepening a need for "authentic grandmother- or mother-cooked meals" (Khare 2012, 249). As journalist Luke Winkie explains,

> It makes me think we need more grandmas on YouTube. Both of mine are gone, which means I'll never be able to experience the fussiness of (my grandmother) on a Thanksgiving afternoon ever again. Thankfully I have … a surrogate abuelita, who brings a generational knowhow that somehow transcends language and makes me feel safe and warm thousands of miles away.
>
> (Winkie 2019, para 5)

It is worth noting here that while this sample of food videos breaks some gender norms with men and women cooks fairly equally represented, intimate family cooking videos are dominated by women while spectacle cooking is dominated by men. When it comes to professional cooking, it is men who are the "chefs" and women who are merely the "cooks" (Herkes and Redden 2017, 125). The images of the genial grandfather, the sweet-faced housewife, and the young farmer cooking in their rural domestic spaces, work to evoke authenticity and nostalgia for an "imagined" simpler life, a back-to-basics, traditional lifestyle that seems pristine and uncomplicated, with everyone knowing their clearly defined roles and place.

Indigenous and Hyper-Local Recipes and Cuisines

Omanamma is a star in her village of Pothupara (in Kerala, a state in South-Western India) and on YouTube. Her channel, run by two young nephews, features a range of local village recipes cooked in the distinctive brass and clay pots of the region. Her recipes are based on ingredients that are hyper-local: tapioca skin, jackfruit seeds, banana stem, as well as local fish and meats such as sardine, mackerel, pearlspot, and mutton and beef. A popular recipe on her channel features two unusual ingredients not often seen in mainstream Indian food media: beef and tapioca. There is very little conversation, and no background music, just ambient sounds like spices being ground or the searing sound of meat hitting a hot pan. Her movements are spare and efficient and she rarely looks at the camera. Brief instructions in English or Malayalam are overlaid on the video. She speaks rarely, and only in Malayalam, the local language spoken in Kerala, but her content appears to transcend ethnic, regional, and language barriers to garner hundreds and sometimes thousands of viewers and comments.

Anita is a homemaker in an unidentified village somewhere in the Hindi-speaking belt of North India. In her videos, she shares local recipes, as well recipes of popular foods from around the country. In one video, she shares her recipe for *patod*, a dolma-like dish made by stuffing, rolling, and steaming *arbi* leaves, a local plant of the *Colocasia esculenta* species. She uses a pumpkin vine to tie the packages closed and demonstrates her steaming technique using twigs and a wide *kadai*. In another video she cooks "snail curry," a traditional village food. As she boils and prepares the snails, she explains that they are considered good for eye health and laments the fact that her children refuse to eat them.

Food Studies scholar Krishnendu Ray draws on Heidegger to emphasize the value of "the non-theoretical, pre-reflective knowledge of carpenters, cooks, poets, and philosophers ... by re-valorizing implicit everyday forms of knowing that are not easily amenable to explication" (Ray 2016, 23). These kinds of videos act as valuable culinary artefacts of localized, traditional cooking ingredients, techniques, and knowledge systems that may be otherwise lost in a rapidly urbanizing and homogenizing food world, and work to "re-valorize" these practices across generations.

Upending the Hierarchies of Taste

In his work on ethnic restaurants in the United States, Krishnendu Ray describes the concept of the "global hierarchy of taste" (2016) wherein the value of a cuisine depends on the economic and military power that a country wields in the world. This hierarchy privileges powerful nations and their cultures and cuisines as more valuable than that of countries with less economic capital. Extending this idea to the cultural politics of taste within a country, one can see how the foods and eating habits of dominant caste and class groups rate higher in the national hierarchy of taste, while devaluing the food habits of lower castes and classes.

This dynamic can be identified in Indian public discourse where vegetarianism is portrayed as ideal, and upper caste foods are normalized as desirable and healthy. Within the enormous range of non-vegetarian foods, a similar hierarchy is imposed, this time in terms of foods to be avoided, where beef (avoided by upper caste Hindus) is the most taboo, followed by pork (avoided by observant Muslims), and other meats such as offal or eels and snails are represented as the most undesirably strange. This ranking renders mutton (in India "mutton" refers to goat meat), chicken, and fish as the least objectionable meats and therefore most mainstream and normal. The disagreements over biryani's true origins, the value of vegetarianism, and the escalation of intolerance against beef consumption, all show how gastro-politics work in the struggle over defining nationhood, citizenship, and identity.

By documenting and displaying these often vilified food traditions, the village food videos are presenting foods and food habits that have been marginalized, dismissed, or made invisible as they do not fit into the mold of mainstream foodways. Tapioca and taro leaves, pumpkin vines and wild mushrooms, snails, eels, and beef fry, are now given an opportunity for their 15 minutes (and more) of fame thanks to these feisty, unabashed videos.

Building Solidarity, Equality, and Intimacy

When we recognize the powerful affective quality of food, we see how it can be deployed in building both solidarity and division within a group. Appadurai argues that food can perform two diametrically opposed functions: it can signify a social relation of "equality, intimacy, and solidarity" or it can reinforce a hierarchy of "rank, distance or segmentation" (1981, 507).

Just as with the battles over biryani and beef, other kinds of food habits have been used to mark certain populations within India as outsiders and second-class citizens. The cultural politics of food traditions can reinstate a hierarchy of social and economic status that legitimizes certain castes and communities as superior and others as inferior, thereby creating distance and constructing a perception of the "other." The village videos work to disrupt this political narrative by sharing recipes, not just of their own communities, but also those of other communities. For instance, some of the beef and pork recipes shared on the village food channels are common to different faiths, showing how certain food habits are not exclusive to specific groups. The dozens of biryani recipes from around the country, cooked by villagers of all religions, counter the political positioning of it as a foreign food. By sharing their cooking and eating rituals with the world, and by inviting viewers into their houses and village greens to (virtually) partake of family meals and community feasts, these YouTubers are building intimacy, and affiliation, showing solidarity and inadvertently working towards greater equality for marginalized communities in India.

Globalization and Capturing the Diasporic Imaginary

When US Vice-presidential candidate Kamala Harris sought to highlight her Indian roots and reach out to the Indian American population, she appeared in a food video with comedian Mindy Kaling, whose parents emigrated from India to the United States in 1979. The 8-minute video showed the politician and the comedian bonding over their shared Indian roots as they made *masala dosa*, a popular South Indian food. The video was widely shared, with nearly 6 million views on Harris's channel alone, showing how the affective aspects of food media can be leveraged to create a shared sense of identity and belonging.

The comments and views on the village food videos show that their appeal crosses national and ethnic boundaries. For example, comments directed at the video "Village Cooking Kerala" are written in English and Malayalam and sent by viewers from around the world. While some commenters are not from Kerala, the most enthusiastic comments are from diasporic Keralites thanking Omana "Amma" for showing them how to make traditional recipes that reconnect them to their roots. Similarly, both Grandpa Reddy and Mastannamma have admirers from around the world, both diasporic and otherwise, supporting Khare's argument that a rising South Asian middle class has pushed region-specific foodways into urban and international markets, changing the dynamics of eating and sharing, as well as working to create a more diverse national cuisine (Khare 2012, 248–250).

Conclusions

Overall, the village food videos act as counterpoints to mainstream narratives of how, why, and what we consume as food. Whereas other media privilege upper-caste and mainstream food practices and construct an image of the ideal Indian citizen, these food videos disrupt that smooth narrative to exuberantly showcase food practices that are local, regional, and specific. These videos "create public geographies through dynamic communication pathways, empowerment and their ability to facilitate interventions – albeit small – on the mediascape" (Goodman and Jaworska 2020, 185). Unlike more self-conscious influencers who may use multiple social media platforms to express their positions on a variety of issues, these videos are mainly single platform entities with an almost determinedly apolitical stance. They do not actively espouse progressive or other activist causes, yet their outreach consists of feeding the poor, an Indian tradition common across religious communities and part of the *sahaj dharma* that Khare (2012) describes.

One way these videos achieve immediacy and appeal is by blurring the realms of private and public, personal and professional. The homemaker, the grandson, and the nephew are (sometimes secondary) actors in the videos, but also the principal producers, camerapersons, and editors. Whereas other research (Goodman and Jaworska 2020, 184–191) has shown how food celebrities and food influencers may self-consciously perform their professional and personal identities in distinct and sometimes separate ways, this sample of videos blurs the public and the private realms and builds intimacy with the viewers by sharing a supposedly authentic "everyday."

By their very existence, village food videos create a space for alternative narratives in the public sphere, rupturing mainstream political and cultural narratives, and raising questions of who has the power to define what is normal and universal, and who is relegated to the exotic and the other. Drawing on our understanding of how counterpublics can challenge dominant or mainstream narratives and open spaces for discourse among marginalized groups, I contend that these village videos function as such subaltern spaces of oppositionality. I see this as happening in two ways. First, these videos push back against the mainstreaming of dominant food cultures and make marginalized foodways visible within the global digital foodscape. Second, by creating these videos within the context of their domestic and community spaces, and by bringing these spaces to the attention of a global audience, the producers/actors are creating new virtual geographies – a subaltern digital counter-foodscape – thereby planting a metaphorical flag on the "augmented" (Manovich 2006, 219–220) digital landscape. Drawing on Appadurai (1988) and Fraser (1990), I contend that these culinary counterpublics work by using food to build intimacy, convey solidarity, and promote the idea of equality among India's many micro-populations and cultures. Digital platforms such as YouTube provide possibilities for developing affinities and interactions inside and outside of national borders not previously possible, offering a digital parasociality (Chen 2016, 232) that creates space for sub-genres such as these to develop and flourish while redefining political and cultural belonging.

References

Amit, Vered. 2007. "Structures and Dispositions of Travel and Movement." In *Going First Class? New Approaches to Privileged Travel and Movement. Vol. 7*, edited by Vered Amit, 1–14. New York: Berghahn Books.

Appadurai, Arjun. 1981. "Gastro-Politics in Hindu South Asia." *American Ethnologist* 8(3):494–511.

Appadurai, Arjun. 1988. "How to Make a National Cuisine: Cookbooks in Contemporary India." *Comparative Studies in Society and History* 30(1):3–24.

Biswas, Soutik. 2018. "The Myth of the Indian Vegetarian Nation." BBC News – India, April 4. https://www.bbc.com/news/world-asia-india-43581122.

Bruns, Axel. 2008. *Blogs, Wikipedia, Second Life, and Beyond: From Production to Produsage*. New York: Peter Lang.

Bruns, Axel. 2015. "Making Sense of Society through Social Media." *Social Media & Society* April 2015. 10.1177/2056305115578679.

Chen, Chih-Ping. 2016. "Forming Digital Self and Parasocial Relationships on YouTube." *Journal of Consumer Culture* 16(1):232–254.

Dumont, Louis. 1970. *Homo Hierarchies*. London: Paladin.

Fraser, Nancy. "Rethinking the Public Sphere: A Contribution to the Critique of Actually Existing Democracy." *Social Text*, no. 25/26(1990):56–80.

Goodman, Michael. K., and Sylvia Jaworska. 2020. "Mapping Digital Foodscapes: Digital Food Influencers and the Grammars of Good Food." *Geoforum* 117:183–193.

Hegde, Radha. S. 2014. "Food Blogs and the Digital Reimagination of South Asian Diasporic Publics." *South Asian Diaspora* 6(1):89–103.

Herkes, Ellen and G. Guy Redden. 2017. "Misterchef? Cooks, Chefs and Gender in MasterChef Australia." *Open Cultural Studies* 1(1):125–139.

Joshi, Shamani. 2020. "How Biryani Became a Political Slur in India." *Vice.com*. December 3, 2020. https://www.vice.com/en/article/dy8yvq/biryani-political-slur-in-india-among-farmer-and-caa-protests.

Kasturi, Sumana. 2019. *Gender, Citizenship, and Identity in the Indian Blogosphere: Writing the Everyday*. Abingdon: Routledge.

Katrak, Ketu H. 2014. "Food and Belonging: At 'Home' and in 'Alien-Kitchens'." In *Through The Kitchen Window: Women Explore The Intimate Meanings of Food and Cooking*, edited by Arlene Voski Avakian, 263–275. Boston: Beacon Press.

Khare, Ravindra. S. 2012. "Globalizing South Asian Food Cultures." In *Curried Cultures: Globalization, Food, and South Asia*, edited by Krishnendu Ray and Tulasi Srinivas, 237–254. Oakland: Univ. of California Press.

Lewis, Tania. 2018. "Digital Food: From Paddock to Platform." *Communication Research and Practice* 4(3):212–228.

Lewis, Tania, and Michelle Phillipov. 2018. "Food/media: Eating, Cooking, and Provisioning in a Digital World." *Communication Research and Practice* 4(3):207–211.

Lupton, Deborah. (2020). "Understanding Digital Food Cultures." In *Digital Food Cultures*, edited by Deborah Lupton and Zeena Feldman, 1–16. Abingdon: Routledge.

Mangaldas, Leeza. 2017. "India's Got Beef with Beef: What You Need to Know About the Country's Controversial 'Beef Ban'." *Forbes*, June 5, 2017.

Manovich, Lev. 2006. "The Poetics of Augmented Space." *Visual Communication* 5(2): 219–240.

Marriott, McKim. 1968. "Caste Ranking and Food Transactions: A Matrix Analysis." In *Structure and Change in Indian Society*, edited by Milton Singer and Bernard S. Cohn, 133–171. New York: Routledge.

Perrier, Maud, and Elaine Swan. 2020. "'Crazy for Carcass': Sarah Wilson, Foodie-Waste Femininity and Digital Whiteness." In *Digital Food Cultures*, edited by Deborah Lupton and Zeena Feldman, 129–144. Abingdon: Routledge.

Phillipov, Michelle, and Katherine Kirkwood. 2018. *Alternative Food Politics: From the Margins to the Mainstream*. New York, NY: Routledge.

Pillai, Pooja. 2021. "Panta Bhat and Masterchef and the Rejection of Culinary Hierarchy." *The Indian Express*, July 14. https://indianexpress.com/article/opinion/columns/pantha-bhat-masterchef-australia-culinary-hierarchy-7403310/

Natrajan, Balmurli and Suraj Jacob. 2018. "'Provincialising' Vegetarianism, Putting Indian Food Habits in their Place." *Economic and Political Weekly*. 53(9):54–64.

Raman, Usha and Sumana Kasturi. 2016. "Performing Transnational Identity Online: Women Blogging from Domestic Spaces." In *Indian Transnationalism Online: New perspectives on Diaspora*, edited by Ajaya Kumar Sahoo and Johannes G. De Kruijf, 41–66. Abingdon: Routledge.

Ray, Krishnendu. 2016. *The Ethnic Restaurateur*. London: Bloomsbury.

Sathyamala, Christina. 2019. "Meat-Eating in India: Whose Food, Whose Politics, and Whose Rights?." *Policy Futures in Education* 17(7):878–891.

Sanghvi, Vir. 2019. "Decoding the Politics of Food Cooked Up over the Years in India." *Hindustan Times*, January 20. https://www.hindustantimes.com/brunch/the-politics-of-food/story-xOz4SgJLPjSyxGpdDSeoLJ.html

Schneider, Tanja, Karin Eli, Catherine Dolan, and Stanley Ulijaszen (eds). 2018. *Digital Food Activism*. Abingdon: Routledge.

Seid, Danielle. 2018. "The 'Anti-Hipster' Feminism of Asian Auntie Cooking Web Series." *Feminist Media Studies* 18(4):779–782. 10.1080/14680777.2018.1478693.

Schultz, Kai. 2018. "World's Oldest Celebrity Chef, an Indian Great-Grandma, Dies at 107." *New York Times*, December 6. https://www.nytimes.com/2018/12/06/world/asia/mastanamma-india-chef-dies.html#:~:text=World%E2%80%99s%20Oldest%20Celebrity%20Chef%2C%20an%20Indian%20Great-Grandma%2C%20Dies,Mastanamma%20got%20her%20big%20break%20at%20age%20105

Steils, Nadia, and Zaika Obaidalahe. 2020. "'Social Food': Food Literacy Co-construction and Distortion on Social Media." *Food Policy* 95(101932). 10.1016/j.foodpol.2020.101932.

Thakur, Arvind Kumar. 2020. "New Media and the Dalit Counter-Public Sphere." *Television and New Media* 21(4):360–375.

Trivedi, Yuvraj. 2020. "Food Politics: Food and Hindutva." *South Asia Journal*, July 1, 2020. http://southasiajournal.net/food-politics-food-and-hindutva/.

Vrikki, Photini, and Sarita Malik. 2019. "Voicing Lived-Experience and Anti-Racism: Podcasting as a Space at the Margins for Subaltern Counterpublics." *Popular Communication* 17(4):273–287.

Winkie, Luke. 2019. "Watching This Grandma Make Mole Is the Comfort Food I Crave." *Vice.com*, October 10, 2019. https://www.vice.com/en/article/ne89jm/watching-this-grandma-make-mole-is-the-comfort-food-i-crave.

Zargar, Haris. 2021. "The Communal Politics of Biryani." *New Frame*, July 12, 2021. https://www.newframe.com/the-communal-politics-of-biryani/.

9 How the Bendy Banana Became a Symbol of Anti-EU Sentiment: British Media, Political Mythology, and Populism

Mary Irwin and Ana Tominc

Misleading claims about threats to and interference in British food by the European Union (EU) played a significant part in constructing the popular Euromyths represented in both tabloid and broadsheet journalism media that contributed to anti-EU agitation and culminated in the UK's withdrawal from the EU following the June 2016 referendum. Over many years, newspapers reported, with barely suppressed incredulity and no little hilarity, that among many other directives issued, interfering Brussels bureaucrats intended to banish any abnormally bendy bananas or too curvy cucumbers from United Kingdom supermarket shelves, ban the tasty, traditional smoky bacon crisp, re-educate the Welsh on how to grow their leeks, and remove the beloved British device the Teasmade, purveyor of the piping hot early morning "cuppa," from the nation's bedsides for being simply too dangerous.

In this chapter, we examine how the first of these, the banana, emerged as a totemic and highly suggestive symbol at the center of both political and popular discourse. As the Commission's Regulation (EC) No. 2257/94 of September 16, 1994, came into force on January 1, 1995, journalists almost immediately began referring to it as "the bendy banana law." Ever since then, the "bendy banana" – in itself a Euromyth – has functioned as the central symbol in a particular type of reporting that used it to frame stories that ridiculed EU regulation politics. These "Euromyth stories" (Henkel 2021) used satire and often misinformation to tap into a sense of British identity, sovereignty, and culture under attack, which gave them persistent persuasive power even after being credibly debunked. They also contributed to the contemporary blurring of boundaries between tabloid and broadsheet journalism; between news, entertainment, and criticism; and between politics and everyday life.

In the context of contemporary popular and political culture, the banana has become an iconic symbol. Bright yellow in color and suggestive in shape, in contrast to more "modest" fruits and vegetables, it is a cheery, cheeky, and comfortingly familiar homely reference, representing something of the self-perceived British character. At the same time, the banana is

DOI: 10.4324/9781003283942-13

also clearly and identifiably an exotic, international product that connects Britain to a less frequently mobilized and deeply problematic colonial historical past. It is therefore not surprising that the frame "bendy banana" emerges, as we will demonstrate, as a foundational myth, an "urtext" that enabled a binary opposition to be established between "us" ("the British," perhaps subliminally more often "the English") and "them" (the EU), crystallizing all that is wrong with how the EU operates, and how much it seeks to interfere in centuries-old, deeply rooted British life.

Much of this reporting built on the British national myth of itself as a sovereign and proud nation that has over the centuries fought wars to save Europe (most recently during the Second World War) and contributed to the overall "civilizing" and betterment of the world (*cf.* Edwards 2019). Through satirical and often misleading reporting, used by both tabloids and broadsheets, the UK media, especially the Eurosceptic and right-wing newspapers, have over the years systematically used Euromyths to represent the British as a "common-sense" nation, unwilling to change its traditions in submission to the EU's bureaucratic rules, using "them" as an "ideological shorthand for imagining how the European 'Other' is destroying our 'thousand year old island heritage'" (Cross 2008) and creating in the United Kingdom "the impression that the British people were being bossed about by Brussels in pettifogging and absurd ways" (Curran, Gabor, and Petley 2018, 248).

Since the monumental 2016 decision to leave the EU, much has been written about the political, economic, and cultural factors that led to and subsequently influenced the outcome of Brexit, including the production and distribution of Euromyths in the press (Henkel 2021; *cf.* also Cross 2008) and in stand-up, sitcom, and political satire (Weaver 2021). However, while the role of food was examined in some of this work, little has been said about its significance in populist media discourse, and especially in Euromyth analyses, even if food generally features as one of the central foci of populist and Eurosceptic right-wing discourse (Demuru 2021). It is not surprising that, out of all the EU regulations reported in the UK media, food-related myths became the perfect vehicle for stirring up anger against the EU – a factor that contributed significantly to the success of the "Leave" vote (Clarke, Goodwin, and Whiteley 2017; Rahman 2020).

In this chapter, we explore the ways in which food was deployed to frame populist media discourses through the emotive symbol of the "bendy banana," rallying its range of connotative and mythic associations to evoke the essence of Britishness and discredit Brussels. Such a usage crystallizes and connects historical British achievements, such as the creation of a sprawling empire, to other seemingly lesser but equally significant markers of Britishness: specifically, Britons' self-proclaimed exceptional ability to seize on the ridiculousness inherent in any situation and, of course, to "always see the funny side" of things.

The Bendy Banana as a Frame: Political Mythology, Media Populism, and Interdiscursivity

The persuasive power of phrases such as "bendy banana" derives from their connotations and ideological meanings that circulate widely within specific historical, social, and political contexts, and that serve as shorthand for complex arguments whose conclusions, while often politically motivated, are presented as natural, inevitable, and grounded in "common sense" (Ducrot 1993). Barthes argued that such narratives function as myth, which "transforms history into nature," masking the historical contingency and political workings of such narratives and transforming them instead into seemingly "innocent" speech (Barthes 1973 [1957], 129, 131). Over time, the "bendy banana" and its associated narratives have come to function as a myth in Barthes' sense of the term, as "ideologically marked narrative[s] which purport to give a true account of a set of past, present, or predicted political events and which [are] accepted as valid in [their] essentials by a social group" (Flood 2002, 44). The "bendy banana" as used in Euromyth stories condenses and represents the "common sense" argument that the EU is an ineffectual and frivolous institution as evidenced by its attempts to impose regulations such as those aimed at policing the curvature of bananas; and it has been made to represent and contribute to the ongoing construction of the imagined national community (Anderson 2016 [1983]; Chilton 2004, 46; Wodak et al. 2009, 22) bound by a shared sense of British identity, sovereignty, and exceptionalism – all of which are being threatened by the EU. In this, the bendy banana functions as an iconic vehicle of political myth, "a symbol through which a specific story and the entire class of myths to which that story belonged can be effectively conveyed" (Flood 2002, 166) without much more than a mention.

The bendy banana was well-suited to Eurosceptic, populist media narratives because it added entertainment and affective value to anti-EU messaging through its humorous, everyday, and close-to-the-heart appeal (Cross 2008). It also provided opportunities for journalists to produce powerfully persuasive stories using interdiscursive strategies that blended hard news with entertainment, straight reporting with satire, and politics with everyday life. Given audiences' broad knowledge of and often emotional investment in discourses outside of politics, this blurring of discursive boundaries and genres allowed these stories to engage large and diverse audiences and tapped into and gave expression to a primal sense of "Englishness" by bringing to political reporting a specific type of humor and satire embodied most famously by the quintessentially English authors Evelyn Waugh and P.G. Wodehouse. These interdiscursive strategies provided as a backdrop to the political messaging a recognizably English worldview that while everyone and everything is intrinsically, ironically funny, the ultimate joke has been played on those not fortunate enough to be English – a worldview that celebrated the exceptionalism of the English while putting the EU firmly in its (inferior) place.

Methodology

For our project, we used the ProQuest International Newsstream to find and explore the usage and recurrence of the term "bendy banana" in the UK press in the context of UK/EU relationships over the period between 1994, when the EU's Commission Regulation (EC) No. 2257/94 directive came into effect, and 2020, when the United Kingdom left the EU. The analysis makes almost exclusive use of newspaper articles and editorial columns, though one reader's letter is included to evidence the extent to which the "bendy banana" and its associated style of writing have become a standard discourse beyond the genre of the newspaper article in writing about EU regulation. The search revealed approximately 100 deployments of this specific term and, with a handful of exceptions, the reference invariably was to this law. The corpus was then manually coded to ascertain in what contexts "bendy banana" was used through this period, including in relation to the type of newspaper (e.g., tabloid vs. broadsheet) and genre of text (e.g., news vs. commentary). As the rest of this chapter demonstrates, with some exceptions discussed at the end, no significant difference was found in the use of this phrase regardless of where it appeared, even though the difference in use had initially been anticipated due to the different production and consumption practices associated with these diverse newspapers and genres.

"Bendy Banana Journalism": Empire, the European Union, and Euroscepticism

Lurking deep in the collective subconscious of British popular culture, the banana is associated with British colonial and post-Second World War history as well as with sexuality and bawdy humor. From the infectious chorus of the evergreen 1910 music hall ditty "Let's All Go Down the Strand … and have a banana" to the popular revival of the 1923 US hit tune "Yes! We Have No Bananas" in the seven-year period during the Second World War when banana imports were banned by the government, to the association of bananas with the British Empire and everything it stands for, bananas epitomize both the perceived greatness of the British past and the nation's character (Piatti-Farnell 2016). The re-importation of the banana in 1946 became synonymous with British victory; the jaunty, juicy banana was somehow representative of the irrepressible British spirit. The banana therefore stands for how particular generations of British people might see themselves: plucky, cheery, sometimes a bit cheeky, rather special and certainly not conformist. This appeal spoke to sections of the Brexit voting population raised in the post-war decades, who prided themselves on the orderliness, pragmatism, and humor of the British national character.

In other contexts, however, the banana also evokes connotations of Britain's colonial past: Shaggy's 1995 remix of Harry Belafonte's 1956

"Banana Boat Song" highlights the connection of bananas with the singer's Jamaican heritage, with one of the banana's places of production, and hence with the consequences of British empire building and exploitation. First imported to England from the Canary Islands (located on the established trade route between Liverpool and West Africa) in the 19th century, bananas were soon after sourced from Jamaica and, later on, Latin American countries (Clegg 2002). Bananas were first planted in the Caribbean and Central America by black smallholders looking for a crop other than sugar, cotton, or tobacco, and who initially sold the fruit to the US export companies. These companies soon established expansive banana growing estates and developed varieties able to withstand overseas transportation and arrive at market ripe and unblemished. Eventually they squeezed the small-scale growers out of the market entirely. While not relying on slavery, as was the case with sugar production earlier in the 19th century (e.g., Mintz 1985), the banana trade system embodied the logic of colonialism: employing black Jamaicans and South Asians, whom the British brought to the Caribbean from India, another of its colonies, as indentured laborers, to work on the plantations (Holt 1992 in Soluri 2006, 149; Soluri 2006) and necessitating British state backing of private enterprise to reduce the corporate power of the United States in Jamaica. As Clegg (2002, 25–26) suggests, while private enterprise was "central in shaping the interest-group dynamic of the Caribbean and UK banana trades," the British government "had come to accept the benefits of 'constructive imperialism,' underpinned by close economic ties between Britain and her colonies."

EU Regulation in the UK Press: Between Factual Reporting, Mythical Entertainment, and Satire

An instructive starting point for analyzing the use of humor and satire in Euromyth articles and editorials published in both tabloids and serious news broadsheets about EU directives on bananas and food more generally can be found in the broadsheet *The Independent*'s contemporaneous interrogation of the tabloid *The Sun*'s now infamous "Euro scoop" editorial of 1994 that inquired "ARE YOU troubled by the size of your bananas?" Cathcart 1994). *The Sun*, Cathcart reported in *The Independent*, "provided a cut-out-and-keep paper banana, allegedly of the new minimum size laid down in European regulations." *The Sun* urged its readers to "See how yours measure up," offering readers a humorous double entendre. Mimicking the British saucy seaside postcard style in which *The Sun* developed this bendy-banana editorial, *The Independent* noted the emerging style of such reporting in which "[a]lmost every joke at the expense of the bureaucrats of Brussels was spiced with double entendre. ... Not since the Commission declared in favour of straighter cucumbers has everyone had so much fun" (Cathcart 1994).

In quoting directly from, and playing verbally with, the tabloid style of *The Sun*, *The Independent* incorporated *The Sun*'s mischievous tone into its own editorial, thus reinforcing the notion that the story and issue were in essence funny, and not to be treated with the gravitas pertaining generally to government regulations. In that same year when "the bendy banana law" came into force, a letter from a reader to *The Independent* bemoaned the EU's ill-judged allocation of time and resources. The letter, printed under the attention-grabbing tabloid style alliterative headline "EU going bonkers over bendy bananas," focused on the EU's shortcomings: "The EC has today hit a new low. It has produced regulations concerning the curvature of bananas while, at the same time, referring proposals for the regulation of the ownership of the media back for further consideration. Is this really worth our while?" (MR 1994).

This co-mingling of the serious and the foolish, the interdiscursive quoting of tabloid discourse within broadsheet reporting, and the resulting difficulty of assigning specific stories into clearly defined genres, constructed what might be seen as a hybrid genre in itself. Jean Quatremer (2016), a journalist at *Libération,* in the aftermath of the June 2016 referendum linked the growing popularity of this type of writing to Boris Johnson, who "managed to invent an entire newspaper genre: the Euromyth, a story that had a tiny element of truth at the outset, but which was magnified so far beyond reality that by the time it reached the reader it was false" (*The Guardian*, July 2016). Johnson, who in July 2019 succeeded Theresa May as UK prime minister and subsequently won the parliamentary election five months later in part by avowing to "Get Brexit Done," had had a long career as a journalist, working as a reporter and political columnist for the conservative newspaper the *Daily Telegraph*, and then as the editor of the conservative-leaning *The Spectator*, where he helped shape Eurosceptic populism by propagating semi-truths about the EU. The journalist Katherine Butler remembers that "[w]hether Johnson believed it or not, the narrative he sold was that elites on the top floors of the Berlaymont [headquarters of the European Commission in Brussels] were engineering a federal superstate in which Jacques Delors would eventually 'rule'" (Butler 2019). As the EU aimed from the 1990s onwards to ease trade within the block by promoting the "regulatory 'harmonisations' of the single market," Johnson "weaponised" the situation and created "a dishonest and xenophobic campaign about British democracy" (ibid.), conveniently side-lining any discussion of the benefits of some of the regulations, such as the protection of citizens from harmful food-related practices and consumers from the purchase of faulty goods.

Although such tabloidization of broadsheet journalism is in line with general trends that indicate more serious news media increasingly orienting themselves towards lifestyle and entertainment features, or indeed, challenging the existence of neat binaries in the first place (Fürsich 2012), much of the reporting about banana regulations went beyond entertainment, crossing the line into ridicule. Imbued with the language, spirit, and sensibility of the tabloid press, representations of "bendy banana law," the EU, and its regulations in the UK broadsheet press promulgated indirectly the Eurosceptic populist agenda decades before the 2016 referendum.

In such a hybrid tabloid/broadsheet genre of semi-truthful reporting, the banana's connotations, especially those related to sex, interdiscursively linked journalistic reporting to tabloid sensationalism and entertainment, and to the literary satire of Waugh and Wodehouse alluded to earlier in this chapter. That is, factual reporting began to be made more palatable and pleasurable by implicitly employing the eloquence and sparkle of literary journalism with the drama and sensationalism of the tabloids. Waugh and Wodehouse are of particular significance here because of their influence on the writing of Boris Johnson who, as a journalist, set many of the standards for such "Eurotainment." Both the upper-class English public schoolboy cadences of Waugh and Wodehouse's writing and their "Englishman-befuddled-by-foreign-laws" perspective shaped Johnson's work and others who emulated his approach. Reporting on bendy banana regulation in the UK news media combined modes that appealed to the British sense of humor and through this, to British identity. As such, EU banana regulation reporting became effective not only because the EU was presented as a threat to "our" national traditions, but additionally, because it was presented as such through a discursive style that British readers associate with and understand as a fundamental part of Britishness.

The Bendy Banana as Myth: Constructing EU Madness and British Greatness

Most articles and columns that contain "bendy banana" in the text follow a loose template where the bendy banana stands as the least "commonsensical" example of EU regulation, functioning as a frame through which other reporting is to be understood. Writing on other EU initiatives presented as similarly nonsensical, these texts use the banana as a reminder of the EU's ludicrousness and silliness, and through this, as an affirmation of the British pragmatic and practical approach to life where "we" possess common sense, and "they" represent varying and ascending levels of madness.

Even if the dominant framing of the bendy banana regulations was at times misleading, by utilizing repetition across time and media it helped construct the myth through which arguments about and representations of the EU could be referenced and understood without being addressed directly or fully. The banana functioned in this way even in the handful of articles that presented issues in more nuanced terms than the established "us and them" binary found in most texts. The bendy banana, then, implies British superiority over the EU. As a potent symbol in Euromyth, it "purveys, reinforms, and validates practices, beliefs, and values which are themselves the products and support of a socio-economic order" (Flood 2002, 164).

As our analysis demonstrates, categorization of the texts based on traditional genre conventions of production and style may not be straightforward since the "madness" of the EU's decision-making processes – rather than the regulation itself – becomes the central theme in both tabloid and broadsheet alike. Even articles that set out to treat the regulations as a serious subject expressed skepticism and employed the vocabulary and perspectives of Euromyth stories described above. While the majority of articles centered around the term "bendy banana" were published in mischief-making tabloids, broadsheet stories about EU food regulations also assumed a lighthearted tone and, as much as the tabloids, used tropes of silly, fussy foreigners that undermined any serious analysis of the issues presented.

"'They' Are Crazy Time Wasters": Ridiculing the EU

The opposition between the "European Other" and the "British Self" is established as a clear binary at the heart of a chronological narrative where the "bendy banana" is almost always employed as representing the EU's desire to impose unnecessary or often ill-considered standards on British products, behaviors and more generally freedoms. One significant element in the construction of the European Other is a lack of good or common sense and appropriate behavior ranging from minor to full-blown meddling, and managerial madness. The EU, it is suggested, is a fussy, sometimes irrational actor. On the opposite pole is the well-disciplined British self whose centuries-old, firmly established, highly rational traditions are being needlessly interfered with and potentially violated by foreign actors. It is notable that in the telling of these stories, the more the supposedly irrational activities of the EU are highlighted, the more this throws into relief the eminently pragmatic, down-to-earth essence of Britishness.

This binary opposition, which is used to structure most of the Euromyth stories, is highlighted well by the journalist and broadcaster Mariella Frostrup. In a 1994 column for the broadsheet *The Times*, she gives evidence to broadsheet "parodic adoption of Euromyth *tabloidese*," as discussed in the section above, and the deployment of EU (then EC) food regulation as the stuff of light entertainment, while at the same time depicting "them" (EU) in the way that had already become characteristic of this journalism. She writes,

> Hot on the heels of insane EC directives regarding over-bendy bananas and kinky cucumbers comes news that the lemon may be the latest casualty of Brussels' time-wasting attentions. Defenders of the fruit are set to take a pre-emptive strike against further legislation by declaring National Lemon Day on November 8.
>
> (Frostrup 1994)

Frostrup deploys here for her quality press audience all the now familiar tropes of Euromyth discourse: the EC's [EU] behaviour is "insane," and

Brussels is "time-wasting." The only sensible course of action, according to Frostrup, is that "defenders" ("we") must enact a "pre-emptive strike" against "them" and their current and future regulations, a representation that is wrapped in the metaphor of war, since in addition to other vocabulary of war, lemons are described as a Brussels "casualty." Frostrup also nods knowingly to the cheeky sexual innuendo integral to tabloid style by referring to the "kinky" cucumber. Like the banana, the cucumber's shape also is suggestive of a penis, while "kinky" is tabloid euphemism for unconventional or slightly "naughty" sexual practices, unfailingly deployed to entertain (notice also the alliteration, a common feature of this reporting). In this short opinion piece, however, written to amuse as much as criticize, Frostrup's column is evidence of EU-sceptic rhetoric used for laughs. At the same time, it demonstrates the implicit absorption into the mainstream press of the entertaining style of writing about the serious subject of food regulation.

The decision to mock dull legislative processes distracted from a distinctly political project without considering the consequences of such reporting for the UK audience's understanding of the seriousness of international regulation treaties. In this vein, a column in the hugely popular and influential middlebrow tabloid *The Daily Mail* "Why Brussels can't say our bananas are too bendy" touts the triumph of the English High Court over the EU after the court ruled in 2002 that the regulation of the shape of fruit was based on a "legal blunder" (Poulter 2002). Poulter made clear how ridiculous this regulation was seen to be in Britain when he wrote, "shoppers and grocers have long thought that European rules on how much a cucumber can curve or a banana can bend were ... well, bananas." What is worthy of note here, buried in "barmy" EU rhetoric, is that the story is concerned with serious information about EU legislation and the high court's decision, namely that "[t]he landmark decision suggests that thousands of standards set by Brussels for the shape and size of fruit and vegetables do not apply," with direct implications for organically grown fruits and vegetables. The typical Euromyth approach, however, means that making jokes and promoting the angle of "us" (English courts) winning out over "them" (EU legislators) obfuscates the serious international economic concerns that this ruling highlights, demonstrating yet again the populist nature of this discourse.

Tabloid reporting and commentaries concentrating on the madness of the EU follow a similar pattern. Just as the 1998 *News of The World* tabloid reporting frames the issues of plastic toy duck regulation as "just another example of Eurocrats gone mad" by referencing the "bendy banana," *The Sun*, too, worries in a similarly constructed piece published in 2000 that an EU ladders ban is a "step too far": "BRUSSELS bureaucrats have unveiled their latest barmy ruling – laying down the law on how to climb a ladder." The piece goes on to argue that the fact that "the daft directive says ladders must be securely anchored to the ground" is self-evident. As before, "barmy" and "daft" are used to position the EU as the inferior other, imposing yet another nonsensical and unnecessary safety rule, and in the process patronizing the hardy, down to earth, sensible British worker, likely also to be the intended audience of this column. Theresa Villiers, British Member of Parliament and member of the Conservative Party, is quoted as a sensible voice justifying the anti-regulation approach: "This is classic Brussels over-regulation and is very silly. It is not the sort of area where the commission should be involved."

In both the published commentary on toy duck and ladder regulations, the "bendy banana" frame is used to underscore that this silliness and time-wasting is a continuous aspect of EU behavior, rather than a single occurrence, even when the regulation in itself may have merited serious consideration. It is also a reminder of the many strengths of the British character as it brings to mind the make-do-and-mend attitude of arguably the strongest touchstone against which solid, down-to-earth British common sense is seen to prevail against European folly and excess: the Second World War.

Only rarely did the UK press concern itself with the consequences of such reporting at the time. In what is a rare piece of reflection, Roy Greenslade (2000), writing for *The Guardian*, suggested that the "years of xenophobic tub-thumping that have already undermined the possibility of a rational choice" when it comes to the Euro, highlight the ongoing anti-Europe bias of the right-wing UK press. Greenslade questioned whether it was even possible to talk seriously about European issues within the hostile media environment which had been incrementally and deliberately developed across tabloids like *The Sun* and broadsheets like *The Daily Telegraph*, highlighting articles such as those about bananas as examples of such reporting.

A later article, Molly Watson's (2006) piece in the Welsh national newspaper *The Western Daily Mail* "Bendy-banana ban? Standardised condoms? Myths undermine EU," similarly stands out as it offers a rare corrective to the litany of facetious commentary on the EU and its attempts to make meaningful safety legislation for its single market. Watson writes that a Welsh MEP has attacked the "silly Euromyths" that attempt to portray the EU as "sinister." Eluned Morgan, who had served as a Labour MEP for 12 years, was quoted as saying, "Euromyths are not only responsible for creating anti-European feelings, but also for drawing attention away from more serious issues." Morgan added that "the people writing the legislation are Brussels administrators who are being driven by consumer demands. It's about protecting the consumer." It is interesting to note that this article comes from a newspaper located in what was to be very significantly a "Remain"-voting city, Cardiff, and in quoting Morgan, documents the views of an MEP who had a clear understanding of what actually occurred within European legislative circles and was concerned that muddled and mixed messages were being circulated. It is, of course, noticeable that even in a sober article such as this, which seeks to warn of the corrosive effects of the Euromyth on voter understanding of political issues of the day, the very first line is "We've all heard the one about Europe banning bendy bananas." In an article purposely designed to bust the Euromyth, its most symbolic object, the bendy banana, has to be evoked to frame the discussion with all the emotions that it had come to embody. It is as if Euromythology has so poisoned the well-stream of discourses around the EU that any discussion of this issue, even one which seeks to banish lies and untruths, must first invoke them in order to disprove them.

Regulation and Satire: Humorous and Sceptical Britain

As noted above, both broadsheet and tabloid newspapers in the United Kingdom presented articles and columns about EU regulation in a similar style. However, even stories that might be deemed nominally more serious or not focused directly on painting the EU as "mad," nevertheless adopt a noticeably begrudging and markedly sceptical tone that draws upon the comedic possibilities of Eurospeak. For example, Colin Brown's 2011 *Independent* article "Knobbly fruit and veg back on menu as EU plans to scrap uniformity laws" reports on the modification of EU rulings on fruit and vegetable specification. This was a fairly straightforward story about the EU making a decision to be more inclusive in terms of its requirements on the acceptable standards for produce. However, the title nods at funnily shaped fruit through the word "knobbly," which is a popular comedic term in the British English lexicon connoting ill-formed British knees. As is the case with most of the texts analyzed in our study, the article is closer to comedy than serious journalism, quoting former Labour EU Minister and committed Europhile Denis MacShane as he integrates Euromyth discourse into the heart of the story by borrowing the jokey faux-comedic tones of his political and ideological foes: "At long last, we are going to get crooked cucumbers in our shops. Hooray for Europe! But I guarantee the Eurosceptics will say that Brussels is abolishing our inalienable right to straight ones" (Brown 2011).

Even the word banana itself sounds attractively comical, pleasantly mellifluous, and poetic to a British/English ear with its repeated melodic "shwa/a/shwa" sounds. To "be bananas," as one of the Eurosceptic articles above shows (Poulter 2002), is to be crazy, foolish, silly, and prone to making ridiculous decisions. It is the perfect word for dismissing the seemingly crazy behavior of the ubiquitous "Brussels bureaucrat," yet another often repeated phrase in Euromyth stories that has pleasingly alliterative connections to other very British English pejorative words for "bananas behavior" such as barmy, bonkers, and bird-brained. That "barmy bureaucrats" would want to mess with the much loved "British banana" is the perfect example of a culturally insensitive organization's lack of understanding of a quirky, individualistic product, rich with national symbolism and significance. If they can try and mess about with the good old British banana – what next?

Conclusion

In this chapter, we interrogated the significance of a piece of fruit – a banana – in the initially barely perceived establishment, development, and then eventual stranglehold of a very particular way of writing and thinking about Europe which, deliberately and deceptively light-hearted on the surface, masked a very pointed and political intent. With reference to what came to be understood as the "Bendy Banana Law," we explored how "bendy banana" was used between 1994 and 2020 in the British press as an emotive phrase to frame articles about EU regulation. Years of misleading, dismissive, and mocking reporting resulted in the widespread belief that the EU and especially its laws were something not to be taken seriously, representing the European Union's distanced and bureaucratic culture as if it were forcefully transforming the British way of life, its culture and habits. These stories offered commentary on the EU's management of its single market that drew from the English literary tradition of Waugh and Wodehouse, which poked fun at overheated foreigners, and from the English bawdy seaside postcard tradition of sniggering smuttiness and "end-of-the-pier" suggestiveness – sexily shaped bananas.

Yet, such reporting also had consequences. In *The Plymouth Argyle Herald*, Sam Blackledge offered an example of its impact on actual voting intentions just before the 2016 referendum. In an article headlined "We want out, say folk at Dave's café," a customer made a direct connection between his wish to vote "Leave" and bendy bananas. When Blackledge asked the customer why he was backing Brexit, he replied: "Bendy bananas; cucumbers; light bulbs; loss of sovereignty; and the creation of a fatal [sic] state which some people might want to describe as steps to a new world order."

The anxieties around sovereignty and a European super or nation-state – which is what might be meant by "fatal state" – may be recognizable political points, but to participate in a momentous national decision in which a core argument is centered around funny fruit demonstrates the power of the Euromyth and the power of everyday topics, such as food, in establishing, maintaining and communicating populist political content.

Acknowledgements

This chapter results from the project "Representing food in UK media during the Brexit Campaign: Policy, regulation and national food myths" which was funded by a Carnegie Incentive Grant (2021–2022). We are grateful to the Carnegie Trust for the Universities of Scotland for their support.

References

Anderson, Benedict. 2016 [1983]. *Imagined Communities: Reflections on the Origin and Spread of Nationalism*. London: Verso.

Barthes, Roland. 1973 [1957]). *Mythologies*. Selected and translated from the French by Annette Lavers. London: Vintage.

Brown, Colin. 2008. "Knobbly Fruit and Veg Back on Menu as EU Plans to Scrap Uniformity Laws." The Independent, June 16, 2008. https://www.independent.co.uk/life-style/food-and-drink/news/knobbly-fruit-and-veg-back-on-menu-as-eu#x02010;plans-to-scrap-uniformity-laws-847911.html

Butler, Katherine 2019. "I was in Brussels When Johnson Peddled His Original Euro Lies – Nobody's Laughing Now." The Guardian, December 10, 2019. https://www.theguardian.com/commentisfree/2019/dec/10/boris-johnson-brussels-europe

Blackledge, Sam "We Want Out, Say Folk at Dave's Cafe: With a Week to Go until Polling Day, Sam Blackledge Visits Porkies Cafe in Whiteleigh to Ask Staff and Customers How They Plan to Vote.", The Plymouth Evening Herald, June 16 2016.

Cathcart, Brian 1994. "The Measure of a Good Banana." The Independent, September 25, 1994. https://www.independent.co.uk/voices/the-measure-of-a-good#x02010;banana-britons-love-a-euroscandal-whether-it-is-true-or-not-writes-brian-cathcart-1451009.html

Chilton, Paul. 2004. Analysing Political Discourse: Theory and Practice. London: Routledge.

Clarke, Harold, D. Matthew Goodwin, and Paul Whiteley. 2017. Brexit: Why Britain Voted to Leave the European Union. Cambridge: Cambridge University Press.

Clegg, Peter. 2002. The Caribbean Banana Trade: From Colonialism to Globalization. Houndmills, Basingstoke, Hampshire, New York: Palgrave Macmillan.

Cross, Simon. 2008. "Hippoglossus Hippoglossus and Chips: Twice Please Love? Adventures in the Underbelly of Euromyths." In Communication Ethics Now, edited by Richard Keeble. Market Harborough, UK: Troubador Publishing Ltd.

Curran, James, Ivor Gabor, and Julian Petley. 2018. Culture Wars: The Media and the British Left. London: Routledge.

Demuru, Paolo. 2021. "Gastropopulism: A Sociosemiotic Analysis of Politicians Posing as 'the Everyday Man' via Food Posts on Social Media." Social Semiotics 31:507–527.

Ducrot, Oswald. 1993. Dire et ne pas Dire. Paris: Hermann.

Edwards, Jason. 2019. "O the Roast Beef of Old England! Brexit and Gastronationalism." The Political Quarterly 90(4):629–636.

EU Ladders "Ban" Is a Step Too Far. The Sun, September 6, 2000.

Flood, Christopher. 2002. Political Myth. London: Routledge.

Frostrup, Mariella. 1994. "Squeezed; Mariella Frostrup's Week." The Sunday Times, October 30, 1994. https://advance-lexis-com.pitt.idm.oclc.org/document/teaserdocument/?pdmfid=1516831&crid=256c9d84-02ef-4a69-958a-5fcedd825c5a&pddocfullpath=%2Fshared%2Fdocument%2Fnews%2Furn%3AcontentItem%3A3T2M-BCT0-00H1-F06V-00000-00&pddocid=urn%3AcontentItem%3A3T2M-BCT0-00H1-F06V-00000-00&pdcontentcomponentid=332263&pdteaserkey=h3&pditab=allpods&ecomp=pz2yk&earg=sr2&prid=822df80b-2287-48ec-8eaa-5e08ee00a4ec

Fürsich, Elfriede. 2012. "Lifestyle Journalism as Popular Journalism." Journalism Practice 6(1):12–25.

Greenslade, Roy 2000. "The Euro's Not for Spinning." The Guardian, July 10, 2000. https://www.theguardian.com/media/2000/jul/10/pressandpublishing.mondaymediasection

Henkel, Imke. 2021. *Destructive Storytelling: Disinformation and the Eurosceptic Myth That Shaped Brexit*. London: Palgrave Macmillan.
Holt, Thomas. 1992. *The Problem of Freedom: Race, Labour, and Politics in Jamaica and Britain, 1832–1938*. Baltimore: John Hopkins University Press.
Hoskins, D.S. 1994. "Letter: EU Going Bonkers over Bendy Bananas." *The Independent*, September 26, 1994.
Mintz, Sydney. 1985. *Sweetness and Power: The Place of Sugar in Modern History*. London and New York: Penguin.
Piatti-Farnell, Lorna. 2016. *Banana: A Global History*. London: Reaktion Books.
Poulter, Sean, 2002. "Why Brussels Can't Say Our Bananas Are Too Bendy; EU Rules on Fruit and Veg Have No Power in British Law, Judges Decide." *Daily Mail*, June 26, 2002.
Quatremer, Jean. 2016. "The Road to Brexit Was Paved with Boris Johnson's Euromyths." *The Guardian*, July 15, 2016. https://www.theguardian.com/commentisfree/2016/jul/15/brexit-boris-johnson-euromyths-telegraph-brussels
Rahman, Muzna. 2020. "Consuming Brexit: Alimentary Discourses and the Racial Politics of Brexit." *Open Arts Journal* 8. 10.5456/issn.2050-3679/2020s05.
Sharp, Marie. 1998. "EU Must Be Quackers." *News of the World*, May 10, 1998.
Soluri, John. 2006. "Bananas Before Plantations. Smallholders, Shippers, and Colonial Policy in Jamaica, 1870–1910." *Iberoamericana* 6(23):143–159.
Strong, Helen and Rebecca Wells. 2020. "Brexit-Related Food Issues in the UK Print Media: Setting the Agenda for Post-Brexit Food Policy." *British Food Journal* 122(7):2187–2201.
Van Leeuwen, Theo. 2005. *Introducing Social Semiotics*. London: Routledge.
Watson, Molly. 2006. "Bendy-Banana Ban? Standardised Condoms? 'Myths Undermine EU'." *Western Mail*, April 24, 2006.
Weaver, Simon. 2021. *The Rhetoric of Brexit Humour: Comedy, Populism and the EU Referendum*. London: Routledge.
Wodak, Ruth, Rudolf de Cillia, and Martin Reisigl. 2009. *The Discursive Construction of National Identity*. Edinburgh: Edinburgh University Press.

10 Heritage, Belonging, and Promotion: Food Journalism Reconsidered

Unni From Andreasen and Alberte Borne Asmusse

In September 2018 and 2019, the Danish regional broadcaster TV2 FYN invited residents in its core region, the island of Funen, to participate in "Smoked Cheese Day," a live journalism event that it organized. On Flakhaven Square in Odense, the largest city on the island and the third largest in Denmark, people attended lectures, workshops, tastings, and demonstrations on how to make *Fynsk Rygeost*, the island's traditional smoked cheese. The event was part of the Odense Food Festival, and its aim was to promote a declining traditional delicacy by demonstrating different ways that *Rygeost* could be used in cooking and by rallying the community around a once treasured but now waning cultural resource. Participants were invited to learn about the cheese, taste it, and cook up innovative and traditional recipes using it as a main ingredient. The station also aimed to explore the causes, cultural significance and economic impact of the declining popularity of this singularly Danish cheese by using the emerging genre of "live journalism," or journalism "performed" before a live audience outside of the confines of a television studio.

Smoked cheese served this purpose well. It is the only cheese originating in Denmark, and it has been produced in the Funen region since the 18th century. It is a fresh cheese made with whole milk then lightly smoked using oat or rye straw and stinging nettles, which gives it a distinctive taste. Historically, the cheese has served as a metonym of Funen food culture, but recently it has been upstaged by international imports to the extent that Arla Foods, the Danish multinational cooperative and one of the largest dairy producers in Scandinavia, has stopped making it. Additionally, most dairies, including local ones, have experienced a decrease in sales, which also threatens this local food. Against this backdrop, the Odense Food Festival and TV2 FYN decided to spotlight the cheese and its cultural significance. Organizers argued that "the smoked cheese is part of the Funen identity; it has been produced on Funen for centuries, and half of all Danish smoked cheese is sold on the island, and, in addition, smoked cheese is Denmark's oldest and only original cheese" (Bøgeholt Lund 2018).

In this chapter, we analyze how TV2 FYN produced an event focused on food that facilitated face-to-face, live and interactive journalism

DOI: 10.4324/9781003283942-14

(e.g., Batsell 2015; Steensen 2014) as a site for developing news that audiences experienced as engaging and valuable (Meijer 2020; Meijer and Bijleveld 2016). We argue that food-related events and journalism content are characterized by a special ability to engage audiences and revitalize a more local or regional sense of community. Moreover, we demonstrate how food became a news item across journalism genres and was covered as much more than just recipes and reviews (Kristensen and From 2012; Voss 2014).

Our analysis also illustrates how TV2 FYN's coverage of the smoked cheese represents not only live journalism but also another relatively new phenomenon in journalism practice and journalism studies conceptualized as "constructive journalism" (e.g., From and Kristensen 2019; Haagerup 2017; Hermans and Drok 2018). Constructive journalism aims to be solution-oriented, guiding audiences and involving them in addressing social problems and needs rather than emphasizing conflict, while at the same time being critical and reflexive (Gyldensted 2015; Haagerup 2017). This approach to journalism can potentially be applied to all news, but some scholars have argued that it is particularly well-suited to, and can be associated with, service journalism and by extension with lifestyle journalism and local journalism, which share similar goals and values (From and Kristensen 2018). These similarities include a focus on dialogue and interaction among members of a community and between media institutions and audiences (see Jenkins and Nielsen 2020; Meijer 2020). We can see this dynamic at work in TV2 FYN's journalism revolving around Funen's smoked cheese.

Finally, in this chapter we explore how food, constructive journalism, and live local journalism events can serve as a relevant and insightful combination to facilitate engagement and community. We also interrogate the potentially permeable boundary between journalism, advertising, and public relations.

Constructive Journalism and Food Journalism in a Local Context

Two strands of research are central to the analysis of how a regional television station incorporates food and makes food and food culture into a journalistic event. First, constructive journalism as both a growing practice and a research field has been important in understanding how journalists and editors implement new strategies to engage and involve audiences and make local/regional journalism (more) relevant (again). Second, media stories about food, which have been a staple of journalism since the early 19th century not least because food constitutes a basic human need (Jones and Taylor 2013; see also e.g., Fusté-Forné and Masip 2019, 129), continue to proliferate and diversify. In scholarly research, food journalism has most often been studied as lifestyle journalism and has been linked to cultural and personal taste and identity. The following analysis adds to these approaches by arguing that food as a specific sub-beat can serve to facilitate community and, in the process, become "valuable news" in a local context.

Constructive Journalism in a Local Context

Constructive journalism was originally developed in journalism practice as an alternative to traditional journalism to be more solution-oriented, less focused on negative stories and conflicts, committed to empowering audiences, and more socially responsible (Ahva and Mikko 2018; From and Kristensen 2018; Gyldensted 2015; Haagerup 2015, 2017). This type of journalism can be seen as one initiative among many to reimagine journalism – and what it could and should be – to meet current needs and remain viable in the future. It is an attempt to solve the contemporary crisis of journalism linked to the declining trust in journalism as an institution, the growing polarization in society, and the overarching complexity of an interconnected world (Mast, Coesemans, and Temmerman 2019). A central aspect of constructive journalism, therefore, consists of new ways of engaging audiences and involving them in addressing community concerns. Constructive journalism has, however, also been criticized for being "uncritical," "happy-news" (ibid., 494). Proponents often counter these arguments by explaining that constructive journalism can be both critical and solution-oriented at the same time.

The definition of and scholarly debate on how to understand constructive journalism is ongoing, but there seems to be consensus that constructive journalism "subscribes to a fundamental, and widely shared, conception of journalism's raison d'étre but rethinks how contemporary journalists could, or should, fulfill their democratic and societal roles" (ibid., 494). More specifically, scholars suggest that constructive journalism is "a form of journalism that is public-oriented, solution-oriented, future-oriented and action-oriented, trying to avoid a bias towards negativity in the news" (Hermans and Drok 2018, 679). However, it has also been argued that constructive journalism shares fundamental characteristics with existing journalistic genres as diverse as service journalism (From and Kristensen 2019), civic journalism (Rosen 1999), peace journalism (e.g., Bläsi 2004; Kempf 2007) and action journalism (Bro 2019), and that "its inherent principles share similarities with other well-known movements in the history of journalism" (Bro 2019, 504). In that sense, constructive journalism is not an entirely new initiative but part of the fabric of recent developments in journalism more broadly and in news more specifically.

One significant difference between traditional news and constructive journalism that has caught the attention of researchers is the way audiences are addressed – and influenced (e.g., From and Kristensen 2019; Gyldensted 2015; McIntyre 2015, 2017). For example, McIntyre (2015) emphasizes the positive effect that constructive journalism can have on audiences and indicates that stories that employ a positive frame and provide solutions motivate people to stay socially engaged while stories that employ a negative frame and do not address possible solutions leave people feeling apathetic. Other studies confirm that constructive journalism can influence audiences on micro, meso and macro levels (Meier 2018). On a micro level, constructive journalism can foster individual feelings of well-being and empowerment; on a meso level, it can facilitate loyalty to the media company by inviting interaction and dialogue; and on a macro level, it can support social and cultural change. More specifically, research on constructive journalism demonstrates a strong connection between the aims of this approach and what people find valuable in local news.

Meijer (2020) identifies five elements common to local news that audiences find most valuable. First, local news should build on reciprocity and audience responsivity as core practices, which, for example, include forging a relationship between news institutions, journalists, and audiences. Second, valuable local news should consistently focus on covering the local area. Third, news items should be told from "within," relying on local sources and giving members of the community the chance to represent themselves and have their voices heard (Meijer 2020, 361). Fourth, valuable local news should foster a sense of place and belonging. As Meijer writes,

> local news that residents value are items that facilitate regional orientation either by visualizing everyday geographical landmarks such as central squares, prominent bridges, highways, public gardens and nature reserves or by providing social and personal landmarks: stories and images of local well-known persons (ranging from shopkeepers to librarians, teachers and street paper vendors).
> (Meijer 2020, 362ff)

Finally, audiences value realistic representations of their community, and local news stories should address tensions and challenges that members of the local community face.

While journalism as a social and cultural institution, business, and practice is weathering profound challenges in an unpredictable, dynamic, global media environment, it has become imperative to reimagine how it can sustainably connect and engage with existing and untapped audiences. Constructive journalism, with its focus on positive framing, audience involvement, and generation of collective solutions to social problems, offers a promising path forward. Combined with a strong community angle and engagement with everyday concerns such as food, it may serve to revitalize journalism at the local level and beyond.

Food Journalism

Food is central to journalism for its life and health-sustaining properties, the pleasures it offers, the risks it poses, the role it plays in maintaining cultural identity, the power it has to confer or withhold social status, its economic and environmental impact, its political implications, and much more. Of lesser yet still significant importance is food's connection to celebrity culture (Jones and Taylor 2013). Well-known chefs, bloggers, YouTubers, social media influencers, reality television show contestants, and other prominent individuals turn food into media content that often draws large audiences. These celebrities and their media in turn often become the focus of profiles and other journalistic coverage.

While scholars have demonstrated that food media in general and food journalism in particular continue to represent a growing sub-beat (Brown 2004; English and Fleischman 2019), research in the field remains relatively sparse. The most dominant analytical approach to food journalism is that of lifestyle (From 2018; Fürsich 2012; Hanusch, Hanitzsch, and Lauerer 2017; Kristensen and From 2012), even though food journalism can – and should – also be evaluated as political or civic discourse that appears in a variety of media, platforms, and genres (e.g., From 2007; Fürsich 2012). As Kristensen and From have shown, the boundaries between lifestyle, cultural, and consumer journalism have blurred over time, and food journalism has long spanned both "hard news" and "soft news" (Kristensen and From 2012; Voss 2014), addressed issues of economy, nutrition, health, and politics (From 2007), as well as lifestyle issues implicated in personal identity construction and cultural taste (e.g., Brunsdon 2003; Kristensen and From 2012). Overall, food and food culture can be approached as an issue of political interest as well as (personal) lifestyles, and food journalism includes many different genres such as breaking news, restaurant and product reviews, dining and how-to guides, recipe stories, profiles, travel articles, among others. All this indicates that lifestyle and food journalism are not defined in opposition to news with little political and civic relevance (see also Fürsich 2012) but as hybrid forms that employ mixed modes of address, sometimes addressing their audience as citizens, sometimes as clients or consumers – and sometimes as both at the same time (Eide and Knight 1999; From and Kristensen 2018, 2019). Thus, food journalism can be centered around subjective and individual narratives, but it can also offer democratic and civic value as described, for example, by Meijer and Bijleveld (2016).

The accelerating hybridization of lifestyle journalism may be linked to broader societal transformations. Various scholars have documented a strong correlation between food, lifestyle, and taste (From 2018; Jones and Taylor 2013), as well as social and cultural identity. Coverage of food can contribute to larger nation-building projects, demarcating exclusion and belonging, and creating an imagined community based on a "powerful system of values" and consumption (Duffy and Ashley 2012, 60ff). Following this line of argumentation, we analyze TV2 FYN and its involvement in and coverage of the Odense Food Festival's celebration of smoked cheese in an exploration of how news media, food events, and the coverage of such events can lead to both a revitalization of news and the construction of community and heritage.

The Case: Smoked Cheese and Constructive Journalism at TV2 FYN

TV2 FYN is one of eight independent regional television outlets in Denmark. Each outlet is supported by licensing funds and acts independently in terms of funding and editorial content; however, each outlet also collaborates to some degree with the central national broadcaster TV2/Denmark as they deliver regional news items to the mother channel. As has been the case internationally, local media in Denmark have experienced a decline in audience and advertising revenue (Svith et al. 2017, 10). However, since 2015, TV2 FYN has maintained a rather stable reach and a 45 percent audience share for its main news broadcast. In its annual government report, the station attributed its ability to retain its audience to, among other factors, the many live events it hosts, a strong digital presence, and a commitment to becoming "the most 'constructive' media house in Denmark" (Pernille Redder and Signe Ryge interview with author June 22, 2021). In pursuit of this latter goal, TV2 FYN launched the project "Together we make Funen better," and in the Fall of 2019 appointed Kristina Lund Jørgensen as editor of constructive journalism. Jørgensen, a former fellow at the Constructive Institute at Aarhus University, identified four central values that act as a compass for constructive journalism at TV2 FYN (Jørgensen and Risbro 2021). These values support journalism that is solution-oriented, nuanced, involving, and critical, and they have led the editorial board of TV2 FYN to organize live events that allow for new forms of journalism that engage audiences in addressing a variety of societal problems and working toward collective solutions. "Smoked Cheese Day" is just such a project, incorporating traditional hard news and political reporting with lifestyle food content and live journalism events as a way to develop and test the potential of constructive journalism. In interviews we conducted with event coordinator Pernille Redder, journalist Signe Ryge, and editor Kristina Lund Jørgensen, they argued that food can facilitate cultural experiences and can serve as a social glue in many different contexts: "It was all about getting the residents of Funen to participate in the event, and thus working with inclusivity was very important ... our aim is to create strong relationships with the residents of Funen and to continue having a dialogue with them" (Pernille Redder and Signe Ryge interview with author June 22, 2021). In other words, food is believed to be instrumental in getting people together in social settings to talk through issues that concern them, and their community and local media are believed to play an active role in this dialogue.

Case Material and Analysis

The case material includes the coverage of the live "Smoked Cheese Day" event organized in conjunction with the Odense Food Festival in September

2019, including a few examples from the "Smoked Cheese Day" in 2018. Moreover, the analysis includes interviews with two TV2 FYN journalists and the constructive journalism editor, all of whom worked on this project. Methodologically, this chapter is based on textual, qualitative analyses of 29 journalistic multimedia articles published by TV2 FYN on its website. These articles were analyzed according to sub-beat, genres, sources, interview techniques, the rhetorical positioning of audiences as citizens, consumers and/or clients (Eide and Knight 1999), strategies of facilitating "valuable news" (Meijer 2020; Meijer and Bijleveld 2016), and strategies of cultural belonging. The latter was specified into four central themes. The "Regional Heritage" theme includes coverage that represents the relationship between smoked cheese and the heritage of Funen objectively, while the "Heritage Pride" theme includes coverage that represents smoked cheese with evident pride as an important local delicacy. The theme "Preservation of Cultural History" includes coverage that emphasizes the importance of smoked cheese to the preservation of Funen's cultural history. Finally, the "Consumption" theme includes coverage in which the (good) taste or nutritional value of the smoked cheese are emphasized or in which the focus is on how the cheese can be used in cooking.

In addition to the 29 articles that we analyzed, social media posts on Facebook and Instagram by TV2 FYN related to the event were harvested and saved (July 20, 2021). One post with the most interaction was analyzed in more detail for evidence of how audiences related to strategies of cultural belonging, but also how they connected to each other and to TV2 FYN. Three semi-structured interviews were also conducted using an online platform: one with event coordinator Pernille Redder and journalist Signe Ryge, and one with the editor of constructive journalism, Kristina Lund Jørgensen. The interviews centered on the aims of the launch of the Smoked Cheese Day, how TV2 FYN evaluated the event, and how the station plans to incorporate food and food culture into future projects.

Analysis: Smoked Cheese between Heritage, Consumption, and Promotion

Our analysis demonstrates how coverage of the smoked cheese as constructive journalism tied to food and food culture becomes not only a way to promote a local food product and a regional media house, but also a way to introduce journalism as a site for community building and heritage. Our analysis is organized into three sections with a focus on how the coverage facilitates cultural heritage, how mixed modes of audience address are used, and if and how social media activity creates meaningful dialogue.

Generally, the coverage of smoked cheese was published in a number of different sections including lifestyle, culture, consumption, health, business, and politics, and covered as a mix of hard and soft news (Kristensen and From 2012; Voss 2014) often in the same article. Most of the coverage in our sample took the form of news articles, although background pieces, consumer guides and product tests were also included. All of the coverage addressed the audience directly in an inclusive, conversational style, employing pronouns "you" and "we" and in so doing, affirmed the importance of facilitating community as a central trope.

Smoked Cheese, Funen Heritage, and Community

The Smoked Cheese Day live event produced by TV2 FYN is an example of "live journalism" – a recent journalistic genre in which journalists present news stories to a live audience outside of a television studio on a theater stage or in the context of community events in order to engage audiences. Live journalism is characterized by insistently being bound to a place and a space where audiences are invited to be participants in a "fairly set and immovable way" (Vodanovic 2020, 4). Moreover, it carries a potential to facilitate loyalty between media institution and audiences because of the interaction and dialogue that it invites, which Meier (2018) has identified as central to constructive journalism. In this specific case, the live event included talks, workshops, tastings, and music, and the festival format and multifaceted activities provided aesthetic and cultural experiences that brought together journalism and the experience economy as defined by Pine and Gilmore (1999). Vodanovic (2020) explained that live-journalism events often rely on three out of four defining elements of the experience economy: entertainment, education, and aesthetic experiences. It can be argued that the Smoked Cheese Day, based on a physical proximity between journalists, invited guests and audiences, and the "performance" of the journalistic story of the possibilities of smoked cheese, becomes a media story in itself.

In the case of the Smoked Cheese Day, food served as the subject of the "story," being placed at the center of the aesthetic and cultural experiences staged in the context of the Odense Food Festival. The journalists argued that food serves as a central and relevant focus of an event because "it is related to identity and people's sense of belonging and community and the strong emotional ties people have to food. There is something about regional food, because it is often related to childhood and family traditions" (Pernille Redder and Signe Ryge interview with author June 22, 2021).

In many of the other live journalism events facilitated by TV2 FYN, food served a supporting rather than starring role. For example, TV2 FYN's editorial board included food in a live journalism coverage of the November 2021 municipal election campaign to attract audiences. As editor Jørgensen explained, "now we are planning events linked to the municipal elections. And we have discussed that it will be central that local food is part of the events – food is a way to attract people and get them involved in societal issues" (Kristina Lund Jørgensen interview with author August 20, 2021). Moreover, the editorial team is planning a series of events that aims to facilitate democratic debate together with other local media, municipalities, and public and private organizations. In this sense, food is often used as a central element in most live journalism events, regardless of the subject of the "story" because food embraces dialogue and community.

Audience Address

TV2 FYN incorporated food into the Smoked Cheese Day live journalism event in a way that addressed audiences primarily as consumers who were encouraged to make buying, cooking with, and consuming smoked cheese a regular habit. However, audience members were also addressed as citizens of the valued local community of Funen who could contribute through their consumption habits to the preservation of an important facet of the island's cultural heritage. Scholars have identified this complex understanding of audience identity and hybrid mode of address as a feature of "service journalism," (Eide and Knight 1999; see also From 2018; From and Kristensen 2018), which recognizes that the roles of "consumer" and "citizen" are experienced as a continuum rather than as distinct categories (e.g., From 2018). This combined mode of audience address is also a key feature of constructive journalism, which presupposes the hybrid identity of audiences as well as active and engaged audience positions (From and Kristensen 2018).

The link between the Smoked Cheese Day live journalism event and constructive journalism is also evident in that it sought solutions to a challenge that had both economic and cultural implications. More specifically, Funen residents were encouraged to visit local shops that had created special food items for the event that complemented smoked cheese, such as specialty chocolates, pancakes, and ice creams, offering a neo-liberal consumption-based solution to preserving history and culture. The event showed Funen residents how they could take responsibility for preserving Funen's heritage by buying more smoked cheese and using it in their everyday lives, and it empowered audiences through constructive journalism to take part in mitigating the negative impact of declining smoked cheese sales on the local economy and its cultural traditions.

However, TV2 FYN did more than encourage audiences to buy more cheese; they also encouraged them to take their support beyond their supermarket carts and kitchens by acting as ambassadors, seizing different opportunities to publicly praise the cheese, explain the importance of buying smoked cheese to preserving a valuable Funen cultural tradition, and doing their part to ensure that smoked cheese is served at every Funen table on every suitable occasion. This ambassador initiative was designed to promote appreciation for the endangered cheese, to raise awareness of its cultural and economic importance to the region, and to motivate Funen residents to engage in solving this threat to the economic and cultural vitality of their island – in the process potentially building a stronger sense of community among its residents.

Social Media Conversations

For the past ten years, scholars have studied the increasing importance of social media to the economic viability and social relevance of journalism institutions (e.g., Nygren 2020). TV2 FYN incorporated a social media strategy into its live coverage of the Smoked Cheese Day event to take advantage of social media's potential to reach and engage diverse audiences, to promote specific articles as well as the TV2 FYN brand, and to facilitate interaction between members of the community. TV2 FYN published posts on their Facebook page and also created a separate Facebook event with links to cheese workshops and practical information about Smoked Cheese Day. On the event page, they also regularly shared articles and videos from their website.

One particular Facebook post elicited 97,000 views, 1,400 Likes, and 234 comments – significantly more comments than other posts that garnered only between 20 and 150 (https://www.facebook.com/tv2fyn/videos/1882453091809631). The post and related article (Jarvel 2018) published on TV2 FYN's website featured Funen resident Jørgen Busander (2018), who created a cookbook of recipes using smoked cheese. He explained in a video that he felt motivated to do so after learning that Arla Foods was planning to stop selling smoked cheese, and how his cookbook was more than just a book with recipes; it was a way to preserve Funen's cultural heritage. He described the cheese as "a piece of cultural history," and said he felt like Funen was collapsing when he heard about Arla's decision (ibid). By featuring a Funen resident and approaching the story "from within," TV2 FYN made the article and post relevant and valuable (Meijer 2020) for audiences, and connected them to the region's collective memory, enabling them to position their lives within the history of the region (Assmann and Czaplicka 1995).

Comments posted to the article and post about Busander and his cookbook demonstrate different types and patterns of interaction and community. First, audiences asked for guidance on where to buy the cookbook and on other consumer decisions. However, TV2 FYN did not respond to these questions; instead, this led to the second type of posting as audience members replied to each other, creating smaller conversations. Third, audiences expressed their opinions, for example lamenting the unfortunate decision of companies to stop selling smoked cheese. Thus, the tone and the mix of themes, genres and modes of address used in the coverage, and not least in social media posts, imitated everyday conversations (Steensen 2014) in a regional community and became part of regional identity construction.

Conclusion

Characteristically and aligned with their goal of being a constructive media house, TV2 FYN has initiated a number of live journalism events and more traditional news coverage to save Funen's smoked cheese, and in the process to extend the boundaries of journalism and explore the potential of both constructive and live, on-location journalism. TV2 FYN trumpeted the success of its efforts as early as 2018, publishing an article under the headline "Optimism in Gundestrup Dairy: The smoked cheese sells again" (Flyttov 2018). In the article, Jørgen Hoff of Gundestrup Dairy was quoted as saying that sales of smoked cheese had increased, and that this was due to improved marketing as well as the activities of "Smoked Cheese Day." Another article, "Smoked Cheese Day: Twice as much smoked cheese is sold from Funen" (Kjær Lindboe 2019) followed up on the increased sales figures and popularity of the Smoked Cheese. Lindboe wrote, "The local goods and regional dishes are gaining ground among Danish consumers, and this is a bright spot for smoked cheese. It is a cheese that you can experiment with and use in different dishes" (ibid).

While the "Smoked Cheese Day" project explored the journalistic possibilities of live journalism and aligned with principles of constructive journalism and the formulated visions of dialogue and community, the project also linked to ongoing debates over the ethically appropriate relationship between journalism, public relations, and advertising, since TV2 FYN's focus on Smoked Cheese favored this product over others, and their coverage provided not only information but also promotion. This tapped into a long-standing debate among journalists and scholars centered on the goals and methods of much of lifestyle journalism, including food journalism, which is much more closely aligned with consumerism than is hard news, and over the question of what types of discourses can count as legitimate and valuable forms of journalism. These are relevant debates that TV2 FYN and the Constructive Institute continue to participate in and develop (Jørgensen and Risbro 2021).

In conclusion, TV2 FYN used Smoked Cheese Day to create a new space for journalism that invited audiences to engage with journalism in new ways, by watching live journalism performances; talking with journalists, business owners, professional cheese makers, chefs, cultural historians – and each other; learning about smoked cheese and Funen's cultural heritage; and enjoying smoked cheese and other local foods. Further empirical studies can illuminate how audiences perceive the links between live-journalism, food and constructive journalism and if and how these types of journalism create senses of belonging and actually brand local and regional news institutions.

References

Ahva, Laura and Mikko Hautakangas. 2018. "Why Do We Suddenly Talk So Much about Constructiveness." *Journalism Practice* 12(6):657–661. 10.1080/17512786.2018.1470474.

Assmann and Czaplicka. 1995. "Collective Memory and Cultural Identity." *New German Critique*, no. 65:125–133. http://www.jstor.org/stable/488538.

Batsell, Jake. 2015. *Engaged Journalism: Connecting with Digitally Engaged Empowered News Audiences*. New York: Columbia University Press.

Bläsi, Burkhard. 2004. "Peace Journalism and the News Production Process." *Conflict & Communication Online* 3(1/2):1–12.

Bøgeholt Lund, Camilla. *Premiere fredag: Oplev Rygeostens Dag for første gang.* [Premiere on Friday: Join The Smoked Cheese Day for the First Time]. *TV2 FYN*. September 11, 2018. https://www.tv2fyn.dk/rygeostens-dag/premiere-fredag-oplev-rygeostens-dag-forste-gang.

Bro, Peter. 2019. "Constructive Journalism: Proponents, Precedents, and Principles." *Journalism* 20(4):504–519.

Brown, Doug. 2004. "Haute Cuisine." *American Journalism Review* 26(1): 50–55,

Brunsdon, Charlotte. 2003. "Lifestyling Britain: The 8-9 Slot on British Television." *International Journal of Cultural Studies* 6(1):5–23. 10.1177/1367877903006001001.

Busander, Jørgen. 2018. *Rygeost: en gammel fynsk specialitet*. [*Smoked Cheese: An old Funnen delicacy*]. Odense: Jørgen Busander.

Duffy, Andrew and Yang Yuhong Ashley. 2012. "Bread and Circuses." *Journalism Practice* 6(1):59–74. 10.1080/17512786.2011.622892.

Eide, Martin and Graham Knight. 1999. "Public Private Service: Service Journalism and the Problems of Everyday Life." *European Journal of Communication* 14(4):525–547.

English, Peter and David Fleischman. 2019. "Food for Thought in Restaurant Reviews: Lifestyle Journalism or an Extension of Marketing in UK and Australian Newspapers." *Journalism Practice* 13(1):90–104. 10.1080/17512786.2017.1397530.

Flyttov, Mie. 2018. Optimisme i Gundestrup Mejeri: Rygeosten sælger igen [Optimism in Gundestrup Dairy: The Smoked Cheese Sells Again]. *TV2 FYN*. September 14, 2018. https://www.tv2fyn.dk/rygeostens-dag/optimisme-i--gundestrup-mejeri-rygeosten-saelger-igen.

From, Unni. 2007. "Forbruger og Livsstilsjournalistik." [Consumer and Lifestyle Journalism]. *Mediekultur* 27:35–45.

From, Unni. 2018. "Lifestyle Journalism." *Oxford Research Encyclopedias*. 10.1093/acrefore/9780190228013.013.835.

From, Unni and Nete Nørgaard Kristensen. 2018. "Rethinking Constructive Journalism by Means of Service Journalism." *Journalism Practice* 12(6): 714–729. 10.1080/17512786.2018.1470475.

From, Unni and Nete Nørgaard Kristensen. 2019. "Unpacking Lifestyle Journalism via Service Journalism and Lifestyle Journalism." In *Lifestyle Journalism: Social Media, Consumption and Experience*, edited by Lucia Vodanovic, 13–25. London: Routledge.

Fürsich, Elfriede. 2012. "Lifestyle Journalism as Popular Journalism." *Journalism Practice* 6(1):12–25. 10.1080/17512786.2011.622894.

Fusté-Forné, Francesc and Pere Masip. 2019. "Food and Journalism: Storytelling about Gastronomy in Newspapers from the U.S. and Spain." In *Lifestyle Journalism Social Media, Consumption and Experience*, edited by Lucia Vodanovic, 129–140. London: Routledge.

Gyldensted, Cathrine. 2015. *From Mirrors to Movers: Five Elements of Positive Psychology in Constructive Journalism*. Lexington, KY: GGroup Publishing.

Haagerup, Ulrik. 2015. *Constructive News*. Hanoi: Innovatio.
Haagerup, Ulrik. 2017. *Constructive News*. Aarhus: Aarhus University Press.
Hanusch, Folker, Thomas Hanitzsch, and Corinna Lauerer. 2017. "'How Much Love Are You Going to Give This Brand?' Lifestyle Journalists on Commercial Influences in Their Work." *Journalism: Theory, Practice & Criticism* 18(2):141–158. 10.1177/1464884915608818.
Hermans, Lisbeth and Nick Drok. 2018. "Placing Constructive Journalism in Context." *Journalism Practice* 12(6):679–694. 10.1080/17512786.2018.1470900.
Jarvel, Andreas. 2018. "Jørgen laver Rygeostkogebog: Jeg elsker Rygeost" [Jørgen Writes a Smoked Cheese Cookbook: I Love Smoked Cheese]. *TV2 FYN*. November 10, 2018. https://www.tv2fyn.dk/rygeostens-dag/jorgen-laver--rygeostkogebog-jeg-elsker-rygeost.
Jenkins, Joy and Rasmus Kleis Nielsen. 2020. "Proximity, Public Service, and Popularity: A Comparative Study of How Local Journalists View Quality News." *Journalism Studies* 21(2):236–253. 10.1080/1461670X.2019.1636704.
Jones, Steve and Ben Taylor. 2013. "Food Journalism." In *Specialist Journalism*, edited by Barry Turner and Richard Orange, 96–107. London: Routledge.
Jørgensen, Kristiana Lund and Jakob Risbro. 2021. *Konstruktiv Journalistik*. Copenhagen: Samfundslitteratur.
Kempf, Wilhelm. 2007. "Peace Journalism: A Tightrope Walk between Advocacy Journalism and Constructive Conflict Coverage." *Conflict & Communication Online* 6(2): no page number.
Kjær Lindboe, Signe. 2019. "Rygeostens dag: Dobbelt så meget rygeost bliver solgt fra Fyn" [Smoked Cheese Day: Twice as Much Smoked Cheese Is Sold from Funnen]. *TV2 FYN*. September 9, 2019. https://www.tv2fyn.dk/rygeostens-dag/rygeostens-dag-der-bliver-solgt-dobbelt-sa-meget-rygeost-fra-fyn.
Kristensen, Nete Nørgaard and Unni From. 2012. "Lifestyle Journalism: Blurring Boundaries." *Journalism Practice* 6(1):26–41.
Mast, Jelle, Roel Coesemans, and Martina Temmerman. 2019. "Constructive Journalism: Concepts, Practices, and Discourses." *Journalism* 20(4):492–503. 10.1177/1464884918770885.
McIntyre, Karen. 2015. *Constructive Journalism: The Effects of Positive Emotions and Solution Information in News Stories*. PhD-diss., University of North Carolina at Chapel Hill.
McIntyre, Karen. 2017. "Solutions Journalism: The Effects of Including Solution in Formation in News Stories about Social Problems." *Journalism Practice* 13(1):16–34.
Meese, James and Edward Hurcombe. 2021. "Facebook, News Media and Platform Dependency: The Institutional Impacts of News Distribution on Social Platforms." *New Media & Society* 23(8):2367–2384. 10.1177/1461444820926472.
Meier, Klaus. 2018. "How Does the Audience Respond to Constructive Journalism?" *Journalism Practice* 12(6):764–780. 10.1080/17512786.2018.1470472.
Meijer, Irene Costera. 2020. "What Does the Audience Experience as Valuable Local Journalism? Approaching Local News Quality from a User's Perspective." In *Routledge Companion to Local Media and Journalism*, edited by Agnes Gulyas and David Baines, 357–367. London: Routledge.

Meijer, Irene Costera and Hildebrand Bijleveld. 2016. "Valuable Journalism." *Journalism Studies* 17(7):827–839. 10.1080/1461670X.2016.1175963.

Nygren, Gunnar. 2020. "De-Professionalization and Fragmentation: Challenges for Local Journalism in Sweden." In *Routledge Companion to Local Journalism*, edited by Agnes Gulyas and David Baines, 158–166. London: Routledge.

Pine, B. Joseph and James H. Gilmore. 1999. *The Experience Economy: Work Is Theatre & Every Business a Stage*. Boston: Harvard Business School Press.

Rosen, Jay. 1999. *What Are Journalists for?* New Haven, CN: Yale University Press.

Steensen, Steen. 2014. "Conversing the Audience: A Methodological Exploration of How Conversation Analysis Can Contribute to the Analysis of Interactive Journalism." *New Media & Society* 16(8):1197–1213.

Svith, Flemming, Peter From Jacobsen, Steen K. Rasmussen, Jakob Linaa Jensen, Helle Tougaard Andersen. 2017. "Lokal- og regionalmediers indhold, rolle og betydning i lokalområder" [Local and Regional Media: Content, Role and Meaning to Local Communities]. Report: Palaces and Culture Agency for the Danish Ministry of Culture.

Vodanovic, Lucia. 2020. "Aesthetic Experience, News Content, and Critique in Live Journalism Events." *Journalism Practice* 16(1):161–177. 10.1080/17512786.2020.1796763.

Voss, Kimberly Wilmot. 2014. *The Food Section: Newspaper Women and the Culinary Community*. Studies in Food and Gastronomy. Lanham, Maryland: Rowman & Littlefield.

Part IV
Recovering History and (Re)producing Memory

11 Patriotic Hens, Tomato Turbans, and Mock Fish: The *Daily Mail* Food Bureau and National Identity during the First World War

Sarah Lonsdale

On March 4, 1918, as Britain wearily faced a fourth year of the Great War, the country's most popular morning newspaper introduced a new service to readers: the *Daily Mail* Food Bureau. In a prominent article at the top of page five headlined "Food Problems," the paper promised that during this time "when food supplies are restricted," the Bureau would help the "housewife, having only the vague idea of the nutritive values of various foods" to feed her family a "balanced" and "sufficient" diet in the present "*Food Battle*." These last two words were italicized to emphasize how the war was now being fought on the Home Front as well as in the trenches of France, inviting the housewives of Britain to see themselves as soldiers engaged in what the paper called a do-or-die "Fight to a Finish." Readers were asked to write into the *Daily Mail* offices at Carmelite House with questions that would either be answered in the paper or through the post. The Bureau would also give public lantern lectures on new sources of food to replace the staples that were now being rationed.

Food controls had gradually been introduced from the earliest days of the war – the sugar trade had effectively been brought under government control on August 7, 1914; official rationing, through coupons, of meat, fat, sugar, jam, and tea began February 25, 1918 (Oddy 2003, 71). Rationing would continue for some foodstuffs right through until the end of 1920, with sugar being the last item to come off the ration in November 1920. Throughout the war years, rising prices, food scarcity, and the regular sinkings of food-importing merchant ships by German submarines had combined to move issues of food to the center of people's concerns. As an illustration of how desperate for advice people were, the *Daily Mail* reported, less than a year after it was established, that the Bureau had sent out 252,977 letters to readers requesting recipes for dishes without meat, fat, or sugar ("Do you need the help of the Food Bureau?" *Daily Mail* February 7, 1919, 7). By the time the Bureau was closed in 1920, the number of letters answered was "in the millions" (Peel 1933, 222).

This represents an unprecedented service from a newspaper to its readers, illustrating a newspaper's role, in addition to providing news, in helping its

DOI: 10.4324/9781003283942-16

readers navigate, as Eide and Knight put it, "the problems of everyday life" (Eide and Knight 1999), even in the early years of mass print journalism. The Bureau was so successful that Dorothy Peel, the *Daily Mail's* women's editor who wrote the wartime recipes, turned much of the advice into a book, *Daily Mail War Recipes*, published in late 1918. The Food Bureau was not the only example of the *Daily Mail's* "service journalism" to its readers on the critical issue of food. We will see that the subject moved gradually from the women's pages to the news and editorial pages as the war continued. Coverage did not only focus on the government's evolving food policy, food prices, and the sinking of merchant ships, subjects one would expect to be covered in a newspaper. As scarcity continued and rationing loomed, the paper published increasing numbers of practical articles on how to find alternative food sources and recipes that made use of limited ingredients as the domestic sphere became an increasingly urgent focus of public discourse.

While it has been established that food journalism, especially in advanced societies, is often designated as "lifestyle journalism" and relegated to the "soft" areas of newspaper features pages and magazine supplements (Duffy and Yuhong 2012; Kristensen and From 2013), this general pattern is disrupted during times of national crisis especially when food is scarce or rationed (Bentley 2001). In addition, scholars have established that lifestyle journalism can have a "democratic and even empowering potential" for readers and audiences (Costera Meijer 2001; Fürsich 2013, 12). Much of the journalism on food published in the *Daily Mail* and other newspapers during the First World War was undoubtedly a kind of lifestyle journalism in that it was about consumption, commodities, and recipes, and it was focused on the domestic realm. This chapter will argue that as the war progressed, and the active participation of civilians was required to avert mass starvation, the *Daily Mail's* food coverage constructed an image of a very different reader than the "clients and consumers" (Hanusch and Hanitzsch 2013, 944) of conventional lifestyle journalism. Crucially, while still focused on consumption, it was all about consuming *less*, rather than more, and because the country was engaged in an existential struggle, it addressed readers much more as public citizens "concerned with the social and political issues of the day" than as individual consumers (Costera Meijer 2001, 194; Hanusch and Hanitzsch 2013, 944).

Food and National Identity

Under the peculiar circumstances of the First World War, the *Daily Mail's* food coverage, in its news articles, editorials, and publication of letters to the editor, became central in the crafting of a national wartime identity for its readers. Not only did coverage of food as a topic break out of the fledgling women's pages and become one of the most important topics in the paper, but both the newspaper and its readers collaborated in using the issue of food as a means of crafting the character of the ideal citizen: patriotic, frugal, resourceful, and selfless – the ideal citizen in wartime to which all readers could aspire.

Scholars have shown how food plays a vital role "in the formation of national identity" through national dishes such as, in the case of Britain, roast beef and fish and chips (Ashley et al. 2004, 80–81). Peter Scholliers has demonstrated food's central role "in the representation and identity of a person" and how this process of identification "operates through various media: the individual, a close and a distance group of declared peers" as well as "remote mediators" including journalists and scientists (Scholliers 2001, 304). In certain circumstances, Scholliers argues that food operates in the process of identification of an entire nation, as the group shares and reinforces common characteristics of an ideal in a "never-ending process of construction" (Scholliers 2001, 6). This process plays out in and through national media: historically through books and pamphlets, and later through mass market newspapers that enabled people "to relate themselves to others in profoundly new ways," to create the "imagined community" bound together through the knowledge that one shares the same values (Anderson 1983, 32).

Food can, however, both bind a nation together and divide it. One way food can accentuate differences within nations is by serving as a marker of social status and class. Bourdieu (1984) initially demonstrated how class differences – and rivalries – can be accentuated through different foods, the working classes eating carbohydrate- and calorie-rich staples such as bread, bacon and potatoes; the bourgeoisie eating exotic, imported and expensive luxuries (Ashley et al. 2004; Bourdieu 1984, 59–70). The specific circumstances of the First World War, however, with the limited range of foodstuffs available to the entire nation, and rationing theoretically restricting the middle and upper classes to the same quantities of food as the working classes, meant that the national diet was more homogenous than it had been for decades, minimizing those class differences and further binding the nation together. Dorothy Peel, Household Department editor at the *Queen* newspaper and later women's page editor of the *Daily Mail*, explained:

> In newspapers, in which descriptions of dishes made of foie gras and truffles, soles and lobsters and unlimited quantities of cream, eggs and butter used to appear, we find recipes for food such as 'cheap brown soup' and a concoction called 'Crowdie', made of the liquid in which mutton had been boiled, onions, oatmeal, salt and pepper.
>
> (Peel 1929, 54)

In other words, the middle classes' diets began to look much the same as the diets of the working classes. The government, very alert to working and lower-middle class concerns that while they went without, the rich would always somehow get around shortages, made great efforts to maintain imports of tinned fruit, a staple more readily affordable and available than fresh fruit. Its propaganda efforts, through the Ministry of Information, also sought to reassure citizens that everyone was in the war effort together. (Hockenhull 2015, 581–582)

The apparent eradication of difference and, through newspapers, the public construction of the ideal citizen through its approach to food, would help bind the nation together in an unprecedented moment of threat and jeopardy. Food writers constructed these changes as a further source of anxiety for middle-class housewives with the *Daily Mail's* new Food Bureau stepping in to provide comfort to these women, reassuring them of their continued status, and advising them on how to appropriately manage their kitchens. Through the *Daily Mail's* leading articles, women were sent the message that their patriotic behavior in feeding their families frugally and helping in food cultivation might earn them "cultural citizenship," and thus they might be deemed worthy of full citizenship, with attendant voting rights that had so far eluded them.

A Nation Tightens Its Belt

After war was declared in August 1914, the prices of staples rose immediately due to panic buying, hoarding, and War Office requisitioning of vast quantities of meat and flour for the army (Oddy 2003, 74). The prices of bacon, sugar, and bread – the working-class staples – all rose, with sugar prices increasing by 80 percent in the first week of the war, although they decreased a few weeks later. The government's budget of 1915 raised taxes on tea, coffee, sugar, and cocoa, effectively restricting consumption of all these goods (Oddy 2003, 74). Real scarcity began after the poor harvest of 1916, which led to the Corn Production Act of 1917 to stimulate the plowing up of lower-grade agricultural land and grassland (Coller 1925, 9–13). Voluntary rationing, which included one meatless day a week, dubbed "National Lent," was introduced in February 1917, and two months later the government passed a Food Hoarding Order in April 1917, giving government agents powers to enter and search private homes for stocks of food. Beginning in 1917, sporadic food riots targeted grocers, shopkeepers, bakers, and butchers, and starvation began to pose a serious threat to the poorer classes (Van Emden and Humphries 2003, 215–216). Official rationing began in February 1918, with first sugar, then meat, butter, cheese, and margarine.

Most British newspapers were enthusiastic supporters of the war, and they would later be held to account for glossing over or trivializing British losses on the battlefield and fabricating numerous stories of German atrocities to such an extent that for many years the reputation of the press was held in very low esteem (Knightley 2000, 83–120). Reader skepticism over newspaper coverage of the progress of the war was widespread and summed up in Vera Brittain's famous memoir of the war, *Testament of Youth* (1933). Brittain wrote, "*As usual* the Press had given no hint of that tragedy's dimensions, and it was only through the long casualty lists, and the persistent demoralising rumours ... that the world was gradually coming to realise something of what the engagement had been" (Brittain 2009, 110, emphasis added). Newspaper mendacities became a popular theme in contemporary wartime novels and, particularly, in the war poetry of Siegfried Sassoon and Wilfred Owen, and the "lying journalist" was soon an established stereotype in popular culture (Lonsdale 2016, 47–71). Yet in the same papers, articles on British victories were joined by the publication of wartime recipes, food-related tips for nursing convalescent soldiers, and suggestions for unusual sources for food. Wartime diaries and letters show that people were very worried about food scarcity, and newspapers, reflecting their readers' concerns, expanded their food and gardening coverage. Even the *Times* published articles, ration recipes and readers' letters on subjects such as alternative sources of fish, using potatoes in place of flour, and hunting for wild game. In many newspapers, the first articles on gardening for food rather than flowers began to appear (Lonsdale 2015, 808–810).

The *Daily Mail*'s First World War Food Coverage

As food became a national obsession, the *Daily Mail* provided intense food coverage in several sections of the paper that fell into three broad categories: news and feature articles written by journalists and specialist contributors, commentary provided by news leaders (the editor's "voice"), and letters to the editor sent in by readers. An analysis of these three categories from 1914 to 1920 reveals a surging interest in food throughout the war years, reaching a peak in 1917 and 1918, and then declining through 1919 and 1920 as controls were gradually removed (see Table 11.1). At the same time, the average number of newspaper pages was reduced by half, from 12

Table 11.1 Number of items containing the word "food" by type of article, *Daily Mail* 1914–1920

Year	News or feature articles	Leader	Letters to the editor	Total
1914	742	20	45	807
1915	1,328	43	105	1,476
1916	1,400	72	153	1,625
1917	2,903	160	492	3,555
1918	2,650	96	301	3,047
1919	2,453	15	118	2,586
1920	1,647	5	89	1,741

in 1914 to six in 1918 as the country experienced a severe paper shortage. Despite this, the number of articles on food still increased, with the issue of food being the subject of more than 6,000 news and feature articles and 256 "news leaders" pieces in 1917 and 1918. Readers' enthusiasm for contributing their opinions on the subject also surged, with nearly 800 readers' letters on food published in the paper in 1917 and 1918. While many of the readers' letters complained about government policy, particularly sugar rationing, this mirroring of coverage between the newspaper's own content and reader contributions implies a close agreement between readers and their newspaper over what issues deserved the most coverage.

News and Feature Articles

News and feature articles written by journalists and specialist correspondents made up by far the largest category, and the thousands of news articles and features about food published in the *Daily Mail* between 1914 and 1920 can be divided into four sub-categories: (1) political articles about food such as government policies, food prices, and trade and import strategies once the German submarines began a campaign of targeting merchant ships; (2) domestic articles about food once commodities such as wheat, butter, and sugar became scarce; (3) articles reporting on food shortages in enemy countries; and (4) recipes.

Political Articles

Political stories dominated coverage in the first two years of the war before the effects of shortages began to be widely felt. Articles explained issues such as the Transatlantic wheat trade ("Wheat for the Allies" January 4, 1915, 8), the government's policy of diverting food stocks to the army ("Butter for the Troops," January 14, 1915, 3; "Patriotic Hens," January 5, 1915, 2) and the intensification of farming to make up for a drop in imports ("Get the Utmost out of the Land" May 23, 1916, 5). As the war progressed, articles covered debates in parliament over whether rationing should be voluntary or compulsory and various attempts by the Food Controller to encourage self-sufficiency on the home front. Details of court cases prosecuting unscrupulous victuallers watering down milk or serving spoiled meat to the troops were also regularly published, reassuring readers that unpatriotic war profiteers would be punished. In February 1918, at the very beginning of official rationing, the paper published details of illegal food hoarding by a Member of Parliament, which included 100 pounds of biscuits, 102 pounds of sugar, and 34 pounds of golden syrup. The MP for West Down, William MacCaw, was fined £400 ("M.P.'s Food Hoard" February 5, 1918, 3). Finally, from early in the war, news articles and features encouraged women to see themselves as part of the effort, doing their bit through personal sacrifice and hard work. The appeal to patriotism through "doing your bit" even went as far as encouraging readers to donate eggs from their "patriotic hens" to speed the convalescence of wounded soldiers by providing them with good nutrition ("Patriotic Hens" January 5, 1915, 4). A similar article inspired by the Food Controller's comments in Parliament urging gardeners to turn their flowerbeds over to vegetable growing stated: "We can undoubtedly fight the Germans with potatoes and beans as well as with shells and bullets" ("Food Vegetables: Gardeners' Duty" March 3, 1915, 3).

Domestic Articles

As headlines translated into real privations, the second category of coverage of domestic food issues began to dominate, with the paper regularly publishing articles on alternative sources of food that housewives could turn to in feeding their families. Women were encouraged to incorporate into their meals foods that had been used in the past but had fallen out of fashion, such as whale steaks and pilchards, as well as more outlandish alternatives, such as substituting seagulls, coots, and moorhens for beef and poultry ("Roast Seagull and Other Quaint Bird Dishes" February 16, 1917, 2), and baking cakes with ground-up roots of bracken ferns rather than wheat flour ("Bracken Fern Cakes" February 22, 1917, 8). These articles inspired readers to contribute letters offering their own tips and advice by the hundreds.

Food Privations in Enemy Countries

The third category of articles, on food privations in enemy countries, quickly became a regular feature of the paper. No matter how bad things were in Britain, these articles implied, things were always worse in Germany ("Germany Day by Day: No Pancakes" January 1, 1915, 9; "Rush for Potatoes: Great Scarcity of Supplies in Berlin" February 13, 1915, 6; "German Food Riots" February 19, 1915, 6). As well as providing news from the continent, these articles helped further the process of constructing and affirming national identity by identifying the "other" against which British citizens could define themselves (Schlesinger 1987, 235). These articles consistently portrayed German troops as more susceptible to the effects of privations than British soldiers, and German civilians, through their participation in food riots, as incapable of the kind of stoic self-control, the "stiff upper lip" fortitude, that was so important to British national identity and pride (Lonsdale 2016, 61).

Recipes

In 1914 and 1915, the *Daily Mail* published 33 and 37 recipes, respectively. These appeared mostly in the women's page but, in 1915, a few appeared as letters to the editor, having been contributed by readers. The number of

Table 11.2 Number of items that contain recipes or directions on how to prepare food, by type of article, *Daily Mail* 1914–1920

Year	News or feature article	Editorial	Letter to the Editor	Total
1914	33	0	0	33
1915	31	0	6	37
1916	22	0	3	25
1917	60	0	7	67
1918	62	1	8	71
1919	33	0	0	33
1920	51	0	0	51

recipes increased to 67 in 1917 and to 71 in 1918, before dropping back to 33 in 1919 (see Table 11.2). In 1920, the number of recipe stories increased to 51, due to the return of a dedicated women's page once paper shortages eased and the paper's pagination increased. Between 1914 and 1920, only one editorial was published that contained a recipe, criticizing the quality of food served to Allied prisoners of war in German prisons and describing the preparation of a thin soup that, the paper argued, was turning British and French prisoners into famished skeletons ("Fair Play for Our Prisoners" May 24, 1918, 2).

In early 1914, before the war started, recipes in the women's page featured luxury or exotic ingredients and were addressed to a housewife anxious to provide delicacies and a tasty range of meals for her family. In 1914, less than 20 years after the paper's launch, it was still trying to shake off the then prime minister's damning epithet that it was "written by office boys for office boys," and made great efforts to attract middle-class housewives (Griffiths 2006, 131).

In its women's page, featuring Paris fashions and luxury recipes, the paper constructed a modern bourgeois identity through careful positioning of the context, ideology, and practice of eating (Rich 2011). Recipes included richly exotic fruit dishes such as banana omelette made with cream and eggs; banana salad made with chopped nuts, lettuce, and parsley (January 27, 1914, 9); and grapefruit salad made with Maraschino cherries, pineapple, grapefruit, and Cornish clotted cream (February 20, 1914, 11). The paper began publishing recipes for the wartime household in early 1915 initially as advice to mothers and wives on how to feed convalescents who had been injured in the fighting ("Milk puddings for convalescents" January 15, 1915, 9). As food rose in cost and began to be scarce, the women's page (which continued to be published until the autumn of 1917) began publishing recipes for "War-Time Meals" as well as alternatives to day-to-day foods once scarcity kicked in. The paper gave advice on making "Herb Drinks" as a substitute for tea (January 27, 1916, 9), suggesting using lime-flower, borage, orange flower, or mint as the government imposed maximum household allowances of a quarter of a pound per person per week for tea. Another recipe, this one for "Mock Fish" gave complicated directions for cooking up softened, mashed and baked salsify (a European edible plant in the daisy family) that contained no fish at all yet required lengthy preparation, to be served in porcelain shells (February 26 1916, 7). Still, in 1916 the emphasis of these recipes was on luxury and keeping up standards despite a certain amount of privation. Gradually recipes focused much more on important basics such as "Nut Bread" (September 26, 1916, 7) and "Sugarless Jam" (September 6, 1916, 7). Potatoes, one of the few sources of carbohydrates that were still plentiful, were often the basis for many recipes ("Potato cakes for breakfast" and "Potatoes with Cheese" July 7, 1917, 7; "Gnocchi of Potatoes" February 4, 1916, 9). In 1918, just as rationing was introduced, a rather desperate "Fish from the Rivers" recipe was published, trying to make river fish, usually rejected in favor of sea fish, sound palatable ("Fish from the Rivers" March 2, 1918, 2).

All these recipes had hitherto been written anonymously but, on February 6, 1918, a new series of ration recipes titled "Food Chat" appeared with the by-line "By a Housewife." The "Food Chat" column was a mixture of news about food, such as what the Americans were eating and the nutritional value of "whale beef," combined with recipes such as "A Cheap Marmalade Recipe" that was made by substituting half the usual quantity of oranges with lemons (February 14, 1918, 4). Three weeks later, on February 28, the author of "Food Chat" was named as Mrs. C. S. Peel, editor of the household department at *The Queen* newspaper, and Ministry of Food lecturer (Peel 1933, 160, 182, 218). Peel, who had been hired by the Ministry of Food during the government's Food Economy Campaign to conduct lecture tours around the country explaining to housewives how to conserve precious food resources, was initially disinclined to accept *Daily Mail* proprietor Lord Northcliffe's invitation to head up the *Daily Mail* Food Bureau. In her memoir she wrote, "I thought I would ask such terms as would not be accepted, so suggested a salary of £1,000 a year and stipulated that I must be allowed to retain the Editorship of the Household Department of *The Queen*" (Peel 1933, 220). Northcliffe accepted and even bettered her terms, indicating how important the issue of food was to the paper and its readers, and also how important it was to the paper's image that the editor of the Household Department of *The Queen*, a paper for elite women, worked on the *Daily Mail* staff.

When the Bureau was announced in the *Daily Mail* on March 4, the paper told its readers that the "new service" would be directed by Dr. J. Campbell, "the scientific adviser and rationing expert at the Ministry of Food." A man's reassuringly scientific and expert voice, presumably, was assumed to have greater authority with readers than that of a woman. All the recipes, however, were written by Dorothy Peel. Peel would later write that she was forever being side-lined at the paper and that women's voices and experiences were belittled or ignored. She wrote,

> It irked me not to be allowed to earn my salary ... I wished to be treated as a person doing a job ... I felt a trifle amused that all these men who were engaged in producing a paper, the success of which depended on the good will of women – should think the opinion of a woman of so little importance.
>
> (Peel 1933, 229)

The purpose of the "Food Bureau" was to provide a service to readers and by so doing to bolster the *Daily Mail*'s image as a paper for the middle classes, even as the recipes and ingredients increasingly resembled working-class fare. The upmarket department store Harrods had first introduced its own "Harrods Food Bureau" in the summer of 1917 as voluntary rationing became adopted as *de facto* by most people ("Harrods Food Bureau" display advertisement, *Daily Mail* August 30, 1917, 1). The Harrods Food Bureau worked to ensure equitable distribution of scarce foodstuffs, organize public lectures for customers on how to make rations stretch, and provide customers with the latest advice from the Food Controller. By mimicking the features of the Harrods Food Bureau, the *Daily Mail* cast itself both as indispensable to its readers and as a trusted source of information for the middle classes.

The recipes Peel wrote for the newspaper and later collected in the *Daily Mail War Recipes* book, published in 1918 by Constable and Co. for one shilling and sixpence, make strange reading today. "Savoury Roast," for example, was a loaf made from eight ounces of butter beans, eight ounces of rice, onions, tomatoes, and just one ounce of minced meat (Peel 1918, 35). Housewives were urged to embellish the roast's presentation to make up for the meager amount of meat and fat. Similarly, another recipe for "Tomato Turban" consisted simply of chopped tomatoes, breadcrumbs, and cornflour mixed together and baked in a ring mold (Peel 1918, 51). Readers were also given advice on how to make cheese from soured milk, how to keep goats, how to make a hay box oven which cooked food through insulation, and how to make syrup sugar from sugar beet. The front cover of the book showed a neat housewife wearing an apron standing in her kitchen, poring carefully over a recipe book titled *Daily Mail*, thus reinforcing the vital help the paper was offering women on the Home Front.

Leaders

The frequency of leaders about food followed the same pattern as other types of articles, peaking in 1917 and 1918 before dropping back after the end of the war. Being the official "voice" of the *Daily Mail*, these leaders for the most part discussed the main political news of the day such as rationing ("The Growing Bread Shortage" April 21, 1917, 4), the sinking of British merchant ships ("What Is Wrong" November 6, 1916: 4), food pricing policy ("Parliament and the Rise in Prices" February 11, 1915, 4), and the blockading of German food supplies ("The Sham Blockade" January 18, 1916, 4). Occasionally leaders promoted the paper's own initiatives, such as offering a £1,000 prize to champion vegetable growers ("1,000 Vegetable Prizes" March 4, 1915, 4) and calling for households to engage in communal pig keeping ("Pigs Not Words" February 28, 1918, 2). The leaders also suggested ways in which women could earn social and cultural citizenship even if they still did not have voting rights (Jensen 2019). Calls for women to join the Land Corps ("A Women's Corps for the Land" January 19, 1917, 4) to help the fight with "food munitions as well as war munitions" ("Sow Now" April 2, 1915, 4) and learn how to cook with inferior cuts of meat ("Learn to Cook" January 8, 1917, 2) all showed women ways they could earn their stripes on the home front. Finally, leaders directed readers' attention to people who broke the rules, hoarders, and profiteers in particular, and the consequences they faced. On the whole, the paper's leaders were supportive of government food policy; the major exceptions were in what its editorial board saw as the Navy's failings in protecting merchant shipping and enforcing blockades of Germany, and the belated legislation to make rationing compulsory rather than voluntary. In many of these critical leaders, the editorial often referred to its readers as also being concerned, such as "as letters in our columns show" ("The Growing Bread Shortage" April 21, 1917, 4), thus reinforcing a positive relationship between readers and paper over matters of national importance.

Letters to the Editor

As we have seen, the number of letters to the editor published in the *Daily Mail* on the subject of food increased steadily through the war years, reaching a peak in 1917 and 1918, and then gradually decreasing as rationing and scarcity eased. The last foods to come off the ration were sugar in November 1920, butter in May 1920, and meat in December 1919 (Oddy 2003, 87). A closer examination of these letters shows readers' concerns can be broadly grouped into four key themes: (1) concern over food waste, (2) desire to demonstrate their patriotism and frugality, (3) helpful hints to share with other readers, and (4) dissatisfaction with government food policy.

The first theme, concern over waste, revealed itself in the early months of the war. For example, letters often suggested that too many parts of vegetables were being thrown away through peeling and aggressive topping and tailing ("Food Waste" February 11, 1915, 4) or that processed white flour should be replaced with wholemeal flour, which used more of the wheat husk ("Standard Bread Tributes" January 28, 1915, 4). The baking of "Standard Bread" made with wholemeal flour had been a long-running *Daily Mail* campaign pre-dating the war, and the paper enthusiastically promoted it beginning in January 1915, quoting experts who claimed this practice would markedly increase the bread supply. Readers responded to the paper's campaign, clearly wanting to show themselves as part of a patriotic and frugal "in-group" of which the paper was a standard bearer.

The theme of frugality and patriotism revealed itself not only in letters informing other readers how to grow more and eat less, but also castigating indulgent cake-eating middle-class women, and in one extraordinary exchange, non-smokers who apparently ate more than smokers ("The Value of Thrift" January 23, 1915, 4; "The Cake Habit" March 17, 1916, 4 and "Are Non-Smokers Big Eaters?" May 10, 1917, 4). Letters complaining about government policy were careful not to object to rationing in itself, which was seen as being unpatriotic, but about specific and apparently ineffective kinds of rationing. Jam makers, particularly, complained that sugar rationing resulted in tons of usable fruit going to waste because it couldn't be preserved (a long-running series of correspondence under the heading "No Sugar for Jam" ran through early 1918). Similarly, pig keepers complained that rationing decreased the amount of available food scraps, which led to thinner pigs that could not provide enough meat in the winter ("Pigs and Officials" July 24, 1918, 2; and "More Pig-Keepers Needed" January 19, 1918, 3).

By far the most numerous letters to the editor shared helpful tips with other readers, through recipes for unusual foods, or tips as to where to find alternative sources of food ("Frozen Whale for Food" February 12, 1915, 4; "Plentiful Whortleberries" July 26, 1914, 4; "The Nutritious Carrot" April 20, 1917, 4; and under a heading of "55 Ships Sunk Last Week," a reader recipe for steamed batter pudding using flaked maize rather than flour, April 28, 1917, 2). Other letters suggest that readers were trying to outdo each other by offering quite outlandish proposals, indicating extreme levels of desperation among British households, particularly in the last two years of the war. One correspondent lauded the taste of young seal flesh as being "as delicate as sucking (sic) pig" ("Seal Flesh as Food" February 15, 1918, 2); another argued that cormorant meat was no different to dark game-bird meat ("Roast Seagull" February 19, 1917, 2); and a third praised sparrow meat in puddings, and advised how to trap and pluck them ("Sparrows as Food" February 10, 1917, 2). These letters revealed readers wanting to show themselves as helpful, resourceful, and "doing their bit" from the home front, which was important to the crafting of national identity.

There is a performative nature to many of these letters, some seeking to shock or provoke, others spotlighting the letter writer as a source of folkloric or age-old knowledge. A letter writer extolling the virtues of gulls' eggs, for example, told readers how as a boy he would climb cliffs to hunt for them ("Gulls' Eggs as Food" February 8, 1917, 4); the writer praising seal made sure to tell readers that he had eaten it himself and could vouch for its flavor. This latter letter provoked a response from Herbert Ponting, a celebrity of the time, famous for being the photographer who had accompanied Captain Robert Scott on his 1910–1912 expedition to the South

Pole. Ponting advised readers on how to catch, skin and cook seals ("Seal Flesh Dishes" February 25, 1918, 2).

This response to a letter by another letter writer was common practice, revealing a community of readers and writers talking to each other often without reference to any newspaper content outside the letters' column: a kind of early 20th century media "echo chamber" that we see today with social media, boosting and reinforcing the views of like-minded people (Boulianne et al. 2020). It has been argued that in the contemporary world of social media "people do not live, any longer *with* the media – but increasingly *in* the media," with anyone able to share and express their lifestyles through their Instagram, Twitter, or TikTok accounts (Hanusch and Hanitzsch 2013, 946). These letters from 100 years ago, in the days before social media, and even before public television and radio, reveal efforts by some readers to occupy a position "in" rather than "with" the media and to become part of a newspaper's war effort. This was achieved by a number of means: either the shocking or performative content of letters, as has been shown above, or by letter-writers aligning themselves to newspaper campaigns such as the one for "Standard Bread." Another *Daily Mail* campaign, advocating for the appointment of a director of pig production, was also enthusiastically supported by letter writers: "Sir: some months ago you began a campaign in favour of a larger production of pigs in this country. You were so far successful that you compelled the government to appoint a Director of Pig Production ..." ("Pigs and Officials" July 24, 1918, 2). None of the letters on the subject of food actually contradicted the *Daily Mail's* editorial position, and so a reader contributing positively to the paper's editorial line could be confident of having their letter published and thus read by millions of people.

A third way that letter writers lived "in" the media was similar to social media practices today: by carefully crafting an anonymous persona that conferred authority to the contributor. For example in the long-running "No Sugar for Jam" debate that ran in the letters pages in early 1918 prior to official rationing, one correspondent, writing about the right time to pick and preserve fruit, signed their letter "An Old Woman of Kent" and another "Resident of Kent," these epithets denoting age-old wisdom and practicality as well as someone living in the so-called "Garden of England" that produced much of the nation's soft fruit harvest (January 21 & 23, 1918, 2). Another correspondent writing about "Food Waste in Ships" signed himself off as "Victualling Superintendent" (January 22, 1917, 4), and a contributor to another long-running correspondence on "Standard Bread" signed themselves off as "Housekeeper," again emphasizing their authority to speak on the subject of food and nutrition (January 28, 1915, 3).

Others used humorous or punning epithets. A contributor to the pig-keeping debate signed off as "Food Hog" ("Keep a Pig" November 3, 1917, 2), while a correspondent advising readers to trap and eat sparrows signed off as "Rustic," denoting either a keeper of country lore or, more likely, used the term in the comedic, Shakespearean sense, meaning a simpleton or joker. Either way, the pseudonym was designed both to preserve the writer's anonymity and add texture and enjoyment to the reading of the letter.

Examined together, these letters provide valuable insight into the relationship between readers and their newspaper at a time of national crisis, with readers boosting and contributing to their paper's coverage on vital issues. The paper, in return, granted a certain degree of democratization to its coverage by allowing readers to publicly assert their expertise in their fields. The gatekeeping control, however, of the editorial board does not show us what kinds of letters were left out.

Conclusion

The *Daily Mail* ended the war with circulation slightly higher than in 1914, and as the highest circulation morning paper in the country, overtaking the *Daily Mirror*, at daily sales of 973,343 in 1918 (up from 945,919 in 1914). Although circulation was down from a wartime peak of nearly 1.2 million in 1916, in early 1917 the paper had increased in price from half a pence to a penny, as many papers had done, to cover the increasing costs of newsprint and reduced advertising income (McEwen 1982, 482). This increased circulation, at a time when disposable household incomes had fallen, shows how popular the paper remained among its readers, despite the widespread view that its coverage of the progress of the fighting in the trenches had been woefully inadequate.

While the role of newspapers in the First World War has been widely criticized, we must also examine the important service these papers provided in helping readers navigate the most severe domestic crisis any of them had ever experienced. Readers evidently turned to newspapers for practical help, even as they felt terrified, or misled, by the war news coverage. Detailed examination of the *Daily Mail's* coverage of food in a variety of sections, from journalist-authored news reports to the editor's leaders, to recipes and readers' letters, reveals a close and mutually reinforcing relationship between the paper and its readers. By encouraging thrift, by enabling women to take on a patriotic role in the war effort, and by sanctioning hoarders and profiteers and defining them as alien "others" at a time of crisis, the paper reinforced the idea of "cultural citizenship," an affective state of national belonging that goes beyond legal rights. By establishing an "ideal" attitude to food and privations, the paper helped its readers "navigate their sense of belonging" and showed women how to "situate themselves through behaviour and practices as worthy of rights," a vital precursor to being given full voting rights (Beaman 2016, 851).

This chapter partly explains why the *Daily Mail* and other papers enjoyed such popularity and how "the British press reached an unprecedented level of importance during the First World War, never to attain such heights again" (McEwen 1982, 459) despite, as one newspaper insider admitted, the fact that newspaper mendacity meant that "You can't believe a word you read" (Montague 1922, 103). Readers and their newspaper worked together, collaborating in crafting a national identity and character that would help win the war. The paper permitted readers a degree of active participation in the production of content, allowing them to share their culinary expertise during the years of most severe privation. However, once the hostilities were over, the *Daily Mail* reverted to its traditional role of provider of information and advice to a passive readership. The Food Bureau not only provided vital advice to readers but also, by deliberately mimicking the features of Britain's pre-eminent department store, allowed the paper to retain its image as a paper for the middle classes, maintaining its one penny readership and advertising revenue.

References

Anderson, Benedict. 1983. *Imagined Communities*. London: Verso.
Ashley, Bob, Joanne Hollows, Steve Jones, and Ben Taylor. 2004. *Food and Cultural Studies*. London: Routledge.
Beaman, Jean. 2016. "Citizenship as Cultural: Towards a Theory of Cultural Citizenship." *Sociology Compass* 10(10):849–857.
Bentley, Amy. 2001. "Reading Food Riots: Scarcity and Abundance and National Identity." In *Food, Drink and Identity: Cooking, Eating and Drinking in Europe since the Middle Ages*, edited by Peter Scholliers, 179–193. Oxford: Berg.
Boulianne, Shelley, Karolina Koc-Michalska, and Bruce Bimber. 2020. "Right-Wing Populism, Social Media and Echo Chambers in Western Democracies." *New Media and Society* 22(4):683–699.
Bourdieu, Pierre. 1984. *Distinction*. London: Routledge.
Brittain, Vera. 2009 [1933]. *Testament of Youth*. London: Weidenfeld and Nicholson.
Coller, Frank Herbert. 1925. *A State Trading Adventure*. Oxford: Oxford University Press.
Costera Meijer, Irene. 2001. "The Public Quality of Popular Journalism: Developing a Normative Framework." *Journalism Studies* 2(2):189–205.
Duffy, Andrew and Ashley Yang Yuhong. 2012. "Bread and Circuses: Food Meets Politics in the Singapore Media." *Journalism Practice* 6(1):59–74.
Eide, Martin and Graham Knight. 1999. "Public/Private Service: Service Journalism and the Problems of Everyday Life." *European Journal of Communication* 14:525–547.
Fürsich, Elfriede. 2013. "Lifestyle Journalism as Popular Journalism: Strategies for Evaluating Its Public Role." In *Lifestyle Journalism*, edited by Folker Hanusch, 11–24. London: Routledge.
Griffiths, Dennis. 2006. *Fleet Street: One Hundred Years of the Press*. London: British Library.
Hanusch, Folker and Thomas Hanitzsch. 2013. "Mediating Orientation and Self-Expression in the World of Consumption: Australian and German Lifestyle Journalists' Professional Views." *Media, Culture and Society* 35:943–959.

Hockenhull, Stella. 2015. "Everybody's Business: Film, Food and Victory in the First World War." *Historical Journal of Film, Radio and Television.* 35(4):579–595.

Jensen, Kimberly. 2019. "Whether We Vote or Not We Are Going to Shoot." In *100 Years of Women's Suffrage*, edited by Dawn Durante and Nancy Hewitt, 55–78. Chicago: University of Illinois Press.

Knightley, Phillip. 2000. *The First Casualty: The War Correspondent as Myth-Maker from the Crimea to Kosovo.* London: Prion Books.

Kristensen, Nete Norgaard and Unni From. 2013. "Lifestyle Journalism: Blurring Boundaries." In *Lifestyle Journalism*, edited by Folker Hanusch, 25–40. London: Routledge.

Lonsdale, Sarah. 2015. "'Roast Seagull and Other Quaint Bird Dishes': The Development of Features and 'Lifestyle' Journalism in British Newspapers during the First World War." *Journalism Studies* 16(6):800–815.

Lonsdale, Sarah. 2016. *The Journalist in British Fiction and Film: Guarding the Guardians from 1900 to the Present.* London: Bloomsbury Academic.

McEwen, John. 1982. "The National Press During the First World War: Ownership and Circulation." *Journal of Contemporary History* 17(3):459–486.

Montague, C. E. 1922. *Disenchantment.* London: Chatto and Windus.

Oddy, Derek. 2003. *From Plain Fare to Fusion Food: British Diet from the 1890s to the 1990s.* Woodbridge: Boydell and Brewer.

Peel, Dorothy. 1918. *Daily Mail War Recipes.* London: Constable and Co.

Peel, Dorothy. 1929. *How We Lived Then 1914–1918.* London: John Lane The Bodley Head.

Peel, Dorothy. 1933. *Life's Enchanted Cup.* London: John Lane the Bodley Head.

Rich, Rachel. 2011. *Bourgeois Consumption: Food, Space and Identity in London and Parish 1850–1914.* Manchester: Manchester University Press.

Schlesinger, Philip. 1987. "On National Identity: Some Conceptions and Misconceptions Criticised." *Social Science Information* 26(2):219–264.

Scholliers, Peter. 2001. "Meals, Food Narratives and Sentiments of Belonging in the Past and Present." In *Food, Drink and Identity: Cooking, Eating and Drinking in Europe since the Middle Ages*, edited by Peter Scholliers, 3–22. Oxford: Berg.

Van Emden, Richard, and Steve Humphries. 2003. *All Quiet on the Home Front: An Oral History of Life in Britain during the First World War.* London: Pen and Sword Military.

12 Influencer before the Internet: The Extraordinary Career of Chef, Editor, and Food Entrepreneur Alma Lach

Kimberly Voss

Chicago-based Alma Elizabeth Satorius Lach (1914–2013) was a food celebrity in her day. If she had come onto the scene decades later, she likely would have had her own magazine, a show on the Food Network and possibly a restaurant. She was a food influencer when this term did not exist yet. This chapter traces her extraordinary career and highlights her contributions to the culinary and media industry. Lach, who graduated from *Le Cordon Blue* cooking school in Paris in 1956, published several children's cookbooks, hosted *Let's Cook,* a children's cooking program on WTTW Chicago (1955), and served as the food editor for the *Chicago Sun-Times* from 1957 to 1964. Through her company, Alma Lach Kitchens, she served as a consultant to several Chicago restaurants and to Flying Food Fare, which provided meals for Midway Airlines, and in the 1970s she opened a cooking school on Chicago's Rush Street. Lach forged her remarkable career at a time when such opportunities for women were scarce. Her perseverance and professional successes illustrate and transcend gender politics and inequality in her respective fields. Shortly after Lach's death in 2013, a reporter described Lach's career as one "that brings back that prefeminist era of female achievement when motivated women accomplished a lot within what was assumed to be their sphere" (Gebert 2013).

Few newspaper food editors save or donate their papers to archives, leaving historians with little evidence of their work. However, after Lach died in 2013, her daughter donated her mother's papers to the Special Collections Research Center at the University of Chicago Library in Hyde Park, a collection that includes more than 3,000 cookbooks, personal notebooks, papers, cooking ephemera, and promotional materials. This collection provided artifacts for "Alma Lach's Kitchen: Transforming Taste," a 2016 exhibition curated by Eileen Ielmini, Brittan Nannenga, and Catherine Uecker along with exhibition designer Joseph Scott. The collection and exhibit provide a rare glimpse into the professional life of a trained chef, cookbook author, food journalist, and media personality whose work escaped the confines of the women's pages. The collection and exhibit can also serve to advance still scarce scholarship on the history of women in journalism, specifically food journalism. Such a project complements recent research on New York food writer Clementine Paddleford (Alexander and Harris 2008), *Chicago Tribune* food editor and the first wine editor in the US Ruth Ellen Church (Voss 2014), and *Milwaukee Journal* food editor, founder, and first president of the Association of Food Journalists Peggy Daum (Voss and Speere 2013). This chapter introduces what has come to light about the extraordinary career of Alma Lach through her archives in the hope that other scholars will take advantage of this valuable contribution to the historical record of women in US journalism, especially food journalism.

Home Economics, Women's Pages, and the Development of Food Journalism

Throughout the history of American journalism, women worked as publishers, editors, political reporters, literary critics, and advice columnists for magazines and major newspapers such as the *New York Herald Tribune, Pittsburgh Dispatch*, the *New York Times*, the *Washington Star*, and many more, well before the establishment of women's pages in the latter half of the 19th century. The growth of women's magazines and newspaper sections in this time period, and the establishment of Home Economics programs beginning in 1914, opened up the field. Many middle-class women were able to work in journalism writing about fashion, furnishings, family – and food, whether it was for newspapers, magazines, cooking schools, or food companies. College home economics programs provided professional training for these women, including copywriting, new technologies, and educating consumers, among others, and their advancement in the workforce was made easier by their focus on non-threatening, traditionally "women's" concerns. For example, home economic graduates often worked in advertising, for women's magazines, and for newspaper women's pages, where food news was located. For decades, universities offered a home economics journalism major or minor for students – who were overwhelmingly female.

Recently there has been an increase in the study of the history of home economics and a re-examination of what the field meant for women. As one scholar wrote: "Home economics has not fared well at the hands of historians. Until recently women historians largely dismissed home economics as little more than a conspiracy to keep women in the kitchen" (Stage and Vincnti 1997, 1). Yet, many students who majored in home economics often went on to significant careers in teaching, journalism, and advertising. In recent years, research has found home economics to be a more complex and diverse field than previously thought. Home economics (initially called domestic science) often focused on skills in the home yet was also a path to a public career. These graduates worked in advertising, teaching, and journalism (Goldstein 2012).

Lach represents women who used home economics to carve a place for themselves in the public sphere. Because the knowledge and skills required of those who worked in the field were associated with traditional unpaid, domestic female work, women were granted authority to write about, teach and otherwise take on gainful home economics employment. Lach pushed back against the limits of what was considered permissible and possible by balancing several roles: writing cookbooks for children, hosting a cooking television show for youngsters, and authoring stories about family dinners, while also writing a French cookbook (representing the epitome of sophisticated professional cooking), acting as a consultant for restaurateurs, and starting not one but two businesses. Her work was a harbinger of the kinds of multi-faceted careers that later cooks and chefs would build in and outside of media. It demonstrates that women were able to build successful careers in food and food journalism at a time when many other professions limited women's involvement by leveraging new opportunities opened up by both home economics programs and newspaper women's pages.

The women's pages have a long history in American newspapers. Most journalism historians note that Joseph Pulitzer started the women's pages in 1891 for the *New York World* to increase advertising revenue for products aimed at women (Gottlieb 2008, 601–602; Marzlof 1977, 207). Other research has found that additional newspapers may have published women's pages at about the same time or even earlier. One of the earliest food columns was produced by the *Milwaukee Journal*, which began covering food on November 25, 1882, in a women's page: "Women and the Home—HER DAILY PAGE," with suggestions for how to boil corned beef and make a wine pudding sauce (Stohs 1995).

Similarly, the *Chicago Tribune* printed a one-paragraph recipe for baked ham in 1849, just two years after it began publishing. The recipe appeared alongside short articles about law reform in England and exploration of the African continent. By 1910, the *Tribune* included recipes and household tips in a daily column called the *"Tribune* Cook Book." The column included instructions on baking and canning, noting that cooking was both an art and a science. In addition, the *San Francisco Chronicle* began its women's page in 1895. Ten years later, the newspaper hired a full-time food editor. Most newspapers continued that trend.

From the earliest days and up through the decades, food journalism provided a way for editors to understand and engage with their communities. In the 1950s, a journalism industry publication advised food editors to become familiar with the tastes and food interests of their readers and to help them by providing recipes sought by the housewife in her constant pursuit of variety, incorporating both humble and luxury ingredients. In 1952, the *Chicago Tribune* wrote that readers were requesting recipes for French pastry, Italian cannoli, and East Indian curry. Readers also wanted to know how to fix potato salad, coleslaw, bread pudding, and corned beef hash.

Yet food editors did more than provide how-to advice for the kitchen. As food production, distribution, preservation, and marketing changed drastically following World War II, readers sought advice and assurance. In

1955, Ruth Ellen Church, Lach's equivalent at the *Chicago Tribune*, described the changes in the food industry during the previous decade as "revolutionary." She noted: "Fully a third of the products and foods we buy now in the supermarket were not even in existence ten years ago: instant puddings, cake mixes, instant coffee, instant dry milk, detergents, the wide array of frozen and pre-packaged foods" (Church 1955). In fact, by the 1950s, one of every three food products available at the grocery store came in a can (Smith 2009, 71–72). Some consumers were concerned about these developments, and Lach regularly sought to assuage her readers' anxiety. For example, she wrote, "When people talk about the 'good old days,' I ask them if they would like to go back to drinking unpasteurized milk, then inquire if they would like once again to eat meats that carry no government stamp of approval" (Campbell 1961, 52).

Although food editors provided much desired and useful information and services for readers, the importance of their work has often been dismissed. In 2004, the *American Journalism Review* covered the increased interest in food journalism, arguing that it had gone upscale after decades of simply serving as a filler section in the paper. The author wrote: "Food journalism has long been an oxymoron with newspaper food pages. Little more than wire service recipe dumps and magazine articles barely scraping deeper than 'what's hot and what's not'" (Brown 2004). David Kamp, in his popular history *The United States of Arugula*, described these journalists as the "Jell-O abusing women's-page ladies" (2006, 10). Characterizations such as these discounted the work found in many women's pages prior to the demise of the sections in the early 1970s, despite evidence that it was these women's page reporters who built the foundation for today's complex, vibrant, and profitable food journalism.

Lach's Early Years

Alma Satorius was born in Petersburg, Illinois, in 1914. She learned to cook at age six on the wood-burning stove in the kitchen of her farmhouse, located on 600 acres in New Salem, Illinois. She was used to home-grown ingredients, contributing to the work of raising chickens for eggs and cows for butter. "Eating local" was not a trend; it was everyday life. As a child, she participated in the youth development program 4-H and took a prize in a cooking contest. Years later, she recalled the important role her mother played in her culinary training: "I owe an incalculable debt. Even today when I go home for a visit, my mother and I spend the late hours of the evening (after the dishes are done, that is) discussing and swapping recipes" (Lach 1998, xxi).

Lach took English classes at the University of Chicago in 1934 and may have taken part in a home economics nutrition project on campus, but she left university after a year. She met history graduate student Donald F. Lach, and they married in 1939. He eventually earned a doctoral degree in

1941 and joined the faculty in 1948. He studied Europe and Asia in the 16th through 18th centuries, which led to significant travel. The couple had a daughter, Sandra (Station 2019).

In 1949, the family moved to Paris after Donald was awarded a fellowship. While there, Lach enrolled in a three-year program at the *Cordon Bleu*. Her husband was excited. "Learn to make a sauce. I am tired of country gravy," he said (Lach 1970). Lach attended classes during the day, and after school she attempted to duplicate the dishes she had been practicing for her husband and daughter. If a dish did not turn out quite right, she reworked the recipe until it was perfect. Years later, she remembered that time fondly: "It was a marvelous escape for a few hours each day" (Claiborne 1968).

Over the next few years, Lach filled numerous notebooks with French recipes and mastered hundreds of sauces before earning her diploma in 1956. By then, she had completed enough classes to earn a *Grande Diplome*, the most comprehensive professional chef diploma conferred by the *Cordon Bleu*. Her training eventually led her to write *Cooking à la Cordon Bleu*, published in 1970 by Harper & Row. The *Cordon Bleu* had not given Lach permission to use its name in her title and after Harper & Row declined to reissue the book it was republished in 1974 by the University of Chicago Press as the *Hows and Whys of French Cooking* with new sections about regional French cuisine. The book included a foreward from famed gourmet and wine expert Andre L. Simon, who gushed, "Cookery books published in the course of my long life may be beyond count, but very few of them were like this one, beyond praise!" (x).

Food Writer, Consultant, and Entrepreneur

Early in her career, Lach published cookbooks for children – her first in 1950, *A Child's First Cookbook*. It included recipes and pictures to make snacks and simple meals. *Life* magazine featured it in a multi-page spread including photos (1950). She went on to write more cookbooks for children, including *The Campbell Kids Have a Party* (1954b), *The Campbell Kids at Home* (1954a), and *Let's Cook* (1956). Cookbooks for children were common in the 1950s and 1960s. For example, Ruth Ellen Church wrote a children's cookbook in 1965 under the pen name "Mary Meade," and famed newspaper food editor Clementine Paddleford wrote a children's cookbook a year later (1966).

Lach's food career was not limited to newspapers and cookbooks; she also made regular television appearances. In 1955, she created, produced, and hosted her own children's televised cooking series, *Let's Cook*, in Chicago. It was first broadcast on WTTW and later moved to WGN-TV. She also appeared regularly as a nutritionist and cooking expert on other television programs. For example, from 1977 to 1978 she was featured on the PBS television series *Over Easy*, and then on the television show *2020* with journalist Hugh Downs where she prepared gourmet dishes for people of retirement age. Downs later won his first Emmy Award for that series. On television, Lach straddled the roles of trained chef and home cook, professional cooking for the public and domestic cooking for the family.

In 1957, Lach was hired as the food editor of the *Chicago Sun-Times*, a daily newspaper with the second largest circulation among Chicago newspapers, second to the *Chicago Tribune*. At the *Sun-Times*, Lach wrote twice-weekly columns about gourmet dishes, tried recipes in her test kitchen, and oversaw food photography. Her section was often promoted by the newspaper, and at one point, a photograph of Lach and her section appeared on the side of a newspaper delivery truck with the slogan: "A Brand New Lift-Out Section: Good Food."

While at the *Sun-Times*, Lach published a cooking booklet, *For Seven Candlelight Dinner*. She explained that her recipes were practical: "And for families with growing children, a special dinner served in candlelight may produce an atmosphere of elegant refinement that will even help Junior to remember his table manners" (Lach n.d., 3). Her recipes included traditional dishes such as rib roast, Cornish game hens, and baked ham – and one for rabbit in a sauce. (Oddly, there is an illustration of rabbits in a classroom doing multiplication.) There were also recipes for pork tenderloin in wine, avocado salad, and asparagus with mint sauce.

In 1958, Lach was recognized in one of the most prominent competitive cooking events in the country – the Pillsbury Bake-Off, which was started in 1949 as the "Grand National Recipe and Baking Contest" and was covered in newspapers across the country. Held at the New York Waldorf-Astoria Hotel, former First Lady Eleanor Roosevelt handed out the top prize. Lach was a winner in 1958 in the food editor category and was awarded a fur coat as part of the honor.

After leaving the *Chicago Sun-Times* in the mid-1960s, Lach founded the Alma Lach Cooking School on Rush Street, focusing first on French cuisine and later introducing classes featuring Asian food. She recalled Chicago Mayor Michael Bilandic and his wife arriving at her school in their limousine and sitting in the back row watching a cooking demonstration. The famed George Bay, who founded Bays Bakery in 1938 downtown and was known for his English Muffins with orange marmalade, also attended Lach's school (Haddix 2007a, 62).

During this time, Lach launched a monthly subscription cooking publication, *Alma's Almanac*. The newsletter included recipes and entertainment tips. Starting in 1972, the monthly *Almanac* provided menu plans and recipes to its subscribers. It also included a culinary crossword puzzle, restaurant recommendations, and wine news, as well as a question box for readers. The annual subscription was $21.50, which would be about $155 today.

In 1968, *New York Times* food editor Craig Claiborne wrote about Lach's cooking. This was significant media attention, as these stories were often syndicated. Claiborne noted that the Lach hosted a couple of small dinners twice a week and held large cocktail buffets several times a year. The story included a recipe for Lach's version of Elaborate Tempura with Alaska King crab legs. Lach told Claiborne that French and Chinese were the best cuisines, and she noted some similarities in the sauces.

In addition, Lach was a founding member of the Chicago Chapter of the *Les Dames d'Escoffier* in 1982 along with *Chicago Tribune* food editor Carol Mighton Haddix and Chicago cookware store owner Elaine Sherman. *Les Dames d'Escoffier* is named after Auguste Escoffier, one of the most innovative chefs in culinary history. The organization is an international philanthropy group of women leaders in the culinary, beverage, and hospitality industries. Current members include a variety of chefs, nutritionists, and journalists. Each year, the Chicago chapter of *Les Dames d'Escoffier* also raises money for scholarships.

Years after the organization's establishment, Lach had the idea for the Chicago members to write a cookbook about Chicago food. They collected recipes, tested, and photographed them. The organization's leaders noted: "For a food group like this, it was almost embarrassing that we never in all these years had pulled together members' recipes into a book. It was long overdue" (Mighton Haddix 2007b). Published in 2007, *Chicago Cooks* included a culinary history of the city and recipes from chefs and home cooks. Lach contributed a recipe for Swedish Lace Oatmeal Cookies – which included only butter, sugar, and oatmeal. She described it as the easiest and best cookie she knew (41). In 2007, Lach was named a "Dame of Distinction" by the organization.

Lach's business portfolio and reputation as an expert in the food world continued to grow when she established her own business, Alma Lach Kitchens, Inc., where she tested recipes, created elaborate menus, and served as a consultant for Midway Airlines – a regional airline out of Milwaukee, Wisconsin – and a number of high profile Chicago restaurants, including the landmark downtown Chicago restaurant, The Berghoff, opened in 1890 by Herman Joseph Berghoff, and the Pump Room, opened in 1938 and located in the Ambassador hotel on the corner of State Parkway and Goethe Street in the city's Gold Coast. The Pump Room was popular among celebrities and was often covered in the press. It was also part of popular culture, with references in The Monkey's 1967 song "Don't Call on Me" and the 1964 Frank Sinatra song "My Kind of Town (Chicago Is)."

Richard Melman, who ran The Pump Room, was responsible for hiring Lach as the restaurant's consultant. "I was a kid and realized I didn't really know what good food was," he said in an interview. "She knew so much, I was enthralled. Her job was just to teach me about food by cooking for me, taking me places to eat, and sitting around and talking." Melman recalled Lach teaching him about caviar. He had included it in the salad bar of his first restaurant but admitted to Lach that he did not know why people got excited about it. This was because the brand he bought cost only $8 a pound and tasted awful to him. She set him straight, "and introduced me to great caviar, and fine smoked salmon, and foie gras," he said. Melman also said Lach encouraged him to start featuring Chinese cuisine, but he did not follow her advice at the time. "The most untapped source of food I know is Chinese food," she told him. "It has so much depth, you ought to start thinking about it." Eventually he figured out she was right about Asian cooking and even opened sushi restaurants in the city (Spiselman 2016).

Lach received several awards during her culinary career. Because she earned the *Grand Diplôme* from *Le Cordon Bleu* cooking school, she was granted membership in the *Légion d'Honneur* by the French government. She was also one of the first American women to be inducted as a member of the *Confrérie des Chevaliers du Tastevin* in 1962. Two years later, she became a member of the *Chaîne des Rôtisseurs*, one of the world's oldest gastronomic societies – founded in Paris in 1248.

Finally, Lach was an inventor who held two patents including one for the "Curly Dog Cutting Board," a maple board that was grooved on one side for cutting hot dogs into curls, catching crumbs when slicing bread, and containing juice when slicing fruit, and that was smooth on the other side for slicing and chopping. Her other patent was for the Walker Tray – designed when she was 90 years old after she broke her leg in an accident. Forced to use a walker until she recovered, she became frustrated with her inability to carry a meal to the table, so she designed a tray that could easily attach to her walker.

Lach passed away at age 99 in 2013. Entertaining and innovating all the way up to the end, she hosted a party just a few weeks before her death. When she died, numerous publications recognized her life's work with articles describing her as a pioneer and highlighting her contributions to the Chicago culinary community. The Chicago chapter of Les Dames d'Escoffier noted: "She was and will always be thought of as a professional's professional, a mentor and a friend" (Reardon 2013).

Conclusion: "Women's Work," Gender Politics, and Archives

Historians have been late to highlight and investigate professional women, especially those working in food industries, home economics, and food journalism. Their work has been overlooked or discounted because it seemed to reinforce a traditional role for women while women's work was devalued (Elias 2008; Goldstein 2012). Yet, women like Lach played significant roles in their culinary communities and in the development of food journalism in newspapers, magazines, television, and branded content. They were also forerunners of today's complex integration of food journalism with other genres of food media along with entrepreneurship. With the rise of lifestyle influencers in the digital era, women are again at the center of activating the private realm for business. This "entrepreneurial femininity" (Duffy and Hund 2015) championed by fashion Instagramers, Mommy bloggers, or food influencers alike is rightly criticized for drawing "upon post-feminist sensibilities and the contemporary logic of self-branding" (Duffy and Hund 2015, 1) while hiding gender, race, and class inequalities. Research on previous female entrepreneurs in the culinary world can add another dimension to understanding the challenges of women in creative businesses. The inclination of influencers to obscure the actual effort, labor, and discipline that goes into this work is not just a problematic branding strategy developed for the digital media economy but a long-established strategic necessity for women entrepreneurs who want to succeed in a male-dominated sector.

Another obstacle to more historic inquiry is the scarcity of archival material since many of the sources of female achievement are not collected or documented by elite outlets, but in unsystematic private collections of flyers, pamphlets, and clips from entertainment or lifestyle media. Archival work of any aspect of what is considered popular culture, as opposed to of official public interest, is a challenge, but the sidelining of women in public life has intensified female absence and symbolic annihilation in historic accounts even more. Had Lach not kept her own material throughout her life and her daughter not donated it, it would have been almost impossible to retrace her impact and influence. Such materials are critical for historical scholarship on the lives of women who are often left out of other traditional historical accounts (Bower 2004; McIntosh and Zey 1989; Theophano 2003).

In this case, Lach was well known in Chicago for her food writing, television appearances, cooking school, consultancy, and entrepreneurship. She was included in the 2017 edition of the *Chicago Food Encyclopedia* published by the University of Illinois Press, and her papers and cookbook collection are now available at the University of Chicago for future research. Hopefully this collection will inspire others, expanding the archival record and formal histories of the women who shaped our culinary culture, food media, and food journalism.

References

Alexander, Kelly and Cynthia Harris. 2008. *Hometown Appetites*. New York: Gotham Books.

Brown, Doug . 2004. "Hautecuisine." *American Journalism Review* 26(1). https://go-gale-com.pitt.idm.oclc.org/ps/i.do?id=GALE%7CA113611644&sid=googleScholar&v=2.1&it=r&linkaccess=abs&issn=10678654&p=AONE&sw=w&userGroupName=anon%7E47bcf72b

Bower, Anna. 2004. "Romanced by Cookbooks." *Gastronomica: The Journal of Food and Culture* 4(2):35–42.

Campbell, Persia. 1961. "Current Consumer Problems." *Food, Drug, Cosmetic Law Journal* 17(1):48–51.

Church, Ruth Ellen Lovrien. "Bobb-Merrill Biographical Questionnaire." Fall 1955. Bobb-Merrill Misc, Box 32: Ruth Ellen Church, Manuscripts Department, The Lilly Library, Indiana University-Bloomington.

Claiborne, Craig. 1968. "Driven to Fine Food by Paris Cold and Ennui." *New York Times*, August 15, 1968. F42

Duffy, Brooke Erin, and Emily Hund. 2015. "'Having It All' on Social Media: Entrepreneurial Femininity and Self-Branding among Fashion Bloggers." *Social Media + Society* 1(2):1–11.

Elias, Megan J. 2008. *Stir It Up: Home Economics in American Culture*. Philadelphia: PA: University of Pennsylvania Press.

Gebert, Michael. 2013. "In Memory of Alma Lach, 1950s Pioneer," *Chicago Reader*, November 6, 2013. https://chicagoreader.com/blogs/in-memory-of-alma-lach-1950s-pioneer/

Goldstein, Carolyn M. 2012. *Creating Consumers: Home Economists in Twentieth-Century America*. Chapel Hill, North Carolina: University of North Carolina Press.

Gottlieb, Agnes Hooper. 2008. "Women's Pages." In *The Encyclopedia of American Journalism*, edited by Stephen Vaugn, 601–602. New York: Routledge.

Haddix, Carol Mighton. 2007a. *Chicago Cooks*. Chicago: Surrey Books.

Haddix, Carol Mighton. 2007b. "An Essential Food Group." *Chicago Tribune*, December 23, 2007:10, 20

Kamp, David, 2006. *The United States of Arugula: How We Became a Gourmet Nation*. New York: Broadway Books.

Lach, Alma. (nd). "Candlelight Dinner." *Chicago Daily News*.

Lach, Alma. 1970. *Cooking à la Cordon Bleu*. New York: Harper and Row.

Lach, Alma S. 1954a. *The Campbell Kids at Home*. Chicago: Rand McNally & Company.

Lach, Alma S. 1954b. *The Campbell Kids Have a Party*. Chicago: Rand McNally & Company.

Lach, Alma S. 1956. *Let's Cook*. Chicago: Child Training Association.

Lach, Amla S. 1998. *Hows and Whys of French Cooking: A Revised and Expanded Edition of Cooking à la Cordon Bleu*. Rev. and expanded ed. Edison, NJ: Castle Books/Book Sales

Marzlof, Marion. 1977. *Up From the Footnote: A History of Women Journalists*. New York: Hasting House Publishers.

McIntosh, William Alex and Mary Zey. 1989. "Women as Gatekeepers of Food Consumption." *Food and Foodways* 3(4):317–332.

Meade, Mary. 1965. *Cooking Fun*. Chicago, Illinois: Chicago Tribune.

Paddleford, Clementine. 1966. *Cook Young Cookbook*. New York: Pocket Books.

Reardon, Joan. 2013. "Remembering Alma Lach." *Les Dames d'Escoffier Chicago*. December 3, 2013. http://www.lesdameschicago.org/2013/12/03/remembering-alma-lach/.

Smith, Andrew F. 2009. *Eating History: 30 Turning Points in the Making of American Cuisine*. New York: Columbia University Press.

Spiselman, Anne. 2016. "Looking Back at Alma Lach, Chicago's Julia Child." *Foodeditor*. November 1, 2016. https://fooditor.com/looking-back-alma-lach-chicagos-julia-child/

Stage, Sarah andVirginia Bramble Vincenti. 1997, *Rethinking Home Economics: Women and the History of a Profession.* Ithaca: Cornell University Press.

Station, Elizabeth. 2019. "Fine Dining Found a Fine Muse in Alma Lach." *Core*, supplement of the University of Chicago Magazine.

Stohs, Nancy. 1995. "A Place at Your Table." *Milwaukee Journal Sentinel*, March 29, 1995. E1

Theophano, Janet. 2003. *Eat My Words: Reading Women's Lives Through the Cookbooks They Wrote.* New York, NY: St. Martin's Griffin.

Voss, Kimberly Wilmot. 2014. *The Food Section: Newspaper Women and the Culinary Community.* Studies in Food and Gastronomy. Lanham, Maryland: Rowman & Littlefield.

Voss, Kimberly and Lance Speere. 2013. "Food Fight: Accusations of Press Agentry." *Gastronomica* 13(2):41–50.

13 *Chef's Table* and a Collective Past: Netflix, Food Media, and Cultural Memories

Diana Willis

Grant Achatz, three-Michelin-star chef and owner of Chicago's Alinea restaurant, proclaims in the Netflix series *Chef's Table*, "To my father, [food] was nothing more than a paycheck. I thought there has to be something more than Western omelets and hamburgers" (*Chef's Table*, "Grant Achatz," Season 2, Episode 1, 10:56). In many ways, Achatz' dismissal of his father's livelihood prepares viewers for the entire series. Through the use of autobiographical, historical, and collective cultural memories, *Chef's Table* depicts food and food practices through a lens of distinction.

This critically acclaimed series explores the lives of celebrated chefs from around the world, such as Modena's Massimo Bottura, Savannah's Mashama Bailey, and Melbourne's Ben Shewry. The show premiered in 2015 and was created by David Gelb, director of the 2011 documentary *Jiro Dreams of Sushi* and founder of the production company Supper Club. It has been praised for its aesthetic approach to food television. Its strategic use of visual imagery contributes significantly to the establishment of a unified sense of narrative time and place and of a collective, shared understanding of the past. Each episode draws on the power of nostalgia while also constituting a practice of mediating memory, of negotiating past and present in the service of contemporary identity construction (Phillipov 2016; van Dijck 2007).

This chapter explores how recollections used to document a chef's past simultaneously allow viewers to embark on memory tourism, encouraging them to "(re)confirm ... notions of imagination and reality" (Reijnders 2011). In a textual and thematic analysis, I examine how the series' use of mediated memories curates the past by cementing personal identities and establishing collective temporal events in dynamic convergences of past and future (van Dijck 2007). The goal of this chapter is to contribute to the intersection of memory studies and food media studies by analyzing the mediated representations of chefs' lives produced by *Chef's Table* as both a key locus of contemporary negotiations of identity and elite authenticity.

The Aesthetic and Narrative Framework of *Chef's Table*

In restaurants, the "chef's table" is located in the working kitchen, reserved for special guests. It is a site of prestige and privilege, one that provides diners with the opportunity to engage in intimate conversation with the chef and enjoy a personalized menu. Echoing that private dining experience, *Chef's Table* uses a documentary approach to introduce viewers to acclaimed chefs from around the world. Each hour-long episode takes viewers on a slow-paced "hero's journey" into the chefs' kitchens and lives. With some exceptions, each episode begins outside of the featured restaurant in a locale that is important to the chef's life and work, an *amuse bouche* so to speak. For example, episode four of season two opens with a scene depicting women making traditional mole as chef Enrique Olvera explains its significance to both Mexican culture and his professional and personal life. These opening scenes are always followed by a series of visual courses, vignettes that comprise the rest of the episodic menu. The "first course" consists of experts introducing the chef to viewers by offering praise and acknowledgment of their trailblazing accomplishments. Next, we meet the chef, either at home or at work, pleasantly reminiscing about their childhood, sharing memories related to the dishes featured in the episode. Viewers are then taken inside the restaurant where the dishes come to life (although there is never a sustained focus on their preparation) or to locations meaningful to the chefs (e.g., Brazilian rainforest, familial mango orchards). Finally, toward the end of the episode, each dish is presented in tasting menu style, one after another, beautifully plated. In cinematic documentary style, *Chef's Table* uses an aesthetic framework to tell its stories. It also relies on sweeping music, slow-motion, and extreme close-ups, techniques that are often associated with "food porn" (McBride 2010; Lindenfeld and Parasecoli 2018; Stein 2016). Yet in *Chef's Table*, these techniques reference a highbrow elegance (Peterson and Kern 1996, 904) that distinguishes it from food media programs typically produced for the Food Network or the Public Broadcasting Service. The show does not intend primarily to educate or to inform. Rather, *Chef's Table* serves as an artistic representation of social and class distinction rooted in the privileging of Michelin stars, critically acclaimed restaurants, and fine dining.

Culinary Capital and Negotiations of Class

The narrative and visual strategies used in *Chef's Table* invoke culinary capital. According to Peter Naccarato and Kathleen LeBesco (2012), culinary capital rests on the premise that food and food practices can serve as markers of social status and ultimately construct social identities. The concept is tied to French sociologist Pierre Bourdieu's ideas of cultural capital, social distinction, and taste. In the 1960s, Bourdieu argued that individuals with access to cultural capital – assets such as education, patterns of speech, style of dress, manners, and other forms of symbolic currency that can promote social mobility beyond economic means – determine what constitutes "good" taste in their society, the demonstration of which in turn can be used to substantiate social status and distinction. Bourdieu mapped this process onto food, specifically the food practices of the poor and the bourgeoisie, noting that "elastic" working class meals were abundant, served with ladles or spoons, and free from rules governing how they should be served. The bourgeoisie meal, in contrast, emphasized rhythmic form, presenting modest portions on small plates in highly choreographed sequence, rigidly organized and ceremonial, and free from the vulgarity of working-class food culture (Bourdieu 1984, 196).

On *Chef's Table*, the bourgeoise meal takes center stage. Exquisitely plated dishes are placed on freshly unfurled tablecloths accompanied by a soundtrack of Antonio Vivaldi's "The Four Seasons." And thanks to its distribution on Netflix, which in 2021 had approximately 75 million subscribers in the United States and Canada and almost 222 million worldwide, *Chef's Table* offers wide and diverse audiences the chance to vicariously dine at the world's best restaurants without concern for cost or accessibility – and affirms the legitimacy and appropriateness of this desire.

With each episode, *Chef's Table* invites viewers into its negotiations of class as it represents, trades in, and makes available to viewers culinary capital, which Naccarato and LeBesco have defined as the process of assigning value to certain foods and food practices, a process which confers status and power to those who can access and accumulate that capital (Naccarato and LeBesco 2012) and which is shaped by conceptions of "highbrow" and "lowbrow" cultures (Peterson and Kern 1996). In *Chef's Table*, culinary capital is demonstrated not only through an appreciation for fine restaurant dining, but also through a commitment to ethical farming practices. For example, Dan Barber, chef and owner of two Blue Hill restaurants in New York state, champions ethical and sustainable farming practices and encourages viewers to use the *best* ingredients derived from *great* farming, without acknowledging the high cost of such ingredients or the reality of industrialized foodways (*Chef's Table*, "Dan Barber," Season 1, Episode 2).

In addition, *Chef's Table* demonstrates culinary capital through a preference for local, native, and often humble ingredients illustrating the ways that "good taste" in contemporary food culture is not bound to the simple economic-class distinctions of the past (Johnston and Baumann 2010). For example, in one episode, Brazilian chef Alex Atala (D.O.M, São Paulo) reflects on the ways individuals learn to cultivate an appreciation or distaste for certain foods:

> I remember very well my first taste of caviar. I said, I don't know if that's good. I remember very well the first day that I tasted tucupi, the juice of manioc flour. And I said … I don't know if I like it. But if caviar

is fancy ... and tucupi is not fancy, it's just because someone told me. There's a cultural interpretation of flavors. (*Chef's Table,* "Alex Atala," Season 2, Episode 5, 00:14:22)

Atala extends his personal negotiations of class to his restaurant, specifically with his "Brazilian Workers' Food," a dish that reflects his working-class roots. The dish includes an edible Amazonian ant, an ingredient native to and popular in the Indigenous Amazon, but traditionally eschewed in fine dining circles and more widely in the West. In this episode, audiences are instructed on how to cultivate an appreciation for this "worker's food" as American restaurateur David Chang suggests that: "If you close your eyes, it tastes delicious" (16:40). In this way, humble, native ingredients are adopted, but then *elevated* by accomplished chefs – a recurring theme across episodes.

Similarly, in another episode, Vladimir Mukhin, an acclaimed fifth-generation Russian cook, looks to the past and old cookbooks for native ingredients worthy of re-introduction to his customers (*Chef's Table,* "Vladimir Mukhin," Season 3, Episode 2). While the obligatory caviar and borscht make an appearance, so do moose lips, honey, smoked herring, and *shchi,* a traditional cabbage soup. Mukhin's sophisticated, upscale take on peasant food is a juxtaposition similarly played out by Mashama Bailey, who elevates the modest breakfast of beef liver and grits popular in the American South. Bailey, chef and partner of The Grey in Savannah, Georgia, explains how liver and grits provided a hearty meal for laborers in the South, calling it the "quintessential Southern breakfast." Yet, beef liver and grits, while able to provide nutrition and sustain the hard work of manual labor, are too unassuming for haute cuisine. Bailey therefore legitimizes the premise of the dish (high protein and humbleness) by transforming it into "something over the top" – foie gras (goose liver) and grits.

While social status is represented in the hauteur of the dishes featured in each *Chef's Table* episode, it is additionally illustrated through the stories the chefs tell about themselves and the food they make, a hallmark of the series. And although the featured chefs come from all walks of life – those of means as well as those of want – the series pays special attention to chefs who have pulled themselves up by their bootstraps. In line with the American Dream, *Chef's Table* sets forth the notion that even a gang member scraping to get by, as in the case of Tim Raue, German two-Michelin star chef and restaurant owner (*Chef's Table,* "Tim Raue," Season 3, Episode 5), can rise to become an internationally renowned chef in fine dining. These narratives of aspiration are carried out through the cultural memories shared in *Chef's Table.*

Cultural Memories and *Chef's Table*

The premiere episode of *Chef's Table* offers an intimate portrait of Italian chef Massimo Bottura, owner of Osteria Francescana in Modena,

Tuscany—widely considered one of the best restaurants in the world. The episode opens in striking fashion: A black screen dated May 20, 2012. Haunting sounds of rumbling and rattling accompany archival news footage of the Northern Italy earthquakes, featuring Modena as the epicenter. Bottura then begins recalling that day, his words juxtaposed with images of thousands of damaged wheels of Parmigiano Reggiano, the prized cheese of the region. He expresses his fears of devastation, not only for the cheese manufacturers, but for the economic livelihood of the whole region. Chef, critic, and cookbook author Faith Willinger emphasizes this intrinsic connection between memory and food: "One of the most important ingredients in [Massimo Bottura's] food is memory. His memory of tasting things and of the way things were made" (*Chef's Table*, "Massimo Bottura," 00:06:34). His remembrances and those of other chefs on the show are significant, for they are more than individual recollections. They are autobiographical, historical, and cultural memories which provide the framework for this episode and the entire *Chef's Table* series.

Food memories represented in *Chef's Table* are multi-sensory, cognitive, and emotional. They can be intense, powerful, and strongly tied to individual and national identities (Holtzman 2006). For the chefs featured in *Chef's Table*, food serves a similar purpose to that of public monuments, erected to construct, negotiate, and maintain collective memory of a shared past (Bartlett 1995; Connerton 2008; Nora 1989). Dishes tied to birthday celebrations, family reunions, and national and religious holidays serve as mnemonic devices. Therefore, food, or specifically the kitchens where we prepare our meals, can simultaneously be called *milieux de mémoire*, environments of memory and *lieux de mémoire*, sites of memory. According to Pierre Nora (1989), the *lieux de mémoire* is based on the premise that memory is not spontaneous, and we must therefore create archives, museums, anniversaries, and other aids that help us to remember. Further, memory is material and mediated. Nora (1989) writes that memory "relies entirely on the materiality of the trace, the immediacy of the recording, the visibility of the image" (13). The memories shared in *Chef's Table* are not simply individual, collective, or enhanced by group memberships. They are culturally constructed.

Cultural memories are generated by "medial externalization," a shared version of the past that is based on communication through media. In its simplest forms, this is represented in oral speech, as when grandparents talk about the *good old days* while looking at photographs with their descendants. Newer, innovative technology, however, has broadened the temporal and spatial landscape, as we now use digital photographs, film, and the Internet, for instance, to support and provide *authentic* collective remembrances (Erll 2010; Hoskins 2001, 2003, 2011). In *Chef's Table*, "medial externalization" is experienced through chefs, family members, friends, and other key actors, as they talk about the "good old days," a trope habitual to *Chef's Table*. For Mashama Bailey, the good old days present themselves in recollections of childhood: "As a child in Savannah, there was just a sense of freedom here. There were kids on stoops and doors were open, and everyone would just run to each other's houses" (*Chef's Table*, "Mashama Bailey," Season 6, Episode 1, 00:09:10). And for Nashville-residing chef, Sean Brock (restaurants Husk and Audrey), medial externalization occurs through remembrances of his father:

> I was born and raised in the Appalachian Mountains of Virginia, deep in the coalfields. I just remember, as a kid, playing in piles of coal all the time. My father grew up very, very, very poor. When he was 11, he had to start working in the coalfields. And that just shaped him into someone who never wanted his kids to grow up poor, so he made sure of that. He never stopped working. But he loved life. He really, really loved life … we had an unbelievable childhood. (*Chef's Table*, "Sean Brock," Season 6, Episode 4, 00:09:18)

With *Chef's Table*, "medial externalization" (Assmann 2010) has no geographic or socioeconomic boundaries. London-based Asma Khan (Darjeeling Express), for instance, recalls her comfortable childhood in India, from time spent with her father in the family's award-winning mango groves to a time she called her name out of a train window while traveling from Calcutta to the Himalayas: "I would call my name out, and the entire mountain would echo my name back to me. That was my moment of freedom, of liberation. I controlled where my life was going. I knew, one day, everybody would know my name" (*Chef's Table*, "Asma Khan," Season 6, Episode 3, 00:00:32). That sense of freedom is similarly relayed in episodes about Magnus Nilsson, Ben Shewry, and Alex Atala. Nilsson grew up in the Swedish town, Jämtland, where his acclaimed, yet now closed, restaurant, Fäviken, was located. Although claiming to have only tolerated the town where he was raised, Nilsson's memories center on hunting, fishing, and spending time outdoors – childhood memories transformed into dishes served at Fäviken. The New Zealand chef, Ben Shewry, reminisces,

> As kids, we had these amazing adventures. When I was eight years old and my sister, Tess, was six, we tramped two hours from our house by ourselves, into the native bush … . We picked wild berries, and we picked blackberries, and we fished for eels in the stream. We did so many amazing things. (*Chef's Table*, "Ben Shewry," Season 1, Episode 5, 00:10:23)

Similarly, the São Paolo chef, Alex Atala, recalls adventures of hunting and fishing in remote Amazonas:

> One of my first memories, to taste and also cook, was with my father and my grandfather. In the old days as a kid, we used to travel to

> remote areas in Brazil and go fishing and hunting in the Amazonas, Pantanal, Atlantic rainforest ... And it was mandatory ... if you kill a fish, if you kill something, to clean the fish and eat the whole entire animal. It didn't matter what we killed. This was maybe my first relation with food ... and cooking as well. It was a way to respect that life and teach how we might respect the natural environment. (*Chef's Table*, "Alex Atala," Season 2, Episode 2, 00:09:25)

Like Nilsson and Shewry, Atala's memories are transferred to the plate. Heart of palm, Amazonian ants, Brazilian honey, these ingredients capture his childhood, and remind us that he is a Brazilian chef.

While most recollections represented in *Chef's Table* are positive, the series does not shy away from significant yet difficult moments or experiences in the lives of the chefs. Instead, they are offered as opportunities to explore the darker days of their upbringings. Berlin chef Tim Raue, for example, shares deeply personal memories of growing up in poverty: "In the age between three and nine, I was growing up in the poorest part of Berlin. I was living with my mother, who was really in poverty. My mother was a nice but intellectually-limited person. She was not able, really, to care about a child" (*Chef's Table*, Season Episode 3, Episode 5 12:23). Raue continues to share stories of physical abuse:

> My father struggled with his job. He became really aggressive and started to abuse me. He did that sometimes twice per week, sometimes daily. I went to a hospital several times, or to the doctor. I was bleeding out of my ears, from my eyes. I was nine years old. My father was beating me. I was alone. (*Chef's Table*, Season Episode 3, E5, 13:16)

Painful memories are not unique to Raue, however, and feature in many chefs' remembrances. Los Angeles chef Niki Nakayama (n/naka) recalls growing up in a traditional Japanese family where she was expected to play a supporting role to her older brother. She also shares the frequent dismissive comments she received for being a female Japanese chef. Melbourne-based Ben Shewry (Attica) recollects a near-drowning incident in New Zealand, and Grant Achatz recalls fighting a rare carcinoma of the mouth, whose treatment rendered him unable to taste. The decision to include these stories perpetuates a sense of resilience among the chefs, the notion that no matter how difficult things may be, it is *always* possible to get ahead.

Autobiographical, Historical, and Collective Memories

Whether uplifting or somber, the cultural memories disseminated in *Chef's Table* fall within three distinct categories, as defined by sociologist Maurice Halbwachs: autobiographical, historical, and collective. Autobiographical memories, based on events personally experienced in the past, have three distinct functions, "to preserve a sense of being a coherent person over time, to strengthen social bonds by sharing personal memories, and to use past experience to construct models to understand inner worlds of self and others" (Bluck 2003, as cited in van Dijck 2007, 3). Historical memories are archived through records, mediated in texts, photographs, performances, commemorations, and festivals (Assmann 2011; Halbwachs and Coser 1992). Lastly, collective memories are "socially framed individual memories and collective commemorative representations and mnemonic traces" (Olick 1999). These three categories are represented in *Chef's Table* throughout the six seasons and are significant for they illustrate negotiations of class, document perceptions of authenticity, and signify chefs' national identities and sources of pride.

Autobiographical memories are always shaped in interaction with other people. They are documented in written or other social records (e.g., photography) to help protect them from fading (Halbwachs and Coser 1992). According to van Dijck,

> Memories are made as much as they are recalled from photographs; our recollections never remain the same, even if the photograph appears to represent a fixed image of the past. And yet, we use these pictures not to fix memory but to constantly reassess our past lives and reflect on what has been as well as what is and what will be. (van Dijck 2007, 100)

Chef's Table relies heavily on photographs; they serve as a mnemonic device for the chefs as they narrate their stories, and as an invitation to the past, all while contributing to the construction of the chefs' personal and cultural identities. This intersection of past and present is a trademark of *Chef's Table*, in how the chefs discuss where they have been and how they came to be. For example, Magnus Nilsson looks at photographs while reflecting on his past: "When you're exposed to it every day, you get blind to that after a while. I never thought it was going to be possible to actually live life here and work with the profession that I had chosen" (*Chef's* Table, "Magnus Nilsson," Season 1, Episode 6, 00:14:34). As with most remembrances, the autobiographical memories on *Chef's Table* generally fall under the themes of family, previous work experiences, relationships, personal setbacks, and of course, food. As French chef and restauranteur Dominique Crenn (*Chef's Table*, "Dominque Crenn," Season 2, Episode 3) asserts, "memory is very important. It's a vehicle to get to know who you are inside" (00:09:17).

In *Chef's Table*, family memories are the most frequent of those shared. Astrid Erll (2011) writes, "family life conveys the cognitive schemata and exemplary stories that help us encode and recall events" (308). The familial stories told in *Chef's Table* not only provide a biographical context, but also create a sense of what childhood food experiences should, and conversely should not, be. Most often, and perhaps unsurprisingly, is that most childhood memories shared on *Chef's Table* are tied to the food a mother or grandmother used to make. Massimo Bottura recalls growing up in a large family and *that* moment when he ate the raw tortellino (filled pasta) his grandmother prepared, "the plate of [my] life" (*Chef's Table,* "Massimo Bottura, Season 1, Episode 1). The vibrant Italian, eight-generation butcher and restaurateur Dario Cecchini, emotionally speaks of his grandmother's food, "everything ... that my grandma cooked was paradise" (*Chef's Table,* "Dario Cecchini," Season 6, Episode 2 00:02:40). Vladimir Mukhin, Russian chef and owner of Moscow's White Rabbit makes a honey cake that pays homage to his grandmother: "I still remember the flavor. The perfect combination of sweet and sour, fried honey and sour cream. The real Russian taste." He describes his creation, his modernization of the dish, declaring, "I give my modernized version next to my grandma's recipe ... My cake can't hold a candle to hers, damn it." (*Chef's* Table, "Vladimir Mukhin," Season 3, Episode 2, 11:21). And then there is Dominque Crenn's contrasting story. Crenn, who owns Atelier Crenn, a three-Michelin-star restaurant in San Francisco, recalls how her father brought her to a Michelin star restaurant when she was nine years old, setting her on the path to becoming an accomplished chef.

The implications of such remembrances are twofold. One, these memories convey a hegemonic sense of the nuclear, or intact extended, family with the matriarch in the kitchen and the father providing culinary escapes. Two, family memories such as these collectively create perceptions that while favorite foods were often made and eaten at home, they are not the types of food to be replicated in the fine dining kitchen. As Willinger argues, traditional ingredients are only acceptable when transformed: "[Bottura] takes what his mother made and turns it into something divine" (*Chef's Table,* "Massimo Bottura," Season 1, Episode 1, 0:06:57). Ben Shewry tells a similar story about Bolognese: "It was a family dish growing up. I wanted to use that kind of technique of making a Bolognese to make something new" (*Chef's Table,* "Ben Shewry," Season, Episode 5, 06:19). Although inherently proud of their upbringings, their desires to provide elevated, sophisticated dishes take precedence. As they are given the opportunity, these chefs, rich in cultural and economic capital (Bourdieu 1984), showcase their privilege and dominant class standing in a gourmet landscape.

Autobiographical experiences are additionally grounded in past education or employment experiences, memories rooted in time and place, providing a sense of the everyday. Dario Cecchini (Season 6, Episode 2) relives his training to become a veterinarian, his dream job. Famed bread baker Nancy Silverton (Season 3, Episode 3) recounts her first job in a college dormitory kitchen. Blue Hill's Dan Barber (Season 1, Episode 2) recalls being fired by Silverton. And Mashama Bailey (Season 6, Episode 1) shares her hardships as a social worker in New York City.

Historical memories are not as frequent on *Chef's Table* but are striking when they do appear. As previously mentioned, the premiere episode on

Massimo Bottura begins somberly – the stark, black screen and the sounds of rumbling followed by news footage of the powerful Northern Italy earthquakes (Season 1, Episode 1). In "Tim Raue" (Season 3, Episode 5), news clips from World War II and 1961 impart the desperation of East Germans trying to escape the construction of the Berlin Wall. The episode featuring the innovative Moscow-based chef Vladimir Mukhin (Season 3, Episode 2) includes video clips documenting the end of the USSR in the 1990s, as well as the Ukraine Crisis in 2014 and the subsequent destruction of banned food imports at the border following sanctions imposed on Russia by the United States. Then there are the salient historical images of the 1938 Art Deco and segregated Greyhound bus terminal in downtown Savannah, Georgia, the very one John O. Morisano bought in 2014 and that he and Mashama Bailey transformed into their restaurant, The Grey. Black and white photographs of segregated buses and "Colored Waiting Room" signs remind viewers of the Jim Crow-era South. They are expertly placed images that reveal the truth about race in America, while simultaneously tackling regional identity, racial identity, and place in a post-2016, polarized Trump America (Medhurst 2020).

Although the archival records in *Chef's Table* often call for moments of somber reflection, they offer lighthearted moments as well. For example, Dario Cecchini gave a stark and ironic tribute to the Florentine steak, a cut that includes the bone, using news footage of a funeral (*Chef's Table*, "Dario Cecchini," Season 6, Episode 2). In 2001, the Italian cattle industry was hit hard with bovine spongiform encephalopathy, or mad cow disease. The consumption of beef products on the bone was banned, so Cecchini held a funeral for the beloved Florentine dish. This is an important, layered historic memory. For one, it represents a significant time and place using archival news footage. Two, the funeral for the Florentine steak, a quintessential Italian dish, addresses national ideologies. The incorporation of historical memories, in video and photographs, illustrates how one item, the Florentine steak, can represent a region, bringing people together to celebrate their individual and collective identities (Stokes and Atkins-Sayre 2016). While covering different moments in time, these historical memories shared by the five chefs echo Halbwachs' (1980) words, "History is neither the whole nor even all that remains of the past. In addition to written history, there is a living history that perpetuates and renews itself through time" (64).

Lastly, collective cultural memories are constructed on *Chef's Table* by the featured chefs, the producers of the series, as well as the audience through the production, circulation, and access to remembrances (Young, Eckstein, and Conley, 2015). There is, however, a distinction to be made between collective and cultural memories. Halbwachs and Coser (1992) illustrate that collective memory is not merely a collection of individual remembrances, but a complex and complementary experience of sharing memories. Moreover, collective memories are constantly changing and transforming, as they do not subscribe to a linear concept of time but are biased toward the present (Steiner and Zelizer 1995). Furthermore, collective memories dedicate time, space, and resources toward the lifetimes of their producers and consumers and are generally represented within an individual's lifespan (Kantsteiner 2002), significant in *Chef's Table*. A cultural memory, in turn, is "a collective concept for all knowledge that directs behavior and experience in the interactive framework of a society and one that obtains through generations in repeated societal practice and initiation" (Assmann cited in van Dijck 2007, 12).

The memories, or stories, recounted in each episode are negotiations of individuality and collectivity (van Dijck 2007), complex mediated memories shaped by the viewers as outsiders looking in. The effect on the viewers is guided by the personal photographs and video reenactments. Pierre Nora (1989) explains that "[m]odern memory is above all archival. It relies on the materiality of the trace, the immediacy of the recording, the visibility of the image" (13). The personal archives shared via *Chef's Table* not only conserve personal memories, but also create collective cultural memories through the production, circulation, and access of the series.

Conclusion

Chef's Table delivers more than recollections and showcases of *haute cuisine*. The visual and narrative format of the show creates a complex web of memories (autobiographic, historical, and cultural) tied to negotiations of class and authenticity while exploring (inter)national identity.

While the *Chef's Table* strives for a multicultural and international approach (chefs from the United States, Sweden, and India, for instance), the series ultimately creates a universal ideal. The childhood memories of upbringing related by the chefs establish personal identity, while simultaneously constructing a strong identity of place as national and regional rootedness. Negative experiences and characteristics (e.g., unrefined taste, deprived upbringing, poverty) or other systemic problems are framed as impediments to personal success and are confined to the past, presumably overcome before each episode's production. These sanitized narratives not only advance the *good old days* chronicles, but match with the production and distribution strategy of Netflix. The series is a perfect example of global non-fiction entertainment that favors programming that doesn't challenge cross-border sensitivities in various markets (Fürsich 2003). The lives of high-end chefs are reified as cosmopolitan, high aesthetic, and quality programming.

The program's narrative also relates to what Gwynne Mapes (2018, 265) calls "elite authenticity," defined as "a condition or positionality which appeals to notions of sincerity, genuineness, naturalness or tradition, but which is rooted in, and only made possible by, privilege and socioeconomic advantage" (272). The cultural memories shared on *Chef's Table* connect especially to what Mapes found in her analysis of the *New York Times'* food section: a rhetorical dimension of "historicity," which is a "focus on origin, longevity and continuity [and] tradition" (271). She illustrates how references to the origins of the restaurateur, strategic use of traditional terminology and memories of cooking with grandmothers and mothers serve to create "nostalgia-producing narratives of origin and continuity [that] serve as examples of the problematic ways in which producers (i.e., restaurants, the media) and consumers (i.e., restaurant patrons, readers) construct authenticity" (274). This storytelling is problematic because it is tied to a post-class ideology that obscures continuing systemic inequalities or understands social and political issues as easily dissolved through individual effort and choice.

Despite its formulaic style and earnest appeals, *Chef's Table* does offer a new perspective on food media. It moves away from the high-energy entertainment programming (e.g., *Chopped* or the oft-maligned *Diners, Drive-Ins, and Dives*) typical of the Food Network. And in contrast to Anthony Bourdain's *No Reservations* and *Parts Unknown*, or similar travel and food shows, the individual vignettes found on *Chef's Table* provide for a valuable insider's look at global cuisines. Although the emphasis is on fine dining establishments, the series sets forth the notion that all cuisines, and their constituent ingredients (Stein 2016,) are to be valued and celebrated, not othered by an outsider-looking-in.

Yet, the politics of *Chef's Table* are not innocuous. The episodes are wrapped in an "authentic" elite discourse high on culinary capital, while cultural memories of family history, rootedness, and locality distance the audience from current systemic problems. By juxtaposing this reminiscence with a refined and cosmopolitan present time tied to personal achievement and (aesthetic) pleasure, the show creates an effective but problematic neoliberal brand for a global streaming audience.

References

Assmann, Aleida. 2010. "Canon and Archive." In *A Companion to Cultural Memory Studies*, edited by Astrid Erll and Ansgar Nünning. Berlin and New York: De Gruyter.

Bartlett, Frederic C. 1995. *Remembering: A Study in Experimental and Social Psychology*. Cambridge and New York: Cambridge University Press.

Bourdieu, Pierre. 1984. *Distinction: A Social Critique of the Judgement of Taste*. Cambridge, MA: Harvard University Press.

Connerton, Paul. 2008. "Seven Types of Forgetting." *Memory Studies* 1(1):59–71. 10.1177/1750698007083889.

Erll, Astrid. 2010. "Cultural Memory Studies: An Introduction." In *A Companion to Cultural Memory Studies*, edited by Astrid Erll and Ansgar Nünning. Berlin and New York: De Gruyter.

Erll, Astrid. 2011. "Locating Family in Cultural Memory Studies." *Journal of Comparative Family Studies* 42(3):303–318. 10.3138/jcfs.42.3.303.

Fürsich, Elfriede. 2003. "Between Credibility and Commodification: Nonfiction Entertainment as a Global Media Genre." *International Journal of Cultural Studies* 6(2):131–153. 10.1177/13678779030062001.

Halbwachs, Maurice. 1980. *The Collective Memory*. 1st ed. New York: Harper & Row.

Halbwachs, Maurice and Lewis A. Coser. 1992. *On Collective Memory*. Chicago: University of Chicago Press.

Holtzman, Jon D. 2006. "Food and Memory." *Annual Review of Anthropology* 35:361–378. https://www.jstor.org/stable/25064929.

Hoskins, Andrew. 2001. "New Memory: Mediating History." *Historical Journal of Film, Radio and Television* 21(4):333–346. 10.1080/01439680120075473.

Hoskins, Andrew. 2003. "Signs of the Holocaust: Exhibiting Memory in a Mediated Age." *Media, Culture & Society* 25(1):7–22. 10.1177/0163443703025 001631.

Hoskins, Andrew. 2011. "7/7 and Connective Memory: Interactional Trajectories of Remembering in Post-Scarcity Culture." *Memory Studies* 4(3):269–280. 10.11 77/1750698011402570.

Johnston, Josée and Shyon Baumann. 2010. *Foodies: Democracy and Distinction in the Gourmet Foodscape*. New York: Routledge.

Lindenfeld, Laura and Fabio Parasecoli. 2018. "Food and Cinema: An Evolving Relationship." In *The Bloomsbury Handbook of Food and Popular Culture*, edited by Kathleen LeBesco and Peter Naccarato, 27–39. London and New York: Bloomsbury Academic.

Mapes, Gwynne. 2018. "(De)Constructing Distinction: Class Inequality and Elite Authenticity in Mediatized Food Discourse." *Journal of Sociolinguistics* 22(3):265–287. 10.1111/josl.12285.

McBride, Anne E. 2010. "Food Porn." *Gastronomica* 10(1):38–46. 10.1525/gfc.2 010.10.1.38.

Medhurst, Julia M. 2020. "Cooking up Southern Black Identity in *Chef's Table*'s 'Mashama Bailey.'" *Southern Communication Journal* 85(4):219–230. 10.1 080/1041794X.2020.1801822.

Naccarato, Peter and Kathleen LeBesco. 2012. *Culinary Capital*. London and New York: Berg.

Nora, Pierre. 1989. "Between Memory and History: Les Lieux de Memoire." *Representations* 26(1):7–24. 10.1525/rep.1989.26.1.99p0274v.

Olick, Jeffrey K. 1999. "Collective Memory: The Two Cultures." *Sociological Theory* 17(3):333–348. 10.1111/0735-2751.00083.

Phillipov, Michelle. 2016. "Escaping to the Country: Media, Nostalgia, and the New Food Industries." *Popular Communication* 14(2):111–122. 10.1080/15405 702.2015.1084620.

Peterson, Richard A. and Roger M. Kern. 1996. "Changing Highbrow Taste: From Snob to Omnivore." *American Sociological Review* 61(5):900–907.

Reijnders, Stijn. 2011. *Places of the Imagination: Media, Tourism, Culture*. Farnham, Surrey, England and Burlington, VT: Ashgate.

Stein, Joshua David. 2016. "'Chef's Table' Season Two: The Good, the Bad, and the Binge-Worthy." *Eater*. May 27. https://www.eater.com/2016/5/27/11794150/chefs-table-season-two-netflix-review.

Steiner, Linda and Barbie Zelizer. 1995. "Competing Memories: Reading the Past against the Grain: The Shape of Memory Studies." *Critical Studies in Mass Communication* 12(2):213–239. 10.1080/15295039509366932.

Stokes, Ashli Quesinberry and Wendy Atkins-Sayre. 2016. *Consuming Identity: The Role of Food in Redefining the South*. Jackson: University Press of Mississippi.

van Dijck, José. 2007. *Mediated Memories in the Digital Age*. Cultural Memory in the Present. Stanford, CA: Stanford University Press.

Young, Anna M., Justin Eckstein, and Donovan Conley. 2015. "Rhetorics and Foodways." *Communication and Critical/Cultural Studies* 12(2):198–199. 10.1080/14791420.2015.1013561.

Index

Note: *italic* page numbers refer to tables.

Aarhus University 172
Abarca, Meredith E. 72
Abbott, Matt 56–59
Achatz, Grant 210, 216
Ad Age Super Bowl Ad Archive 35, 37
Adams, Carol J. 36
ad hoc restaurant 88
Agyemang, Brianna 19
Alexandra's Kitchen 25
Ali, Maxine 124–25
Alinea restaurant 210
Aljazeera America 9
#AllLionsMatter 68
All Together Now 2021 74–75
Alma Lach Cooking School 204
Alma Lach Kitchens, Inc. 205
"Alma Lach's Kitchen: Transforming Taste" (exhibition) 199–200
Alma's Almanac 204
Almiron, Núria 68
Ambassador Hotel 205
American Constitution Society 1
American Dietetic Association (ADA) 118–19
American Journalism Review 202
Andreasen, Unni From xi, 13, 167–80
Andrés, José 87, 91–92
animal rights 138–39
Anitaji ka Kitchen 141, *142*
Appadurai, Arjun 136–37, 140, 148, 150
Apple 37, 116, 121–22, 127
Arla Foods 167
Armytage, Samantha 122
Art Deco 219
Asimov, Eric 104, 106–7
Asmusse, Alberte Borne x, 13, 167–80

Association for Education in Journalism and Mass Communication 3
Association of Food Journalists 200
Atala Alex 212–16
Attica 216
Audrey 215
Australia 10; Aborigines of 73; environmental conflict and 53–54; Evans 12, 115–27; food sovereign voices and 67, 70–74; Gibson 12, 115–27; scandals and 115–26; *When Inclusion Means Exclusion* report 74–75
Australian Consumer Law Act 116
Australian Medical Association (AMA) 120–21, 127
autobiographical memories 216–20
Avery, Jill 88

bad boys: Bourdain and 1, 11–12, 86; culinary capital and 85–89; to heroes 85–89; Ramsay and 86; Soler on 89; Stevens on 86
Bad Influencer: The Great Insta Con (BBC documentary) 116, 121–22
Bailey, Mashama 210, 213–15, 218
"Ballpark Peanuts, A Classic Pleasure, Are Benched For the Season" (Severson) 106
"Banana Boat Song" (Belafonte) 157
bananas: bendy 153–64; British greatness and 159–60; colonialism and 156–57; Euromyths and 13, 153–64; iconic symbol of 153–54; imports of 157; Indian food and 146; omelettes and 190; populism and 155; "Yes: We Have No Bananas" song 156

Barber, Dan 212, 218
Barilla Center for Food and Nutrition 2
Barthes, Roland 155
Bartone, Tony 120–21
Batali, Mario 86
Baumann, Shyon 69, 86
Bay, George 204
Bay of Fundy: Conservation Council of 58; Deer Island and 51, 53–54, 56; environmental conflict and 11, 48–61; Fundy Footpath and 53; Fundy Salmon Recovery Project and 55–56; Grand Manon and 51; Passamaquoddy Bay and 51, 56; Saint John River 53; seafood and 11, 44, 48–61
BBC 122–23
Beard James 117–18
Beer, Maggie 119
Beggs, Alex 35
Belafonte, Harry 156–57
Bell, David 7
Bendy Banana Law 153, 158–59, 164
Bennett, Lance W. 30
Berghoff, Herman Joseph 205
Besh, John 86
Bijleveld, Hildebrand 171
Bilandic, Michael 204
Bio Charger lamp 123
Birthing Kit Foundation 126
Blackledge, Sam 164
#BlackLivesMatter: COVID-19 pandemic and 109; influencer activism and 9–10, 19–22, 25–30, 109; political ideology of 19
#BlackOutTuesday: Agyemang and 19; amplifying/muting content and 24–25; education and 23; Floyd murder and 19; influencer activism and 10, 19–31; personal experience and 23–24; racial issues and 10, 19–31; self-reflexivity and 25–26; social media and 19–31; themes of 23–27; Thomas and 19
Blair, Tony 115
blogs: branding and 20–22; calculated content of 21; celebrities and 119, 125; Denmark and 171; empty statements and 26; Indian food culture and 139, 144–45; influencer activism and 20–31; labor intensive nature of 21; Lach and 207; Mommy 207; politics and 7–11; protest language and 27–30; *Saveur* Blog Awards 22–23; scandals and 119, 125; self-promotion and 21, 23, 26–27; self-reflexivity and 11, 20, 23, 25–26, 28–31; social media and 7–11, 20–31, 119, 125, 139, 144–45, 171, 207
Blythman, Joanna 66
Bočák, Michal 69
Bon Appetit 35, 95
Boston Globe 42
Bottura, Massimo 210, 213–14, 218–19
Bourdain, Anthony: attacks on celebrities by 86; as bad boy 1, 11–12, 86; environmental conflict and 49; *Kitchen Confidential* 86; *No Reservations* 118, 221; *Parts Unknown* 221; politics and 1–2, 5, 11–12, 118
Bourdieu, Pierre 86, 211–12
Brady, Tom 42–43
brand strategy 25–30, 207
Brexit 13, 146, 154, 158, 164
British media: bendy banana and 153–64; Brexit and 13, 146, 154, 158, 164; class and 155, 159; consumerism and 158, 162; consumption and 156; Euromyths and 13, 153–64; framing and 159; identity and 153, 155, 159; labor and 157; menus and 163; politics and 153–55, 158, 161, 163–64, 184, 188–89, 192; populism and 153–64; satire and 157–59; sex and 156, 159, 161, 164; tabloids 153–63
Brittain, Vera 187
Brock, Sean 215
Broma Bakery 24
Brown, Colin 163
Brown, Tara 124–25
Brunswick News Inc. (BNI) 52, 57
Bubba Yum Yum: The Paleo Way for New Mums, Babies, and Toddlers (Carr and Padarin) 125–26
Budget Bytes 24

Campbell, Allen 42
Campbell, Colin 96
Campbell, J. 191
Campbell Kids at Home, The (Lach) 203
Campbell Kids Have a Party, The (Lach) 203

Canada: Bay of Fundy 11, 48–61; *Chef's Table* and 212; Commissioner for the Environment and Sustainable Development and 55; environmental conflict and 11, 48–61; First Nations and 50; Labrador 50, 60; New Brunswick 11, 50–61; Newfoundland 50, 52, 60; Nova Scotia 50, 52; Prince Edward Island 52

capitalism: culinary philanthropy and 85, 89, 94, 97; food sovereign voices and 67, 69, 72, 75; Intergovernmental Panel on Climate Change (IPCC) and 67–68, 73; Super Bowl and 36, 44; values of 12

Cargle, Rachel 28

Carr, Charlotte 125–26

Cathcart, Brian 157

CBC New Brunswick 57

CBS Sports 37

Cecchini, Dario 218–219

celebrities: Australia and 12, 115–26; bad boys and 85–89; blogs and 119, 125; class and 115; commercialism and 116, 121, 127; consumerism and 116, 118, 126; cookbooks and 115–16, 121, 124–25; COVID-19 pandemic and 117, 123–27; education and 119; Facebook and 116, 123, 127; influencer activism and 10, 116, 118, 121–27, 140; Instagram and 116, 127; lifestyle media and 115, 124; meat and 120; nutrition and 115, 118–25; Paleolithic diet and 116, 123, 126; public personalities of 122–24; recipes and 125–26; scandals and 115–27; sensational narratives of 122–24; social media and 115–18, 123–27; tabloids and 115–18, 122; visibility and 124; vulnerable communities and 124–27. *See also* specific celebrity

Centers for Disease Control and Prevention 118–19

Chaîne des Rôtisseurs 206

Chang, David 213

Chauhan, Maneet 92–94

Chef's Table (Netflix): accomplishments of 210, 212; aesthetics of 211; autobiographical context of 216–20; Canada and 212; class and 211–13, 217–21; collective memories and 216–20; consumerism and 220–21; consumption and 219; cookbooks and 213–14; COVID-19 pandemic and 12; culinary capital and 211–13, 221; cultural memories and 213–16, 220–21; education and 211, 218; ethics and 212; family and 217–18; farming and 212; historical perspective and 216–20; identity and 13–14, 210, 219–20; indigenous people and 213; inequality and 221; labor and 213; menus and 211; narrative framework of 211; negotiation of class and 211–13; nutrition and 213; politics and 221; racial issues and 219; recipes and 218; strategy of 220; subscriber demographics of 212; sustainability and 212; visibility and 214, 220

Chicago Library 199

Chicago Sun-times 199, 204

Chicago Tribune 200–5

Child's First Cookbook, A (Lach) 203

Chopped (TV show) 221

chronic traumatic encephalopathy (CTE) 36

Chuen, Lorraine 70

Church, Ruth Ellen 200, 202–3

citizenship: changing concepts of 5–6; culinary philanthropy and 85–97; *Daily Mail* Food Bureau and 186, 193, 196; food sovereign voices and 69; India and 147; *New York Times* and 112; politics and 5–6, 11, 13

Civil Eats 2, 9

Claiborne, Craig 204–5

Clark, Melissa 103–5

class: British media and 155, 159; celebrities and 115; *Chef's Table* and 211–13, 217–21; culinary philanthropy and 88–89, 94–97; *Daily Mail* Food Bureau and 102, 185–86, 190, 194; food sovereign voices and 66, 75; India and 136, 140, 147–49; influencer activism and 21, 25; Lach and 200, 207; middle 21, 66, 97, 115, 149, 185–86, 190, 194, 200; *New York Times* and 108; politics and 5–6, 9; poverty and 76, 108, 216, 220; Super Bowl Food and 38 climate: Asimov on 107; Brady and 42; farmers and 39; food journalism and 8, 11, 14; food sovereign voices and 66–68, 73, 77; global protests and 109; greenhouse gases and 67; Intergovernmental Panel on Climate Change (IPCC) and 67–68, 73; *New York Times* and 107, 109; pollution and 51, 55, 57, 67, 108; Super Bowl and 39, 42–43

CNN 35, 39, 118

Cocking, Ben 48–49

Cohen, Jaclyn Alexandra 89

collective memories 216–20

Columbia Journalism Review 2

Combs 90

commercialism: celebrities and 116, 121, 127; environmental conflict and 51, 56; fishing and 51, 56; food sovereign voices and 73; influencer activism and 7, 20–21, 25–30; journalism as watchdog on 3; Super Bowl and 11, 34–44

Confrérie des Chevaliers du Tastevin 206

Connell, Daniel J. 89, 94

Conservative Party 162

constructive journalism: food journalism and 168–71; Smoked Cheese Day and 13, 168, 172–77; TV2 FYN and 168, 172–73

Consumer Affairs Victoria 116, 126

consumerism: British media and 158, 162; celebrities and 116, 118, 126; *Chef's Table* and 220–21; culinary philanthropy and 85–86, 95–97; *Daily Mail* Food Bureau and 184; Denmark and 171–77; food journalism and 3–7, 10–12; food sovereign voices and 66–69; hyper 66; India and 139; influencer activism and 20, 28; Lach and 200, 202; *New York Times* and 100; Super Bowl and 35, 41, 43

consumptagenic food system 66

consumption: British media and 156; celebrities and 115; *Chef's Table* and 219; culinary philanthropy and 94–97; *Daily Mail* Food Bureau and 184, 186; Denmark and 171, 173–76; environmental conflict and 48; food journalism and 4–14; food sovereign voices and 66–69, 74; heroic 94–97; India and 136–39, 147; lifestyle and 4, 6; *New York Times* and 102, 108; Super Bowl and 34, 37, 40–42; sustainability and 7 (*see also* sustainability); YouTube and 135

Contois, Emily x, 11, 34–47

cookbooks: celebrities and 115–16, 121, 124–25; *Chef's Table* and 213–14; Denmark and 176; food sovereign voices and 72; India and 140; influencer activism and 26, 29; Lach and 13, 199–207; self-promotion and 26; social media and 26, 29

Cooke Aquaculture 51, 54, 56, 59–60

Cookie and Kate 24

Cooking à la Cordon Bleu (Lach) 203

Cooking App 102–3

Cooking Gene, The (Twitty) 2

Cooking Light magazine 9

Cooks, Leda 69

Corn Production Act 186

Coser, Lewis A. 219

Cosmopolitan magazine 121

Couldry, Nick 71

Courier Mail, The 121

Courtenay, Will 36

COVID-19 pandemic 11; Bio Charger lamp and 123; #BlackLivesMatter and 109; celebrities and 117, 123–27; *Chef's Table* and 12; coping with 103–5; culinary philanthropy and 85–97; education and 88; Evans and 124, 127; farming and 85, 87; food sovereign voices and 70; gender issues and 12, 85–90, 97, 101–2, 112; Gibson and 124, 126; heroes and 85–97; labor and 87; marginalized food workers and 70; media coverage themes of 100–8; *New York Times* and 100–5, 100–12; politics and 91; racial issues and 87; strategy and 110–11; struggling with 105–7; Super Bowl and 11, 34, 38, 43; sustainability and 91–92, 107–8

crabs 51, 205

"Craft Distillers' Boom Goes Bust" (Risen) 106

Craig, Nephi 74

Crenn, Dominique 217–18

critics 2, 36, 87, 111, 200, 214

culinary capital: *Chef's Table* and 211–13, 221; negotiation of class and 211–13; philanthropy and 85–89, 95, 97

culinary kitchen chats 72
culinary philanthropy: capitalism and 85, 89, 94, 97; citizenship and 85–97; class and 88–89, 94–97, 211–13; consumerism and 85–86, 95–97; consumption and 94–97; COVID-19 pandemic and 85–97; ethics and 85, 87, 89, 94–97; framing and 85–87, 91, 97; heroes and 85–97; inequality and 85, 88, 91, 94, 96–97; lifestyle media and 85–86, 95–96; masculinity and 85–91, 96; meat and 87; menus and 95; moral issues and 87, 96–97; nutrition and 91; social media and 95; visibility and 87, 97
"Curly Dog Cutting Board" (Lach) 206
Cusack, John 37–38

Daily Mail Food Bureau: citizenship and 186, 193, 196; class and 102, 185–86, 190, 194; consumerism and 184; consumption and 184, 186; farming and 188; Food Chat and 191; identity and 183–86, 189–90, 194, 197; Instagram and 195; intense food coverage of 187–88; leaders and 192–93; letters to the editor 193–96; meat and 183, 186, 188, 192–94; moral issues and 187; national identity and 184–86; nutrition and 183, 189, 191, 194–95; politics and 184, 188–89, 192; rationing and 183–88, 191–95; recipes and 183–92, 194, 196; social media and 195; sugar and 183, 186–88, 191–95; war effort and 13, 183–97
Daily Mail War Recipes 184, 192
Daily Mirror 196
Daily Telegraph, The 158, 162
Dalits 138
Darjeeling Express 215
Daum, Peggy 200
DeDauw, Esther 89, 94
Deer Island 51, 53–54, 56
Dehaene, Michiel 72
Dejmanee, Tisha x, 10–11, 19–33
Delish magazine 2
Delors, Jacques 158
Denmark 10; blogs and 171; constructive journalism and 168–71; consumerism and 171–77; consumption and 171, 173–76; cookbooks and 176; education and 174; ethics and 177; Facebook and 173, 176; food journalism reconsidered in 167–77; framing and 170; Funen region and 13, 167–68, 172–77; identity and 167–68, 171, 174–76; influencer activism and 171; Instagram and 173; nutrition and 171, 173; politics and 171–73; recipes and 167–68, 171, 176; Smoked Cheese Day 13, 167, 172–77; social media and 171, 173, 176; strategy and 176; sustainability and 170; TV2 FYN and 13, 167–68, 171–77; YouTube and 171
Deuze, Mark 6
diabetes 120
Diners, Drive-Ins, and Dives (TV show) 92, 221
discrimination 9, 68, 87, 138, 145
Diversity in Food Media: New Voices on Food (Lam) 71
domesticity: *Daily Mail* and 189; lifestyle media and 12, 20, 100–12, 135; politics of 100–12; public quality and 110–12
Donelly, Beau 116, 121–22, 126
"Don't Call on Me" (The Monkeys) 205
DoorDash 39
Downs, Hugh 204
dude food 11, 35, 41

Easter 94
Eater.com 95
Eating Well magazine 9
Economic Hardship Reporting Project (EHRP) 76
Economist journal 2
education: #BlackOutTuesday and 23; celebrities and 119; *Chef's Table* and 211, 218; COVID-19 pandemic and 88; Denmark and 174; environmental conflict and 59; experience and 8, 22–23, 174, 218; food journalism and 3; Instagram and 22–23, 27, 29; lifestyle media and 4; personal experience and 23–24, 29, 108, 217
Ehrenreich, Barbara 70
Eide, Martin 184
Eleven Madison Park 88–89
Elle magazine 121–22
Emmy Awards 204
Energy East pipeline 57

E! News 36
entrepreneurs 7, 90, 203–6
environmental conflict: Australia and 53–54; Bay of Fundy 11, 48–61; Bourdain and 49; commercialism and 51, 56; consumption and 48; education and 59; farming and 50–59; India and 139; lifestyle media and 48; politics and 48–49, 59, 61; pollution and 51, 55, 57, 67, 108; pulp mills and 49, 54–55; seafood and 11, 48–52, 56, 59; social media and 57; strategy and 53–54, 61; sustainability and 48–49, 55, 59–60; travel journalism and 11, 48–61
E! Online 35
Epicure (newspaper section) 119
Escoffier, Auguste 205
ethics: *Chef's Table* and 212; culinary philanthropy and 85, 87, 89, 94–97; Denmark and 177; food journalism and 4, 7; food sovereign voices and 67–68, 76; India and 137–38; influencer activism and 26; *New York Times* and 104; sustainability and 104
ethnicity 9, 70, 146–48
Euromyths: bananas and 13, 153–64; British media and 13, 153–64; constructing British greatness and 159–60; Johnson and 158–59; tabloids and 13, 153–63
European Union (EU): Brexit and 13, 146, 154, 158, 164; Empire and 156–57; regulations of 13, 154, 163–64; ridicule of 160–63
Euroscepticism 154–59, 163
Evans, Pete: activated almonds and 120; alt-right ideology of 116; background of 115–16; conspiracy theories of 116; COVID-19 pandemic and 124, 127; credibility and 116; fad diets and 116; fall of 116; fines of 126–27; legitimacy and 119–21; *The Magic Pill* 116–21, 124, 127; *My Kitchen Rules* 116, 123, 127; public personality of 122–24; scandal of 12, 115–27; Twitter and 120; vulnerable communities and 124–27

Facebook: celebrities and 116, 123, 127; Denmark and 173, 176; Evans and 116; India and *142*; Pew Research on 21; scandals and 116, 123, 127; social media and 21, 116, 123, 127, *142*, 173, 176

fad diets 116
Fakazis, Elizabeth x, 1–16
farming: COVID-19 pandemic and 85, 87; *Daily Mail* Food Bureau and 188; environmental conflict and 50–59; food sovereign voices and 66, 68, 73–76; India and 138–39, 144–46; Lach and 202; *New York Times* and 106–7, 112; politics and 9, 11; Super Bowl Food and 39; sustainable 9, 11, 55, 59, 66, 74, 212
Fäviken 215
Feed Me Better petition 115
femininity 13, 20, 207
feminism 21, 28
Fieri, Guy 88, 91–93
First Nations 50, 73–75, 91–92, 108
Fiske, John 5, 111
Flore, Roberto 91
Floyd, George 19
Flying Food Fare 199
Food & Wine magazine 1, 35, 37
Food, Inc. (film) 120
Food 52 2
Food and Agriculture Organization (FAO) 67
Food and Environment Reporting Network (FERN) 2, 8–9
food deserts 8, 30, 73, 75, 108
foodie culture 70, 110, 119, 139
Food in Jars 25
food insecurity 11, 67, 76
Food in the Anthropocene: EAT-Lancet Commission on Healthy and Sustainable Food Systems report 66, 68
food journalism: Association of Food Journalists 200; citizenship concepts and 5–6; climate and 8, 11, 14, 67–68; constructive journalism and 13, 168–77; consumerism and 3–7, 10–12; consumption and 4–14; *Daily Mail* Food Bureau and 184; Denmark and 167–77; development of 200–2; domesticity and 12, 20, 100–12, 135; education and 3; environmental conflict and 48–49, 61; ethics and 4, 7; food sovereign voices and 70–71; framing and 1 (*see also* framing); indigenous people and 2, 12; Lach and 200–2, 206–7; lifestyle media and 3–7, 11, 14; local context and 168–71; media concept and 7–8;

models of 70–71; *New York Times* and 100–12; political engagement of 1–14; problems of Western 70–71; recipes and 8; reconsidering 167–77; as site of negotiation 8–10
Food Network 35, 40, 66, 89, 92, 199, 211, 221
Food Nouveau 25–26
foodscapes: Bočák on 69; digital 140; food sovereign voices and 69; Indian 135, 140, 145, 149–50
food sovereign voices 11; Australia and 67, 70–74; capitalism and 67, 69, 72, 75; cheap food and 67; citizenship and 69; class and 66, 75; climate and 66–68, 73, 77; commercialism and 73; consumerism and 66–69; consumption and 66–69, 74; cookbooks and 72; COVID-19 pandemic and 70; ethics and 67–68, 76; farming and 66, 68, 73–76; food journalism and 48–49, 61, 70–71; food resistance and 59–71; foodscapes and 69; framing and 67; gender issues and 70, 75; identity and 69, 72; indigenous people and 66–67, 73–75; labor and 67, 70; lifestyle media and 70; mainstream media and 71–73; meat and 66, 68; menus and 67; moral issues and 67–68, 73; nutrition and 66; politics and 67–75; recipes and 68, 70, 72; social media and 66; Super Bowl Food and 67, 70, 75; sustainability and 66, 72, 74–75; towards better media for 75–77; veganism and 66–68; vegetarianism and 66, 68; violence and 68, 74, 76
Food Sustainability Index 2
Food System Exposés (FSEs) 120
Forbes magazine 88
For Seven Candlelight Dinner (Lach) 204
framing: British media and 159; constructive journalism and 170; culinary philanthropy and 85–87, 91, 97; Denmark and 170; food sovereign voices and 67; influencer activism and 23; *New York Times* and 108–9; politics and 1–2, 11–12; Super Bowl and 38
Fraser, Nancy 145, 150
Friedman, Ken 86
Frostrup, Mariella 160
Fundy National Park 61

Fundy Salmon Recovery Project 55–56, 61
Fun Fearless Female award 121
Fürsich, Elfriede xi, 1–16, 49, 50, 100–14, 158, 171, 184, 220

Gandhi, Rahul 140
Gannon, Michael 120
gastro-politics 12, 125, 137–40, 147
Gazzaniga-Moloo, Jeannie 118
Gelb, David 210
gender issues: citizenship concept and 5; COVID-19 pandemic and 12, 85–90, 97, 101–2, 112; dude food 11, 35, 41; food sovereign voices and 70, 75; India and 136, 138, 146; influencer activism and 21, 27; Lach and 13, 199, 206–7; lifestyle empowerment and 6; masculinity 3, 36–43, 85, 87–91, 96; *New York Times* and 101–2, 112; #MeToo movement and 9, 86, 97, 109; Super Bowl and 11, 36–43; "women's work" 206–7
Gibson, Belle: background of 116; *Bad Influencer* and 116, 121–22; cancer fraud of 116, 121; COVID-19 pandemic and 124, 126; credibility and 116; Donelly and 116, 121–22, 126; *Elle* and 121; Fun Fearless Female award 121; legitimacy and 121–22; public personality of 122–24; scandal of 12, 115–27; smartphone app of 116, 124, 126; *Sunrise* and 121–22; Toscano and 116, 121, 126; Turner on 122–23; vulnerable communities and 124–271; *The Whole Pantry* 116, 121, 127
Gilligan, Carol 96
Globe and Mail 53
Glynn, Tracey 50, 57–58
GMO 76
Goldberg, Lena 88
Gómez-Barris, Macarena 75
"Good Appetite, A" (Clark) 105
"Good Wine Leads Back to Nature" (Asimov) 106–7
Gordon, Aubrey 121
Govender-Ypma, Ishay 75–76
Grande Diplome 203, 206
"Grand National Recipe and Baking Contest" 204
Grandpa Kitchen Channel 141, *142*

Gravy 2
Green, Anthony 66
Greenslade, Roy 162
Grey, Sam 73
Grocer, The 66
Guardian, The 158, 162
Guilliatt, Richard 122, 126
Gundestrup Dairy 177

Habermasian philosophy 145
Haddix, Carol Mighton 205
Halbwachs, Maurice 216, 219
Hanitzsch, Thomas 3–4
Harper & Row 203
Harper's Bazaar magazine 89
Harrington, Stephen 118
Harris, Jessica 2
Harris, Kamala 148
Harrods Food Bureau 192
hashtags 19, 26, 29, 31
Hayes, Liz 123
Hedge, Radha 144
Hell's Kitchen (TV show) 86
"Here's a Salad that's Negotiable" (Clark) 105
heroes: bad boys to 85–89; culinary philanthropy and 85–97; good citizenship and 85–97; masculinity and 88–91; narratives of 91–94
"Heroic Story of How José Andrés' Charity Feeds 250,000 People a Day in a Pandemic, The" (Wofford) 91
High on the Hog (Harris) 2
Hindus 136–38, 147
historical memories 216–20
Ho, Colin 71
Ho, Soleil 2
Hobbes, Michael 121
Hockenhull, Stella 185–86
Hoff, Jørgen 177
Hollows, Joanne 7
Holt, Douglas B. 90
Home Economics 200–2
HOP Strings Craft Brewery 94
Hows and Whys of French Cooking (Lach) 203
Huffington Post 36, 38
Hugos 116
hunger 66–67, 88
Huntsman Marine Science Centre and Aquarium 55
Hurricane Maria 87
Husk 215

identity: bendy banana and 153–64; British media and 153, 155, 159; *Chef's Table* and 13–14, 210, 219–20; citizenship and 5–6 (*see also* citizenship); *Daily Mail* Food Bureau and 183–86, 189–90, 194, 197; Denmark and 167–68, 171, 174–76; digital 20–21; food sovereign voices and 69, 72; Funen 167; India and 137–38, 147–48; influencer activism and 19–21, 26, 28, 116; politics and 4–6, 9, 13; social media 116; Super Bowl Food and 36, 43
Ielmini, Eileen 199
I Love to Eat (Beard cooking show) 117–18
immigrants 1–2, 108
Independent, The 52, 157–58, 163
India 10; Appadurai on 136–37, 140, 148, 150; blogs and 139, 144–45; citizenship and 147; class and 136, 140, 147–49; consumerism and 139, 158; consumption and 136–39, 147; cookbooks and 140; digital foodscape of 140; environmental conflict and 139; Facebook and 142; farming and 138–39, 144–46; foodscapes and 135, 140, 145, 149–50; foodways of 136–37; gastro-politics of 12, 125, 137–40, 147; gender issues and 136, 138, 146; Hindus 136–38, 147; identity and 137–38, 147–48; indigenous recipes and 143, 146–47; influencer activism and 140–41, 149; Instagram and 139, *142*; Jainism 137; labor and 137; meat and 137–38, 141, 144, 146–47; moral issues and 136–37; Muslims 147; recipes and 135, 140, 143–48; social media and 135, 137, 139–43, 149; subaltern culinary counterpublics 144–49; taboos 12, 138, 147; vegetarianism and 12, 137–38, 147; village foods and 12, 135–50; violence and 138; visibility of food cultures in 135–39; YouTube and 135, 140–50
indigenous people: Australian 73; *Chef's Table* and 213; First Foods and 73; food journalism and 2, 12; food sovereign voices and 66–67, 73–75; Indian recipes and 143, 146–47; Native American 50, 73–75, 91–92, 108

inequality: *Chef's Table* and 221; culinary philanthropy and 85, 88, 91, 94, 96–97; Lach and 199, 207; *New York Times* and 106, 112
influencer activism 11; Agyemang and 19; amplifying/muting content and 24–25; #BlackLivesMatter and 9–10, 19–22, 25–30, 109; #BlackOutTuesday and 19–31; blogs and 20–31; branding and 20–22; celebrities and 10, 116, 118, 121–27, 140; class and 21, 25; commercialism and 7, 20–21, 25–30; consumerism and 20, 28; cookbooks and 26, 29; Denmark and 171; education and 23; ethics and 26; Floyd murder and 19; framing and 23; gender issues and 21, 27; identity and 19–21, 26, 28, 116; India and 140–41, 149; Instagram and 19–27; labor and 21, 26; Lach and 199, 206–7; lifestyle media and 29; moral issues and 30; nutrition and 22; personal experience and 23–24; politics and 19–31; protest language and 27–30; racial issues and 19, 26–27, 29; recipes and 20–21; *Saveur* Blog Awards 22–23; scandals and 116, 118, 121–27; self-reflexivity and 25–26; social media and 19, 21, 26, 28–31; strategy and 19, 25, 27–30; Thomas and 19; veganism and 22; visibility and 19–25, 28–31; YouTube and 21
Inside Development (Green) 66
Instagram: amplifying/muting content and 24–25; branding and 20–22; celebrities and 116, 127; *Daily Mail* Food Bureau and 195; Denmark and 173; education and 22–23, 27, 29; empty statements and 26; Evans and 116; India and 139, *142*; influencer activism and 19–27; Lach and 207; personal experience and 23–24; Pew Research on 21; politics and 7; popularity of 21; protest language and 27–30; scandals and 116, 127; self-promotion and 21, 23, 26–27; self-reflexivity and 25–26; social media and 7, 20–27, 116, 127, 139, *142*, 173, 195, 207
Intergovernmental Panel on Climate Change (IPCC) 67–68, 73
Irving, J. K. 52
Irwin, Mary xi, 13, 153–66

Jainism 137
James Beard award 86–87
Jamie's School Dinners (TV show) 115
Janmohamed, Zahir 2
Jiro Dreams of Sushi (documentary) 210
Johnson, Boris 158–59
Johnston, Josèe 69, 86
Jones, Steven 7
Jordan, Nicholas 71
Jørgensen, Kristina Lund 172
Joy the Baker 23

kadai 135, 141, 143, 147
kale 36, 38
Kamp, David 202
Kasturi, Sumana xi, 135–52
Kaufman, Michael 88
Keller, Thomas 88
Kerala 141–43, 146, 148
Khan, Asma 215
Khan, Sabiha Ahmad 11, 67, 71–73
Khare, Ravindra S. 136, 146, 149
Kirkwood, Katherine xi, 12, 115–31
Kitchen Confidential: Adventures in the Culinary Underbelly (Bourdain) 86
Kitchenista 27
Kitchen Nightmares (TV show) 86
Klassen, Branden 86
Klion, David 1
Knight, Graham 184
Koslow, Jessica 110
Krishna, Priya 104
Kristensen, Nete Nørgaard 171
Kwantlen Polytechnic University 86
Kwong, Kylie 119

labor: British media and 157; *Chef's Table* and 213; COVID-19 pandemic and 87; food sovereign voices and 67, 70; immigrant 1; indentured 157; India and 137; influencer activism and 21, 26; Lach and 207; *New York Times* and 106–7, 111; politics and 1, 8; slave 68, 75–76, 110
Labrador 50, 60
Lach, Alma: achievements of 13, 199–207; awards of 206; background of 199, 202–3; blogs and 207; *Chicago Sun-Times* 199; on Chinese food 205–6; class and 200, 207; as consultant 203–6; consumerism and 200, 202; cookbooks and 13, 199–207;

as entrepreneur 203–7; farming and 202; food journalism and 200–2, 206–7; as food writer 203–6; gender issues and 13, 199, 206–7; home economics and 200–2; home economics and 200–2; inequality and 199, 207; influencer activism and 199, 206–7; Instagram and 207; labor and 207; *Le Cordon Bleu* and 199, 203, 206; *Les Dames d'Escoffier* 205; *Let's Cook* 199, 203; lifestyle media and 207; meat and 202; menus and 204–5; *New York Times* and 200, 204–5; nutrition and 202–3, 205; papers of 199–200; patents of 206; politics and 199–200, 206–7; recipes and 201–5; television appearances of 203–4, 206; women's pages and 200–2
Lach, Donald F. 202–3
Lach, Elizabeth Satorius 199
Lach, Sandra 203
Lam, Lee Tran 71
Lane, Robert 96
La Via Campesina 71–72
Lawson, Nigella 119
Leavitt, Nicole 57
Le Bernardin 87
LeBesco, Kathleen xii, 11–12, 85–99, 211–12
Le Cordon Bleu 199, 203, 206
Légion d'Honneur 206
Les Dames d'Escoffier 205
Let's Cook (TV show) 199, 203
Lewis, Tania 6, 7, 115, 139
LGBTQIA+ 89
Life magazine 203
lifestyle media: celebrities and 115, 124; culinary philanthropy and 95–96; domesticity and 12, 20, 100–12, 135; education and 4; empowerment and 6–7; environmental conflict and 48; food journalism and 3–7, 11, 14, 101–3; food sovereign voices and 70; influencer activism and 29; Lach and 207; *New York Times* and 100, 102, 109, 112–13; politics and 3–7, 11, 14; scandals and 115, 124; vulnerable communities and 124–27
Lindsey-Warren, Tyrha M. 118–19
Little Plantation, The 26
Livestock Long Shadow report 67
lobster 51–52, 56–57, 151–54, 185
Lofaso, Antonia 92–93

Lonsdale, Sarah xii, 13, 183–98
Los Angeles Times 35, 40
Lupton, Deborah 139
Luzzini, Johnny 86
Lynch, Lazarus 26–27

MacCaw, William 188
MacGregor, Roy 53–55
MacShane, Denis 163
Madera, Kasia 122–23
MAD symposia 73
Magic Pill, The (Evans) 116–21, 124, 127
Maintenance Phase 121
Mann, Alana xii, 11, 66–82
Mapes, Gwynne 106–7, 220–21
masculinity 3; culinary philanthropy and 85–91, 96; danger and 36–37; heroes and 88–91; Super Bowl and 36–43; vegetables and 37–38
Mastannamma 141, 148–49
MasterChef 54, 140
McAllister, Matthew 37
McBride, Anne E. 91
McGaurr, Lyn xii, 11, 48–65
McMillan, Tracie 70
meat: celebrities and 120; culinary philanthropy and 87; *Daily Mail* Food Bureau and 183, 186, 188, 192–94; food sovereign voices and 66, 68; India and 137–38, 141, 144, 146–47; Lach and 202; National Lent and 186; *New York Times* and 105; Super Bowl and 35–43; #yes2meat 66
Medium Rare 89
Meijer, Irene Costera 5–6, 111, 170–71
Melman, Richard 205–6
Men's Health magazine 37
menus 8, 104; British media and 163; *Chef's Table* and 211; culinary philanthropy and 95; food sovereign voices and 67; Lach and 204–5; Super Bowl 11, 34–44
#MeToo movement 9, 86, 97, 109
Michelin stars 88, 118, 210–11, 213, 218
Midway Airlines 199, 205
Mihesuah, Devon 74
Miller, Donella C. 108
Millie's Cuban Café 89
Milwaukee Journal 200
Mims, Ben 40
Mook, Nate 91–92

moral issues: culinary philanthropy and 87, 96–97; *Daily Mail* Food Bureau and 187; food sovereign voices and 67–68, 73; India and 136–37; influencer activism and 30
Morgan, Eluned 162–63
Morisano, John O. 219
Most Inspiring Women You've Met This Year (Elle) 121
Mother Jones magazine 2, 9
MSNBC 2 118
Mukhin, Vladimir 213, 218–19
Muslims 1, 147
"My Kind of Town (Chicago Is)" (Sinatra) 205
My Kitchen Rules (TV show) 116, 120, 123, 127
"My Seder Menu" (Roman) 104–5

Naccarato, Peter xii–xiii, 11–12, 85–99, 211–12
Nakayama, Nika 216
Nannenga, Brittan 199
Nation, The (journal) 1–2
National Football League (NFL) 34, 36, 38
National Lent 186
National Public Radio 9, 89
National Restaurant Association 88, 92
Native Americans 50, 73–75, 91–92, 108
Nawabs Kitchen 141, *142*
Netflix: *Chef's Table* and 12 (*see also Chef's Table*); food journalism and 8; *The Magic Pill* 116–21, 120–21, 124
New Brunswick: British occupation of 50; crab and 51; First Nations and 50; French occupation of 50; lobster and 51; as Maritime Province 50; Saint Andrews 51; salmon and 50–51; tourism and 11, 50–61
"New Faces of Restaurant Hospitality, The" (Stevenson) 106
Newfoundland 50, 52, 60
Newman, Lenore 73
New Republic, The (journal) 9
News of the World 161
New Yorker 2
New York Herald Tribune 200
New York Times: "At Home" section and 100, 103, 111; citizenship and 112; Claiborne and 204–5; class and 108; climate and 107, 109; consumerism and 100; consumption and 102, 108; Cooking App of 102–3; COVID-19 pandemic and 100–12; domesticity and 101–2, 110–11; ethics and 104; farming and 106–7, 112; food journalism of 100–12; framing and 108–9; gender issues and 101–2, 112; inequality and 106, 112; labor and 106–7, 111; Lach and 200, 204–5; lifestyle media and 100, 102, 109–13; meat and 105; neoliberal vs. holistic positions and 108–12; nutrition and 104; politics and 100–12; Rao and 86–87; recipes and 100–5, 111; strategy and 110–11; Super Bowl and 34–35, 40; sustainability and 104–9; Wednesday Food section 100, 103; YouTube and 100
New York Times Magazine 103
New York World 201
Nickel-and-Dimed: On (Not) Getting By in America (Ehrenreich) 70, 76
Nilsson, Magnus 215–17
Nimmo 90
n/naka 216
Nom Nom Paleo 23, 25
Nora, Pierre 214, 220
No Reservations (Bourdain show) 118, 221
Northcliffe, Lord 191
Nova Scotia 50, 52
nutrition 2; celebrities and 115, 118–25; *Chef's Table* and 213; culinary philanthropy and 91; *Daily Mail* Food Bureau and 183, 189, 191, 194–95; Denmark and 171, 173; food sovereign voices and 66; influencer activism and 22; Lach and 202–3, 205; *New York Times* and 104; Super Bowl and 35, 41–42

Oatly 41
Odense Food Festival 167, 171–74
Oh Lady Cakes 29
Olien, Jessica 104
Oliver, Jamie 115, 119
Omanamma 146
Osteria Francescana 213–14
Ouelette, Laurie 6–7, 109
Over Easy (TV show) 203

Padarain, Helen 125–26
Paddleford, Clementine 200, 203
Paleolithic diet 23, 25, 116, 123, 126
Palestinians 1
Panayides, Fanos 123
Pan Macmillan 115
Parts Unknown (Bourdain show) 221
Pascoe, Bruce 73
Passover 94, 105
PBS 203
Peel, Dorothy 184–85, 191–92
Penguin 116, 121–22, 127
Perelman, Deb 25
personal experience 23–24, 29, 108, 217
PETA 68
Petroni, Christian 92–94
Pew Research 21
Phillipov, Michelle 48
Philport, Tom 2
Pillsbury Bake-Off 204
Pittsburgh Dispatch 200
Plymouth Argyle Herald, The 164
Polish, Jennifer 68
politics: bendy banana and 153–64; #BlackLivesMatter 9–10, 19–22, 25–30, 109; #BlackOutTuesday 10; blogs and 7–11; Bourdain and 1–2, 5, 11–12, 118; British media and 153–64, 184, 188–89, 192; *Chef's Table* and 221; citizenship and 5–6, 11, 13; class and 5–6, 9; COVID-19 pandemic and 91; *Daily Mail* Food Bureau and 184, 188–89, 192; Denmark and 171–73; domesticity and 101–2; environmental conflict 48–49, 59, 61; Euromyths and 13, 153–64; farming and 9, 11; food journalism and 1–16; food resistance and 59–71; food sovereign voices and 67–75; framing and 1–2, 11–12; gastro 12, 125, 137–40, 147; gender 206–7; identity 4–6, 9, 13; India and 12, 125, 137–40, 147; influencer activism and 19–31; Instagram and 7; labor and 1, 8; Lach and 199–200, 206–7; lifestyle media and 3–7, 11, 14; *New York Times* and 100–12; populism and 9, 153–64; racial issues and 9; scandals and 115–18; social justice 1, 9, 22, 28–29, 139; social media and 1, 7–8, 12; Super Bowl 34–44; sustainability and 2, 7, 9, 11–12; YouTube and 8, 12
pollution 51, 55, 57, 67, 108
Ponting, Herbert 194–95
populism: bendy bananas and 155; British media and 153–64; politics and 153–64; Trump and 9
poverty 76, 108, 216, 220
Prince Edward Island 50
ProQuest International Newsstream 156
Public Health Association of Australia 126
pulp mills 49, 54–55
Pump Room 205

"Quarantine Exposes Hapless Home Cooks" (Krishna) 104
Quatremer, Jean 158
Queen newspaper 185, 191

racial issues: #BlackLivesMatter 9–10, 19–22, 25–30, 109; #BlackOutTuesday 10, 19–31; *Chef's Table* and 219; COVID-19 pandemic and 87; ethnic 9, 70, 146–48; Floyd murder and 19; food sovereign voices and 67, 70, 75; influencer activism and 19, 26–27, 29; politics and 9; protest language and 27–30; segregation 138, 219; slavery 68, 75–76, 110; Super Bowl and 38; violence and 19
Racist Sandwich Podcast, The (Janmohamed) 2
Ramos, Jessica 112
Ramsay, Gordon 86
Rao, Tejal 86–87
Raue, Tim 213, 216, 219
Ray, Krishnendu 147
recipes: celebrities and 125–26; *Chef's Table* and 218; *Daily Mail* Food Bureau and 183–92, 194, 196; Denmark and 167–68, 171, 176; food journalism and 8; food sovereign voices and 68, 70, 72; hyper-local 146–47; Indian 135, 140, 143–48; influencer activism and 20–21; Lach and 201–5; *New York Times* and 100–5, 111; Super Bowl and 34–35, 39–41; YouTube and 8, 12, 21, 135, 140, 146, 148

Redder, Pernille 172
Reddy, Narayan 141, 148–49
Red Rock Adventure 56
Red Rooster 89
Restaurant Employee Relief Fund 92–93
Restaurant Hustle 2020: All on the Line (documentary) 92, 94
Rethink Food 88
Ripert, Eric 87
Risen, Clay 106
Roman, Alison 104–5
Runner, The (student publication) 86
Ryan, Maureen 102
Ryge, Signe 172

Saint Croix Courier 57
salads 35–38, 105, 190, 201, 204–5
salmon: Bay of Fundy and 50–61; exports of 51; Fundy Salmon Recovery Project and 55–56; as king of game fish 50–52; Little Salmon River 53; local stakeholders and 56–59; smoked 206
Salon.com 86
Salyuk, Alina 89
Samuelsson, Marcus 89, 92–93
Samways, Kurt 55–56
San Francisco Chronicle 2, 201
Satterfield, Stephen 2
Saveur 22–23, 95
scandals: Australia and 115–26; blogs and 119, 125; Evans 12, 115–27; Facebook and 116, 123, 127; Gibson 12, 115–27; influencer activism and 116, 118, 121–27; Instagram and 116, 127; Kowlow 110; lifestyle media and 115, 124; politics and 115–18; social media and 115–18, 123–27; tabloids and 12; violence and 118
Scholliers, Peter 185
Schwarz, Joshua 126
Scott, Joseph 199
Scott, Robert 194–95
Scrinis, Gyorgy 42
seafood: Bay of Fundy 11, 48–61; crab 51, 205; discursive alignments over 59–60; lobster 56–57, 151–54, 185; salmon 50–61, 206; sustainability and 48–61; UN Fisheries Observers and 70
Segerberg, Alexandra 30
segregation 138, 219
self-promotion 21, 23, 26–27

self-reflexivity 11, 20, 23, 25–26, 28–31
Sen, Mayukh 2, 9
Serious Eats 2
Seven Network 116
sex: British media and 156; chefs and 86, 90; harassment and 1, 8, 86; #MeToo movement and 9, 86, 97, 109; Super Bowl Food and 36
sexism 9, 86, 97, 111
Sexual Politics of Meat, The: A Feminist-Vegetarian Critical Theory Adams) 36
Shaggy 156–57
Sherman, Elaine 205
Shewry, Ben 210, 215–16, 218
Sifton, Sam 35
Silverton, Nancy 218
Simon, Andre L. 203
Sinatra, Frank 205
60 Minutes Australia 117, 123–25
slavery 68, 75–76, 110
Smith, Phoebe 53
Smitten Kitchen 25
Smoked Cheese Day: constructive journalism and 13, 168, 172–77; Funen region and 13, 167–68, 172–77; heritage of 173–75; live coverage of 13, 167–68, 172, 174–77; social media and 176; themes of 173
social justice 1, 9, 22, 28–29, 139
social media: amplifying/muting content and 24–25; #BlackOutTuesday and 19–31; blogs 7–11, 20–31, 119, 125, 139, 144–45, 171, 207; celebrities and 115–18, 123–27; cookbooks and 26, 29; culinary philanthropy and 95; *Daily Mail* Food Bureau and 195; Denmark and 171, 173, 176; education and 22–23, 27, 29; empty statements and 26; environmental conflict and 57; Facebook 21, 116, 123, 127, *142*, 173, 176; food sovereign voices and 66; hashtags 19, 26, 29, 31; India and 135, 137, 139–43, 149; influencer activism and 19, 21, 26, 28–31; Instagram 7, 20–27, 116, 127, 139, *142*, 173, 195, 207; personal experience and 23–24; politics and 1, 7–8, 12; protest language and 27–30; regulations and 157–59; scandals and 115–18, 123–27; self-reflexivity and 11, 20, 23, 25–26, 28–31; Smoked Cheese Day and 176; TikTok 195; Twitter 19, 68, 120, 139, *142*, 195; visibility and 21

Soler, Pascual 89–90
Son of a Southern Chef 26–27
Special Collections Research Center 199
Spectator, The 158
spice 140, 146, 157
Sports Illustrated 35, 37
Sprouted Kitchen 23
Sqirl 110
starvation 69, 184, 186
Stein, Rick 119
Stevens, Ashley 86
Stevenson, Kim 106
strategy: brand 25–30, 207; *Chef's Table* and 220; COVID-19 pandemic and 110–11; Denmark and 176; environmental conflict and 53–54, 61; framing and 1 (*see also* framing); influencer activism and 19, 25, 27–30; Netflix 220; *New York Times* and 110–11; protest language and 27–30; social media 176; survival 110
sugar 205; *Daily Mail* Food Bureau and 183, 186–88, 191–95; exports of 157; film on 120
Sun, The 157–58, 162
Sunday Life (newspaper section) 119–20
Sunrise (TV show) 121–22
Super Bowl: capitalism and 36, 44; class and 38; climate and 39, 42–43; commercialism and 11, 37–44; commercials of 34–43; consumerism and 35, 41, 43; consumption and 34, 37, 40–42; COVID-19 pandemic and 11, 34, 38, 43; dude food 11, 35, 41; farming and 39; food rules for 35–38; framing and 38; gender issues and 11, 34–43; identity and 36, 43; LV 38–43; masculinity and 36–43; meat and 35–43; menus and 11, 34–44; *New York Times* and 34, 35, 40; NFL and 34, 36, 38; nutrition and 35, 41–42; politics of 34–44; racial issues and 38; recipes and 34–35, 39–41; veganism and 36–43; vegetarianism and 36–43; violence and 37, 41
Super Size Me (film) 120
Supper Club 210
supply chains 2, 43
sustainability: *Chef's Table* and 212; COVID-19 pandemic and 91–92; Denmark and 170; discursive alignments over 59–60; environmental conflict and 48–49, 55, 59–60; ethics and 104; farming and 9, 11, 55, 59, 66, 74, 212; food sovereign voices and 66, 72, 74–75; Food Sustainability Index 2; *New York Times* and 104–9; politics and 2, 7, 9, 11–12; seafood and 48–61

tabloids 8; British media 153–63; celebrities and 115–18, 122; constructing British greatness and 159–60; Euromyths and 13, 153–63; scandals and 12
"Taking Comfort in a Familiar Wine" (Asimov) 104
Tanis, David 103–4
Taste Makers: Seven Immigrant Women Who Revolutionized Food in America (Sen) 2
TB12 Diet 42
Teran, Daniel 89
Testament of Youth (Brittain) 187
Thanksgiving 35, 89, 146
That Sugar Film 120
Therapeutic Goods Administration (TGA) 123, 127
#TheShowMustBePaused 19
Thomas, Jamila 19
Thompson, Craig 90
Thompson, Derek 41
Thug Kitchen 68
TikTok 195
Tilzey, Mark 72
Times, The 160
"Together we make Funen better" project 172
Tominc, Ana xiii, 13, 153–66
Tornaghi, Chiara 72
Toscano, Nick 116, 121, 126
tourism: gastro 73; memory 210; New Brunswick and 11, 50–61
Tourism New Brunswick 50–53, 59
travel journalism: environmental conflict and 11, 48–61; MacGregor and 53–55; nuanced approaches and 49; Wilkinson and 53–54
Tribal Foods 141, *142*
Trump, Donald 9
Tseng, Esther 87
Turner, Pixie 122
TV2/FYN: Denmark and 13, 167–68, 171–77; live journalism of 13, 167–68, 172–77; Smoked Cheese Day 13, 167, 172–77

238 Index

2020 (TV show) 203–4
Twitter 19, 68, 120, 139, *142*, 195
Twitty, Michael 2

Uber Eats 39
Uecker, Catherine 199
Ukraine 219
UN Fisheries Observers 70
United States Department of Agriculture (USDA) 76
United States of Arugula, The (Kamp) 202
University of Chicago 202–3
University of New Brunswick 56
Unwin, Mike 52
USA Today 35

veganism: food sovereign voices and 66–68; influencer activism and 22; Super Bowl Food and 36–43; taboos 12, 24, 68, 138, 147
vegetarianism: food sovereign voices and 66, 68; India and 12, 137–38, 147; Super Bowl Food and 36–43
Vietnam War 90
Village Cooking Channel 140–41, *142*, 148
village food: Appadurai on 136–37, 140, 148, 150; authenticity 145–46; bananas and 146; gastro-politics and 12, 125, 137–39, 147; globalization and 148–49; grandfather trope 143–44; grandmother trope 143; hierarchies of taste 147; hyper-local recipes and 146–47; India and 12, 135–50; intimate home cooking 144; *kadai* 135, 141, 143, 147; Khare on 136, 146, 149; legitimacy of 138–39; Mastannamma and 141; narrative of 140–49; nostalgia and 145–46; Reddy and 141; rural setting of 142–43; solidarity and 148; spectacle cooking 144; subaltern culinary counterpublics 144–49; traditional methods 142–43; visual vocabulary of 140–49
Villiers, Theresa 162
violence: discrimination and 8–9; food sovereign voices and 68, 74, 76; India and 138; racial issues and 19; restaurant 1, 8; scandals and 118; Super Bowl Food and 37, 41
visibility: celebrities and 124; *Chef's Table* and 214, 220; culinary philanthropy and 87, 97; digital 21; Indian food cultures and 135–39
Vos, Tim P. 3–4
Voss, Kimberly xiii, 13, 199–209

Walker Tray 206
Wall Street Journal 66
Wanderlust 53
Washingtonian 91
Washington Post 9, 35, 39, 41
Washington Star 200
Watergate 90, 101
Watson, Molly 162
Waugh, Evelyn 155, 159, 164
WEIRD (Western, educated, industrialized, rich, democratic) nations 66, 68
Western Daily Mail, The 162
WGN-TV 203
What's Eating America (TV show) 2, 118
Wheelhouse, The 89
When Inclusion Means Exclusion: Social Commentary and Indigenous Agency (All Together Now 2021) 74–75
Whetstone magazine 2
White Rabbit 218
White Witnesses 74–75
Whole Pantry, The (Gibson) 116, 121, 124, 126–27
Why Voice Matters (Couldry) 71
Wilkinson, Guy 53–54
Willinger, Faith 214
Willis, Diana xiii, 13–14, 210–23
Wilson, Korsha 9
Winkie, Luke 145–46
Wodehouse P. G. 155, 159, 164
Wofford, Benjamin 91
Woman Who Fooled the World, The: Belle Gibson's Cancer Con and the Darkness at the Heart of the Wellness Industry (Donelly and Toscano) 116
women's pages 200–2

World Central Kitchen 91–92, 97
World Expeditions 53
WTTW 203
Wyllie, Kylie 121, 124–25

Yeatman, Heather 126
#yes2meat 66
"Yes! We Have No Bananas" (song) 156

YouTube: consumption and 135; Denmark and 171; Indian food culture and 135, 140–50; influencer activism and 21; *New York Times* and 100; Pew Research on 21; politics and 8, 12; recipes and 8, 12, 21, 135, 140, 146, 148

Zimmern, Andrew 2, 118

For Product Safety Concerns and Information please contact our EU
representative GPSR@taylorandfrancis.com
Taylor & Francis Verlag GmbH, Kaufingerstraße 24, 80331 München, Germany

www.ingramcontent.com/pod-product-compliance
Lightning Source LLC
Chambersburg PA
CBHW051354290426
44108CB00015B/2013